ECUMENOPOLIS
the Inevitable City of the Future

ECUMENOPOLIS
the Inevitable City of the Future

Books in This Series

ANTHROPOPOLIS City for Human Development by C. A. Doxiadis *et al*.

ECUMENOPOLIS The Inevitable City of the Future by C. A. Doxiadis
            and J. G. Papaioannou

BUILDING ENTOPIA by C. A. Doxiadis

ACTION for Human Settlements by C. A. Doxiadis

ECUMENOPOLIS
the Inevitable City of the Future

C.A. DOXIADIS and J.G. PAPAIOANNOU

W·W·NORTON & COMPANY · INC · New York

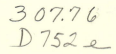

To Walker Cisler
for his vision in initiating large-scale planning
for energy and human settlements

Acknowledgements

The authors wish to express their sincere thanks to all those who contributed essentially, in one way or another, to the building up of the body of knowledge used by the Athens Center of Ekistics in general, and by the authors in particular, in connection with this book. First and foremost they wish to thank Mrs. Myrto Antonopoulou-Bogdanou (Greek architect-planner and ekistician) who has been working with the City of the Future research project since 1960, and since 1964 as its Project Manager, and who, among others, developed several aspects of the Ecumenopolis theory, worked out its maps in their final form, supervised many graduate students working for the project, and contributed many other studies.

Then the team of experts that participated in the intensive early discussions on the project (mainly in 1961 and 1962), that clarified many of its basic issues: Dr. R.L. Meier (U.S. chemist, economist, sociologist, environmental planner and generalist) who contributed several original papers and interacted in many constructive ways with the project's research team throughout the life of the project; Prof. J. Tyrwhitt (British architect and ekistician), who contributed several papers, supervised several graduate students, summarized repeatedly the research findings for the journal EKISTICS, and interacted in many ways with the project's research team; Prof. J. Matos Mar (Peruvian anthropologist), who surveyed many cities in S. America for the project and contributed several interesting ideas; Prof. H. Fathy (Egyptian architect), who surveyed many cities in Africa for the project and contributed several interesting ideas; Prof. M. Gomez Mayorga (Mexican architect), who surveyed several cities in Mexico and Central America for the project; Prof. G. Gutenschwager (U.S. geographer and planner), who surveyed several cities in the U.S. for the project.

Then Mr. V. Nikitopoulos (Greek civil engineer) for his detailed studies on the future of water supplies; Mr. M.G. Ionides (British civil engineer) for his studies on development of water resources; Messrs J. Piperoglou and L. Athanassiou (Greek economists) for their economic studies; Prof. Brian Berry (U.S. geographer) for his studies on megalopolis theory and on U.S. megalopolises; Dr. C. Goudas (Greek mathematician and astronomer) for his mathematical studies on Ecumenopolis; the late Mrs. M. Carr (British anthropologist) for her social studies and her interaction with the research team; Mrs. C. Huws-Nagashima (Welsh-Japanese geographer) for her studies on the Great Lakes Megalopolis, on the Japanese Megalopolis, on air transportation, etc.; Mr. G. Papageorgiou (Greek architect-planner) for his work on Ecumenopolis in Greece.

For valuable advice, Prof. J. Gottmann (French geographer) for his advice on megalopolises, Dr. A. Toynbee (British historian) for his historic perspective of the future of Human Settlements, Dr. H. Ozbekhan (Turkish-U.S. systems analyst) for his methodology on projections and automation, Dr. J. Platt (U.S. neurobiologist and generalist) for general projections, Dr. S. Havlick (U.S. geographer, ecologist, and planner) for studies in ecology, Mr. P. Psomopoulos (Greek architect-planner and ekistician) for his supervision of several graduate students, and for his participation in several seminars and discussions. The authors also want to thank most specially Mrs. A. Freme-Sklirou (British-Greek secretary), who has meticulously and systematically kept all the project's archives, carried out documentation on it, and carefully typed and edited (for the English language) all internal reports (258 reports totalling some 9,500 pages) of the project and the earlier, more extensive versions of the text of this book, and also Mrs. A. Moschona and Mrs. L. Hadjidakis, who prepared the bulk of this project's maps and graphs (totalling 1,600 drawings).

The authors also wish to express their special appreciation to Mr. C.H. Ripman, who prepared a careful intermediate complete version of the text and illustrations of this book, condensing previous versions, editing them, and introducing many novel ideas and new formulations of basic concepts in it.

On the production side of this book, the authors wish to express their warm thanks to Miss K. Pertsemlidou (Greek architect) for her careful and systematic work on the coordination of the illustrations, tables, figures and other data used in this book; Miss E. Kaliata (Greek secretary) for her most careful and systematic coordination of the work on the final text; Mrs. L. Green (British writer) and Miss D. Harvey (British editor) for their editing of the English text of, respectively, the two final versions of this book, Mrs. A. Moschona (Greek graphic arts specialist) for the drawing of the illustrations of this book, and Mr. N. Avronidakis (Greek international relations specialist and Director of the Athens Publishing Center) for the careful supervision of the printing of this book.

Finally, the authors wish to express their thanks to the *Ford Foundation* for extensive financial assistance in various stages of this project, to the *Athens Center of Ekistics* within which the *City of the Future* research project was developed, and to *Doxiadis Associates* for their multiple collaboration in many aspects of this project.

Special Contributors
to the "City of the Future" (COF) Research Project
of the Athens Center of Ekistics

Out of the many contributors, beyond those mentioned in the Acknowledgements, to the studies of the "City of the Future" research project, the following ones, to whom the authors extend their thanks, are specially mentioned, with an indication of the area of their main contribution(s):

Regional Studies

Mr. John Bayly (Australian architect-planner) — Ecumenopolis in Australia
Mr. G. Clarke (Australian architect-planner) — Ecumenopolis in Australia
Prof. T. Shibata (Japanese economist) — Japanese cities
Prof. J.A. Khan (Pakistani geographer) — Settlement patterns in Bangladesh
Prof. P. Kormoss (Belgian geographer) — W. Europe
Prof. M.A. Rege (Indian planner) — Indian cities
Mrs. A. Kolars (U.S. geographer) — Cities in E. Africa

Mr. J. Kolars (U.S. geographer) — Cities in Turkey
Mr. S. Hatiras (Greek civil engineer) — Addis-Ababa
Mr. O. Yakas (Greek architect-planner) — Melbourne
Mr. L. Stylianopoulos (Greek civil engineer) — Zürich
Mr. G. Candiotes (S. African planner) — Johannesburg
Prof. S.G. Shiber (Kuwaiti planner) — Kuwait
Mr. J. Cordes (Argentinian architect) — Buenos-Aires
Prof. A.W. Baxter (U.S. education expert) — Copenhagen

Special Study on the Great Lakes Megalopolis

Mr. C. Kakissopoulos (Greek civil engineer), coordinator
Mr. Th. Vournas (Greek statistician), principal component analysis
Mr. A. Drymiotes (Greek civil engineer and computer programs specialist), similarity analysis and computer work
Mr. I. Tazartes (Greek civil engineer and computer analyst), computer work
Mr. J. Frantzeskakis (Greek civil engineer), transportation and computer work
Mr. A. Simeon (Greek architect-planner), team member
Mr. A. Kollaros (Greek architect-planner), team member
Mr., Ph. Costas (Greek-U.S. geographer-planner), general studies
Mr. S. Arion (Rumanian architect), presentation of results

Special Studies

Prof. R. Fakiolas (Greek economist) — U.S.S.R. and China
Mr. J. Glyniadakis (Greek economist) — Economic projections
Mr. A. Thronos (Greek economist) — Economic projections
Mr. J. Melidis (Greek economist) — Economic projections
Dr. D. Simeon (Greek power engineer) — Energy studies
Dr. A.N. Christakis (Greek physicist and systems analyst) — Studies on models
Prof. B. Newling (U.S. geographer) — Studies on density
Prof. J. Osman (U.S. philosopher and theologist) — Social and administrative studies
Dr. L. Lehrman (U.s. sociologist) — Social studies
Prof. M.C. McCrumm (U.S. systems analyst) — Control theory

Documentation (special documentation studies on various aspects of the project)
Mrs. Ch. Anemoyannis (Greek librarian)
Mrs. A. Martin-Papazoglou (U.S.-Greek librarian)
Mr. R. Rooke (British librarian)

Graduate Students (who conducted research within the framework of the "City of the Future" Research Project as trainees in the Educational Programs of the Athens Center of Ekistics)

Mr. M. Perović (Yugoslav architect-planner) — Gulf Megalopolis of the U.S. (Gravity Models with varying exponents, Principal Component Analysis, projections)
Mr. J.R. Stewart (Australian architect-planner) — Numerous studies on various aspects of Ecumenopolis; Ecumenopolis in China
Messrs R.C. Quinn and J.J. Reid (Irish architect-planners)-Ecumenopolis in Ireland
Mr. B.J. Rae (New Zealand architect-planner) — Ecumenopolis in New Zealand
Mr. K. Dahlström (Swedish architect-planner) — Ekistic development in S. Sweden
Miss R. Hirschon (S. African geographer and anthropologist) — Several studies on physical geography related to Ecumenopolis

Mr. J. Verbouwhede (Belgian architect-planner) — Ecumenopolis in N.W. Europe

Mr. T. Doi (Japanese architect-planner) — Megalopolis and Ecumenopolis in Japan

Mr. P. Ofori Nyako (Ghanaian planner) — Ecumenopolis in W. Africa

Mr. W. Pharaon (Egyptian architect-planner) — Nile Valley area; W. Europe

Mr. L.A. Reddy (Indian civil engineer) — Megalopolis in S. India

Miss G. Bachman (U.S. social scientist) — Migration patterns as related to Ecumenopolis

Mr. G. Sheather (Australian architect-planner) — General systems theory of the Great Lakes Megalopolis (1st part)

Mr. P. Mardones (Chilean architect-planner) — Megalopolises in Central Chile and in the U.K.

Mr. P. Compagnoni (Australian architect-planner) — New capitals; Australia

Mr. D. Van Havre (Belgian political scientist) — Methodology of projections for Ecumenopolis

Mr. V. Curtin (Irish economist) — Athens area

Mr. D. Saikia (Indian architect-planner) — Densities

Mr. D. Hardy (British geographer) — Recreation in Ecumenopolis

Mr. J. G. Ximenez (Mexican architect-planner) — Ecumenopolis in Mexico

Mr. R.V. Pryor (U.S. social administrator) — Administrative aspects of the Japanese Megalopolis

Mr. M.O. Elsammani (Sudanese geographer) — Migration and water economy in the Sudan

Mr. K.A. Balla (Sudanese geographer) — Megalopolis-Ecumenopolis in the Sudan

Miss S.L. Higman (U.S. social scientist) — Population, health and social standards

Mr. P.W. Pratt (U.S. architect-planner) — Brasilia

Mr. B.E. Roe (Norwegian architect-planner) — Densities

Mr. M. Nakamura (Japanese architect-planner) — Philippines; China; U.S. West Coast

Mr. Sh. Murota (Japanese architect-planner) — Japanese cities; Indonesia

Mr. M. Deobakhta (Indian architect-planner) — India

Mr. S.V. Singh (Indian architect-planner) — Amritsar-Calcutta Megalopolis

Mr. K.P. Singh (Indian architect-planner) — India

Mr. S.G. Thakur Desai (Indian architect-planner) — India

Mr. M. Bhatia (Indian economist) — India

Mr. R. Bahe (Indian architect-planner) —India

Mr. G. Luna (Mexican architect-planner) — Megalopolises in Mexico, Central Ameria, Brazil, and other parts of S. America

Mrs. B.A. Charron-Ximenez (French urban sociologist) — Central France

Mr. R. Bussière (Canadian mechanical engineer) — U.K.; densities

Mr. N. Findikakis (Greek architect) — Near and Middle East

Mr. C. Crantonellis (Greek architect) — Mediterranean region; U.K.

Mrs. M. Potiris (Greek architect-planner) — Densities; metropolitan boundary definitions

Mr. F. Hall (U.S. architect-planner) — Historic cities; new cities

Mr. P. Subrahmanyam (Indian civil engineer) — Urban transportation

Mr. G.P. Melnicove (U.S. architect-planner) — Great Lakes area

Mr. J.W. Kikaire (Ugandan economist) — Uganda

Mr. D.R. Baxter (British architect-planner) — U.K.

Miss U. Oelsner (U.S. planner) — New cities

Mr. D. Botka (Czech architect-planner) — E. Europe

Mrs. E.C. Yamoah (Ghanaian physical planner) — N. Africa

Mr. G.M. Peter (Greek-Canadian civil engineer-planner) — Megalopolises in Canada

Mr. S. Kumar (Indian civil engineer) — Centers and functions

Mr. S. El Jadr (Iraqi planner) — Iraq; U.S.S.R.

Mr. R.G. Fuher (U.S. architect-planner) — Densities

Preface

This is the second of the four red books which try to help the understanding of what is going to happen to our human settlements and what we can do to save them. It deals with the inevitable changes in their scale from the small polis (town or city of the past) to the present-day megalopolis and to the City of the Future or Ecumenopolis[1]. The first book covers the concept that we need a City for Human Development or, in a broader sense, the city we need as humans, *Anthropopolis*[2]. The third book faces the problem of how in order to avoid disasters we can turn Ecumenopolis into Anthropopolis, and it is called *Building Entopia*, that is, the city that combines our hopes and goals with reality. The fourth book is dedicated to the ways in which we can move from just talking and writing about ideas, dreams and theories towards action, and is called *Action for Human Settlements*.

The concept of the City of the Future was born in the Athens Center of Ekistics in the year 1960. By the end of the 1950's we could not see any progress being made anywhere in the world in attempts to deal with the urgent problems of our cities. People did not even seem to be concerned, and at that time, when we tried to draw attention to the urban crisis, we were accused of frightening people.

We therefore asked ourselves: what is going to happen? Are we going to go on living in the cities of the present which get increasingly worse with every day that passes because of their continuous growth, or are we going to live in those utopian cities which so many people talk about, but which never actually get built because they cannot and because many even should not be built? We did not know the answer, so we decided to become more serious about it and begin a research project to find out. This project entitled "the City of the Future", has now lasted for fifteen years, and is still continuing: it should never really end.

The first internal document[3] on the subject was published by the Athens Center of Ekistics in July 1961 as an outline of our thoughts and procedures in the hope that we might challenge our collaborators to respond and start making their own suggestions. We gradually mobilized forces and resources to try and learn as much as possible from every discipline and every part of the world. We began to present our new findings in seminars, lectures, symposia, conferences, articles and books in order to try and get our messages across to as many people all over the world as we could. We needed other people's reactions to confirm or reject our estimates and our interpretations.

The detailed findings of the research project "The City of the Future" are included in 260 internal reports totalling some 9,500 pages, and illustrated by some 1,600 drawings (maps, graphs, etc). They have been repeatedly summarized in various forms (e.g. for international conferences, in the journal EKIS-TICS, etc.). This book is a broader summary of the work and is, therefore, much less the official report of the project and much more a personal view of its two authors. Since, however, these were continuously and deeply involved in the project, and responsible for it, this attempt at a first comprehensive synthesis purports to sum up the total experience gained through the research project and to present it, for the first time, in as unified a vision as this seems possible at the present stage of evolution of ideas around the central concept of "the City of the Future".

We think we are now ready to present our findings in a way that can convey our whole experience of this subject and answer some basic questions about what the City on the Future will be like, not just in the form of a series of hypotheses — which they were at first — but as conclusions about which we can be certain. In doing this, we also hope to challenge those who have different ideas to present them in a similar way, and so help humanity to escape the confusion it is in about living in cities today. We think this can best be done by trying to see clearly what road we are on, where it is inevitably leading us, and what alternatives we have for our future in the city.

In presenting this road we are on today, we have followed the most probable assumptions and selected the most probable upper limits. In the predictions of a global population, for example, we speak of 15 to 20 billion[4], although the present United Nations forecast is for 12 billion and there are some serious studies, such as Lester R. Brown's *In the Human Interest*[5], which set goals of six billion, although we do not know if we can attain them. In making such assumptions we are always aware that nobody can be certain about such a remote future, but in trying to serve the future of humanity we have to prepare for the most probable upper limits. We cannot allow ourselves to repeat the great crime in dealing with urban planning in every city of the world of failing to face the real growth with the permanent excuse of planners who say: 'we have been reckoning on a successful control of growth'. We have the obligation to be realists and to prepare ourselves for the greatest probable crisis. If, following the United Nations world population conference held this August (1974) in Bucharest, humanity manages to develop population control plans capable of facing such problems as very rapid growth in some areas and the decline of the working classes in others, and the global population will not grow as much as we predict in this book, we can be very happy because those dealing with cities will have an easier task and therefore they will be able to carry it out more successfully.

The situation is very similar concerning predictions about new types of controls in energy and income growth, but with one difference: although it is certain that slowing down the population growth can be very helpful in many ways, it is not necessarily so for energy and incomes. Our future may be much happier if there is no such slow-down, provided we can also develop the technology to eliminate the problems resulting from such growth and leave only the benefits that derive from the availability of more resources. Thus we can foresee such a probable high rate of growth without being daunted by the pessimistic prediction that technology will not be able to catch up with our future needs, for if it does not, then growth will be limited anyhow by its own balancing process and the task of those who have to face the problems of the future may be easier.

The conclusion is clear: to face the future of human settlements in a realistic way we have to prepare ourselves by predicting the most probable road that will be taken by population, energy, incomes and technology at their highest growth levels and the corresponding formation of human settlements merging into the City of the Future. In this way, we can prepare ourselves to deal with the most difficult and most dangerous situation that might occur by building Ecumenopolis in the proper way and with a proper ecological balance for the sake of humanity, and if in fact growth does not reach this high level, then we are going to be even more successful in dealing with Ecumenopolis, our inevitable City of the Future.

C.A. Doxiadis, J.G. Papaioannou
Athens, August 1974

Table of contents

List of illustrations

List of figures

Part One

Developing Urban Detroit Area, Vol. 1, The Detroit Edison Company, Detroit, Michigan, 1966, fig. 36)

33. Superimposed commuting fields in northeast of U.S.A.

    (source: drawing based on the 1960 Census data recording movements of people in all major American cities, prepared by Brian J. Berry, University of Chicago, April 1967, for the Social Science Research Council Committee on Areas for Social and Economic Statistics, in cooperation with the Bureau of the Census, U.S. Department of Commerce)

34. Northern Ohio Urban System — generalized population density (1960)

    (source: the "Northern Ohio Urban System" project, Doxiadis Associates, Athens)

35. Daily urban systems

    (source: drawings by Doxiadis Associates, Athens, based on projects: "E-tude de la Région Méditerranéenne," France; "Plan de Ordenación de la provincia de Barcelona y Gerona", Spain; the "Northern Ohio Urban System", U.S.A.; the "Urban Detroit Area", U.S.A.)

36. Linear system of the Megalopolis of the eastern seaboard of U.S.A., 1963

    (source: C.A. Doxiadis, *Ekistics: an Introduction to the Science of Human Settlements*, Oxford University Press, New York, 1968, fig. 82)

37. Japanese megalopolis, 1960

    (source: T. Doi, "Megalopolis in Japan", RR-ACE:123, August 30, 1967, internal report)

38. Great Lakes and Eastern Megalopolises

    (source: the "Great Lakes Megalopolis" research project, Doxiadis Associates, Athens)

39. Schematic cross-section (AA) through Great Lakes Megalopolis for component 1

    (source: the "Great Lakes Megalopolis" research project, Doxiadis Associates, Athens)

40. The increase of forces in Detroit, Michigan, 1870-1970

41. Growth of per capita indicators for metropolitan Athens, Greece, 1870-1970

    (source: the "Capital of Greece" research project, Athens Center of Ekistics)

42. The three forces conditioning the shape of urban systems

43. The built-up areas of cities

44. New York area, 1963

    (source: drawing based on fig. 81 from C.A. Doxiadis' *Ekistics: an Introduction to the Science of Human Settlements*, Oxford University Press, New York, 1968)

45. The real city of New York, 1963

    (source: C.A. Doxiadis, *Ekistics: an Introduction to the Science of Human Settlements*, Oxford University Press, New York, 1968, fig. 81)

46. Decreasing farmland in the Urban Detroit Area

(source: the "City of the Future" research project, Athens Center of Ekistics)

Part Five

List of tables

4. Past number of settlements by broad categories (also urban and rural)
5. Structure of past global population by broad settlement categories (also urban and rural) in % of the total global population
6. Yearly growth rates of past global population by broad settlement categories (also urban and rural)
7. Present distribution of settlements by size categories (1960) for the entire globe
8. 1940-1960 trends of growth in the metropolitan areas

Appendix 2

1. Global population projections, 1950-2225 (revised March 1974)
2. Global population projections, 1950-2225 (revised March 1974) (average growth rates)
3. Urban population according to assumption F-20
4. Geographic distribution of global population
5. Total global population by settlement types and sizes
6. Global income projections — model S-20l
7. Global income projections — model F-20m
8. Global energy consumption per capita — model S-20l
9. Global energy consumption per capita — model F-20m

Appendix 3

1. Size definition for megalopolises and larger settlements
2. Emergence of the megalopolis, 1960-2000: number of megalopolises and small eperopolises
3. The first megalopolises: list of emerging "true megalopolises" (both "normal" and "small") 1960-1975
4. The first small eperopolises

N.B.   In accordance with the international tendency, throughout this book we have used the American billion which is 10^9.

1. Our goal

Our goal has been to clarify the picture of the City of the Future as much as possible, not in terms of what each one of us hopes will happen, but in terms of what Anthropos[1] is actually going to build; that is, not in terms of our personal utopias, which are unpredictable and in most cases unimportant for mankind in general, but in terms of Anthropos' action, which can be predicted.

The first question which arises is whether there are any predictable trends in this field, and the answer is definitely: yes, there are. The City of the Future will not be built in the Himalayas, nor even in the Alps, nor will it be built on the ocean, despite the fact that there will be some weather and sports stations on the mountains, and some scientific and resource-collecting stations on the ocean. It is true that there are some characteristics of our subject which are predictable, and some which are not: universal desires are predictable, individual ones are not; biological needs can be predicted, 'fashions' cannot. Our goal is to define those features which are predictable, and so turn from vague theorizing about the subject to a realistic approach to it.

The second question is whether the attempt to predict our future like this makes any sense: and the answer is that mankind has done it many times in the past, and managed to get even further. Anthropos cannot have lived in villages for thousands of years without working out what his future was going to be, and then trying to act in order to achieve it. He certainly began to act by trial and error about ten or twelve thousand years ago, and then one day he found the right road and discovered the village. The same thing must have happened with the formation of his towns and cities, which were born some six thousand years ago or even earlier. He may have failed at first, and then managed to solve his problems, but the fact is that he did solve them. We do know that in ancient

2

Part One

The concept of the City of the Future

Greece, for example, the cities created before the sixth century were not ideal — even Athens had its problems. Then people began to understand what the city was to be, and the day came when Hippodamos was able to conceive the City of the Future as a whole and help people to build it.

The third question is whether what was possible for small villages and small cities is also possible today for the big cities that are exploding into the colossal cities of the future. The answer to that was given as early as 1781 in Washington D.C., and in 1856 in Barcelona, where people had the courage to foresee growth and to plan successfully for their cities of the future which they then predicted would be ten times larger than their present ones.

If Anthropos has had the ability at certain times during thousands of years to predict the future of his settlements, then it is unreasonable to assume he has now lost it.

Is it really important to concentrate so much attention on the City of the Future? If we remember that the big problems humanity faces today are achieving peace, producing enough food and developing a successful system of life, we can see that the city is involved in all of them. It is the indispensable foundation for any system of life; it is a very important factor in the production of food; and a more rationally-built and better-fed world has much more hope of achieving peace. We will never achieve peace if we do not build a better world and the city is the practical foundation for such a world. So the City of the Future is of the greatest importance for mankind and should have the greatest possible attention concentrated on it.

Why is it so important for us to discuss not what each one of us hopes Anthropos will build, but what Anthropos is actually going to build?

The world today gives people more opportunities for individual freedom with every day that passes, so we hear more conflicting individual views about the problem than ever before. Some people say: "I love the city", others: "I hate the city". Many people, as groups, may complain loudly about such things as air pollution, but when they are actually given the chance to reduce it — as they were recently by the organization of computerized car-sharing pools in Los Angeles — they showed that they really were against it by their total refusal to use the system[2]. Another example of the confusion between theoretical statements and practical reality came up when we had long sessions with different scientific groups, each of which insisted that our cities would not survive unless we organized them according to one philosophical theory or another. They all neglected the one essential without which any city would be dead in seconds — and that is oxygen.

We can be sure that what Anthropos will actually build will not correspond to any individual theory, much less to individual interpretations of any particular type of person. The city Anthropos builds will correspond to Anthropos' real desires. So we must understand what Anthropos really is as a biological and

3

psychological organism. When Anthropos is driven by his desire to save energy in his movements, to consider his economic interests, to respond to the actual geographic conditions around him, these are the things that really count when he decides what action he will take. So this is our goal, to understand what sort of city it is that Anthropos is actually going to build — that is, to find what the inevitable City of Anthropos is to be.

In order to be as objective as possible we did not let ourselves be influenced by the findings of any specific group either in the arts or in technology, nor even by our own opinions about what ought to be done in the future. At the beginning we did think of dividing this study into two sections: the first (with which we are dealing at present) to cover the inevitable City of Anthropos; and the second to deal with what we ourselves consider should be done — that is, with the desirable City of Anthropos. However, we finally decided to separate these two projects completely. Although we have worked on the subject of human settlements for forty years, and therefore do have personal views about it, and although the consulting office of Doxiadis Associates International, with which the Athens Center of Ekistics is closely associated, is involved in the construction or reconstruction of hundreds of cities around the world, we still thought it much more useful at this point to dissociate what is inevitable about the city from what we believe to be desirable. What matters here is what humanity is actually doing; what we ourselves are doing is another matter.

To be certain that we attain this goal we must first clarify our subject in order to avoid the three grave mistakes often made in similar projects, which are:
1. confusion as to what the City of Anthropos actually is;
2. vagueness about the period of time represented by the "future" we are discussing;
3. lack of any systematic approach for trying to understand this future.
We will therefore proceed to define the following:
1. the real City of Anthropos;
2. the future which can realistically be faced as a period of time;
3. the systematic approach which can actually be followed.

2. The real City of Anthropos

There is a good deal of confusion in our minds when we talk about any individual city. Some of us are thinking about its built-up area, others of its administrative boundaries, and so on. There is much greater confusion when we think about "the city" in abstract, because each of us is thinking in a different way and most of our concepts are oversimplified and basically wrong.

In actual fact, no city in the world exists on its own. Not even the smallest town of the past could exist within its own walls, or even within the limits of its own surrounding countryside, unless it was properly connected with villages round about, or even with distant villages if the connections were by sea. If such connections do not exist, then we are not talking about a city at all, but about a village within its surrounding fields.

The real city is a system of human settlements covering a much greater area than we usually realize; a system of which the built-up part, which we usually call the city, is only very small in terms of area.

There are several ways in which we can define the spatial limits of the real city. One of these is to think of the area within which the city receives and exchanges goods. Another is to think of the area under its political, administrative, cultural or religious influence. Still another way to define the city's limits is to think about the daily system of movements — or the kinetic fields — of the citizens moving out from the city, and those from outside moving in and traveling home in the same day.

We still do not understand what the real dimensions of the city are. We wonder, for example, why Constantinople — the great capital of an empire — fell so easily to the Turks in 1453. The answer is that by that time the empire had gradually been reduced to a very small area after centuries of fighting, and while the city of Constantinople still retained the same walls which had earlier contained perhaps one million people, it was really a city of less that 50,000 people[3]. The empire had disappeared, so the city was really a dwarf wearing the clothes of a giant.

The city is really a system: its substance is formed by a system of linked human settlements. This is the reason why at first we called this project "The Settlement of the Future", and later "The Universal Settlement"[4]. These titles might be said to be more exact; however, both for symbolic reasons — since the term "city" appeals more to the imagination — and because all these settlements are in fact gradually being unified into one global system, we now speak of the City of the Future. However, it must be understood that we do mean to indicate the whole system of settlements that is contained within this city, as well as all the many types of landscape around them.

When we talk of the system of human settlements, we are really talking about the system of our life. This life system consists of settlements of all sorts, from a single shelter to a big city, from the built-up part of a village or a town to the forests from which people get their timber, from the settlements themselves to their system of interconnections across land and water. Since we cannot identify the system of our life in any easier way, we can think of it as the system of our settlements, which then becomes the image representing our life. Do we not have an image of our own body — even fully-clothed — when we say: "This is *me*"? Yet while we do this, we fully accept that we are not thinking of ourselves as our body alone, but of our whole organism, including our senses, our mind, and our soul.

In the past, the capital city of a city-state might properly be defined in terms of its central and total area, but this can no longer be done since there are no more isolated city-states. A city today may draw half the forces which sustain its life from within its own state, and the other half from the whole world beyond. Singapore is certainly not the thriving city it is today because of the 578 sq. km (225 sq. mi.) which represent the actual area of its state; if world trade declines, Singapore cannot go on existing in its present form. The systems which exist today are much more complex than those of the past, but we have to understand them.

Cities, then, are systems of human settlements, and in order to understand these systems, we must realize that human settlements are unique complex biological individuals. Like all natural organisms, they have a characteristic life-cycle of birth, growth, maturity, decline and death; but unlike most other organisms, the time of their withering and dying is not foreordained. Since their basic genetic material, that is, Anthropos himself, is subject to constant renewal and modification, in a sense human settlements are potentially immortal — if Anthropos manages to build them in balance with the whole system of life.

6

Human settlements are a great deal more than static, built-up areas. Settlements are *processes*, systems in a continuous state of flux as they react to the myriad influences of growing populations, evolving technologies, changing conditions of the natural environment, and successive social, political and cultural institutions. As dynamic, metamorphic entities, they cannot be understood through analysis of their separate parts, no matter how exhaustive or detailed. Since human settlements cannot be separated from the life-streams of their inhabitants — sleeping, interacting, producing, loving, growing — the analysis of settlements cannot be separated from the fourth dimension, that of time. A three-dimensional understanding which leaves out time cannot possibly cover the most essential characteristic of human settlements, which is their intense aliveness. The attempt to analyze cities in terms of their static structure rather than their dynamic functions has been one of the main reasons why Anthropos has progressively lost real understanding of his great urban organisms, and therefore lost control over their evolution.

Human settlements are synergetic phenomena: that is, the behavior of their whole system cannot be understood or predicted from an analysis of any one of the elements which compose them. The essential nature of settlements results from the fusion and interactive balance between their container — or physical structure — and their contents — or Anthropos. The proper study of settlements must therefore revolve round the analysis of the dynamic balance of these two elements.

Existing disciplines are simply not broad enough to cover settlements as a whole, nor do they possess the necessary dynamic analytical tools. There are a multitude of special professions concerned with one or more aspects of settlements — town planner, architect, civil engineer, urban economist, sociologist, traffic engineer, artist, administrator, and so on — but there is a critical shortage of established theory on the subject as a whole, and of people trained to relate the facts together on the holistic level.

Since no discipline existed to deal with human settlements in this way, C.A. Doxiadis proposed the creation and refinement of the new discipline which he called *ekistics*[5]. It was to be devoted to the study of human settlements and to their dynamic and evolutionary processes. Whether this new approach of ekistics qualifies as a discipline, a science, a methodology, or a philosophy is immaterial; indeed, ekistics, by its very nature, must be a science relying in various degrees on one or more of the other sciences. Even if today ekistics is not yet a fully-grown science, it is developing fast in this direction, and this makes us confident that before long it will fully qualify as a science in its own right. The important thing is that ekistics is one response to our immediate need for some sort of unified approach with which to tackle the growing crisis that threatens our urban civilization.

Aristotle stated that the main function of settlements is to make their inhabitants happy and safe, and it is difficult to find a better basic definition, although C.A. Doxiadis has tried to add a few more particular notions in *Anthropopolis*. The quality of the human life within it is the only acceptable standard of measurement for the success of a human settlement. As Protagoras is reported to have said: "Man is the measure of all things"[6], a sentiment to which John Dewey gave a new reformulation two thousand years later when he said: "Humanity is not, as once thought, the end for which all things were formed; it is but a slight and feeble thing, perhaps an episodic one, in the vast stretch of the universe. But for man, man is the center of interest, and the measure of importance."[7] A science of human settlements must move beyond the purely descriptive role into that of the prescriptive if it is to help Anthropos regain as much control as possible over the evolution of his settlements. The central task of ekistics must be to search for a real understanding of the factors which make a settlement successful in human terms, and put that understanding to work in the creation of such settlements.

A successful settlement can only be created by achieving a dynamic balance between Anthropos and his total environment. Anthropos' happiness is intimately related to the ease and satisfaction with which he can adapt to the physical background of his life, so we must try to establish a balance between the various elements of a settlement which will enable Anthropos to adapt easily to them. On the other hand, human beings do not remain the same during the whole course of their lives — they evolve and develop — so settlements must cater for such changing needs, and leave each person free to develop as an individual in the highest and most creative ways possible for him according to his own desires and aptitudes.

Well-meant urban experiments have often proved disastrous simply because people did not realize that findings which had been calculated for one size of human settlement could not be applied to one of a different size. Conclusions which hold true for an urbanized region, for example, are rarely valid for a neighborhood, and solutions which might be appropriate for the problems of the metropolis may have catastrophic results if blindly transposed to deal with the problems of the village. We must therefore classify all the human settlements that exist into categories of sizes before we can begin to work out the correct solution for each one.

The need for such a classification scheme had been known for some time, but unfortunately most classifications now in existence suffer from critical defects. They differ from profession to profession, so that it is hard to compare them. Geography, economics, urban sociology and town planning, for example, classify settlements in radically different ways, each according to their special interests. We can hope that our intended meaning is clear when we speak of the "polis", "metropolis" or "megalopolis", although the way each definition is used in various disciplines and countries can be quite different, and the meaning therefore may be different for each person talking of them. Existing classifications also usually fail to cover the entire spectrum of settlement sizes — the smallest and largest units being most frequently omitted. Indeed, several units which do have a separate meaning are not blessed with any name at all. A third common defect in most classifications is that they fail to reflect the essential four-dimensional nature of dynamic settlements.

Ekistics, as a discipline concerned with metamorphic processes, required an analytical set of scales based on dynamic morphology — a classification scheme which would reflect the evolutionary nature of settlements and the natural stages of their growth. The first problem to be encountered in the creation of such a scheme was simply to determine what constituted a settlement. What was to be included?

We have already said that a human settlement consists of two basic components: Anthropos, who is the content, either alone or in great numbers leading to societies; and the physical settlement with its surrounding environment, which form the container, and which consists of both natural and man-made elements. These two fundamentals can be further subdivided into five elements, which we will call henceforth the *five ekistic elements*. They are:

Nature: the total natural environment which provides the basis for the creation of settlements and the context in which they function.

Anthropos: the inhabitant, as an individual.

Society: the systems of interactions between Anthropoi.

Shells: the structures which shelter Anthropos, his functions and activities.

Networks: the natural and man-made connective systems which serve and integrate settlements, such as roads, water supply and sewerage systems, electrical generating and distribution facilities, communications facilities, and economic, legal, educational and political systems.

Anthropos' building activities have exerted their greatest effect on the quality of human life through the Shells and Networks he has created, while perhaps the element of Nature has suffered most in this process, although recently both Society, and even more, Anthropos himself, have shown symptoms of distress.

Shells and Networks alone are totally inadequate to represent what a human settlement actually is. This realization led to the eventual conclusion that *any space* in which human activity takes place must be considered to be an integral part of at least one settlement. Any specific area may indeed be related simultaneously through different human activities to several different settlements or scales of settlement. Thus, almost every area belongs to some form of settlement. There are a few major exceptions, such as the Polar areas, the Amazon jungles, the high mountains and the great deserts, where Anthropos cannot at present live for extended periods, and which are only tenuously related to any specific settlement — although even these areas are connected to the political systems created by Anthropos and certainly influence his natural environment.

9

There are also minor uninhabitable regions scattered around the globe. All other regions are very clearly related to specific human settlements, and this cannot be ignored in the formulation of a classification scheme.

The full range of sizes of human settlements must include units as small as a bed, where Anthropos settles for one night, and as large as the entire surface of the planet. Experimentation showed that a linear scale would be inappropriate to such a wide spectrum, so, on the basis of practical experience, a set of divisions was worked out resulting in a set of quasi-logarithmic scales, one for each of the ekistic elements. The scales for population and area, which have been used most commonly in the "City of the Future" project, are presented in a simplified way in fig. 1. The smallest and indispensable unit is individual Anthropos. Anthropos is not a settlement by himself, since he is only one of its elements, but he does have personal Shells (such as his clothing, his furniture, or his private vehicles), and he carries around him a minimum bubble of "personal space" which is quite clearly defined for any given individual in any specific situation[8].

Ekistic unit	1	2	3	4	5	6	7	8	9	10	11	12	13	14	15
Community class				I	II	III	IV	V	VI	VII	VIII	IX	X	XI	XII
Kinetic field	a	b	c	d	e	f	g	A	B	C	D	E	F	G	H
name of unit	Anthropos	room	house	housegroup	small neighborhood	neighborhood	small polis	polis	small metropolis	metropolis	small megalopolis	megalopolis	small eperopolis	eperopolis	Ecumenopolis
population	1	2	4	40	250	1.500	9.000	50.000	300,000	2M	14M	100M	700M	5,000M	30,000M

1. ekistic logarithmic scales and grid for population and area

10

Starting with Anthropos, we reach the conclusion that we can deal with the following fifteen ekistic units[9]:

1. Anthropos, as an individual
2. room, which is taken as corresponding to one or two people under normal conditions
3. house
4. housegroup
5. small neighborhood
6. neighborhood
7. small polis
8. polis
9. small metropolis
10. metropolis
11. small megalopolis
12. megalopolis
13. small eperopolis
14. eperopolis
15. global system (whole planet) or Ecumenopolis

Analysis of the area covered by each of the fifteen categories resulted in the quantification of an ekistic logarithmic scale for area, and tabulation of the average number of people living in settlements of each category generated an ekistic logarithmic scale for population. On the logarithmic scales the width of each step is constant, being proportional to the (quasi-) constant ratio of the average values of the phenomenon measured at the two consecutive levels. It can be seen that for the population and area scales the ratio between successive hierarchical levels is generally in the vicinity of 1:7 (between 1:5 and 1:9), which is in accordance with the theoretical precepts of central place theory[10].

Certain discontinuities may be found in both scales. In the smaller units especially, the central place theory is less applicable, and this in itself is a lesson that the way Anthropos organizes his settlements is not the same in all units of space. In the population scale the Anthropos-to-room and room-to-house unit ratios were determined on the basis of global averages — estimated at approximately two rooms per house unit, and about two people to a room. On the area scale there is a major discontinuity between the area of the house unit and that of the typical group of house units, and another jump at the level of the small megalopolis — the first truly regional settlement consisting of an interconnected system of urban centers functionally integrated with a broad surrounding region.

For the presentation of comparative data in the form of histograms, the ekistic logarithmic scales may be replaced by the corresponding ekistic grids, the steps of which have been standardized to constant values in order to facilitate the undistorted presentation of such data.

When we divide the human settlements of the entire globe according to this classification we see at once that at the present moment they are moving up in size from the metropolis to the megalopolis. We might therefore be tempted to ask ourselves: should we not limit this project to the study of the megalopolis, since it seems that the megalopolis is to be the City of the Future?

We cannot say this, however, since we have not yet defined what we mean by the word "future" in terms of this project. Until we have done so we cannot say what the form of the city will be at that time, and to assume that it will be the megalopolis would be to limit ourselves wrongly. We must first define all the dimensions of our subject before we try to study it: we therefore proceed to define our use of "future" in the following section.

3. A realistic definition of the future

We are confused in talking about our future unless we are clear how long or short a period we mean. We may say that it is impossible to change the city at all in the future — and that could be true if we meant one year from now. However, if we meant ten or twenty years hence, then it would not be true at all, since we could certainly change our city if we had twenty years in which to do it. Our definition of the "future" must be a useful one. It is pointless for us to discuss some time as near as tomorrow, or as far away as a thousand years from now. There would be no point in this study concerning itself with the eventual freezing of the earth, since that will not take place for millions of years.

There are two ways to go about deciding how far into the future we should look. The first is to consider the units of time most naturally related to the things we are studying. If we were dealing with the life of one human being, for instance, we would not need to look forward for more than a hundred years; if we were dealing with some particular insects, then a single year would be long enough. The second way is to try to see what phase of development our subject is in at this moment, and to study that phase until its end. This is like climbing a high mountain and being unable to see the top, let alone knowing if there is another range of mountains beyond it. It is reasonable for us to try and decide how long we will take to reach the top of the mountain we can actually see, and then reconsider the next step ahead when we have reached the top and can see what lies before us. In this study we try to use both these methods.

We decided that a reasonable basic unit of time to use was that of one generation, that is, between 25 and 30 years. In order to analyze all the different aspects of settlements we decided we would need to cover as a whole a span extending for 250 years. The reasons why we did so are these:

Few settlements have a life span as short as one or two centuries. Many have a continuous existence of several millennia. Their average lifetime, according to one of our own estimates, has been close to 800 or 1,000 years. A single year therefore, or even a decade, would be far too brief a time unit to be used in a broad study of settlement evolution. Almost no part of the physical structure of settlements has an effective life span as short as a decade. Urban houses usually last for at least 30 years. Public buildings — churches, banks, hospitals, government facilities — generally last for considerably longer, for a century or more. Networks, such as roads, drainage systems and power-lines, which have the most influence on the physical structure of settlements, change most slowly of all. Landownership patterns and public roads change so little that, despite frequent additions and repairs, the main layouts of Networks change hardly at all over very long periods of time.

Thus the general structure of settlements tends to remain stable for long periods. While it is true that most settlements are now rapidly expanding into the surrounding countryside, their most developed and mature sections change slowly, and it is these older established parts that give settlements a great deal of their individuality. A century, then, is about the minimal period of time we can give ourselves in order to study the processes of change throughout a whole urban organism, including these older established areas.

A second argument also supports the choice of a century as a minimum period of time. Human settlements, like human populations, evolve through S-shaped cycles of growth, as one might expect from their biological nature. Mankind is clearly in the middle of a period of wild acceleration, a period of rapid growth and change which our research indicates is likely to continue for one or two more generations. A decelerating phase should follow, less tumultuous but still far from stable, of approximately the same duration. Eventually human population must reach a relatively stable and balanced equilibrium with global natural environment.

Since many important variables — such as use of resources, incomes, energy consumption, pollution, international tension — are intimately linked to population growth, it would be unreasonable to adopt a time horizon, the end of which would fall right in the middle of the wildly ascending branch of the population curve. The period of rapid change must be studied in its entirety, and also enough of the stable conditions that follow to give a picture of the equilibrium in its final and sustainable form. So any period of less than a century would be inadequate.

A set of future dates was therefore chosen to be used consistently throughout all our projections. The year 2000 was included to make it easy to compare our results with those of other studies which are often based on this date. The year 1960 was used as a base point because, when we began this study in 1960, this was the most recent date for which reasonably complete global data existed.

The year 1975 was chosen because it is both approximately halfway between these two dates and close to the time this study will be presented. Further dates were added at 25-year intervals in order to facilitate broad comparisons to such concepts as "the middle" or "the first quarter" of the century. This gave us the final series: 1960, 1975, 2000, 2025, 2050, 2075, 2100, 2125, 2150, etc.

The nature of the population growth curve suggested that it could be divided into three periods corresponding to the accelerating, decelerating and stable phases. The general form of the curve indicated that significant deceleration of population growth is unlikely to set in much before the year 2000, but that by 2100 convergence on some form of global ecological equilibrium will be well under way. At the beginning of the 22nd century, the final consolidation of human settlements around our globe into a unified system is expected to occur.

The basic unit of time for our study was therefore taken as 25 years, the lower limit of time for one generation. Then we must look forward for at least 100 years from 1975 in order to see the end of the period during which most of the things which go to make up today's settlements — the people and buildings — will have been replaced. We will need a further 150 years after that in order to reach the top of the mountain we are climbing at this moment, the period that will cover the stabilization of those forces still in the process of violent action today. In all, therefore, we need to look forward for 250 years, from 1975 to 2225. This is our definition of the future for the present study.

We must next answer the question: can we make any predictions for such a period of eight or nine generations, or 250 years?

In thinking about the future we confront ourselves with a very basic subject of speculation. Are we entitled to speak about the future? Can we actually say anything about the future? There is an old Greek saying: "The common man knows the present, some wise men know tomorrow, but only God knows the future." Is it not, therefore, a daunting task to give ourselves? Do we perhaps venture outside our domain into that of God when we try to talk of the future?

We do think that it is a big task: but we do not think we should not attempt it. After all, the "tomorrow" some wise men were said to know about was not defined as being just one day from now, it could be several years hence — and Anthropos is always trying to grow wings in order to fly higher and higher in his eternal struggle to achieve something better.

To achieve our goal we must start from somewhere positive. A realistic way to begin is to try and connect the present situation of all types of settlements in all countries and areas, and under all systems, with their future situation. If our predictions are not realistic, then it will be found impossible to make such connections. Since the whole work has tried to select only those solutions which are necessary and possible, we now have the task of tracing the best road connecting the present situation with future trends.

The future is a *most mysterious proposition*. Since the dawn of history Anthropos has been caught up by the desire to know his fate before it happens to him. Oracles and priests, fortune-tellers and mystics, have been his constant companions in his endless search for an understanding of what tomorrow, and the day after, will bring.

With the advent of the scientific age Anthropos has added sophisticated calculation techniques to his repertoire of tools for harvesting knowledge for the future. Nevertheless, many people remain firmly convinced that the future cannot be accurately foretold, even by the new oracles — and in many respects they are right, although in some others they are certainly not. We are now in a position to forecast the decline of several diseases, the increase of incomes at certain rates, and so on. The term "future" is so complex that we have to be very careful before stating if we can forecast it or not. This book represents an effort to find out as much as we can about the future; in a sense, it cannot help but be a treatise on certainty and uncertainty. It is not really surprising, in the light of past efforts on the topic, that the public should regard books on the future — and in particular on such a dubious subject as the future of human settlements 250 years hence — with the uncomfortable feeling that they can never be more than pure speculation about the unknowable probability distribution of innumerable alternatives. The "City of the Future" project endeavors to prove them wrong.

With his characteristic insight, Mark Twain once observed: "The future is not what it used to be." The future is an incomplete image, shimmering and shifting elusively, never quite the same. But it is by no means totally indeterminate. There exist definite limits to what might be, although the limits themselves are in a constant state of flux. As the present materializes, the indeterminate continuously becomes determinate, and as each succeeding moment of "now" is added to the enormously complex body of facts of the past, its addition changes the number of things which control the range of possible futures.

Human decision and action are becoming steadily more important in determining what will in fact emerge from the mists of uncertainty and become the present. As Anthropos grows ever more powerful, so the extent to which he can influence his own future grows. Anthropos has already wrested a measure of control over his destiny from the unknown which once totally surrounded him. For the first time he now has sufficient means to sterilize or even destroy the biosphere — that extraordinary thin film of organic life which clings to the surface of his planet on the borderline between dead rock and dead vacuum. The exercise of such tremendous power, whether for good or evil, with or without intention, automatically influences the probable future of the biosphere in which the human race must live.

Anthropos is continuously making his own future. Almost every action he takes has repercussions which will far outlive it. Every institution and act of legislation concerned with the physical environment has some lasting effect on it. Every individual building which is created, every road or factory or dam which is built, commits its surroundings not just for its own lifetime alone, but for the often much longer time during which it will have an influence. Those houses and offices which are built today will largely predetermine the physical plan of our settlements for at least the next hundred years; the parks and industrial areas, roads and sewers built today will create conditions which will last for several centuries. So the physical structure of those settlements we are creating will, insofar as human settlements may be said to determine the quality of human life lived within them, influence the nature and quality not only of our own lives, but of those of our descendants.

In order to move beyond general and intellectually courageous concepts to specific estimates, we have to distinguish what the forces are which are actually shaping the City of the Future. When we do this we can recognize the existence of four different futures[11] for everything about which we are talking within the city (fig. 2). The first of these futures is the constant one, represented by things like the mountains, which we cannot change, or the fundamental properties of matter and energy. The second future is represented by those elements which are inherited from the past but which are declining and will be gradually eliminated, such as the present generation of people, or houses which are in a dilapidated state, or the cultural traits and technological inventions which have been

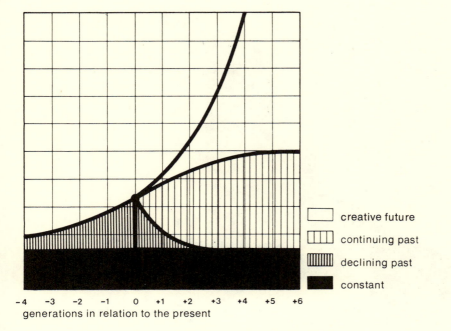

creative future
continuing past
declining past
constant

-4   -3   -2   -1   0   +1   +2   +3   +4   +5   +6
generations in relation to the present

2.   the four futures of human settlements

superseded: that is the declining past. The third future is represented by the continuing past, such things as the children of the present generation who are influenced by parents now alive, houses being built according to the patterns of existing ones, or roads which are existing today and will go on being used. The fourth future is the creative one: this is the future which will come into being because of things that do not exist at all today — new ideas, new technology, new developments. It is this creative future which in fact makes all the real difference between the past and the future, and which marks the difference between Anthropos and animals, since they cannot influence their future in this way, whereas Anthropos can. Anyone who insists on thinking about only one of these futures is either an extreme conservative, who will not admit that life changes at all, or else an extreme radical, who believes life can be changed overnight. Our cities, however, are biological systems, and we must therefore deal with continuity and change. With the passing of time we can effect greater and greater change.

When we look at these four futures, we can see that there are some forces which can certainly be predicted — particularly in the first two futures; that there are reasonably predictable forces in the third future; and forces which will require our imaginations in order to predict them in the fourth and creative future. If we try to make a probable projection of all the forces of human settlements into the future (fig. 3), we can see that we can be quite certain about such a

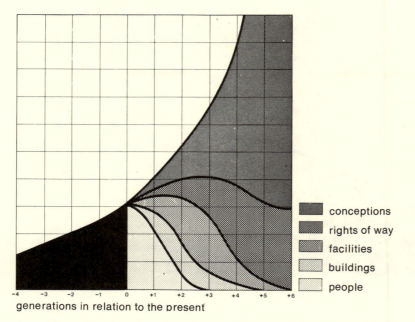

conceptions
rights of way
facilities
buildings
people

generations in relation to the present

3.   probable projection of present forces into the future

18

projection of several forces for a few generations ahead, and that therefore we have a sound foundation according to which we can think about the fourth future.

In order, therefore, to lay the proper foundations, we must first predict all those things that are predictable. It is simply cowardice to avoid the obligation to predict because of a fear that something unpredictable might happen.

We now reach the point at which we must ask: how about the fourth future, the new and creative one? Here we must use our imagination, since, as René Dubos very well said: "To imagine is an act which gives human beings the chance to engage in something akin to creation."[12] If we have the courage and ability to imagine what the fourth future will be, we will help ourselves to see not only where we are going, but also what we must create in order to get there in the best possible way. We will really be opening roads that will allow the creation we need to take place.

4. The dimensions of the City of the Future

We had to define the future we were going to discuss before we could decide the size of settlement unit that was going to become the "city" in this future. From the viewpoint of today, it looked as if this settlement would be the megalopolis. If we were speaking of a future a few decades from now, we might concentrate on the problems of some small cities of the old-fashioned type, many big cities, many metropolitan areas and a few emerging megalopolises. However, when we come to think about the future of 250 years hence, we see that nothing less than the area of the whole earth will do, since already some of the world's new central cities, such as New York, London, Tokyo and Rotterdam, together with their financial networks, cover the whole globe. In several generations from now these Networks will have become so interwoven it will be impossible to separate them without endangering the whole of mankind.

Ekistic unit	1	2	3	4	5	6	7	8	9	10	11	12	13	14	15
Community class				I	II	III	IV	V	VI	VII	VIII	IX	X	XI	XII
Kinetic field	a	b	c	d	e	f	g	A	B	C	D	E	F	G	H
name of unit	Anthropos	room	house	housegroup	small neighborhood	neighborhood	small polis	polis	small metropolis	metropolis	small megalopolis	megalopolis	small eperopolis	eperopolis	Ecumenopolis
population	1	2	4	40	250	1.500	9.000	50.000	300.000	2M	14M	100M	700M	5.000M	30.000M

(Vertical axis years: 1900, 1950, 2000, 2050, 2100, 2150)

4. changing focus of the "City of the Future" project

Even today, many problems which affect human settlements are global ones that can no longer be dealt with by divided national authorities. Barbara Ward and René Dubos have given an analysis of the fatal flaws which, to date, have prevented our economic and political mechanisms from dealing adequately with global environmental problems[13]. As human activity increases, our oceans, our atmosphere and our climate are placed in increasing jeopardy, and the need for a global response becomes a clear ecological imperative.

Human settlements show a metamorphic consolidation into ever larger units with the passage of time (fig. 4). We will go into this phenomenon in detail later. At present, the megalopolis is indeed the most important category, but later on emphasis will shift to the small eperopolis, then to the eperopolis and finally to Ecumenopolis itself, the linked system of human settlements of all sizes which will extend over the whole globe. We must therefore understand our whole life system, which will extend over the whole earth, from the villages — which are suffering or disappearing today — to the very largest types of settlements.

The conclusion is quite clear: because the present phase of Anthropos' evolution will end with the creation of one unified system of life, and because we have already begun to build this system, the City of the Future must have the dimensions of the whole globe.

5. Our method

Since we wanted to find out not what we, the authors, hoped would happen to human settlements in the future, but what was actually going to happen to them, we tried to develop a research method which would achieve this as accurately as possible.

Before we go on to describe it, we must deal with the possible question: how can you call this a research project, since you cannot check your conclusions? It is certainly true that we cannot check conclusions as scientists can in a laboratory. We can, however, check the continuing processes which lead to those conclusions, since we live in the actual subjects of our study — human settlements — and can observe those processes going on all round us. We, the authors, have therefore been studying the development of such processes continuously during the two generations which have elapsed since we ourselves began to live in human settlements, during one generation since we began to study settlements seriously, and during half a generation during the progress of this study itself. We have therefore had the opportunity to check if our predictions have been along the right lines or not.

What kind of research is this, then? It can only be called an ekistic research project. It does not belong to the science of physical planning, since it creates a new framework. Nor does it belong to economics, social sciences, geography, or any of the technical, political or administrative sciences. It belongs to the science of ekistics, which aims to study all the aspects of human settlements covered individually by these other sciences.

We had, therefore, to use every possible method of research, from realistic ones following up phenomena and experimenting with them in various ways to developing abstract models. We also used the method of publicly announcing our findings in order to get the comments of as many people in as many fields as possible, since it is just not possible for any one person or group to have enough knowledge or experience to deal with this enormous subject of human settlements alone.

We were very much aware that the greatest danger, when starting such a new project as ours, was that of imposing damaging limitations on ourselves by formulating a detailed design of research in advance. We knew that the road before us was far from clear, and we wanted to make sure we were not committed to any ideas about our subject, or to any of the solutions to its problems, before we began. We therefore chose an approach that would leave us complete freedom, both in the concept of our problem and in working out its solutions. We recognized that in doing it this way we might end up without any specific answers at all, but we believed this danger to be less serious than the possibility of limiting our thought in advance. Any research project which tries to open up new frontiers of thought must preserve its freedom of concept in this way. The process of opening up new frontiers is what counts, not the achievement of specific goals.

We believed that within the subject of ekistics too many things are already taken for granted, and we wanted to take nothing at all for granted. Later on we discovered that a similar attitude is being developed in the physical sciences today. Thomas H. Johnson, a former Director of Research of the Atomic Energy Commission, has said: "The more specifically one tries to define the practical purpose of a research, the more indefinite becomes its bearing on the important questions of science, and the less reason a scientist can find for doing it."

Since it is imperative to retain such freedom of concept, it is also important not to define this project as belonging either to basic or to applied research. We are not making any innovation here. Researchers in the physical sciences have already discovered, and are coming more and more to believe that "a new mating of basic and applied research can lead to unsuspected and far-reaching insights that neither applied nor ivory-tower research would be likely to uncover separately"[14]

Nor did we allow ourselves to decide in advance that we were concerned with the problems of "urbanization". We did not want to assume that our solutions would be in terms of urbanization alone. We did not want to be bound to the study of any one category of settlement — such as cities or megalopolises — any more than to the attitudes of any one discipline. Our use of the word 'City' in our title *Ecumenopolis: The Inevitable City of the Future* is only indicative, as we have already emphasized. We use 'city' to stand as the symbol of Anthropos' organized system of life, and do not limit our project to the idea of the city as it is usually understood today.

For similar reasons, since this is an ekistic study, it has covered human settlements of all sizes in the ekistic scale, and has included the subcomponents and elements of systems of settlements and the Networks which connect them. We could not deal with aspects of human activity not directly related to human settlements in any detail however, so many specialized studies in other fields will be needed before any sort of total picture of the urban future of humanity emerges. All we could do was to synthesize some of the knowledge from other fields that could clarify some implications for this future.

Interest in scientific methods of analyzing the future has recently grown throughout the world in a spectacular way. The feasible length of forecasting has risen dramatically in many fields, and books and terminology have proliferated. Each discipline and profession has, however, concentrated on developing its own techniques. Many of these, often of great ingenuity and sophistication, are available, but unfortunately most of them are only applicable to the problems for which they were devised. Little had been published on the long-range research on the future of human settlements when the "City of the Future" project began, so we were forced to develop an ekistic methodology, and a plan of research and set of analytical strategies to deal with our own needs and objectives.

Since we are forced to use continually the word "prediction" when describing our methods, we must begin by trying to clarify our thinking about the possibilities of prediction. When making projections into the remote future, it is necessary to generalize; the more specific one tries to be, the less reliability can be attached to conclusions. Something like Heisenberg's Uncertainty Principle in physics seems to apply to ekistic projections: the further one tries to advance into detail, the more imprecise and elusive the behavior of the phenomena under study. The further one tries to look into the future, the greater are the number of small-scale elements we become unable to determine; the vision blurs, until only the basic outlines of the form of the remote future can be perceived. What we say of time also applies to space. Projections which deal with very large units — the whole earth, continents or very large regions — are much safer than projections relating to small areas, and the smaller the area the more elusive it becomes. Forecasting the future is like trying to throw things a great distance: a feather can only be thrown a few feet, while a good piece of rock can be heaved for a hundred yards. The smaller the phenomenon projected, the less its "inertia", and the less sure one can be of the actual path it will take into the future.

It is reasonably safe to make predictions about some things — for example, economic trends within a certain nation or within humanity as a whole. We have now learned enough about the evolution of certain aspects of economics to make it not unreasonable for us to assume a certain evolution will take place under certain conditions within a certain period of time.

It is even more possible to make predictions about the physical facts related to our cities — the total investment in them, and the actual structures within them. It would be unreasonable for us to assume in advance such an unpredictable event as a destructive war, and unless we have such a war we will not demolish the wealth invested in our cities overnight. So the major part of every city that exists now will go on existing until each part has completely outlived its usefulness, both economically and culturally. We do, therefore, have the ability to make predictions about such elements of our cities for a reasonable period of time. If we assume the average life of a building is one century in cities all over the world, and facilities created now will last even longer on average (providing proper maintenance takes place), then it is reasonable for us to attempt to make predictions about the buildings and facilities in our cities for a period between one century and a century and a half from now, when they will either still exist or will be created.

As we have said earlier, the larger the units of space with which we are dealing, the more accurate the prediction. The further we move up the ekistic scale from the neighborhood towards the megalopolis and small eperopolis (fig. 5), the more we can rely on rational solutions being made, and therefore on estimates about them. Within the smaller ekistic units, such as the room or even the housegroup, we must depend more on people's individual desires and emotions. This is why we have not dealt so fully with small units in our study, but have concentrated our attention on the largest scales of settlements, such as megalopolis and Ecumenopolis, as well as on those variables which lend themselves to quantification and projection with some degree of reliability into the remote future.

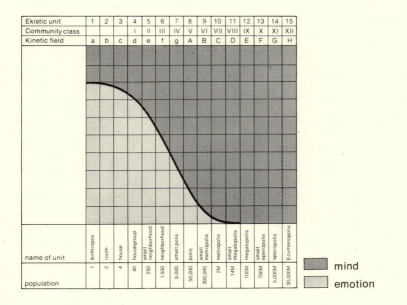

5.   probable validity of predictions by ekistic unit

We can see that it is also more possible to make accurate predictions about Shells and Networks (fig. 6) than about anything to do with Society, and that economic and technological forecasts are more reliable than political or cultural ones. Knowing such things makes it easier for us to know where we can make reliable statements, and where the present state of our knowledge makes it difficult or even impossible to predict.

We believe, from the study of many interesting projects on the future evolution of mankind, that it has now been established how difficult it is to predict anything directly related to the evolution and future of Anthropos himself. Even things easiest to describe and directly related to numbers, such as the total future population of the earth, or the total population of any nation or continent, seem difficult. We know that every specific attempt to predict such things has tended to be wrong. Let us remember the population forecasts prepared before the last war, one of which, for example, stated that the population of England and Wales would be below 30 million people by the year 2000. This is already a very low estimate, because the population is already 48.6 million although we have 26 years still to go. In this instance, we even failed to predict the possible evolution in terms of numbers of people for the near future.

Practically every method used to predict population growth has failed because of great changes which have taken place in the life-patterns of the people who

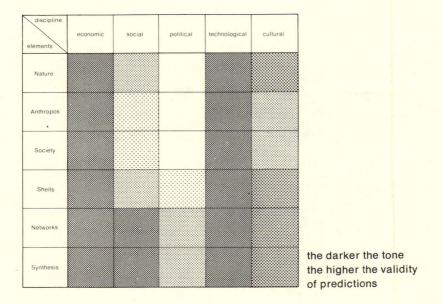

the darker the tone
the higher the validity
of predictions

6. probable validity of predictions by disciplines and ekistic elements

were creating families. The situation is such that scientists like P.B. Medawar have wondered whether all the predictions about future population, such as those for England, will have to be changed ten or twenty years from now, if and when we see new and unexpected increases. We might then have to think of dangers of over-population even within what we have been calling the "older population groups". This development has in fact actually come to pass since he made this speculation. So we now know enough about our ability to predict the evolution of mankind itself to be certain that we cannot be sure about specific estimates. People like P.B. Medawar even suggest that we will have to learn much more by studying "the process of foretelling rather than what is actually foretold"[15].

If we ask ourselves, then, how much we can rely on our predictions, we would answer in terms of our own evaluations, which are related to the size of the ekistic units and to the five elements of human settlements to which those predictions refer. The larger the size of a unit, the more reliable the prediction will be, and predictions that are concerned with Shells and Networks will be far more reliable than those concerned with Anthropos or Society.

There are, of course, many people who, when trying to design cities of the future, rely totally on their imagination. Often, when we find ourselves unable to predict something, we wonder if we cannot simply imagine what would happen. Let us try to think about the imagination and how much it can really help us with these problems.

A long experience of this subject and dedication to it has led us to the following conclusion: in dealing with human settlements, which are biological systems created by Nature and Anthropos, we must find the laws that govern them. Would it be reasonable to suppose that imagination alone discovered the law of gravity, or any of the laws in biology or astronomy? It can be useful to have the imagination to see what is happening, and why it happens, but we must also observe the actual phenomena themselves, the falling apple or the rotating moon; the use of the imagination on its own is naive in terms of science.

Our study of human settlements through ekistics has convinced us that Anthropos follows certain principles and laws[16] in forming his settlements. Our imagination should therefore be used to understand these age-old processes and see where they are leading us, rather than to give form to our personal desires, and then confuse these with Anthropos' real needs and the real trends. It is these real needs and trends that actually shape our city.

To succeed in our difficult task we do sometimes need to use our imaginations in the way poets do, since we often need the courage of interpretation a poet has when, as Edith Sitwell said: "Like Moses, he sees God in the burning bush when the half-opened or myopic physical eye sees only the gardener burning leaves."

We can also remember Thoreau's statement that: "As the dead man is spiritualized, so the *imagination* requires a long range. It is the faculty of the poet to see present things as if also past and future, as if distant or universally significant."[17] We can realize, then, that the imagination cannot be excluded from such an effort as ours, but it must be used only when it helps the scientist to widen his views, and not when it attempts to turn him into an artist — which is a completely different thing.

So let us see that we are faced with the task of making predictions about a composite phenomenon, the city as a whole, which is composed of two elements, Anthropos and his Society, and all the physical aspects of the city. We must recognize that the value of the predictions we make about each of these two elements must perforce be different. It will perhaps be possible for us to develop a methodology for predicting the future of our cities so that we can see what their certain evolution will be unless we take action to avoid it. We will then be able to take that action. The evolution of animals and plants takes place without their being able to do anything to avoid or change it, but Anthropos can act, and can change his future.

We have, then, built and tested models of the remote future of Anthropos, and made outlines for the revolution towards that future which we consider highly likely, in recognition that, by their nature, different aspects of the future are not equally susceptible to numerical projection. Some, such as population, we have been able to treat in some detail, although we can never be sure what will happen in this area. Others, such as the nature of future political systems, remain completely beyond our methodological grasp. The coverage of our study is of necessity uneven, but it is to be hoped that subsequent work will further refine its reliability and extend its coverage, correcting our mistakes and filling in the worst gaps.

When dealing with individual cases, we have tried to select examples from all continents and areas throughout the world with people who have recently been exposed to the actual conditions and problems in urban settlements. We have covered all continents, and have come into contact with all types of human settlements in many nations, in many different stages of development, in many cultures, and under different types of economic, social, political, technological and cultural conditions.

We have, however, had to face one big limitation from the start: because of the difficulties of communication it was not possible for us to study China or Russia directly, nor some of the countries of Eastern Europe for which no data are published. Few things exist in the bibliography on problems of interest to this project in these countries. When we consider that Eastern Europe is developing under distinct political, social and economic theories, we must recognize that a basic weakness in our project at its present phase is not to have covered one big area of the globe, and more especially one that is developing under a separate system. We must state, therefore, that our present project is based mainly on very detailed experience gained on all five continents of Western-aligned countries, and only to a limited extent on information gained from countries within the Eastern Bloc. It is to be hoped that this basic weakness can be overcome, either through collaboration with representatives from the Eastern Bloc — which would be preferable — or through permission that may be granted for studies to be made of similar problems within these countries.

We did also think at first that it might be useful to select one city born in our time and now growing into the future, and had thought of taking Islamabad for this purpose[18]. We later decided, however, that we would leave this for a later specific case study of the City of the Future in order to remain as objective as possible in this present study and avoid being influenced by a major project of Doxiadis Associates in which we ourselves are so deeply involved.

Our first aim was to try and predict what would happen on this earth by the end of the time we had set, supposing that everything continues to happen according to the present trends. This would be to assume that humanity will not think of any better policies for its cities, will not work out better programs for their development, and will not implement policies and programs with any greater effectiveness than it does at present. This is relatively easy to predict, so long as we assume that the problems, policies and programs are all going to remain just the same as they are now.

However, it is also necessary to predict what may happen within the period set if new forces become active, that is, if population sizes, economy or technology develop in unprecedented ways, or in ways which we cannot expect as most probable. This is, of course, an extreme case, but in it we are faced with much greater difficulties in prediction, since by definition we must assume the inclusion of unknown forces. Predictions which include such unknown factors may, of course, be wrong. We can only try to outline the possibilities of an evolution which may happen under new conditions but which may in fact never arise.

Also, in order to be like the two-headed eagle which can look back as well as forward[19], we made a study of all past types of settlements as well as those of the present. Only by so doing could we learn about the processes of their development so that we could make extrapolations into the future.

During the first two or three years of this project the objectives of the study even were revised several times. Preliminary explorations were made in many directions to feel out areas of analysis which it would be necessary to include in any study of the future of human settlements. We gathered a wealth of data on the historical evolution, current trends, achievements and problems of many cities throughout the world through a special series of surveys, one of which, covering about one hundred cities, was carried out within the Athens Center of Ekistics. This knowledge was supplemented by that obtained during the planning work of Doxiadis Associates on such projects as Rio de Janeiro, the Urban Detroit Area, the Rio de la Plata region, and other areas around the world. These preliminary probings culminated in the first formulation of the Ecumenopolis concept, and the first detailed statement of this was made in public by C.A. Doxiadis in June 1961[20]. Both the Ecumenopolis concept itself and the accumulated data were subjected to intensive scrutiny in a series of discussions among a group of experts, mainly in the summer of 1961 but also during the following summer and on numerous subsequent occasions, with a small nucleus of the project's team guiding the effort and keeping track of developments.

In the second stage of the project, many more detailed studies were carried out attacking single aspects of the future, exploring and isolating independent approaches, providing many refinements to the overall view given by the Ecumenopolis concept, correcting erroneous hypotheses, and generally adding detail and extending the coverage of the project. A long series of continuous feedback processes began, constantly recycling ideas and findings and reformulating hypotheses. Additions, corrections and revisions were made, based on the evolution of ideas and findings within the project and on the incorporation of new views and techniques developed in other fields. These findings have been included in 135 main internal reports totalling 5,679 pages, and 123 subsidiary ones totalling another 3,791 pages, or a total of 258 internal reports with 9,470 pages, and a total of 1,715 maps, graphs and other drawings.

While the project was mainly concerned with the largest scales of urbanization — continental and global — many smaller scale studies were also worked out, ranging from subcontinental to regional. The degree of detail and sophistication attained in these case studies varied considerably, but in most cases they gave a valuable insight into the local texture and layout of Ecumenopolis. A few of these case studies contributed valuable clarifications and refinements to the general methodology. The methodology itself evolved gradually by trial and error until it reached its present state, an eclectic synthesis of a variety of techniques drawn from many fields, rather than a complex elaboration founded on any single technique.

Our first detailed statement of the Ecumenopolis concept was made, as we have said, in 1961, but as the project evolved it became clear that all our work was converging to further strengthen the initial insight. The vision of Ecumenopolis was being strengthened by new findings and new conclusions as we saw further and further into the future. One of the most remarkable findings of this study was just this fact, that several different methods of approach, which were developed within it, all seemed to converge towards the same final picture of Ecumenopolis, and therefore to reinforce it. What is more, these different methods of approach were found to be truly independent of one another, which made their value in strengthening the conclusion still greater. We will give a short description of some of these methods of approach here. They will be described in detail later on.

One of our first methods of approach was to determine the degree of habitability in the future of the areas into which the globe was divided. We then decided what the maximum density of population would be for each area according to its degree of habitability. From this we could work out what was the maximum capacity of each area to sustain a population. We assumed that at some remote future point the actual population in each place would come close to this maximum, given enough time for economic and technological development, and providing other limiting factors (discussed later) did not interfere. When we added up all these maximum populations we could discover the final maximum population of the globe according to the habitability of its various areas alone, and also what the distribution of this population would be by broad areas. It became apparent that, once reached, this maximum population would remain stable — or quasi-stable — for a relatively long period, since the global capacity to sustain human settlements would have become saturated.

Another method we used was to try and work out what the geometric pattern would be of the distribution of human settlements in the remote future. We found an optimum pattern corresponding to a system of axes and centers of ekistic development over the globe. The optimum pattern was the one which would allow the maximum communication and interaction within the large-scale system which, it was anticipated, would develop as a major ekistic network. It was also the most economical arrangement, and the one which gave the best advantages from the point of view of environmental conservation, social interaction and other aspects. We saw that this would have to be a hierarchical system, with more or less the same structure at all its highest levels. When we had determined this pattern, we discovered a common denominator between it and the previously developed habitability pattern, so that the network was more developed in the more habitable areas and less in the less habitable ones. This led us to a mutual refinement and enrichment of both approaches.

A third method was the "evolutionary" approach. We recognized the emergence of the new large-scale ekistic units, such as the (predominantly linear) megalopolis at a regional scale, and extrapolated the trends they represented. We found that larger and larger linear formations were likely to develop forming larger and more completely interconnected ekistic networks. The striking fact is that the final, stable and fully interconnected network, covering the entire planet, was found to be the same as the one resulting from the previous method. So the pattern that would develop according to that established by historical evolution coincided with the one worked out according to a theoretical geometric pattern. Both expressed, in a way, through the Ecumenopolis image the major geographic constants provided by coastlines, mountains, climatic regions, and so on, as these affect human habitation of the globe.

The evolutionary approach was a unified study conducted on the global scale. Another approach consisted of various independent regional studies, carried out on smaller or larger scales. In every case it was found that each such regional study came to inscribe itself neatly within the more generalized pattern resulting from the previous global approach. Minor adjustments proved necessary in some cases, "correcting" either the global or the local pattern, or both. By and large, however, the congruence of these two independent methods of approach was remarkable, thus reinforcing the final Ecumenopolis picture.

We also developed different models for Ecumenopolis according to various assumptions as to future economic, social, political, technological or cultural developments. What was remarkable was that, save for the most extreme of these assumptions, the bulk of the Ecumenopolis models which resulted showed a similar basic structure: the location and the course of its major axes and centers were found to remain practically invariant for all these varying assumptions, which confirmed the objective and stable nature of the basic structure of Ecumenopolis. This invariance formed another reinforcement of the conceptual independence and unity of Ecumenopolis.

We also carried out projections for some of the factors and resources which might restrict the ultimate total population of the globe, such as economic and energy development, food, water, minerals, and environmental conditions. A striking feature of our results was that every one of these factors, given enough time for economic and technological development, would allow population figures even higher than those arrived at according to the habitability method. Given enough time, the earth could produce enough food to feed a population larger than the one consistent with the conditions of habitability of its various areas. The same is true for water, energy and other resources, and also for the preservation of the environmental balance between Anthropos and Nature. Clearly then, it is habitability itself which is the most restrictive factor on future population, and the projections made according to habitability remain valid and need not be corrected for other factors at the time of Ecumenopolis. On this assumption we developed projections for each such factor congruent with those developed for habitability. We were left with a system of interrelated projections for these factors which were internally consistent, and could be used to describe the corresponding aspects of Ecumenopolis and further strengthen the concept.

Many other partial studies that were made could be inscribed within the overall concept of Ecumenopolis, and their convergence towards this same goal was one of the major proofs of the validity of the concept of Ecumenopolis itself. Moreover, (and this is very important), no partial study among the many carried out within this project ever resulted in an outcome conflicting with the picture of Ecumenopolis, or even leading to a drastic revision of any of its basic features.

We hope to stimulate discussion and criticism of our methodology and vision as a part of our method. This will be most useful for the further refinement of our ideas, and the eventual solving of our problems. In 1961, as we have said, we started circulating specific proposals to our collaborators on the whole research project, and at the beginning of 1963 we presented our ideas and findings to international conferences and symposia in order to get as much criticism as possible and check every aspect of our effort[21].

The result was that some eminent people, such as Arnold Toynbee, who had himself independently predicted the universal trends[22], agreed with our predictions. Others disagreed completely. Others simply failed to understand what we were talking about and attacked the concept of Ecumenopolis as if it were something we had made up, rather than something we had worked out from researches on the facts.

The general pattern since then is clear and somewhat unexpected. Whereas in the early '60's the reaction at international conferences and symposia to our ideas was strongly negative, indeed they were often wildly attacked, a very marked change has taken place within a relatively short time. Our ideas began to be accepted, more and more so with time, and the number of exceptions to this trend has gradually been reduced. Many outstanding scholars and thinkers have got to the point of agreeing, in broad terms, with the essence of our ideas — even if they disagree on points of detail — and the general climate of opinion in both academic and practical areas seems to have turned to general acceptance of the broad principles underlying many of our findings.

What we still have not had is any specific criticism of the predictions we have made in terms of the people, forces, or the spatial formation of the City of the Future. Indeed, some people who before had been making very different predictions of their own (such as that cities would be built on the sea, as in the Gulf of Tokyo project) have, since 1965, begun to design their own parts of universal systems in silent acceptance of what we had predicted — or, what is more important, for lack of any argument against it.

Twelve years have now passed since our official presentations and publications. We have still had no valid arguments made against our facts: we hope for them.

We have opened an analytical door on the remote future of human settlements, in the hope that we have clarified the basic elements of Anthropos' possible futures, and shown what factors are likely to limit him and the importance and gravity of the problems before us all, so that we may find ways of meeting the crises mankind will have to face in the coming decades. It is hoped that the unavoidable deficiencies and imperfections which must accompany such an exploratory work will be balanced by the contribution we make in opening up an unexplored field in which scientific knowledge is so badly needed.

The goal we have set ourselves, and the methodology we selected, are certainly very ambitious. To those used to walking on safe ground, the description of this project must have created the fear that it would require the work of more people and more resources than are known to most research projects. We knew from the start what the extent of our own limitations were in terms of time, funds available, experience, numbers of people. We did not think this a good reason not to begin, nor to limit our work to something more specific.

We began with the belief that our main purpose was to open up new ways of thought, and that new horizons could not be opened by the imposition of any limitations. The important thing for us was to start out along this new road, not necessarily to walk too far or to reach the final destination too fast. So this project was begun, and was brought to the present stage of completion. We feel it better to accept that such a report must contain weaknesses than to avoid making it because of the fear such weaknesses will be recognized and criticized. Such a fear might have tempted us only to walk on safe ground, but safe ground is known ground, and it is the basic aim of our research project to move out into the unknown.

We therefore faced all the limitations which will be recognized by the reader — and many others which perhaps will not — and all the dangers involved in such a wandering in the darkness in the conviction that we must make this venture into the unknown. We did it, and we are satisfied with the results we present here.

Such a statement does not by any means imply that this work is finished. On the contrary, it is only beginning. If we want to achieve our goals, we must follow up and report on all our findings in a systematic way, so that we can become more and more accurate, and so that we can transmit our messages to everyone.

This report is simply the end of the beginning of research on the City of the Future.

6. The process of this study

The process of this study, which lasted for 15 years, was as might be understood from the methodology, very complex. We had to learn about, calculate and test many things for several different periods, in many sizes of settlements, and in various parts of the world. There is no need to describe this process in detail here, since the reader can see its results in the documents it produced which are referred to in Appendix 1. The present publication follows the same process, and so will help the reader to understand how it took place in the simplest possible way.

We start in Part Two by presenting the past of human settlements and the lessons that can be derived from that past, not for the future — since that is impossible — but for recognizing what the principles and laws are that Anthropos has followed in the formation of his settlements. We have a very specific set of facts derived from Anthropos' experience during the thousands of years of his life within his various types of settlements (of which there may have been as many as 20 million thus far, providing us with a rich laboratory in which to work), from his first nomadic ones to the metropolis as it was before the invasion of the machine — and these facts lead us to reach very specific conclusions about what happened during this development and how it happened.

In Part Three we look at the settlements and, more specifically, at the city of the present, which was born in 1825 when the first railway carrying passengers ran in Northern England between Stockton and Darlington; we recognize the changes that occurred, the outcome for the different types of settlements, the problems that resulted, and the new approaches made by Anthropos, by the examination both of individual cases and of the situation as a whole. We then draw conclusions about our present crisis.

Before looking at the settlements of the future, we look in Part Four at those forces which shape them, and which define their destiny. We begin by looking at the earth itself, since it constitutes the actual container within which our settlements must be fitted. We follow with an account of technology and economic development, since these define the dimensions of the population. We try to discover the balance that is needed between all these, and draw conclusions about the evolution of the whole system of the life of Anthropos.

Then in Part Five we turn to the settlements of the future and study their most probable evolution during the next few generations which are our direct concern. We draw conclusions about the new dimensions, new systems of life, and new solutions which can be foreseen.

Ecumenopolis is the universal settlement towards which our whole evolution is leading and which will be reached within a few generations. In Part Six we try to understand how far our forecasts can go in speaking of the dimensions, systems, structures, new problems and solutions for the balanced city that humanity needs.

We end by looking ahead in the Epilogue and by proposing specific decisions for the action which is needed everywhere, as there are no "developed" and "underdeveloped" settlements today as some people believe; there are simply human settlements, all trying to get out of the same present impasse of great change and confusion into a new and balanced situation.

7. Conclusions

It may be helpful to summarize here the conclusions of our whole project. We must see these conclusions as a system leading us towards an overall concept of great importance and must not be confused by the lack of detail which exists, or by Anthropos' inability to foresee minor events. We can be certain about the long-term future of the Himalayas, but we can have no idea, for even as far ahead as tomorrow, what curtains will hang in the window opposite ours.

The main conclusions are the following:

One: The main trends of present technological and economic progress cannot, and should not be reversed. This means that a universal system of life will be formed, with a population which will stabilize at between 15 and 25 billion, and which will cover 25-35 million sq. km (10-14 million sq. mi.) with the built-up parts of its settlements if Anthropos fails to see what is happening in time and take action; or 7.5-15 million sq. km (3-5 million sq. mi.) if Anthropos retains his age-old ability to solve his basic problems.

Two: Such an evolution will gradually create one global settlement, which we have called Ecumenopolis or, as Arnold Toynbee has also called it, World City[23]. We can see it drawn on the map of the earth in a way which represents the settled areas in terms of their densities of population, since this is as far as we can go at present (fig. 7).

There are some people who are allergic to new words, and if they wish they can use, instead of Ecumenopolis, the expression: "the potential area for the development of the main body of human settlements on the whole earth". The truth is, however, that whatever we decide to call it, Ecumenopolis, with its general characteristics, is inevitable.

The general concept and layout of Ecumenopolis which have been developed within this project are established beyond any possible doubt as a valid image of the future of urbanization on this planet. Since, however, there are a number of different detailed models of Ecumenopolis which are compatible with the general image, it is less certain which of the detailed variants will in fact evolve with the passage of time.

The reader must approach our statements, fully aware of their conditional nature, in a rather flexible frame of mind. Conclusions have been framed in terms of orders of magnitude instead of exact figures. The "precision" of these conclusions has nothing whatever to do with the sort of precision which can be obtained in such fields as physics or engineering. The mind may boggle, but

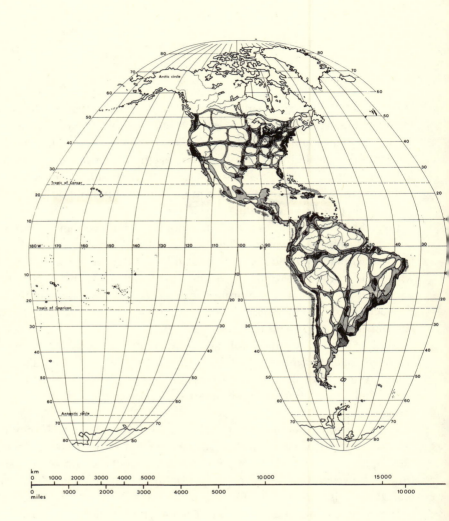

7.   Ecumenopolis 2100 A.D.

 high density

medium density

low density

deep ocean waters (practically no continental shelves)

deep ocean waters (greater depths)

39

margins of 50% and even 100% are quite acceptable when it is impossible to be more accurate. For some variables not even such crude accuracy could be obtained, and the only thing which could be quantified was an upper and lower limit to the variable's behavior — but even this is a useful finding. In some cases no quantitative statements at all could be made, and the most that could be said was that the variable in question will grow, diminish, or fluctuate uncertainly. Yet even such a limited insight can sometimes make a valuable contribution towards pinning down aspects of the future of human settlements.

One further thing requires caution: most of the graphs and large-scale maps which appear throughout this book have been provided as schematic illustrations. They are not intended to be accurate to the last detail and should be considered as subject to the same margins of error as individual statements. It is impossible to draw the fine details of large-scale maps of the future with any meaningful degree of precision, just as it is impossible to calculate the exact paths of curves representing the future behavior of projected variables. The curves of the various graphs have been smoothed and normalized and the maps have been drawn in order to make general trends as clear as possible, and this should be borne in mind at all times.

We are right in the middle of a transitional phase from the cities of the past to the City of the Future, a phase which may last about ten to twelve generations or about 300 years. Since about 150 of these years have already passed, we are exactly in the middle of the period in 1975. Our confusion today is the same as the confusion of the first hunters, when they were inventing cattle-breeding and farming and starting to form the first villages, or that of the first farmers, when they started building cities. They succeeded in their efforts, so we can do the same, and we will do so. When this transitional phase is over, and we reach Ecumenopolis, we will once more move into an era of static settlements, and out of the era of dynamic settlements in which we are today. By that time, the walls of the City of Anthropos will be formed by the area beyond the atmosphere where there is not enough oxygen for him. He will travel beyond these walls, but he will only be safe inside them.

The foundation for all our statements is not simply what we have learned from Anthropos' achievements in the past, but also the very important fact that we are moving from the phase of civilization to that of ecumenization. This is a big revolutionary change, which will be gradually understood and welcomed by everyone on this globe — if his or her mind is not frozen. The big change is that while civilization meant advantages for the citizens inside their cities but exploitation for the farmers living outside, ecumenization will for the first time create conditions in which all people can be equal all over the earth — equal not only according to their political constitutions, but in actual fact. There will no longer be some people inside and others outside: everybody will be inside the City of Anthropos.

Part two

The settlements of the past

8. Learning from the past

Any serious attempt to understand anything related to human settlements can only be based on past human experience since we do not know the future and the present is too short a span to form a basis for study. Experiment for us, in the sense in which physics can make experiments to discover such things as the laws of gravity, is not possible, since human settlements do not have a short enough life span. In any case, since we are dealing with human beings, as in medicine we must be careful not to undertake any experiments which may create dangers for Anthropos.

We must learn from human experience, and discover where we have come from and exactly what principles and laws Anthropos has followed during the two million years or more of his history. Even if we doubt that we can learn anything from Anthropos' earliest stages, because he was then changing from a primitive animal into contemporary Anthropos, the state in which we now know him, we do know that he has not changed at all over the past few tens of thousands of years, so we can at least rely on the experience of Anthropos over the last 40,000 years or so.

This is the only possible scientific approach.

Do we know enough about the past to reconstruct the full history of human settlements? The answer is definitely, no. During the course of only the last 40 years, during which the authors have been studying settlements, many changes have been made in the chronology or location of many events in the human story, from Anthropos' birth and origins to his actions. If we think only of the discoveries that have been made by archeology during the 1960's, we see that there have been new findings all over the world and must recognize that we cannot really speak of the full history of all human settlements. The cases of Lepenski Vir in Yugoslavia and Çatal Hüyük in Turkey[1] have revolutionized our views and they are enough to convince us that any statement we might make about where, for instance, a certain housetype came into being or how it developed can only be very tentative and should never lead us to form definite conclusions. There must be so many more settlements still to be found we must recognize that we can only speak in terms of evolutionary trends — because we do know these trends, and for some areas of the world and some periods we know them very well.

It is from these evolutionary trends that we can reach certain conclusions about such questions as the formation of the room. We cannot say exactly where the room was born, nor when, nor how; but we can say that no matter how it was born it always tended towards its present form[2], and from this we can learn what we need about present and future trends.

In order to try and find out what some of these evolutionary trends were, and to learn as much as possible about settlements of the past from the point of view of ekistics, we tried to study some (out of the probable total of about 20 million) of those settlements that were easily accessible to us.

We wanted to find out their dimensions, their systems of life and their structures. An understanding of such things about the earlier stages of our human settlements is essential if we are to guide their future organic evolution for the benefit of Anthropos. Although this research is still in its early stages, patterns, concepts and values have already begun to take shape, and since these coincide in many ways, they are not limited in validity to any specific time or area. These same patterns, exhibiting local and temporal variations and repeating themselves at greater, or at different intervals of time, have appeared and reappeared across the face of the globe. Since there is no reason to think they will suddenly stop forming in the same way, it is central to the study of the future of human settlements that we should investigate and evaluate these patterns.

During the recent wild and unbalanced growth of settlements, many of the valuable achievements and qualities of past settlements have been lost. Urban life today, as is often said, would benefit if it could be more like life in the beautiful and balanced cities of the past, such as Florence, or achieve something of the harmony between Nature and Anthropos of the successful village. Yet it is pointless for us to try and bring back any one element or aspect of a settlement of the past which we admire; the life of every element depends on the complex interweaving of the whole structure. We therefore studied the settlements of the past for two reasons: to discover what were the values they possessed that have been lost; and to find out what the total structure of their life and all the complex balancing of conditions were, which enabled them to achieve such a quality of life. Only in this way, we believed, would we be able to avoid the futility of trying to recreate single good elements from past settlements in isolation from the context essential to them, and have some real hope of recreating the values of the past that might satisfy the real needs of Anthropos in the human settlements of today.

We have been lucky during this study to have been based in Athens, a city which is many thousands of years old and at the center of a country which probably contains the largest number of past human settlements to have been found and studied, and from which we can learn. We have, therefore, often used Greek examples, but this does not endanger our conclusions since Greece is not an extreme case of a country with a single and isolated civilization. It has witnessed many developments and been subject to many influences; it has been at the top of the human pyramid and also very far down; many civilizations have come into it from the south and east, as well as from the west and the north; and it has faced many problems. More than this, Greece has always been representative of many countries, since it lies in a central area which contains the geographical settings of many types of civilization, from mountains to plains, valleys, islands and sea coasts. It is not very rich (nor could it be), nor is it very poor; it is therefore very close to the "average" of the world in general, so the many facts we have concerning its history can be useful in reaching general conclusions.

The "Ancient Greek Settlements" research project[3], which has been under way for the last six years, has given us the opportunity to make estimates which can be of practical use for universal generalizations. The Greek micro-cosmos has been helpful to us in understanding trends in our much greater global cosmos, but it has not been our only basis for study; we have used everything we could from all over our globe to come as close as possible to reasonable conclusions.

9. The first settlements

We do not really know when the first settlements began, since we cannot be certain even about the date of the appearance of Anthropos. It was only recently we learnt that Anthropos began his life at the Olduvai Gorge, and elsewhere in East Africa, more than two million years ago. It seems that the earliest sign of an Anthropos-built shelter is found in Olduvai. It is a primitive structure giving protection at least from the winds which dates back 1.8 million years[4]; and there are several other East African settlements that are about one million years old, or even older.

What we can assume about the greater part of these two million years is that there are no signs of organized Anthropos-built settlements, and that: "So long as men have to depend exclusively on what they can divert from wild nature, whether by hunting, catching or various forms of collecting and gathering, narrow boundaries are set to their development."[5]

The situation is different for the period of about the last 40,000 years, since in it we have the remains of the advanced paleolithic peoples, who left a good deal of evidence allowing us to conclude that between c. 35,000 and 10,000 B.C., in Europe and southwest Asia at least[6], there were organized systems of life and settlements about which we can speak.

The people of this era were all hunters and food-gatherers, and lived in bands — that is in groups of "somewhere between thirty and a little over one hundred individuals"[7]. This allows us to speak of an average band of 70 persons. This group of 70 persons is the basic unit with which we have to reckon for the majority of hunters and food-gatherers, who lived in their own territories at densities ranging from one person per 100 ha (250 acres) to perhaps one person per many hundreds of hectares. So we can make the reasonable assumption that hunters and food-gatherers lived at an average density of one person per 300 ha (750 acres). This is what we term ekistic unit 4 (community class I). (Anthropos alone is ekistic unit 1, and room, including two people, is ekistic unit 2, while house is ekistic unit 3).

Such people usually live in bands, which are very often territorial; they stick to their own territories, and sometimes do not even allow members of other bands to pass through them. There are some bands which are not territorial and which share wider areas of some hundreds of square kilometers with others, and yet others with what Coon calls an "anomalous type of organization"[8] which live as composite bands. There may be many other variations, but the fact is that we can speak of the general phenomenon of territorial bands which probably cover an average territory of about 21,000 ha (52,500 acres) or 210 sq. km (80 sq. mi.) each.

If we try to conceive how a number of such bands live within a total area, we can think of the territory of each as represented by a circle, so that the total area will be covered with a pattern of circles which, as they touch one another, will tend to form hexagons, since this shape minimizes the effort which must be expended on movement within each territory. The radius of each will be about eight kilometers and the resultant pattern of settlements is shown very simply in fig. 8. This could have been shown on a very small scale, but for reasons of comparison with those which follow we present it in the same standard scale. It is interesting to note here that we have at least one case where the aborigines of Australia "dig shallow wells at points within a day's walk of each other"[9]. This makes sense, since we will gradually learn that Anthropos has always considered one day's walk to be somewhere between 16 and 23 km. Anthropos did not ride animals or use vehicles in this phase, so we can speak of his average rate of travel over flat ground as being 4 km (2.5 mi.) per hour. This will be much less, perhaps 3 km (2 mi.) per hour, over an average type of landscape which may range from flat land to cliffs or from open land to bush. Such assumptions mean that the average distance between the centers of two territories was about 20 km (12 mi.), and that the time needed to reach the territorial boundaries of each band and return back to the center after hunting was of the order of five hours — which seems to be a reasonable maximum day's effort for a hunter.

The Anthropos-created settlements of this period are not known as a whole. There is, however, enough knowledge to allow us to state that they ranged from simple living-floors (as in the Olduvai site)[10] to many settlements of shelters of all types, from individual ones for a single person and average-sized ones for families to very large ones for groups of families. There is nothing special to be learned from these facts except that Anthropos begins by building his settlements in almost all possible ways, not by knowledge but through experimentation.

We should not think, as we very much tend to do today, that only our contemporary human settlements have problems. We can be certain that early Anthropos also had his big problems. He certainly had pollution — from food left in his caves, and from the bodies of his own dead until in the Neanderthal phase he learned how to make burials, even if only in shallow trenches under the floor of his caves[11]. Another of his problems must have been what we today call "social isolation", and this he solved gradually — at least in some cases — by not remaining within the territory of his own band for at least some part of the year. We could also mention the problem of the great expenditure of human energy he needed to make in order to collect his food. He may not have been polluting the environment in this way, but certainly it often deprived him of the energy he might have had available for creative endeavors.

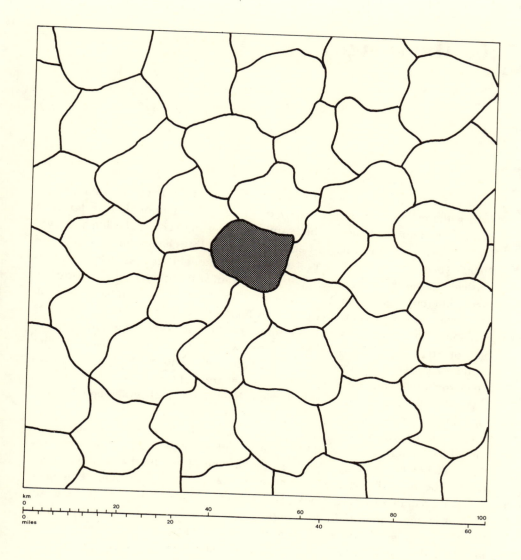

km
0 ⊢┬┬┬┬┬┬┬┬┬┤ 20   40   60   80   100
0
miles ⊢┬┬┬┬┬┬┬┬┬┤ 20   40   60

▓▓▓ territory of a band
average radius ~ 8 km

8.   a theoretical pattern of territorial organization of bands

10. The villages

After hundreds of thousands of years of nomadic life in bands as a hunter and food-gatherer, although the capacity of the earth to support him in terms of numbers had not yet been reached, Anthropos began to change his life in a revolutionary way, and the villages began to appear. This change began more than 10,000 years ago, and whereas it was at first thought to have happened exclusively in the "fertile crescent", it is now known that the change occurred in many different areas — in Asia Minor and the Middle East, in Iran, Afghanistan and several areas of central Asia, in the Indian subcontinent and in Indochina and South China as well as in Meso-America (that is, in Mexico) and the northern part of South America. Even in Europe, we are beginning to discover, this change occurred more than 8,000 years ago[12], and with every year that passes we learn more about how it happened in other areas of the world.

We can state, therefore, that Anthropos-built permanent settlements (excluding minor efforts undertaken earlier, which may have been permanent for a certain period or season of the year) are at least 10,000 years old, and appear or spread in different ways around the world in different periods. So we recognize that while Anthropos began with one major type of life, he then shifted to two types: the nomadic, and the permanently-based, Anthropos-built settlement.

This revolutionary change took place, it seems, at about the same time as Anthropos learnt about the domestication of animals and plants, that is, the cattle-breeding and agriculture which still interest him today. Desmond Morris calls this "mixed farming", and says: "an all-out reliance on meat would give rise to difficulties in terms of quantity, whereas an exclusive dependence on crops would be dangerous in terms of quality"[13].

This complete alteration in Anthropos' way of life had a great impact on all the dimensions of his life, the numbers of his population, his economy and his territorial needs.

The number of people in a community gradually increased from a band of about 70 to villages with anything from 10, 15 or 20 families, or to even several hundred families. The average for a village would seem to be 700, and there could be up to a few thousand people. We have cases in which archeological evidence shows positively that there were 2,000 people in a village or initial urban settlement, in Jericho III, for example, at about 7000 B.C.[14]. In fact we can now see from many recent excavations that we should think of a much wider range in terms of population size for the village phase of human settlements than for the hunting and food-gathering phase. Agricultural settlements ranged from those with 20 or 30 people — perhaps with even less than ten in isolated farms such as those in Crete — to a few thousand, several thousand and perhaps even more than 10,000 in cases like that of Çatal Hüyük[15] which definitely had a population of several thousand even before 6000 B.C.

We are not certain when the village turned into a town. It does seem that villages began small and increased very rapidly in population size[16]. Certainly many always remained small, and probably the average size only changed slowly. What actually happened in terms of our ekistic scale is that Anthropos moved up from being able to live only in settlements of ekistic unit 4 to being able to live also in those of ekistic units 5 and 6 — that is, from being able to live only in a community class I to being able to live also in communities of class II, III, and perhaps even IV.

The greatest change was in terms of the amount of land required for the production of food for each person. It now becomes clear — as we have learnt from cases such as those in Europe[17] — that probably about 0.5 ha (1.25 acres) was enough land to provide food for one person under mixed farming. This means that the total area needed per person for Anthropos' survival was now 600 times less than was needed when he was a hunter and food-gatherer only.

We begin to understand, therefore, that this great revolution led to a new type of social organization which we can describe in the following simplified way: The average size of a band of 70 persons changed to an average village of 700 people — that is, the community became ten times larger; the average amount of land required to feed one person decreased from 300 ha (750 acres) to 0.5 ha (1.25 acres) — that is, it became 600 times smaller. So the area needed for the community changed from the 210 sq. km (80 sq. mi.) needed by the band to the 3.5 sq. km (1.4 sq. mi.) needed by the village — that is, the area became 60 times smaller. Such an extreme shrinkage in the amount of land used did not, however, take place in reality, since, as we have seen already, Anthropos did not live by farming alone, but also from cattle-breeding. We can therefore speak of an average village territory of about 21 sq. km (8 sq. mi.) that is, of an area ten times smaller than the hunter's, as is proved in the specific case of Greece[18].

Such villages spread out their territories over the available land to form the hexagonal patterns first analyzed by Christaller[19] for Bavaria, and then found to be valid in many parts of the world, such as in Greece and elsewhere[20]. Such a pattern is shown in theoretical form in fig. 9 in a way allowing comparisons with other patterns such as those of hunters (fig. 8). We should always remember, however, that this is a theoretical pattern, and that in reality the various territories can be as different as those shown in fig. 10, which exist in contemporary Greece, but are probably quite similar to ancient ones.

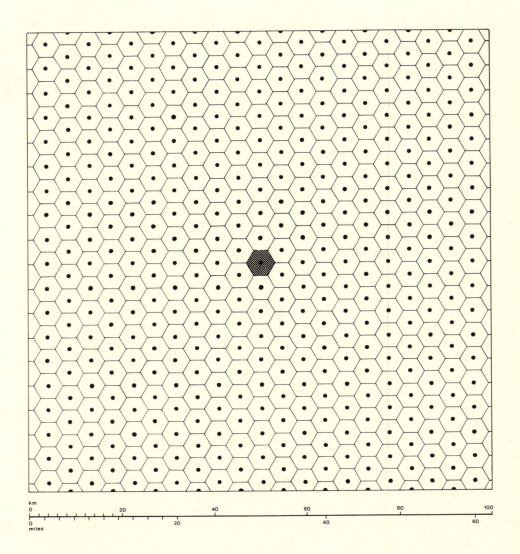

km
0   20   40   60   80   100

0   20   40   60
miles

▓▓ territory of a village

9.   a theoretical pattern of territorial organization of villages

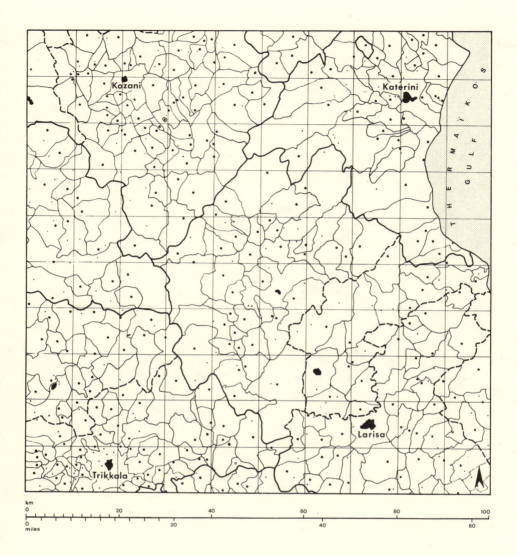

the average size of the territory of the modern and probably the ancient Greek village is
21.8 sq. km

10.   actual pattern of territorial organization of villages
        in modern Greece

These villages at first may have been created and spread out in either continuous or discontinuous patterns, but in the end they always formed systems making continuous use of the whole available territory, both arable and non-arable[21]. A study of many cases all round the world proves that although the actual territories of any two villages were never exactly the same, they always tended towards the same average size when large areas were considered. This is because although the territories of some villages might be very small, as in irrigated areas with a high land yield, those of others would be much larger when life depended a lot on cattle-breeding and hunting.

The variety which existed in villages in terms of numbers of population and size of territory is even greater when we consider the structure of the built-up section (or Anthroparea). We also refer to this as the central part of the village, not because it is always at the center of the territory, but because the life and human energy of the community are concentrated there.

The reason for this variety seems to be that Anthropos always tried to find personal solutions to the problems of the built-up section of his village under the influence of the local conditions and traditions and his own creativity, and this naturally led to an immense variety in the sizes and structures of what he built, and in the densities at which his buildings were created. Proof of this can be seen in the fact that the number of built-up settlements in any area is often more than the number of actual villages, since people may live together in the social sense that they use common facilities and form one political unit, though their houses may be widely spread over their territory in anything from single ones to groups.

It may be reasonable to assume that the larger the built-up part of a settlement, the longer it tends to survive, since over many thousands of years we find many more settlements superimposed in the same place than single houses. Anthropos probably tried many different sizes for the built-up parts of his settlements, but it was the larger sizes that more often than not were repeated.

The structural patterns of these villages are also very different. They range from those with a very low density, when the dwellings are round huts or houses with special roof structures, to those with a high density, usually when the houses have orthogonal constructions. There are houses without even any streets between them since the entrances are in the roofs, as at Çatal Hüyük[22], etc.

Some patterns are concentric and centrifugal — like the villages in ancient Crete — while others are orthogonal; some tend to create compact forms, while others are very spread out, as some in the Far East for example. There are many other patterns, from linear forms to completely round or square ones.

In general we can speak perhaps of average densities of about 200 people per ha (80 per acre) in the built-up area (or Anthroparea), if we remember that this may range from a few tens to several hundreds.

When we look at single buildings the great variety is also apparent, whether we consider size, type of construction, materials used or their subdivision into small units and forms. Europe alone presents us with a great variety of housetypes[23] and the range increases enormously when we look at the entire globe.

Some of the problems of the hunter have now been solved — in particular that of the huge expenditure of energy he needed for survival. The problem of social isolation has been solved to a lesser degree, since the average number of people in a community is ten times larger, and the distances between them are smaller — but this change is not so big, and is not valid for everyone.

Thus the big revolution meant that Anthropos could feel safer, have a permanent settlement, and spare time to begin to enjoy life. Therefore he had greater opportunities for the creation of new and more satisfactory solutions for his life.

11. The towns

Sometime after the development of villages we see the development of the first urban settlements. When this happened is uncertain for two reasons: firstly, because there is never full agreement as to when a settlement ceases to be a large village and becomes a small town in the many successive stages of superimposed settlements like those that form the tels of the Middle East; and secondly, because the continual discovery of new settlements is always giving earlier dates for the birth of the first towns. We can only be certain, therefore, that towns follow the creation of villages at a period between hundreds and one or two thousand years, and that this period varies for different areas of the world.

There are many theories and reasons — ranging through economic, commercial, administrative, cultural, religious, psychological or social — for the appearance of towns. We are not in a position to say if any is correct, but we can state that the creation of a town means a definite strengthening of all these activities, and that a greater percentage of the population moves from farming and cattlebreeding into being town dwellers. Towns therefore serve a wider area which includes several villages.

The fact is that towns appear when Anthropos acquires greater technological ability and an organizational capacity, and expresses this in several ways.

The town itself is a central urban settlement which has a population of a few thousand people, and as an economic, commercial, cultural, religious and social administrative center serves a wider area than a village. Whether political unification precedes or follows the other developments, whether it is decided by all the people or by a few oligarchic families, or even by a tyrant or king, cannot be answered; most probably all these things happened in different places and in many ways. It should be made clear, therefore, that while we are speaking of a town — which in Greek is *polis* — we are not using the term in its political sense but in the broad sense which defines a type of settlement. In ancient Greece, for example, towns and even cities perhaps appeared as early as the Minoan and Mycenean eras, while the *polis* as a political unity of equal citizens appeared much later, probably at the end of the 6th century B.C.[24], several centuries after the beginning of the Iron Age and the new Greek culture.

The fact is that when the town appeared it almost always survived and became the center of a system of villages in every sense of the word. This town marks the shift from Anthropos' ability to create villages, that is, settlements up to the size of ekistic unit 6 (community class III) to his ability to create settlements of the size of ekistic unit 7 (community class IV).

These are new types of communities which comprise the villages that are served by the central town as well as that town itself. They should never be seen as independent units in the same way as the systems of living that existed prior to this phase could be seen as independent. The band or the village could survive by itself for ever; the town depends on several other communities and cannot survive except as the center of such a system.

These systems certainly began in many ways with many different dimensions in terms of area and population, but it does seem that they always tended towards standardization. Comparisons we have made in nine very different civilizations, ranging from China through Asia and Europe to the Maya culture, show that in the Persian Empire the average distance between towns was from about 15 km (9 mi.) up to 22.7 km (14 mi.) [25].

More specifically, in the case of Greece during the classical period[26] and in Palestine in the Early Bronze Age (3000-2300 B.C.)[27] for which we have more data, we see that the average distance between towns ranges from 16.2 km (10 mi.) in Greece to a maximum of 22 km (13.6 mi.) in Palestine. Such conclusions are being strengthened by contemporary studies like the one made for East Anglia in 1972[28] where the average distance between towns was seen to be 19 km (12 mi.).

On the basis of such comparative studies we can see that the theoretical pattern of the systems of living represented by the towns and their villages is based on hexagonal patterns. The pattern shown in fig. 11 shows the situation in ancient Greece, and represents a theoretical image of towns created as the centers of village systems around the world. In such cases the average distance between a village and a town is 5.22 km (3.25 mi.), or one hour's walk for a person or a horse-driven vehicle. The system depends on this distance. Otherwise the area per person is the same as before, except that a higher technology allows more people to live off the area, the total of which is now in the order of 150 sq. km (58 sq. mi.) since it includes six to seven villages.

It is interesting to note that when about two centuries ago the American Congress decided to create a pattern of "townships" for the organization of settlements in the Middle West, it came to the conclusion that the best pattern was that of 6 X 6 miles square (10 X 10 km), which meant — since many farmers did not live in the few villages that existed but on their own farms — that the maximum distance from the center was again that which could be covered in one hour, that is, slightly more than 5 km (3 mi.). We can see an example of the application of this principle in the State of Michigan in fig. 12.

The population of the theoretical average town, taken as a system, can be con-

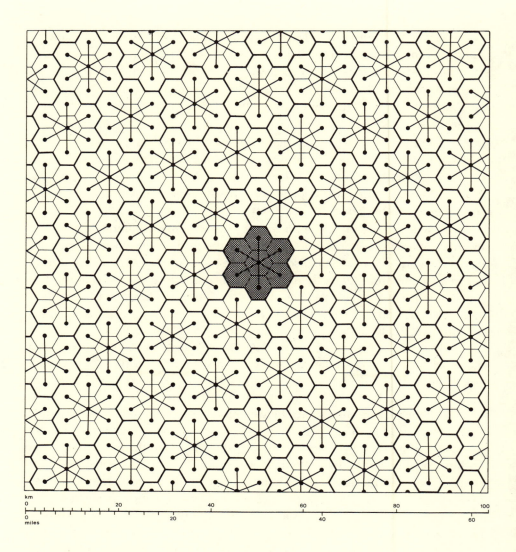

km
0   20   40   60   80   100
0   20   40   60
miles

▨ territory of a town

11.   a theoretical pattern of territorial organization of towns

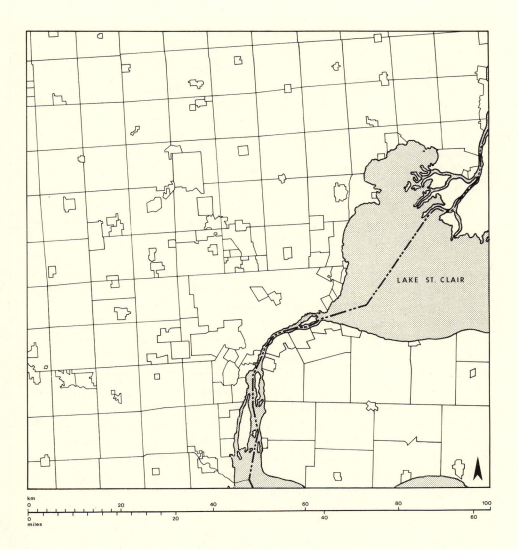

LAKE ST. CLAIR

```
km
0        20        40        60        80        100
|  |  |  |  |  |  |  |  |  |  |  |  |  |  |  |  |  |  |  |

0              20                40                60
miles
```

12.   territorial organization of townships in Michigan, U.S.A.

sidered to be in the order of 7,000 people — that is, six villages of 700 people each and a central town of about 3,000 people. So the same area of land, which before had a population of 4,900 people (seven villages of 700), now has an increase of 2,100. It has therefore increased by 43% in terms of the population providing its central functions. Once again it must be stressed that these are only rough estimates of an average situation; in Minoan Crete, for example, a very small proportion of the total population lived in the central settlements, though up to 50% did in other places.

It is during this stage of his evolution that Anthropos invents the wheelcart — perhaps first in Sumer at the beginning of the fourth millennium B.C. Even earlier he had managed to move over water by creating the dug-out boat[29]. Such inventions meant that he increased his ability to serve other places lying beyond his own village territory.

The location of a town is almost always central to the area it serves — for obvious economic, administrative and defensive reasons. Whether there is a great or a little need for defense decides whether the site of a town is in a plain or on a hill — a hill even that cannot be reached at all easily.

There are numerous variations in the structures of towns. Some develop from the growth of villages, while others are created in new places and experiment with new structures that correspond more readily to the needs of larger settlements. This is the case with Mohenjo-Daro in India, where around 2600 B.C. Anthropos was courageous enough to create a much larger town with an almost pre-conceived overall structure which could also be called a city.

Most of such towns go through a period of dynamic growth and then become static, as the area in which they are situated ceases to grow, or the necessity for the villages or the central town to grow further lessens. It is in such static towns — which can survive for hundreds or thousands of years — that Anthropos learns to build better settlements by striving continuously to work out more satisfactory solutions to living, sometimes even after the total destruction of his settlement in war.

One effort to build a more satisfactory structure is represented by fortifications which offer three advantages: better defense, more elaborate structure, and better living conditions. When a town is dynamic most of the available energy probably goes towards growth, but when it becomes static Anthropos has time to spend energy trying to attain a higher quality of life.

At the beginning, only few additional human needs were served by the town. People were unused to living in such a way, and few of their actual needs were served; indeed, quite often only the needs of the ruler were served. Gradually, however, more and more general human needs were served, this being a direct result of the growth of the town and those functions concentrated within it.

The town really made Anthropos aware of his additional needs — both group and individual. Some needs already existed in the rural population, some first became conscious within the urban population. From the moment when the town was created, every major development took place within it and radiated back to the villages. Thus the town played an important role as a center of evolution and development, serving all the non-agricultural needs of the community and realizing the trend of needs within the agricultural and urban populations.

In general we can say that the town gave rise to an expression of hitherto unsuspected human needs and managed, after trial and error, to serve many of them — but mostly those of the town-dwellers. We should not forget that the town serves everyone within its territory in some way, but that the further out anyone is from the town, the less they receive of the services of the town. The town is a pyramid composed of the services it supplies, but the pyramid also represents the exploitation of the outlying members by the central ones.

12. The cities

After the appearance of towns we begin to witness the appearance of the first cities, and then their continuous growth. When this happened we do not know exactly, for the same reasons why we do not know the exact date of the birth of towns, and for one additional reason: we have never agreed on what the difference is between the town and the city. One thing is certain, the cities are larger and more complex than the towns, and they appear later than the first towns. We could make the tentative assumption that cities appeared in the fourth millennium B.C. — that is, at the same time as the literate civilizations of the Near East. They grow more and more from this time on, especially when they appear within primary civilized societies which give them many incentives for growth. All we can assume on the basis of today's facts is a normal rate of growth towards ever larger urban settlements. Such facts as we do possess today may be completely changed by the archeological findings of tomorrow.

The phenomenon of the appearance of cities has been explained in many ways giving rise to many theories. We can only explain it in terms of Anthropos' increasing technological and organizational capacity — taking technological in the broadest sense to include such things as the development of writing — which helped him to create larger territorial systems.

Cities are larger than towns: in a simple way, we can say that they increase in size from a few thousand people to tens of thousands, and much later to hundreds of thousands. They do this by becoming the functional centers not only of a few villages (as did the towns of ekistic unit 7), but of many tens of villages and their towns, to become cities of ekistic unit 8 with an average population of 50,000 and a maximum population of 150,000. A "large city" belonging to ekistic unit 9 can consist of hundreds of villages and tens of towns, and a few cities as well, in which case it will have an average population of 300,000 and may reach a maximum population of one million.

With the growth of cities, the economy and social organization also develop more and more. One thing that makes this growth more easily understandable is the political organization of independent units into city-states. City-states are certainly born with the appearance of some towns — as we know from examples in Mesopotamia, Palestine and Greece — but they become really more apparent to us when they grow larger, and when their central towns turn into cities.

Cities are often the political centers of their area, and always the administrative ones — even when their rulers prefer to behave like feudal lords and live outside the city itself. Their populations can reach more than 50,000, as did Babylon and classical Athens, or hundreds of thousands, as did Alexandria, until they reach what tended to be the maximum limit for a city of the past, which was probably about one million.

This limit of one million inhabitants seems to have been reached, or at least approached, a few times in history; for example, in Rome in the time of Christ, later in Constantinople, in Teotihuacan in Mexico, and even in China in Chang-an and Peking, as well as in Angkor-Wat in Cambodia for a shorter period. The one million maximum was also reached by London in the year 1800, and perhaps by Tokyo around the same time, but both of these are so close to the city of the present that we shall deal with them in a later chapter.

Today, the figure of one million inhabitants does not sound very great and does not seem to us anything out of the ordinary. However, in the past any city which reached such an enormous population, with the political organization and achievements which went with it, was admired as something unique. It is very important for us to understand that the concept of the "big city" has been something different for every era of past history. In the year 486 B.C., for instance, the poet Pindar called a city with a population of only close on 50,000 people "the megalopolis Athens"[30].

For 6,000 years the average size of cities has been growing even larger because they have become the centers of much larger territories. Theoretically we can see the continuation of the territorial growth from a town to a city which controls the area of seven towns to become ekistic unit 8 (community class V) in fig. 13, and then to a large city which controls the area of seven cities to become ekistic unit 9 (community class VI) in fig. 14. In practice, although the

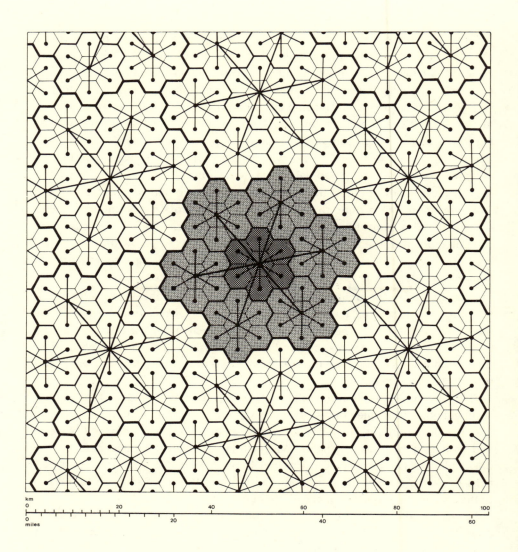

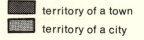 territory of a town
territory of a city

13.   a theoretical pattern of territorial organization of cities

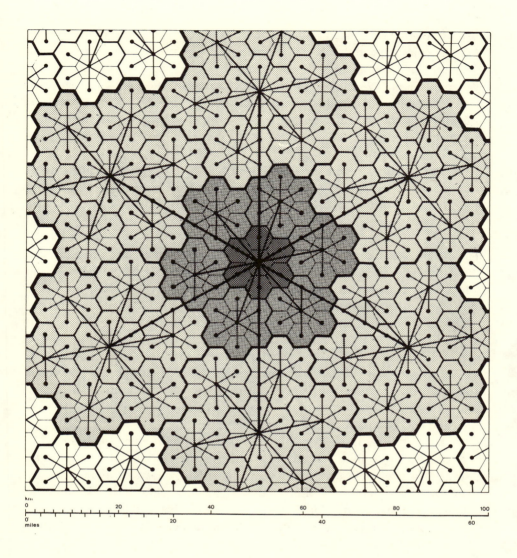

km
0   20   40   60   80   100

0   20   40   60
miles

- territory of a town
- territory of a city
- territory of a large city

14.   a theoretical pattern of territorial organization of large cities

existing towns had created patterns quite close to the theoretical ones by the time the cities appeared, this did not happen in a systematic way, since the local geography and the abilities of each group of people to grow in various ways was so different. We can see the pattern of a real situation in fig. 15 where we have been able to reconstruct the political boundaries of several city-states for a central part of ancient Greece, ranging from the smallest possible class — that is, of towns up in the mountains — to cities of higher degrees of territorial and central importance.

We can follow the evolution of cities on this scale of territorial presentation until we reach those with a few tens of thousands of people, such as Corinth (fig. 15), with a territory of several hundreds of square kilometers. To understand the real territories of the larger cities, and finally of those reaching the one million mark, we must change the scale used up to now from 100×100 km (60×60 mi.) to a scale of $5,000 \times 5,000$ km ($3,000 \times 3,000$ mi.) for Rome and Constantinople, and even larger ones for the Mongol Empire of China[31].

It is quite clear that the greater the territory becomes, the more the size of the central city increases, but it does not increase at the same rate as it reaches the larger dimensions. While a city can increase in population by 20% when its small territory doubles, it may increase only by 1% when its territory increases as part of a great empire. How much effect expansion in territory will have on the central settlement depends on the distance at which such growth takes place from the central settlement. Again, this distance will have more or less effect according to the amount of territory, and the technology, economic development and energy possessed by that central settlement.

We must add that historical evolution has meant the rise and decline of cities in direct relation to their real territory — as has already been mentioned in the case of Constantinople (Part One: 1). Many complexities also existed because of the interwoven networks of economic, cultural, religious, political and other interests. We should not forget that it is very probable that: "there are no great civilizations anywhere in the world that were invented independently without outside stimuli"[32].

Because of this complexity, the patterns of hierarchical territorial organization changed when the general conditions became different. Rome, for example, created cities of importance in the coastal areas of the Near East, but these cities declined after the Arab conquests when the cities of the interior became more important.

The location of cities was always central to their real territory, as was the location of towns. We should always remember, however, that the majority of larger cities were built beside lakes or on sea fronts, so that they were central to their whole system of life. Corinth, for example, was at the periphery of the land territory of its city-state, but as the city also depended on its colonies all around the Mediterranean, its built-up area (Anthroparea) had to be on the coast.

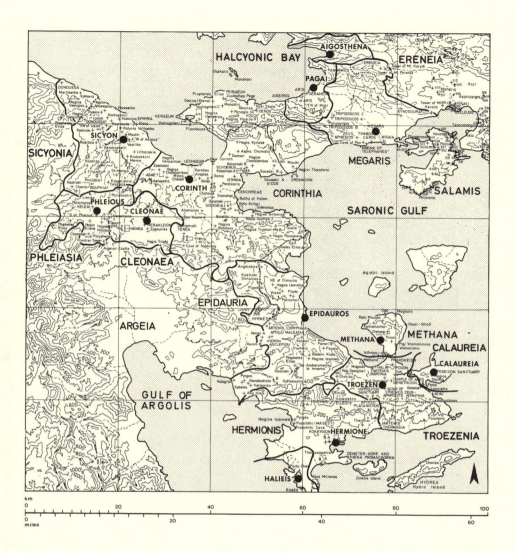

15.   territorial organization of several city-states in the central part of ancient Greece

The case of London was similar, if it is seen not as the capital of England, nor of the two islands since it is geographically located at the edge of their land territory, but as the capital of an empire depending on sea connections. It is even probable that this will remain so in the future, since London is the closest major outlet of the British Isles to the large system of settlements of northwest Europe.

The structure of cities follows the same principles as those of towns, but is more often in the form of a natural radial concentric system, which creates many problems when the city grows too much. This happened to ancient Rome, the center of which became overloaded with traffic and suffered enormously. It is clear that traffic congestion is not only a modern experience, but an ancient one too. When Anthropos had occasion to create cities on the basis of a plan, it was always according to orthogonal systems. The first examples of these are in classical Greece, where Hippodamus designed orthogonal systems, and they were repeated when the Romans created their colonies. They were very apparent when Teotihuacan was conceived in Mexico in the 2nd century B.C. and went on developing until the 6th century, or in Chang-an (6th century) and later Peking (10th century) in China, and again in Angkor-Wat in Cambodia (13th century). In all these cases of big capitals, a properly conceived orthogonal grid structure was adhered to.

Most cities, like most towns, are static for the longest period of their lives. Only during the transitional phases of growth of their territory do they become dynamic. They then reach their new size, and once more become static. During their dynamic phase, as is natural, the whole city, or at least the new parts of it, would not be protected and often had no walls; whilst in their static phases the cities are well protected inside walls and are able to take care of their overall structure and their everyday problems.

The fact that most cities were enclosed by walls is probably one basic reason why people's concept of the whole cosmos was so often of an unmoving world, whose boundaries were circular ones. This concept occurred on many occasions in antiquity and more recently in medieval times.

As is natural, the growing cities served new needs and also created many problems. Many people who were urban dwellers might gradually become weak, and newcomers, who needed time to become adjusted to this way of life, might take over from them. Any change in the whole system could easily mean the rise or decline of the central city, and for these reasons the city was never as stable as the villages of the countryside which might often remain the same for long periods. The city, therefore, was the center of change, progress, and of all the problems that follow from these things. The problems of the villages were, in contrast, related to isolation and lack of change.

The situation of constant change created many social problems in the cities, which were always in need of slaves or low-cost labor and therefore exploited their newcomers in various ways. This was true of the earliest up to the largest cities of the past, and is a basic reason why the revolutions which became necessary always started in the cities. Suffering and change took place in the same centers.

The situation was the same from the technological point of view. The problems of traffic congestion first appeared in the cities, which suffered from over-congestion and the noise created by wheelcarts. It was therefore in Rome towards the close of the 1st century B.C. that the earliest known forms of traffic control seem to have appeared.

Corresponding situations existed in the quality of human life in cities. In contrast to villages, where almost the whole population was in constant contact with Nature, a large proportion of the people living in cities came to spend their time without any contact with surrounding Nature at all. This led to a new demand — the creation of public gardens, parks and other open spaces, and the increased importance of the private garden. When it was not possible to have a garden — as was often the case — then those who could afford it abandoned the city and went to live on the outskirts where they created villas with private gardens. We have examples of this development in many ancient cities which suffered from the type of pressures Anthropos cannot stand.

These ancient cities did achieve a great deal: they managed to preserve the human scale in their buildings, squares and streets so that people moving in them felt at home, and they managed to preserve a good balance between their various elements. However, there was often a good deal of misery and squalor within them, a low level of cleanliness and public health. The general standard of living was infinitely lower than that within the "rich" cities of today.

13. The global situation

For at least some hundreds of thousands of years Anthropos has managed to live on this earth by creating all sorts of settlements, from temporary ones to permanent ones, and from very small to very large. He probably founded more than 20 million permanent settlements, of which some 14 million still survive as living organisms, and of which we see the remains of another one million. We are therefore in a position to attempt an understanding of the global situation, although with the passing of the years we shall know more and more. One thing is certain, and that is that the container — the whole globe — has not changed in its dimensions, although at times the climate, and the relation between the land and the sea and the flora and fauna have changed; but these changes have been very small during the last 11,000 years following the end of the Pleistocene era. We are therefore now able to try to make a general estimate of the global situation in the different periods.

The total population of the earth before the beginning of the agricultural revolution around 10,000 years ago has been estimated in several ways, and the figures obtained range from tens of thousands of people at the beginning, some millions of years ago, up to 16 million people just before the agricultural revolution (Appendix 1, tables 1, 4). We cannot know how accurate these estimates are, because with the passing of time we are bound to find new data on life, perhaps in hitherto unsuspected areas; but at present we must reckon on these figures for lack of better ones.

On the other hand, we have enough knowledge to state that the whole earth — which now has an area of about 74 million sq. km (28.5 million sq. mi.) of usable land — could probably have reached the point of supporting 350,000 bands of men, with 25 million people at an average density of one person per 300 ha (750 acres), or 3 sq. km (1.2 sq. mi.).

If the real population was only four million 25,000 years ago and 16 million 10,000 years ago, then we can state that for obvious reasons Anthropos managed to reach a population which was 16%, and later 64%, of the capacity of the whole earth. This means that although as a hunter-fisher he inherited almost the whole earth[33], he did not cover the whole area of usable land in it — and this is quite a natural assumption to make.

Then came the villages. The estimates of the population of the whole earth in this period between 10,000 and 8,000 years ago speak of a population starting around 16 million and ending with 80 million. Once again, however, we find out more with every day that passes and cannot rely on these estimates as being completely correct.

On the other hand, using the estimate that one person needs 0.5 ha (1.25 acres) to live from, and that today subsistence agriculture "occupies 40% of the total land area under cultivation and supports over half the world's population"[34], which means that each person is supported by 0.25 ha (0.60 acres), we can reach the conclusion that the total area of cultivable land could have supported 3.5 million villages, with a population of 2.5 billion people at the density at which they then lived.

If this is true, then Anthropos, with the development of villages, reached only 3.2% of the earth's capacity to support him in numbers. He did not therefore reach the same proportion (16% and later 64%) of its capacity as he had before. This is a reasonable assumption, because even if some day we should find that the population at this time had reached 100 million, or 200 million, that would still be only 4-8% of the global capacity. It does make sense, since Anthropos the hunter with his technology had hundreds of thousands of years to spread round the earth against only the 2,000 years we consider it took to spread the new technology of Anthropos the farmer and cattle-breeder. The revolution was a very important one, but there was not time for its completion.

The total capacity of the globe of 2.5 billion given above corresponds to 3.5 million villages each with an average population of 700 and an area of 21 sq. km (8 sq. mi.). How many such villages may actually have been created we do not know, but our general estimate is for many even smaller settlements which could correspond to about 600,000 typical villages, or 17% of the earth's global capacity.

Then came the change created by the towns. Until about 3000 B.C. the direct benefits of this change affect no more than 1% of the total world population, and no more than 7% until the middle of the first millennium B.C. (Appendix 1, tables 1, 4). If we wonder about these low percentages, we should not forget that even today a certain percentage of people — the nomads and inhabitants of remote villages — do not receive any advantages from towns since there are none within their systems of life.

This change meant that the global container could have supported 600,000 towns and villages instead of around a possible 40,000 to 50,000, or 7-8%. This was because although an estimated 600,000 typical villages could theoretically have produced 100,000 towns, not all of them reached the stage of urbanization.

We do not speak here of the theoretical 1:7 relationship between town and villages, because in practice mountains and seas did not allow this, so that it is closer to reality to reckon one town to every six units, that is, to five villages. The change to towns could have meant an increase in the global capacity of an order of perhaps up to 50%, due to improved technology and organization such as the creation of irrigation systems in the Middle East. In all, therefore, about 3.75 billion people could have been supported.

Then came the cities, and this change could have meant an increase in the capacity of the global container to support 100,000 towns and cities, and perhaps an additional 33% of people, that is, a total of five billion people, due once more to a continuously increasing technological and organizational capacity. Possible limits were not reached, however, except in small areas of the earth where long periods of peace and development allowed it. The whole surface of the earth looked rather like a sea on which there were islands covered by populations which had reached the accepted limits. These "islands" covered various sized areas of land, depending on the degree of development of its corresponding civilization.

In practice, the creation of cities did not change the global distribution of population among villages and urban settlements to any important degree. The fact that great empires which had many tens of millions of inhabitants managed to have a capital city of hundreds of thousands only means an additional urban population equal to 1% of the total. Thus we can make a general assumption that the majority of the population of the globe remained rural and continued to live as nomads or in farming settlements, and that the urban population may have reached up to 10% of a theoretical 30%. The cities came and created civilizations, but the majority of people remained outside, receiving some indirect benefits, but being exploited for the benefit of the centers. Even within the cities a large proportion of the population lived under conditions of misery and squalor, deprived of most of the benefits of an urban civilization.

The whole evolution of global population (fig. 16) shows that the capacity of of the earth to support people increased from 25 million to five billion over a period of 10,000 years. The actual population varies, but at the end of the second phase (that is, in 1825) reaches a total of one billion. This means that at the end of both major phases — that is, the nomadic and the agricultural-urban ones — the population reaches only between 64% and 20% of the capacity of the earth to support it. If these estimates are realistic, this is because these changes occurred only in some parts of the earth, and whilst in the nomadic era they reached quite a high level, in the agricultural-urban one there was no time or occasion to reach the same level.

The corresponding evolution of the distribution of the global population (fig. 17) demonstrates that the urban population in settlements with more than 2,000 people may have reached 10% of the total at the beginning of our era, around

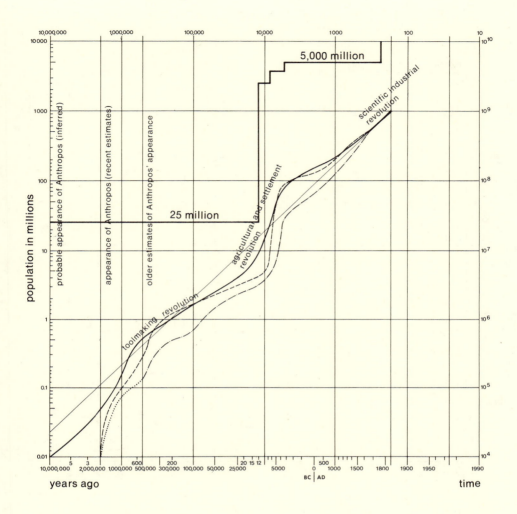

16. **historical evolution of global population**
doubly logarithmic graph

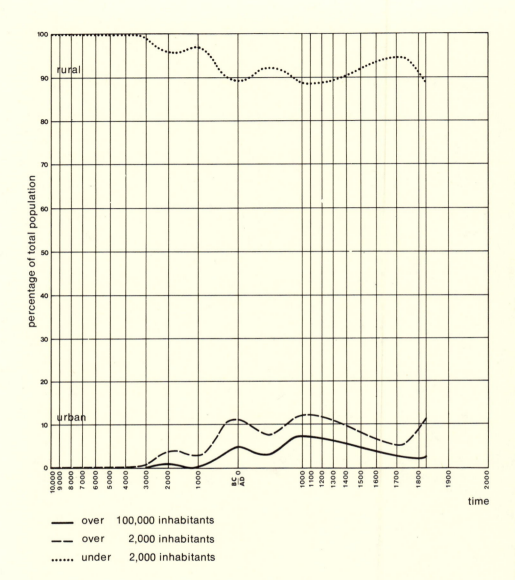

17.   historical evolution of global population by settlement
       size

— over   100,000 inhabitants
-- over   2,000 inhabitants
..... under   2,000 inhabitants

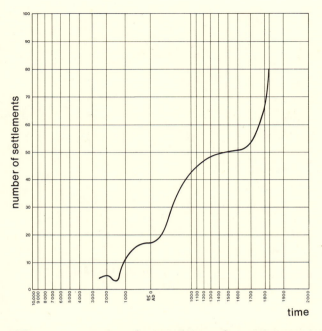

number of settlements

time

18. growth of number of settlements with population of more than 100,000

1000 A.D., and also at the end of this phase, around 1800 A.D. From 500 B.C. until the beginning of the 19th century, the proportion of the earth's population living in rural settlements (with less than 2,000 inhabitants) remained stable at close on 90% of the whole with some minor variations. Of the urban 10%, the proportion of those living in small towns (population between 2,000 and 10,000) grew during this period from about one third of the total (3%) to about one half (5%). It is interesting to note that the settlements which were rising in numbers almost continuously were those with more than 100,000 people (fig. 18).

The average population of all settlements over the whole earth has been growing steadily since historical times (fig. 19). In 1960, the average size of all human settlements was 215 inhabitants, a low figure because of the inclusion of some 14 million small units such as isolated farmsteads and nomadic settlements counting a total population of about three billion. Again using the figure of 2,000 inhabitants to distinguish between an urban and a rural settlement, the average urban population in 1960 was about 14,500, while the population of the average rural settlement was about 120. Comparable figures based on our estimates for the period between 1000 B.C. and 1000 A.D. give 7,000 to 8,000 as the average size of an urban population, and 70 to 80 as the average of a rural one; the overall average population size for all settlements at that time, therefore, was between 80 and 90 people (fig. 20).

19.   probable average size of settlements

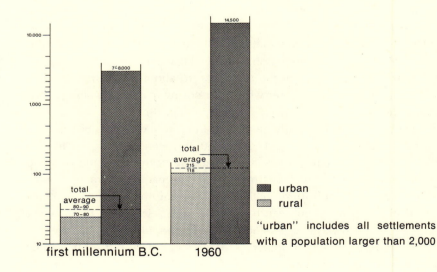

20.   average size of settlements

14. Conclusions

The historical trends are now clear: Anthropos was born and developed on the earth, which formed a limited container for him, and which he managed to conquer and develop in some areas for his own benefit.

Although we notice a constant and pressing urge to expand into the available space, Anthropos never filled this container completely, since his numbers never reached more than 64% of the earth's capacity to support him. However, while this is true of the global situation as a whole, it is not true for certain parts of the earth where Anthropos did reach the limits of the container, as we know from the many crises that occurred, usually expressed in the form of war. Since Anthropos did not have the means to find out about, or reach other parts of the earth whose areas could have supported the increasing population, he either formed colonies or attacked other people's territory in the areas he knew when there seemed no other solution.

In his efforts to survive, however, not only did he conquer land, but he gained knowledge also. So, by increasing his technological and organizational abilities he increased the capacity of the earth to support him in greater numbers by as much as 200 times over 10,000 years.

The most recent crisis in terms of numbers reached by Anthropos was after the scientific and industrial revolution which brought Western Europe (as a container) to the limits of its capacity to support its population. This led to the last phase of national and political colonization, but it also created the opportunity to enter a new era — as we shall see in the next Part.

Throughout all his efforts, Anthropos has followed the same five principles in creating the system of life expressed in his settlements.

The first principle is his need to maximize his potential contacts with other human beings and with natural resources of all kinds. If he had not been following this principle throughout history, the size of his community would not have moved up continuously from bands of about 70 people to villages of 700, towns of thousands, and cities of up to a million. As soon as he had the opportunity (which was given by larger territory and his own better abilities) to create larger settlements, he did so. When such larger settlements declined, it simply meant that Anthropos at that point had ceased to be able to achieve the best he had wanted. The physical realities of the system he could create and support at that time forced him to go back to a smaller size of settlement.

The second principle is the minimization of the effort needed for everything he does. If he had not been following this principle, Anthropos would not have broken up the area of territory he had as a hunter (210 sq. km or 81 sq. mi.) into ten villages, thereby losing some of it. But he did not want to commute so far every day, so he abandoned 90% of the territory he once had in order that he would not have to walk for more than half an hour each day to reach his fields. Then when he created his famous cities he reduced this half-hour's walk of the farmer to the ten-minute's walk of the urban dweller inside his city.

Each time he invented a system that would save him most energy. The system of nomadic pastoralism created by some shepherds and cowherds in the early centuries of the second millennium B.C. was a commuting system, as Arnold Toynbee has very well stated[35]. The same was true of the invention of horse riding and the use of chariots, which were invented to save human energy and which then contributed to the growth of towns into cities. Indeed, these cities were internally organized into a hierarchical system of communities so laid out as to economize on the amount of energy needed for the movements of their inhabitants.

According to his first principle Anthropos tried to reach settlements of one million people, and perhaps more, in order to maximize his contacts; but because of his second principle he could not achieve this as a permanent solution. The energy needed to sustain settlements of this size was too high, and they were therefore only achieved a few times under the greatest empires, their decline coming easily when the empire was no longer able to survive. Anthropos reached the limits of large human organizations and large settlements: he could not go beyond this size with what he then knew of technology and organization.

This principle is also demonstrated by Anthropos' technological efforts to save energy in all his endeavors. We learned recently that as early as 500,000 years ago Anthropos created "pits that had been scooped by hand from sand, connected by channels four inches wide and four inches deep to catch rainfall"[36].

The third principle is the optimization of protective space. In order to follow this principle Anthropos always tended to get as far away as possible from anything that disturbed him or created dangers for him. This principle explains the location of many settlements, and of the people within settlements. People want to be close together in order to maximize their potential contacts (first principle) and also in order to minimize their use of energy (second principle); on the other hand, they also have a need to be apart from one another, both because of their desire for privacy and their need for safety. At this point, a synthesis of the various principles begins.

The fourth principle is the balance between the five elements of human settlements — that is, between Nature, Anthropos, Society, Shells and Networks. If Anthropos had not followed this principle, he would not have survived. Although, for example, he did burn forests as a hunter and as a farmer in order to survive, he nevertheless kept the balance by leaving enough forests to serve all his needs for oxygen, water, wildlife, and everything else he got from their existence.

It is characteristic of this principle that Anthropos' ideal cities have always been seen as static — from the city conceived by the Chinese sage Lao-Tzu to those of Plato and Sir Thomas More with his Utopia[37], or to the conceptions of our own day. Anthropos has always dreamt of achieving a balance; as St. Thomas Aquinas said very clearly: "A stable society must integrate the town and the countryside."[38] Anthropos never desired a lack of balance.

The fifth principle is the achievement of a proper balance between the four previous principles. The best example of this is seen in Anthropos' attempts to · arrive at the proper densities for his systems of life. When he lived in times of great physical danger he lived at higher densities, but when the danger was reduced, those densities were also reduced. He never went beyond certain low limits of density, however, because to have done so would have been to disregard either the first, the second, or the fourth principle. Under certain conditions he would allow himself to be squeezed tightly (disregarding the third principle), but as soon as these conditions passed he returned to his balanced systems of life.

One proof of the consistent application of this principle is that the physical structure of settlements has always exhibited a great resistance to sudden change, and because of this the slow population growth rates of the past were highly significant. The physical structures of towns can only adapt when the population is stable or grows slowly and predictably. Although the settlements of the past were subject to sudden disruption, and although following disasters and during times of colonization they grew very fast, they did grow incomparably more slowly in terms of population than do the settlements of the present. Their physical structures therefore had time to adapt, since they were rarely subject to periods of rapid change. In this sense we are justified in calling them static in comparison with settlements of today.

The implications of this slow rate of change were far-reaching. Slowness in growth meant greater stability in most aspects of life — in institutions, beliefs, values, customs and culture. Since change took a long time it was possible for adaptive processes to take place, and for a balance to be created between Anthropos and his environment. Obviously, this normal pattern would be disrupted during periods of upheaval, but so long as such disruption was not complete the settlement would resume its normal life after a period of reconstruction and reorganization. We might say that these settlements possessed extraordinary capacity for balance and a great inherent vitality derived from their surroundings as well as from their own nature.

The settlements of the past were always developing, and by a system of trial and error Anthropos in each case always found the best solution for each era and area. Each new type of settlement he created always had big advantages over those of his previous ones, and this is the reason why he abandoned the earlier types. New types of settlements also had many weaknesses, especially during the earliest times of their formation, since Anthropos did not yet know how to deal with their bigger dimensions and greater complexity, but most of these difficulties were overcome gradually. Each new type also had weaknesses in relation to Anthropos' dreams and ideals of what a settlement should be, and this is the reason why, whenever he was given the opportunity, Anthropos always took another step towards the creation of an even better, more satisfactory solution.

Part three

The settlements of the present

15. The great change

The evolution of human settlements was quite normal for 10,000 years, but then the day came when a great change took place: the first settlement of a totally new type, the first settlement of the present, was born. The day on which this happened was the 27th of September 1825, since this was the day when the first railway to carry passengers ran between Stockton and Darlington in the north of England. It was on this day that a new force entered human settlements and completely changed their destiny.

These new settlements may be said to have been subconsciously conceived when the scientific and industrial revolution began, so we might say that their day of conception came in 1765 when Watt invented the steam engine. However, the new cells themselves only began to appear when in 1825 the first passengers were transported on a railway line without the use of human or animal energy.

The steam engine was followed by the appearance of many other types of machines which were used by Anthropos to save his own energy on land, sea or in the air. We could therefore have divided this era into phases according to the use of railways, automobiles, and airplanes — except that they are often used simultaneously, though in different ways by various countries in differing stages of evolution, so such a division is not helpful. What matters is for us to understand the very big change that occurred with the use of mechanical transport resulting in the creation of human settlements as different from the villages and cities of the past as these had been from the nomadic settlements before them. Not only does the size of populations change, but the scale of the territories involved changes out of all proportion. We can therefore say that humanity entered a third era of human settlements in 1825. The first era of nomadic settlements lasted for hundreds of thousands of years; the second era of permanent Anthropos-built settlements lasted for 10,000 years; the settlements of our own era have lasted for just a century and a half, so either this is to be a very short era or else we are just at the beginning of it.

The most important characteristic of the new settlements is that they have become dynamic. We have moved from the era of the static city into that of dynapolis. In the past, as we have seen, cities often went through a period of dynamic growth and change, but this period lasted for only a short time, and once it was over they settled back into a static state. Today, more and more cities are not only becoming dynamic, but continuously dynamic, so that they never stop changing and growing. For the first time in history, settlements are not only three-dimensional but four-dimensional, since they exist continuously within the fourth dimension of time.

We can see what happens by noting the changes that occur in the basic dimensions of settlements when all the movements, instead of being made at one basic speed — that of Anthropos and of animals — are made at the many different speeds of Anthropos with his various types of machines. It is as natural for the Anthropos who uses machines to connect his cities together and form them into urban systems as it was for Anthropos when he was a pedestrian to form the small romantic cities of the past. The small isolated cities of the past are therefore becoming interconnected today. Their inhabitants can move faster, so their daily systems of movement — which are part of their total fields of movement, or kinetic fields — are growing and forming systems of cities, which in turn give birth to new cities at the places where these fields of movement cross. The static city of the past is changing, first into a city which grows concentrically, then into one which grows especially in certain directions, and finally into an urban system (fig. 21).

We must recognize that we are living in a period of enormous explosion, not only in terms of population, but also in terms of area covered, energy used, communications made, and confusion created. It is an explosion of unique dimensions, which is creating new settlements and new problems.

An example of the degree of confusion which has arisen is the fact that we no longer understand what our "city" actually is. We could have understood what it was very easily up to about two centuries ago, but not since then. There are two reasons for the change that has happened to the city: first, the population has spread way beyond the old city limits, and is now living in, and building over much larger areas than ever before; and second, many people who live well outside the old built-up area of the city — in small towns, villages or farms in the countryside — are today able to participate in the life of the city because they have cars. If we consider the city of today as consisting only of its built-up area (fig. 22a) or even as the area under the administration of the city authorities (fig. 22b), we fail to understand it completely. A citizen of any one city will participate in the life of many other human settlements in the surrounding area (fig. 22c). A farmer living in the countryside now does the same; his wife may work in a nearby city, his children go to school in other towns or cities, and he himself may belong to a club in the central city itself (fig. 22d). People today live not so much in cities, but in urban systems.

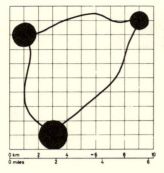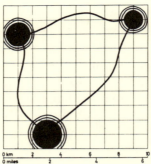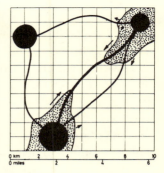

- inhabited built-up areas within a radius of less than ten minutes

- inhabited built-up areas growing because of increase of population

- inhabited built-up areas
- paved road
- directions of easier traffic and therefore increased number of choices
- ten-minute kinetic field by machines

phase A: pedestrian kinetic fields only

phase B: pedestrian kinetic fields only

phase C: pedestrian and mechanical kinetic fields

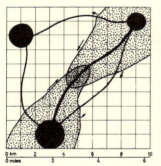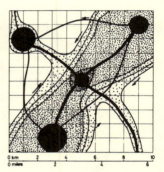

- inhabited built-up areas
- paved road
- directions of easier traffic and therefore increased number of choices
- number of choices increases much more with overlapping kinetic fields

- inhabited built-up areas
- paved road
- directions of easier traffic and therefore increased number of choices
- a new center is created in the area of increased choices

- inhabited built-up areas
- paved road
- directions of easier traffic and therefore increased number of choices
- a new center grows in the area of increased choices

phase D: pedestrian and mechanical kinetic fields

phase E: pedestrian and mechanical kinetic fields

phase F: pedestrian and mechanical kinetic fields

21.   from a city of pedestrians to an urban system

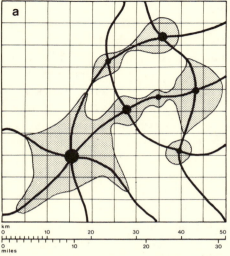

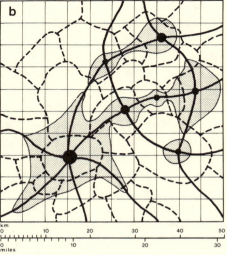

the real city no longer consists of its built-up area only

nor of the area under its administration

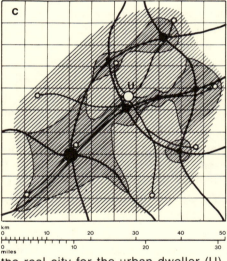

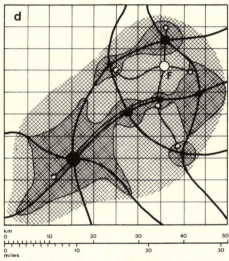

the real city for the urban dweller (U) covers a much wider area

and so does the real city for the farmer (F)

built-up areas — (a, b, c, d)

main transportation lines

administrative boundaries

the entire urban system of urban dweller (U) — (c)

the entire urban system of farmer (F) — (d)

22. the change from city to urban system

We must try to get out of our present state of confusion, and we can be helped to do so by realizing three basic mistakes we have made in the past. The first mistake is that of trying to understand an elephant by taking it to be a mouse, that is, trying to understand the new big urban systems by thinking of them as if they were the small static cities of the past. The second mistake is that of using old methods when trying to deal with new problems, especially in terms of finance, energy and manpower. The third mistake is that of trying to deal with the city, which is our most important organism for expressing our system of life, without having any very clear concept as to what our aims for a better human life really are.

We must therefore make an effort to understand what the city of the present really is — or rather, since to refer to "the city" only increases our confusion, what the settlements of the present really are. This may seem difficult, but if we start without prejudices, we can see that it is really much easier to do this than to understand the past, since we only have what has been left behind of the past to study, whereas we ourselves are living in the present, and the longer we do so the more we learn about it. It is not easy to make a diagnosis of any of the diseases of the past, but we suffer from the symptoms of those of the present ourselves, so we can understand them, as long as we do not — as often happens today — think we know the cure before we have undertaken a full analysis of everything that is happening and made a proper diagnosis.

We have the settlements of the present in our laboratory available for study, and they are much easier to deal with than the settlements of the past referred to in Part Two, since they are still alive and we can observe them in all their vital complexity. We can evaluate them by measurement and analysis, and in some cases even by experiment.

As we described in Part One, we have drawn on data we collected about the forms, achievements and problems of present settlements in order to find out what are the forces within them that will determine their future development. Our greatest difficulty was in finding data which could be validly compared; population statistics, for instance, exist for many hundreds of settlements, but for other urban characteristics there are no figures at all. By our own researches, therefore, we supplemented the deficiencies of existing information, making a survey of about one hundred cities during the early days of our project, and many later studies of individual cities, groups of settlements and special regions. As a preparation for practical action we also made use of the many studies of specific cities and regions prepared by Doxiadis Associates in very considerable detail.

In the following pages we briefly summarize our findings on the dimensions of our system of life and all our settlements today. We try to describe the values they still possess, as well as their problems. The settlements of today are the platform from which we will later launch our probe into the future.

16. New dimensions

The settlements of the present have acquired completely new dimensions in every respect. Before this period, the largest city Anthropos had ever created had been one of about one million inhabitants — that is, he had reached the limits of ekistic unit 9 (community class VI). Today, he has created a great many metropolises of ekistic unit 10 (community class VII), many small megalopolises of ekistic unit 11 (community class VIII), and is already beginning to create megalopolises of ekistic unit 12 (community class IX). Although it took Anthropos more than 8,000 years to take the previous three steps that brought him from settlements of the size of villages to those of large cities, it has taken him only 150 years to take the three similar steps in our present era. This is the big change which has taken place, and which has been called the urban explosion.

Every aspect of life has been affected. The changes which have occurred in terms of population have not only affected the cities; they have been changes of a much broader nature, taking place in many different ways. The total population has grown very much, but its distribution has also changed, so that the total urban population has grown at the expense of the rural population. The regional distribution of population has also been very different from place to place, and we doubt if these changes have been properly understood.

One example of these changes can be seen from the research we did to discover what urban America actually is in terms of population[1]. If we look at graphs comparing the growths of population between 1900 and 1970 of settlements categorized according to their population size, we get a picture of what the growth has been within each category (fig. 23). This, however, is not a true picture of urban America today, since these calculations were based on a definition of non-urban dwellers as being people who live in places with small populations, although such people may live only five or ten miles from the big cities and therefore participate in every aspect of city life.

If we take only those people who live within the metropolitan areas to be urban dwellers, then in 1960 they numbered 119 million, or 67% of the total American population, and had increased to 136 million or 68% of the total by 1970. If, however, we include all those people living within the daily systems of movement of urban centers as inhabitants of urban systems, then in 1960 there were 171 million of them, that is, 96% of the total American population then, and were estimated to have become about 196 million, or 97% of the total by 1970 (fig. 24).

In America, the average central city of the Standard Metropolitan Statistical Area (SMSA) had a population of 274,000 in 1960. If, however, we include all those people living within the daily systems of movement of the central cities, that is, the inhabitants of the city as it really is today, then this average rises to 930,000, or becomes 3.4 times as many. This is a much larger figure than that which is usually given for an urban population, but it is a much more realistic one. People have increased mobility today; if they want to reach a certain place they do so, and in ever larger numbers. So urban America is already embracing 97% of all the American people, and spreading out its arms to the rest.

The attraction of big urban centers has been so great and has resulted in so many changes that it is no longer even possible to compare cities, since we are no longer certain how far any city extends. The City of London, for example, had only 4,767 inhabitants in 1961, while the total area under the London County Council had 3,000,248. It is therefore no longer possible to say which city is the largest. The United Nations Demographic Yearbook puts Shanghai first in 1970 with 10,820,000 people, Tokyo next with 8,841,000, New York with 7,895,000 and Moscow with 7,050,000. These figures are only indicative, however, since Tokyo, for example, with the highest speed railway in the world, is estimated to serve 17 million people. We can make only one certain statement: that there are several urban systems in existence which have passed the mark of 10 million people and are heading for 20.

This phenomenon of growth has not only affected the big cities; almost every major city has become dynamic. The most rapid growth of population has taken place within cities, and the larger they are, the greater that growth has usually been (fig. 25). Many rural centers still do increase in total population, but at slower rates. There has been a clear global shift of population from rural to urban areas, especially during the last few generations, and a shift within urban areas themselves from the smaller towns to the larger cities. Settlements with under 1,000 inhabitants, for example, had a yearly growth rate of 0.28% around 1800,

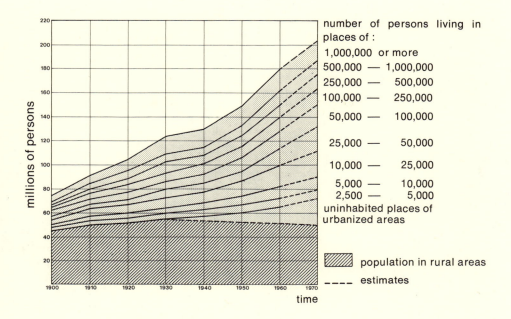

23. urban and rural population in conterminous U.S.A. according to the Bureau of the Census

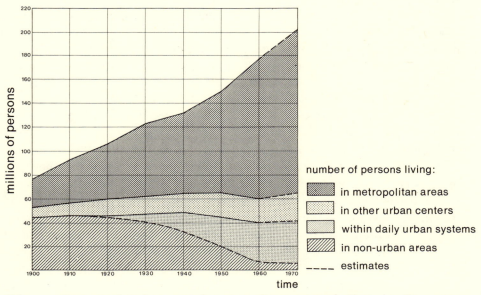

24. the real urban and non-urban population in the conterminous U.S.A.

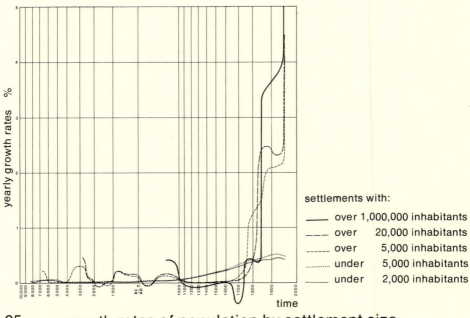

settlements with:

——— over 1,000,000 inhabitants
– – – over   20,000 inhabitants
- - - - over   5,000 inhabitants
············ under   5,000 inhabitants
——— under   2,000 inhabitants

time

25.   growth rates of population by settlement size

which rose to a maximum of 0.45% in the first half of the century, but is now showing a slight decline in rate of growth for the first time in human history, from 0.45% to 0.41%. In contrast, cities with populations of over one million, which grew at an annual rate of 0.4% around 1800, showed an average yearly growth rate of 5.1% during the decade between 1950 and 1960. Settlements of intermediate sizes show rates of growth varying directly with their size. For the period between 1950 and 1960, cities with over 20,000 inhabitants showed yearly growth rates of 4.5%, and towns over 5,000 a growth of 4.05%. Villages of under 5,000 people grew at a rate of only 0.497%, and still smaller mountain villages further down the scale have been losing population at high rates. All these phenomena are shown in table 5, Appendix 1, and are based on studies made by the Athens Center of Ekistics.

The maximum settlement size on earth just before the birth of the new settlements at the beginning of the 19th century was just over one million inhabitants, and this had been reached only by London and probably by Tokyo and Peking, that is, a total of three cities. The number of cities with one million inhabitants had risen to 19 by 1900, to 90 in 1950, to 141 in 1960, and was around 190 by 1970 (fig. 26a). The relative growth in importance of such large cities can be gauged from the following facts (fig. 26b, 26c): in 1900 they contained 2.2% of the total world population (35 million people); by 1960 this percentage had risen to 12.5% (370 million people); and by 1970 it had reached 16.2% (590 million people).

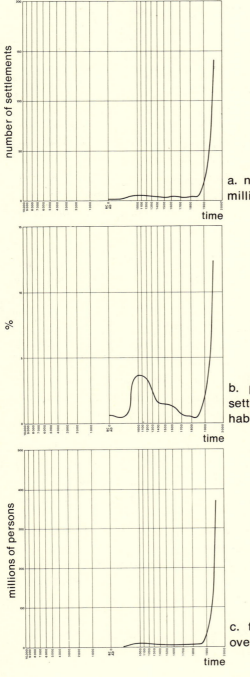

a. number of settlements with over one million inhabitants

b. percentage of world population in settlements with over one million inhabitants

c. total population of settlements with over one million inhabitants

26.   growth of large cities

The newest and largest form of settlement, the megalopolis, is the one which exerts the highest attraction on people from all other areas, and is the class of settlement now growing at the highest rate. In 1960 there were 11 megalopolises under formation, with a total population which was 8.5% (250 million) of the world total.

These general changes in population structure took place in different ways in different countries and cities according to the particular factors that affected them individually, such as increasing political independence, or rapidly rising incomes. There are cities, like Dakkar and others in West African countries, where the population doubled in the five years between 1945 and 1950[2].

There are more settlements now, and they are larger, but there have also been important changes in the demographic characteristics of populations. In general, households become smaller as the level of incomes and degree of urbanization become higher. Before 1800 the average household in rural and low-income areas had over five members. Today, and especially in the high-income areas, there has been a progressive drop, from an average of four people to three, and in some cases even to two people per household. This conclusion takes the household as the conventional nuclear family and does not take into account types of family organization found in non-western cultures which can differ widely from western patterns, nor recent trends within the western world towards experiment with unconventional types of household such as community living or other ways of returning to the extended family.

Life expectancy has increased dramatically. A life span of 20 to 30 years was common among primitive and prehistoric people, but as the standard of life and level of incomes have risen, this span has gradually increased. It is not that the biological life span has actually increased, but that more people live to be old, so that in several countries the normal life span is now 70 or even 75 years. As a result, the age structure of populations as a whole has changed radically (fig. 27a). The proportion of older people over 65 has been rising steeply and continuously. There are therefore certain problems in assimilating such increasing numbers of old people into societies; often with enormous injustice to the elderly and to the detriment of their societies, they are termed "non-productive". In the lowest-income countries, elderly people represent 2-4% of the total population, 7-8% in the middle-income countries, and reach 12-13% in the highest-income European countries where the increase in this percentage has been quite rapid in recent years (fig. 27b). In the large cities of these areas the percentages of elderly are even higher.

In contrast, the proportion of children under 15 years old has become smaller as incomes have risen. Children represent 40-50% of the total population in low-income countries. In the high-income countries they only represent 20-30% and even this percentage has shown a decrease in recent years, especially in the more advanced areas. In the larger cities the percentage of children is again lower.

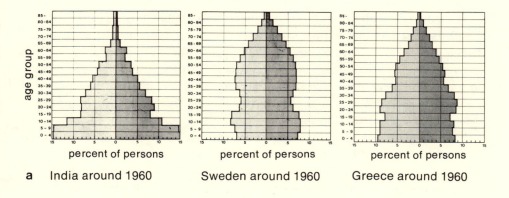

a India around 1960   Sweden around 1960   Greece around 1960

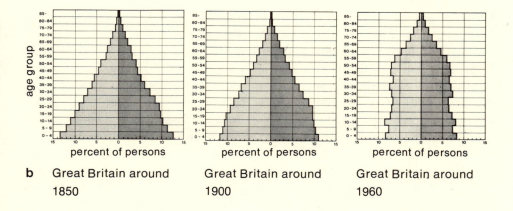

b Great Britain around 1850   Great Britain around 1900   Great Britain around 1960

males
females

27.   age structure for different countries

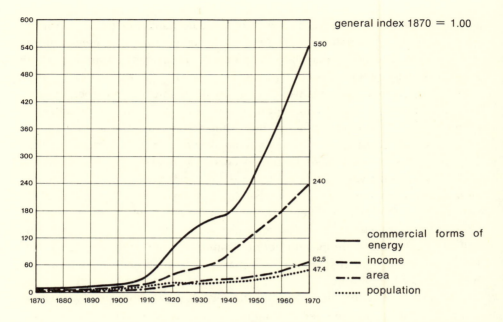

general index 1870 = 1.00

commercial forms of energy
income
area
population

40.   the increase of forces in Detroit, Michigan, 1870-1970

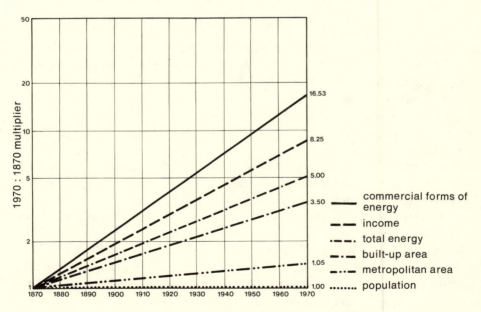

commercial forms of energy
income
total energy
built-up area
metropolitan area
population

41.   growth of per capita indicators for metropolitan Athens, Greece, 1870-1970

With fewer children and more old people, the percentage of active people (those between 15 and 65) has risen with the rising levels of income from between 45% and 55% to between 60% and 70%. There are more active people in urban than in rural areas, and more in large settlements than in small ones. In the U.S. in 1950, the percentage of active population (those between 19 and 64 years) was 51.3% of the total in the rural areas, but 64.2% in cities of over three million inhabitants. In 1961 in Canada the proportion of those between 15 and 64 years old was 54.4% in rural areas and 61.7% in cities of over 100,000 inhabitants, and in 1955 in Japan it was 59% in agricultural areas and 67.2% in metropolitan areas.

Birth rates, which are steadily decreasing with the rise in development and urbanization, remain noticeably higher in rural than in urban areas. Death rates also show an initial decline with the rise in development, but then later show a greater similarity in urban and rural areas. The diverse trends in the total structure of rural and urban populations is accounted for by the fact that while birth rates in towns are markedly different from those in the country, death rates are more similar.

Great changes have also occurred in the economic sphere. Although urban incomes have increased, urban people have become less rich than they used to be in proportion to country people, at least in the high-income countries (fig. 28). In countries with an average level of income, those people living in small villages may have less income than those living in large cities at a ratio of about 1:4; and in low-income countries, those in towns are even richer in comparison to those in villages. In high-income countries the disparity in incomes may be as low as 1:2. This fact, however, does not seem to have tarnished people's image of the "golden city".

The value of urban land has increased incredibly as a result of the continual migration of people from the country to the cities (fig. 29). Most of this money, however, has found its way into the pockets of a relatively few people who own or speculate in such land.

Big social changes have also taken place. Not only are populations and incomes growing in an unprecedented way, but as the last economic example demonstrated, some people are getting all the benefits of this growth while others get none, or very few of them, at least in countries with free economies.

Another example of the social changes is the formation of new groups of people within society in quite an unprecedented way. In the traditional societies of the past every village had its village "idiot". He may have been a real idiot, or he might in fact have been a genius, but the important thing to the villagers was that he was different from everyone else. If we call country people the green people, and town people the red people, then those odd people are the blue people. As the average village had, let us assume, 500 inhabitants, this blue person would be one in 500. Therefore a big modern city with ten million

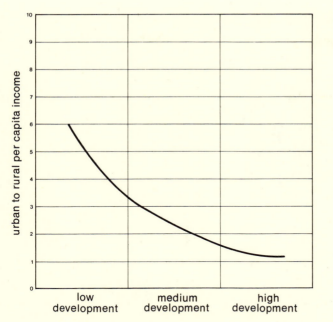

28.   ratios of urban to rural per capita incomes for entire
       countries, circa 1960, by level of development

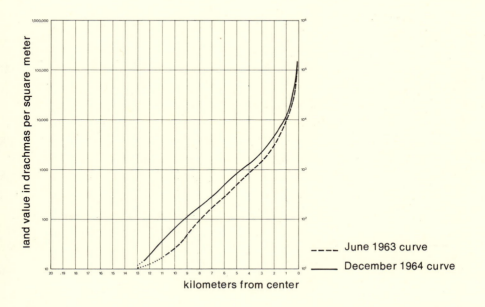

_ _ _ _ June 1963 curve

_____ December 1964 curve

kilometers from center

29.   land value increase in relation to distance ﬧrom city
       center for Athens, Greece

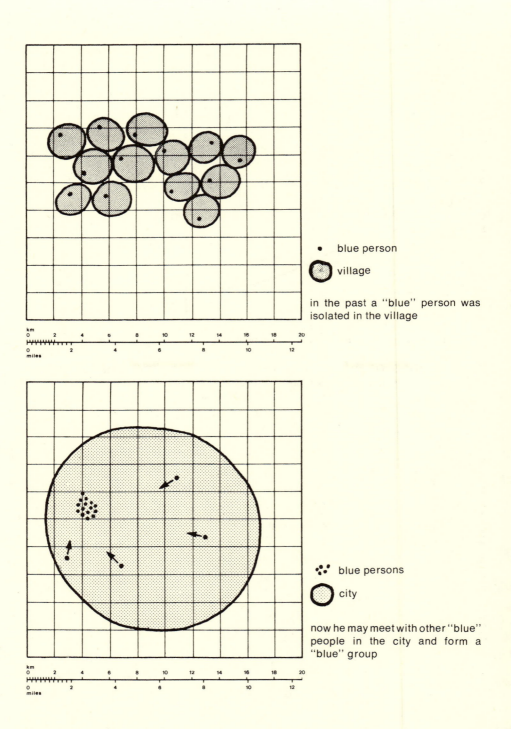

• blue person

village

in the past a "blue" person was
isolated in the village

km
0   2   4   6   8   10   12   14   16   18   20
0   2   4   6   8   10   12
miles

blue persons

city

now he may meet with other "blue"
people in the city and form a
"blue" group

km
0   2   4   6   8   10   12   14   16   18   20
0   2   4   6   8   10   12
miles

30.   new formations of social groups in urban areas

people will have 5,000 blue people of every kind, 5,000 geniuses, or idiots, or people who think and behave differently from everyone else. In the villages these people would be isolated, but in the big cities they can find other people similar to themselves and come together to form groups who think in similar ways or enjoy the same activities (fig. 30). The Woodstock Festival was an example of this. All those people who wanted to get together with others in an open space and listen to a particular kind of music were able to get together and do so because of present-day mobility. There were 400,000 of them out of 200 million Americans, or one out of every 500. It was not so much a herald of social change, as some people referred to it, as a demonstration of how different structures of society are made possible because of increased numbers and mobility. We must understand this and be prepared to face completely new social phenomena.

17. New systems of life

The big revolution that has taken place is that we have entered an era with entirely new systems of living. These new urban systems, small megalopolises of the size of ekistic unit 11, first emerged as functionally coherent units in the 1940's. Their growth in area has been far greater than their growth in population or incomes.

The systems of the past extended over areas based on daily fields of movement that covered, in round numbers, about 210 sq. km (80 sq. mi.) for hunters, 21 sq. km (8 sq. mi.) for farmers, and 150 sq. km (58 sq. mi.) for town-dwellers. The urban systems of today have reached areas of tens of thousands of square kilometers, that is, they have become hundreds of times larger than any systems of the past. Such systems are emerging all over the globe at different speeds according to the types of transportation systems in use, and are continuously increasing in area at a rate of 3-7% and more every year[3].

In order to make this case clear, we shall consider some details from a study of some typical American cities carried out in 1971[4]. This was based on the 1960 census data, which recorded movements of people in all major American cities[5]. When the limits of the daily fields of movement of 11 typical American cities (not including any of the largest ones) are superimposed, we can see that whereas in the past urban life involved the people who lived at a walking distance of about 1 km (0.4 mi.) from the city center, and the farmers who served the city at a distance of about 5 km (3 mi.), now there are people driving into American cities from as far out as 203 km (127 mi.), that is, from over 50 times further than ever before. The size of the average system has grown from the average for an American township of about 100 sq. km (36 sq. mi.) to about 26,000 sq. km (10,200 sq. mi.). The system has therefore become more than 250 times larger than the American township of the past, and 164 times larger than the institutional American city. In this case, also, the area has increased 2.12 times faster than the population.

This change can be better understood if we compare fig. 31, which has fig. 11 superimposed on it at the same scale, with fig. 13. We can now see two things: first, the daily field of movement of the average American city (not including the largest ones) is much larger than the whole territory of many city-states of the past with all their towns and villages, and even larger than the total territory of many of the early empires; second, whereas the Network of connections between the central city of the past and its surrounding territory formed very thin radial lines, the whole area today is covered by large numbers of strong connecting lines in all directions. Not only has the territory blown up into new dimensions, but the system has been transformed into a completely new type of organism.

This is a global phenomenon. We can see among others, from the 15 metropolises studied at the Athens Center of Ekistics[6] and the 49 included in the Urban Detroit Area and the Northern Ohio Urban System studies[7], that the total area covered by these systems grows at a greater rate than their population (Appendix 1, table 8 and fig. 32). So if we consider the urban systems as total organisms rather than looking only at parts of them, we can see that urban density is dropping continuously all over the world.

Growth of the systems, however, is a very small problem compared to what has happened because of this growth. The most complex change, and one which has been completely overlooked, is that while the fields of movement of people living in various settlements of the past did not overlap, so that their settlements remained separate systems of life, today the fields of movement of many settlements are overlapping more and more. People therefore no longer belong to one village, town or city, but to many, since they can reach many settlements in different directions within the limit of one hour. A clear example of this can be seen in the case of several of the cities in the northeast of the U.S.A. (fig. 33).

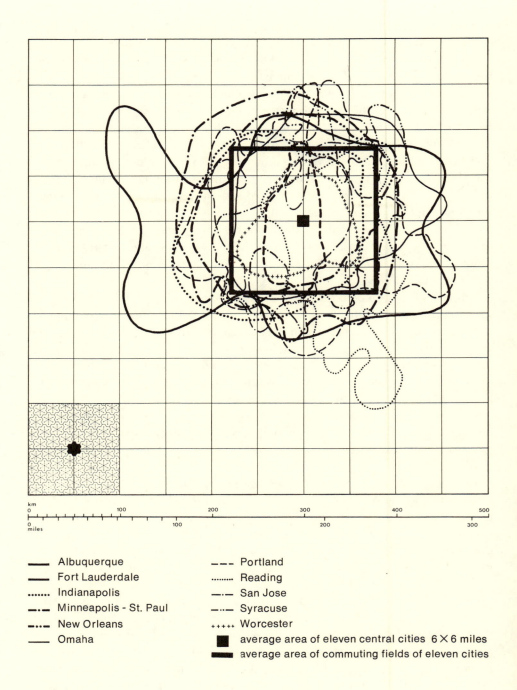

—— Albuquerque	——— Portland
—— Fort Lauderdale	········ Reading
······· Indianapolis	—·— San Jose
—··— Minneapolis - St. Paul	—···— Syracuse
—···— New Orleans	+++++ Worcester
—— Omaha	■ average area of eleven central cities 6 × 6 miles
	▬ average area of commuting fields of eleven cities

31.   commuting fields of eleven American cities in 1960

(and comparison with villages and towns of the past)

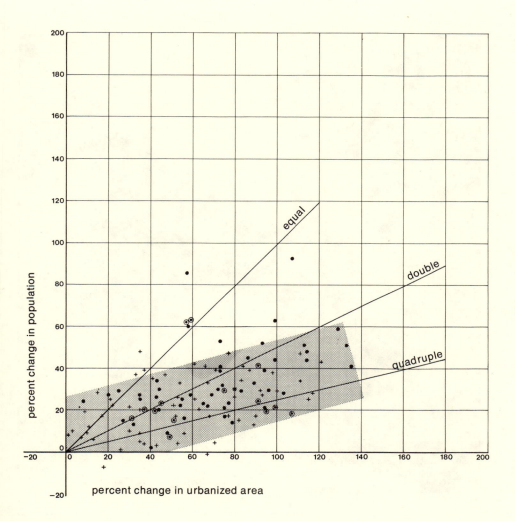

urbanized areas of:

+   50,000 - 200,000 persons in 1960   ▓ zone of maximum frequency

•   200,000 - 1,000,000 persons in 1960   ✳ mean for all urbanized areas

◉   1,000,000 and over

32.   changes in area and population in urbanized areas of the U.S.A, 1950-1960

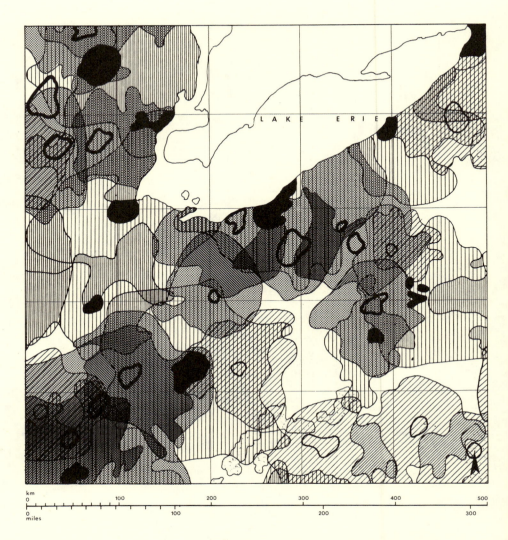

LAKE ERIE

percentage of tract residents commuting to central city:

	50% or more	some commuting
principal metropolitan centers		
centers within metropolitan fields		
independent centers with less than 50,000 population		
national parks and forests		

33.   superimposed commuting fields in northeast of U.S.A.

We are now witnessing a further jump in size to much larger daily urban systems, moving up from the city to the metropolis and to the small megalopolis. Such small megalopolises form ekistic unit 11 (community class VIII). Since they are a global phenomenon appearing everywhere, they are now referred to as daily urban systems.

The case of the Northern Ohio Urban System is typical since here we can see the emergence of one system from several separate cities such as Cleveland, Akron, Canton, Youngstown, Lorrain, Erie (fig. 34). With Cleveland as its metropolis, this system has a population of 5.6 million, and covers 43,700 sq. km (17,000 sq. mi.). Recent studies in which we have been involved have shown the emergence of a similar system in southern France, extending from Italy to Spain, with a population of 5 million and an area of 59,000 sq. km (23,000 sq. mi.) (fig. 35a). Another, in Catalonia, Spain, with Barcelona as its metropolis, has a population of 5 million and covers an area of 32,000 sq. km (12,500 sq. mi.) (fig. 35b). In southeastern Michigan, the Detroit daily urban system has 8 million people and covers an area of 59,000 sq. km (23,000 sq. mi) (fig. 35d).

The formation of ever-larger systems does not end with small megalopolises or daily urban systems. Once Anthropos started to conquer space through the use of machines, he went on finding ways of doing so ever more effectively. He moves further outwards with every day that passes, causing the appearance of even larger systems, the first of which — in the northeast of the U.S.A. — was called Megalopolis by Jean Gottmann[8]. The very name given to it is significant, since the same impression which was given to people in the 5th century B.C. by a city of 50,000 people (Part Two: 12) is now being given to us by a city with tens of millions of people.

Unlike the daily urban systems of the present, which usually form concentric systems within areas of not more than 500×500 km (300×300 mi.), the megalopolises, which cover larger areas within $1,000 \times 1,000$ km (620×620 mi.), tend to form linear systems from the interconnection of several daily urban systems (fig. 36).

A second emerging megalopolis is the Japanese one. In 1966, the year of its consolidation into one continuous unit from Tokyo to Yahata, its population was 69.2 million, its area 76,000 sq. km (47,200 sq. mi.) and its population living at a density of 9.1 inh. per ha (3.7 inh. per acre), and it had four main centers. This megalopolis is shown in fig. 37.

An attempt was made to study megalopolises in the Athens Center of Ekistics, and some of the conclusions that were reached are presented in Appendix 3. It is essential that we understand the emergence of this new type of settlement. In particular, we made a more detailed study of the Great Lakes Megalopolis.

We took an example from the Great Lakes Megalopolis study in order to illustrate how the area of a megalopolis may be distinguished from its surrounding territory as a functionally coherent whole. We picked out a series of 40 variables,

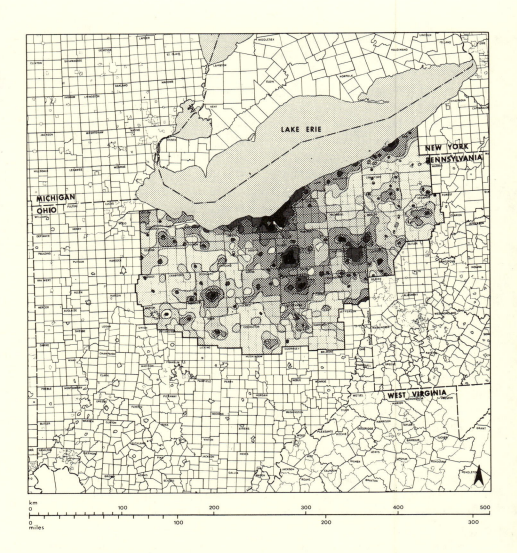

population per square kilometer:

	0 — 19
	20 — 39
	40 — 199
	200 — 399
	400 — 1,999
	2,000 and above

34.   Northern Ohio Urban System — generalized population
       density, 1960

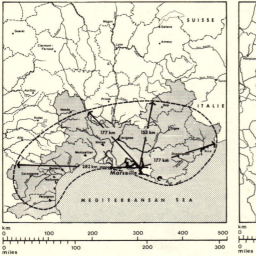

a. Southern France

b. Catalonia, Spain

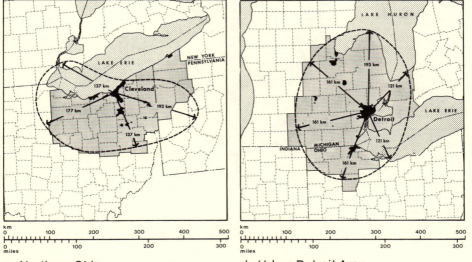

c. Northern Ohio

d. Urban Detroit Area

35. daily urban systems

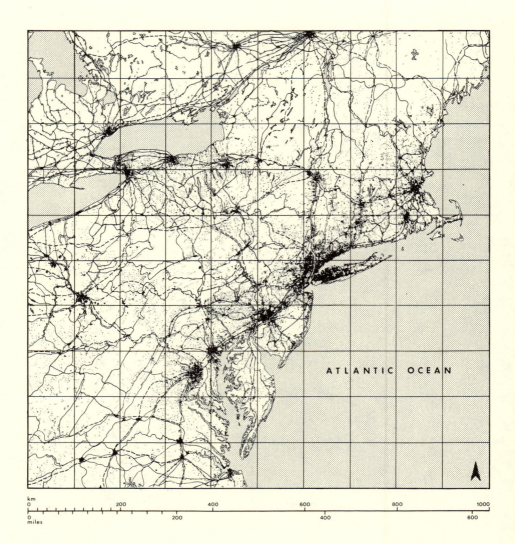

```
km
0          200         400         600         800        1000
├─┴─┴─┴─┴─┴─┴─┴─┴─┤
0                  200                   400                   600
miles
```

36.   linear system of the Megalopolis of the eastern sea-
       board of U.S.A., 1963

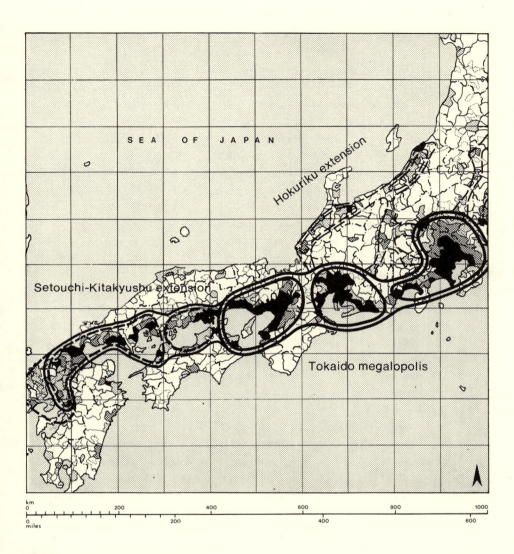

■ overlapping of three factors

▨ overlapping of two factors

░ overlapping of one factor

note: the three factors are:
   — population density more than 300 inh./ha
   — increase of population more than 5% between 1960-1965
   — production of yearly additional value more than
      10 trillion yen in industry

37.   Japanese Megalopolis, 1960

which were expressing to a greater or a lesser extent the degree of urbanization in any area, using data drawn from many fields such as sociology, economics, demography, transport, etc. Then, applying among other techniques the method of Principal Component Analysis (an analytical statistical method particularly suitable to multivaried situations), we brought to light distinct and characteristic patterns for Component One — a new derived variable representing the degree of urbanization in each area which synthesizes the pertinent information contained in each original variable into a meaningful index (fig. 38). When we then made a cross-sectional analysis of the whole land area, on which these various degrees of urbanization were represented like contours on a map with the peaks of urbanization standing up like mountains, we could see the shape of the megalopolis (fig. 39). We can see two clear discontinuities which take the form of a very steep decline in the value of Component One at the boundaries of the axial portion of the megalopolis, and a lesser, but still significant decline at the limits of its functionally dependent surrounding region.

We can now clarify one point: none of the systems of life presented here (figs. 31, 33, 34, 35, 36, 38) is comparable with any presented in Part Two dealing with settlements of the past. These figures do not show the total territories of these new systems, as earlier figures showed those of the bands (fig. 8), villages (fig. 9), towns (fig. 11), and cities; nor do they represent their built-up areas only. The new systems contain a mixture of built-up and non built-up areas, of urban areas and rural areas, in fact a mixture of everything, with only their definition as daily urban systems (ekistic unit 11) and of interwoven daily urban systems for the megalopolises (ekistic unit 12) to distinguish them.

We can compare them with the settlements of the past only in terms of the daily fields of movement, and that is to compare them with the territories of villages and towns only. If we want to think of them as we did of the cities, as centers of organization which extend beyond their daily fields of movement in terms of their total territory, then we must think in terms of larger areas that are not even measurable at present. London, for example, was once the capital of an empire, but it now lives by economic relations with the whole world. New York, Rio de Janeiro, Accra, Shanghai and Melbourne are similar cases. We can measure their built-up areas, and we can measure their daily urban systems, but we can only mentally conceive the global relationships which keep them alive because of their many interwoven Networks. What happens on a small scale with the interwoven fields of movement of various cities (fig. 33) happens on a big scale with interwoven economic fields. The life system of the city in fig. 13 can therefore only be properly compared with the whole global system of Singapore, and not with the small territory of its political state.

The basic, and perhaps the only cause for this change from cities to urban systems has been the use of mechanical energy for transportation. It began with the railways in 1825, which developed systems both on the surface and under-

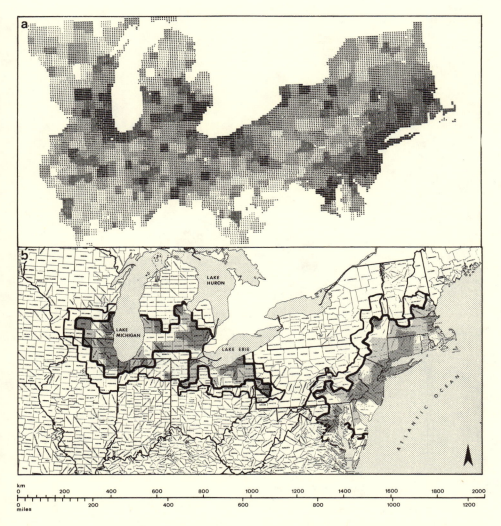

a. Principal Component Analysis:
   component 1, alternative 4

b. Great Lakes Megalopolis definition
   (main portion)

standard units

7.0
5.0
3.0
1.0
-1.0
-3.0
-5.0
-7.0

———— Great Lakes Megalopolis,
       Northeastern Megalopolis

———— study area

▨ urban clusters

▩ urban centers

38.   Great Lakes and Eastern Megalopolises

107

b. section

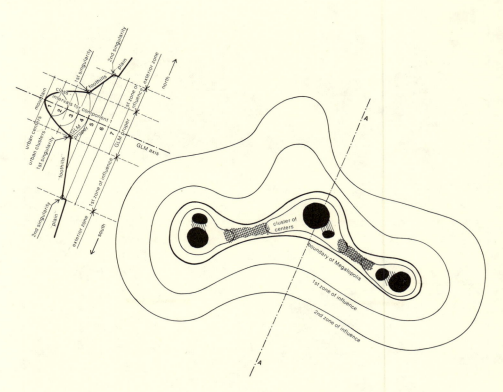

a. schematic plan

▨ intra-cluster peripheries
▨ megalopolitan confluence zones

39. schematic cross section (AA) through Great Lakes Megalopolis for component 1

ground, and intensified with the arrival of the automobile, invented by various people in different countries in the 19th century and coming into general use in the 20th. So we can say that the settlements of the present turned into urban systems because of the arrival of the railways 150 years ago, and the car 75 years ago. Although steam engines were in fact used for ships even earlier, in 1817, their use has not yet played an important role in the formation of urban settlements, although it has strengthened those situated on lakes, rivers or by the sea. The use of the airplane has not had any great effect on their formation either, although it too has strengthened those systems with important airports.

Once we realize what the basic cause is for the appearance of major urban systems, we must see that they will continue to grow in area all over the globe with every day that passes, even if no new people are added to them. So long as incomes and technological innovations go on increasing, each new machine will be able to take Anthropos further out from the center, and Anthropos, since he always follows his first principle of maximizing his potential contacts, will move ever further outwards.

We can see proof of this fact in the statistics dealing with trips. Everywhere, more trips are being made per person, the distance of trips is becoming greater, the duration longer, and the speeds and time spent on the road are increasing. Such increases range from very low to very high, and imply big changes in every aspect of life, which have had a direct effect on the physical formation of the system. For the first time in history, this formation does not depend just on the topography and the people, but on the direct influence of the transportation networks on everything else.

Speeds today are very high compared to those of the past. We can speak of an average speed of 100 km (60 mi.) per hour for people moving in automobiles in many urban systems of the world, and 200 km (120 mi.) per hour for those using the best railway in operation — that running between Tokyo and Osaka. This means that speeds used in these new systems are already 20 to 40 times higher than those of the past, and such speeds are continually increasing, producing enormous changes as a result.

The formation of the new systems has·been caused basically by new methods and speeds of transportation, but changes have also occurred because of new technological inventions in general. With every day that passes, new inventions give Anthropos new choices, both in the products of industry and in communication systems, so that new conditions are continually being created.

Having looked at just some of the things involved in the emergence of these new systems, such as population, incomes, territories and transportation, we can understand that the interaction between them and their influence on other phenomena is important, and will lead to changes of all sorts.

We tried to study what has been happening to several urban variables over a period of one century, between 1870 and 1970, in two urban systems belonging

to countries with very different situations, Detroit, Michigan, U.S.A., and Athens, Greece. We tried to relate the growth rates of various things for a period long enough to eliminate temporary and local fluctuations. We found that while population has grown rapidly, its growth has been surpassed by such things as the metropolitan commuting area, literacy, elementary and secondary education, total energy consumption, incomes, and commercially marketed energy.

This rapid growth began in the 19th century, intensified during the first third of our century, and redoubled its speed during the second third. The absolute change in population and in technological innovation is completely without precedent. What is more, the general acceleratory trend shows no signs of slackening. In Detroit over the last 100 years (1870-1970), the population has grown 47.4 times, the area 62.5 times, incomes 240 times, and commercial energy 550 times (fig. 40). In Athens, those things which have grown most are: population 53.2 times, area 74.7 times, incomes 345 times, commercial energy 695 times, and higher education 4,960 times. A comparison of the multipliers obtained for the period 1870 to 1970 for these indicators, expressed on a per capita basis, is shown in fig. 41.

18. The many different settlements

The result of the changes in dimensions and the appearance of new types and new systems of life has been a radical and continuous alteration to all existing human settlements.

The number of existing nomadic bands diminishes continuously all round the world. When such bands cross a new highway under construction, they are confronted with the challenge to join the labor force and make the huge jump of 10,000 years of historical development. Villages, too, are disappearing everywhere[9], especially in the most remote areas. Once farmers are given the opportunity to join a team for some special effort, as were the *decasegi* (Japanese farmers working away from home) in preparing Japan for the Olympic Games, it is doubtful if they will ever return to their villages. Villages are not being deserted for the first time in history, but it is the first time they are being deserted on a global scale and in a permanent way. The era of the traditional village is over.

People everywhere are tending towards the creation of urban systems of all sorts, and therefore every urban system, from city up to metropolis, small megalopolis and megalopolis, is continuously spreading outwards with continuously decreasing densities of population, creating many dangers for the areas of countryside it invades. In an attempt to understand these phenomena we carried out an analysis of many cases all over the world and our conclusion was very clear: that the trends are the same everywhere.

The location of these new or changing settlements has been affected by the changes which have taken place While in the past the tendency was for people to live as close to the center of their settlement as they could in terms of direct distance, they now tend to come close to in it terms of time. This may mean that they live at a greater distance from the center but closer to the new lines of high-speed transportation. In following the first two principles of maximum potential contact and·minimum effort, they first came close to the new railway lines, and now are close to the highways. Also, once they are given the opportunity, people tend more and more to select a location for purely esthetic reasons, to achieve a better climate, or to obtain a pleasant view of the whole natural environment around them.

Defense, which according to the third principle of the optimization of protective space played an important role in the selection of the location of settlements in the past, has played only a small one in determining the location of those of the present. It did affect such cases as that of Paris in the first half of the 10th century, or Germany before World War II when new factories were often built in small isolated cities, or Asia where cities like Peshawar in Pakistan, for obvious reasons, had to keep their defense systems (still expressed by walls) intact.

The location of the settlements of the present, therefore, is beginning to be influenced by three things according to the new forces which shape them: the attraction of existing urban centers; the attraction of high-speed transportation lines; and the attraction of areas with esthetic values (fig. 42). Because of the influence of these new forces, settlements are acquiring completely new forms as physical systems everywhere in the world where machines are beginning to play an important role. The phenomenon starts on a small scale — as we can see, for example, in the building-up of settlements all around Lago di Como on the branch of the river di Lecco from Bellagio — and then spreads until the system becomes very large.

As a result of all these factors taken in combination there has been a complete change in the structure of all settlements today, a phenomenon that has not been understood and so has led to the chaotic situation in which we are living. No urban system of the present has managed to understand the colossal changes which are taking place, or prepared itself to deal with them properly. We can understand why if we look at a schematic presentation comparing the built-up areas of cities of the past and present (fig. 43). The largest cities actually planned in the past did not exceed the size of Peking in 1300 A.D. New York today is 200 times larger than this; nobody prepared for such an increase.

Yet even this is misleading, since New York is presented here as being a compact built-up area (fig. 43), whereas in reality it is spreading over the open countryside around it, so that a more realistic image would be the one shown in fig. 44.

Even this is not the true image of the real city of New York today, since people commute to it from as far away as Philadelphia and other cities, so that in order to see it we have to change to a figure at a different scale (fig. 45). On this scale we can begin to understand how the structure of the countryside around all such growing urban systems has changed also. The case of the Urban Detroit Area demonstrates how the amount of farm land there has been receding during our century (fig. 46).

Yet, once again, it is still impossible to understand the real size of the structure of our settlements today unless we move to an even larger scale of 1,000 × 1,000 km (620 × 620 mi.), in order to be able to study such large and complex systems as the Northeastern Megalopolis of the U.S.A. (fig. 36) and the others which were shown earlier on the same scale (figs. 37, 38).

We can finally get the real image of the completely different situation which actually exists today if we look at a map on the scale of 5,000 × 5,000 km (3,000 × 3,000 mi.), by which we can see the formation of new types of settlements in every area (fig. 47).

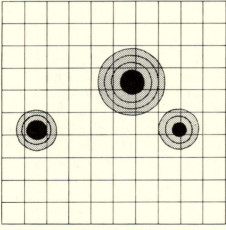

a. the attraction of existing urban
   systems

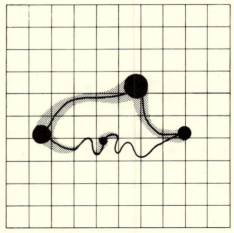

b. the attraction of existing lines of
   transportation

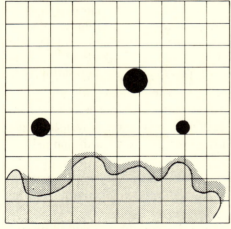

c. the attraction of esthetic forces

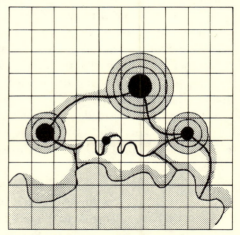

d. the total system of attractions

42.   the three forces conditioning the shape of urban
       systems

name	date	area in sq. km	area
village	700 B.C.	0.40	.
Athens	400 B.C.	1.80	.
Alexandria	150 B.C.	9.00	.
Rome	A.D. 200	13.60	•
Constantinople	A.D. 800	21.60	•
Peking	A.D.1300	52.70	•
Athens	1960	126.00	○
Paris	1960	1,105.00	⬤
Tokyo	1960	2,235.90	⬤
Moscow	1960	3,880.70	⬤
London	1960	6,476.40	⬤
New York	1960	10,074.40	⬤

43.   the built-up areas of cities

km
0   20   40   60   80   100   120   140   160   180   200
0 miles   20   40   60   80   100   120

44.   New York area, 1963

116

ATLANTIC OCEAN

```
km
0          100          200          300          400          500
0               100              200              300
miles
```

45.   the real city of New York, 1963

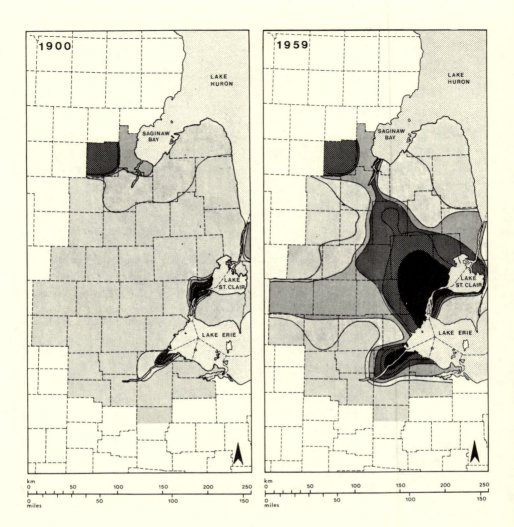

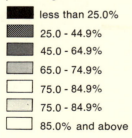

percentage of farmland:

■ (black)	less than 25.0%
▒ (dark)	25.0 - 44.9%
▓ (medium)	45.0 - 64.9%
▒ (light)	65.0 - 74.9%
□	75.0 - 84.9%
□	75.0 - 84.9%
□	85.0% and above

46.   decreasing farmland in the Urban Detroit Area

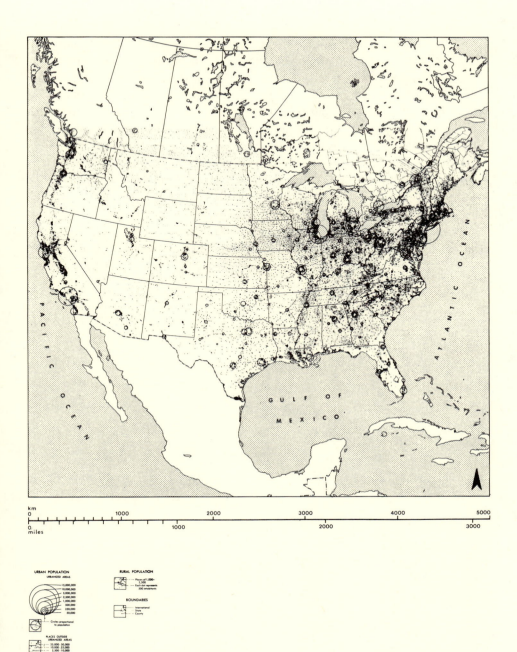

each dot represents 500 inhabitants

47.   distribution of population in conterminous U.S.A. and
        southern Canada, 1960

Even these complex situations might have been easy to deal with had they remained static, so that Anthropos had time to understand them and ameliorate the bad things that were happening. They are not static, however. All human settlements have now become so dynamic, so much action is being taken by everyone, from private people to government sectors, with every minute that passes, that it is very difficult for anyone to understand the settlements of the present, and that is why the confusion about them is so great all over the world.

The case of Athens, which changed so greatly between 1940 and 1970, that is in just one generation, is not unique; on the contrary, it is characteristic of what is happening all over the globe since Athens happens to be close to world averages from many points of view, as detailed comparative studies of the Athens Center of Ekistics have shown. We have moved from the era of the static city, occasionally passing through a dynamic phase and then consolidating once more into a static form, into the era of dynapolis, where all cities are in a phase of continual change and growth.

19. The problems

Every type of settlement has problems today, as they have always done. A settlement is a very complex developing organism, so it could not be otherwise. Every human being has his problems, and so does every settlement. There are problems concerned with Nature, Anthropos and Society, and others concerned with the Shells and Networks created by Anthropos. These problems are obvious; the difficulty is how to classify the most important ones in order to concentrate our attention on them.

Methods have been developed for classifying problems, and by using them we can gradually learn how to understand our problems in the right way instead of just seeing them in whatever the fashionable way of the day happens to be — as, for example, concentrating on air pollution and forgetting the equally big social and human problems that exist. These methods also show us that the larger a settlement is, the more problems it has, so that while in practice we can concentrate on two or three problems in the villages, we have to deal with 30 to 60 in the large cities.

We can now briefly summarize the problems for each type of settlement of the present. For nomads the problem might be said to be that they are gradually disappearing; yet this is not a problem for the nomads themselves at all — it is a problem for Society as a whole, since it is Society which would like to keep the nomads in existence as it prefers to have examples of all types of Society alive and available for study. There is also the problem of the so-called new nomads, people who live in motor caravans and move from city to city, especially in the U.S.A. These people are not real nomads, but they have found that this solution is cheaper than buying a house in the city where they have a job. Several of them suffer from the problems of real nomadic peoples, and others simply prefer this kind of life.

The present situation of village people is similar to that of the nomads, though not in such an extreme way. The villages are disappearing because their inhabitants are happier elsewhere. The problems are that when the villages do survive, everyone living in them suffers from the lack of many services and amenities, and when they disappear, Society as a whole loses some production advantages, and many cultural values.

As for the small towns, they may be suffering from the problems connected with growth or, more often, from those of decline.

Cities, since, as we have seen, we have now entered the era of dynapolis in which all cities are growing and expanding, are usually suffering from all the problems resulting from the ever-increasing invasion of new forces, all their resultant pressures, and the all too rapid rates of growth.

We begin a systematic study of the problems concerning each of the five elements of settlements today with those concerning Nature, and with the influences of Anthropos' action on Nature on land, water, air and climate.

There is no need to dwell at length on the many problems concerned with pollution and the environment which have received so much attention recently, but there may be need to draw attention to some aspects of the problems concerned with Nature that are often overlooked. For example, it is not only Anthropos that creates problems for Nature, Nature also creates problems for Anthropos. There are many areas of the globe with bad climates, like deserts and polar zones, and Anthropos suffers from living in them and is therefore abandoning them. It is time we remembered this fact and took some action in this direction. A second point is that there are other forms of pollution of the environment besides those on which we tend to concentrate. It is true that the air is chemically and physically polluted by machines — but it is possible for us to clean it, should we decide to do so. If, however, we pollute the urban landscape by building huge towers rising to our city skies, how can we ever clean that up?

We must therefore consider the whole range of problems connected with Nature, those created by Nature for Anthropos as well as those created by Anthropos for Nature, and those concerned with all the interconnected elements of Nature itself — land, water, air, climate, and the animal and the plant worlds.

We can describe the way in which Anthropos' actions are adversely affecting Nature in the following way: When energy is used, waste products are created, and pressures are exerted on Nature. Pollution does not automatically result, but only when the rate of the production of waste matter exceeds the capacity of the system to remove, purify, or convert it.

The enormous increase in both material consumption and the use of energy, which has come with our present technological civilization, has unintentionally put greater strains on the natural homeostatic processes of the environment than they can cope with.

This has produced undesirable changes, not only in each subsystem which is affected, but throughout the whole complex of which each is a part. Too much organic waste passed into a lake overloads the subsystem responsible for its biological decomposition and eventually the whole body of water may die.

Pollution of every sort — gaseous, particulate, radioactive, light, thermal, noise, vibration and trace — now exists quite extensively. The list grows daily as new and unsuspected effects are brought to our attention. Anthropos is continually producing new stable chemical compounds for which the environment has no natural processes of neutralization.

Cities must breathe. In doing so they vent gaseous and particulate wastes into the air, forming an envelope above them which maintains their temperature and humidity higher than that of the surrounding country and reduces normal daily and seasonal variations. Simply breathing the atmosphere of Paris is as harmful as smoking two packs of cigarettes a day. Under certain conditions, concentrated air pollution can result in numerous deaths.

Cities must also drink. Water-table levels have been modified by digging deep foundations and mining groundwater deposits. Patterns of run-off have been altered by the impervious surfaces of roofs and streets as well as by sewer systems and drainage projects. Widely increased consumption of water threatens to exhaust supplies in arid climates, and has forced cities to draw their supplies from ever greater distances. Water is also returned to the environment bearing with it dangerous trace elements such as DDT, lead, mercury and chromium, which then enter various biological food chains and can accumulate in living tissues. Rachel Carson painted a grim picture of the effects of such trace pollutants in *Silent Spring*[10].

Cities must also work. Even the generation of excessive noise and vibration constitutes pollution, overtaxing nerves and over-stimulating the senses of the people who live in cities.

It is at present technically possible to neutralize or to eliminate almost every polluting factor which has been mentioned. Exhaust fumes can be cleaned, water can be recycled, noise and vibration can be eliminated by better building construction. However, such things are expensive to do and no economic system has yet been devised which can assess these costs, or force the responsible individuals and institutions to pay for them. The same difficulties are encountered under competitive and centralized economic systems. The industries and cities responsible for the biological decline of various lakes, for example, did not cause this to happen deliberately — but were never forced to make their consumers pay the full price for the prevention of such pollution. Whom should they pay, and how much?

Until such questions are answered, pollution control cannot hope to be very successful; but we have cases which prove that once we know the best and most economic technological solution, a program can be worked out for the application over a given number of years of proper economic measures that will deal with such problems.

The next major category of problems concerns those that affect Anthropos himself directly. The recent changes that have taken place in our systems of life have had many effects on Anthropos, some good and some bad.

There have been some noticeable physiological transformations in the human organism. Advances in public health have meant that many human beings with defective genes now survive to reproductive age, when in earlier days they would have died without having children. On the other hand, it is now possible for people to attain their full physical potential, as was not the case earlier. Average bodily dimensions and weight have increased, first and second dentitions and sexual maturation take place earlier, and these changes are more marked among urban than rural children.

The quickening tempo of urban life with its rapid alternation of so many diverse activities has increased stress, producing a rise in the occurrence of nervous breakdowns, mental illness, and the use of drugs.

While infectious diseases have been practically eradicated from the cities of high-income countries, degenerative diseases, such as cancer and cardiovascular conditions, have increased. So also have venereal diseases, arthritis, baldness, and symptoms resulting from increased stress on vision and hearing.

Changes in nutrition, with more sugar, alcohol, animal protein and rich food, have led to an increase in obesity, bad teeth, ulcers and other defects. The absorption of pollutants has also produced subtle poisoning and degeneration in the human body.

Unused functions tend to atrophy. Urban Anthropos, living in a stable, controlled and artificial environment, is losing the normal homeostatic or balancing functions of his physiological mechanisms. His body is also degenerating from lack of essential exercise.

Some of these pathological changes pose a mounting threat to the other advantages of urban life. We must examine all the new problems which concern Anthropos in every phase of his life, including those nine months before he is born, until the day of his death. It is clear that Anthropos has solved many of his old problems by changing his systems of life, but he has created many new ones. This is quite a natural thing to have happened, but we should not accept these changes as inevitable. There are positive signs that we shall eventually be able to win most of the battles in these new areas, provided we increase our efforts in the right direction.

Society has also suffered many changes, but we are not sure that these have been properly understood. Inaccurate statements are often made. We speak, for example, of the problem of the urban poor all over the globe. We forget, however, that these people did not become poor and a problem just because they came into the cities. They did not come into the big cities like Calcutta and Bombay, and others in Europe and the U.S.A., because they were rich and liked cities; they came because they were already poor and abandoned in their remote and unpromising rural areas. The urban poor are not an urban problem, but simply a more apparent expression of the age-old problem of the poor in general.

Changes in society are many and continuous, and we can only mention a few of them here. One is the formation of low-income ghettos, which is beginning to happen in the centers of many urban systems. The cases of Detroit (fig. 48) and Cleveland (fig. 49) are characteristic of many large cities. The same thing is happening in the core areas of megalopolitan centers (fig. 50) as the study made by Brian J.L. Berry demonstrated[11].

a cross section by concentric zones

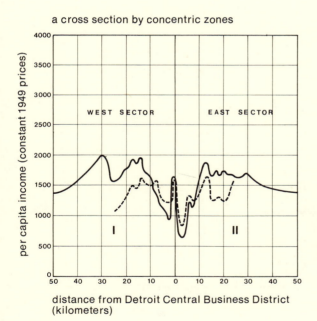

distance from Detroit Central Business District (kilometers)

key to cross section plan

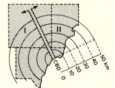

----- 1949
——— 1959

curves are derived on the basis of average values for concentric zones at various distances from the Detroit CBD east and west of Woodward Avenue

48. distribution of per capita income in the central region of Detroit, Michigan, 1949 and 1959

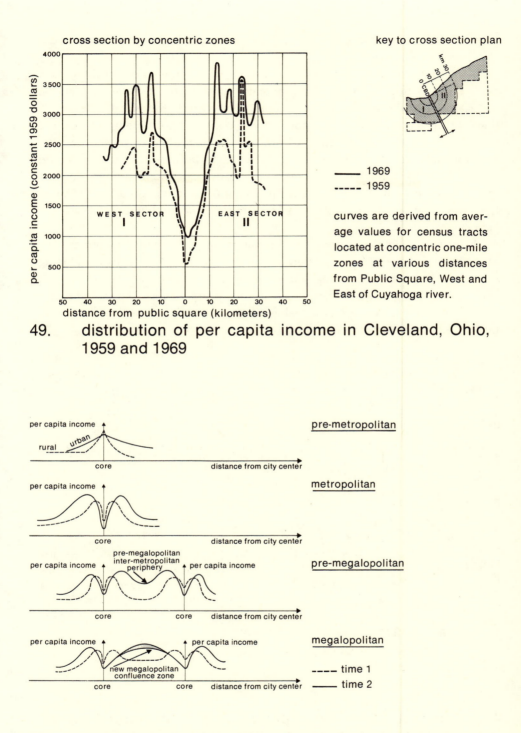

cross section by concentric zones

key to cross section plan

per capita income (constant 1959 dollars)

WEST SECTOR
I

EAST SECTOR
II

distance from public square (kilometers)

—— 1969
----- 1959

curves are derived from average values for census tracts located at concentric one-mile zones at various distances from Public Square, West and East of Cuyahoga river.

49. distribution of per capita income in Cleveland, Ohio, 1959 and 1969

pre-metropolitan

per capita income
rural   urban
core   distance from city center

metropolitan

per capita income
core   distance from city center

pre-megalopolitan

per capita income   pre-megalopolitan
inter-metropolitan
periphery   per capita income
core   core   distance from city center

megalopolitan

per capita income   per capita income
new megalopolitan
confluence zone
core   core   distance from city center

----- time 1
—— time 2

50. postulated changes in per capita income gradients

a cross section by concentric zone

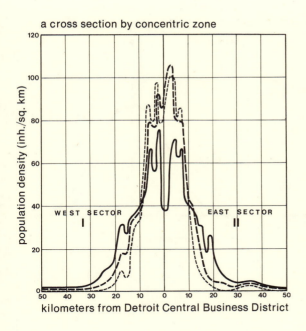

population density (inh./sq. km)

WEST SECTOR
I

EAST SECTOR
II

kilometers from Detroit Central Business District

key to cross section plan

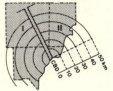

------ 1940

--- 1950

——— 1960

curves are derived on the basis of average values for concentric zones at various distances from the Detroit Central Business District east and west of Woodward Avenue

51. distribution of population density, Detroit SMSA, 1940-1960

People are moving outward from the centers of all overloaded urban systems, as we can see in the case of Detroit (fig. 51). Therefore, although business remain in the center, there is a corresponding tendency for industry to be transferred to the outskirts (fig. 52). This is only natural, since industry tries to keep in balance with the existence of people it is willing to employ at corresponding incomes in its immediate environment.

A further problem of great social importance which has been overlooked until recently has been created by the automobile. Whereas in the past all the inhabitants of a city, rich or poor, had the same degree of mobility, since in the earliest days they all walked, and later some used horse-driven vehicles which had almost the same speed, today, people who have have cars are able to visit very many more places than their neighbors who do not (fig. 53).

Such changes lead to new segregations within human settlements according to age-groups, race, religion and other factors, which greatly increase the tensions of life. On the other hand, the old neighborhood ties are being broken. Because of their increased mobility and the increased possibilities for human contact, as well as the physical degradation of the neighborhood (motor cars control the streets), people no longer feel so involved with their own neighborhood but come to be more in touch with the larger urban systems.

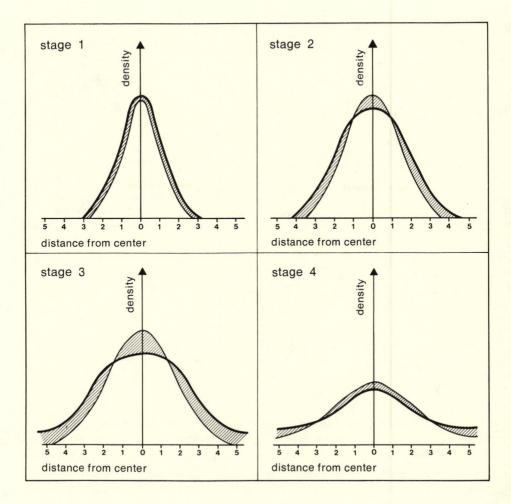

stage 1

density

distance from center

5 4 3 2 1 0 1 2 3 4 5

stage 2

density

distance from center

5 4 3 2 1 0 1 2 3 4 5

stage 3

density

distance from center

5 4 3 2 1 0 1 2 3 4 5

stage 4

density

distance from center

5 4 3 2 1 0 1 2 3 4 5

population distribution
industrial employment distribution

52.   characteristic stages of population and industrial employment decentralization

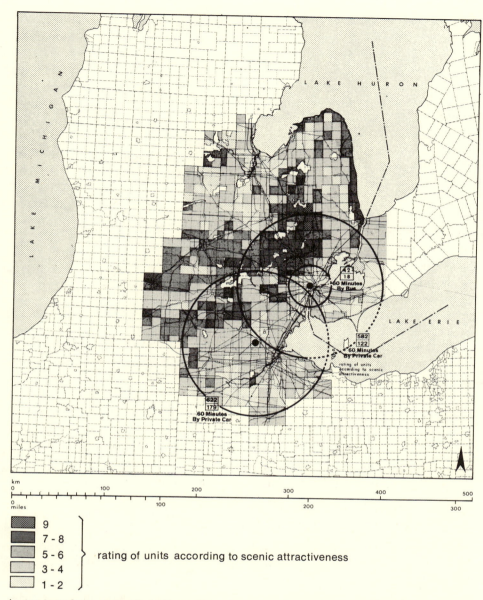

▓	9
▓	7 - 8
▓	5 - 6
░	3 - 4
□	1 - 2

rating of units according to scenic attractiveness

In one hour from central Detroit a person with a car may reach his choice of 122 area units with a total scenic attractiveness rating of 582. By bus he can choose among only 18 units with a total scenic attractiveness rating of only 42. In the suburbs the person without a car does not have public transportation readily available to him, but the car owner may reach his choice of 119 units with a total scenic attractiveness rating of 622.

53.   kinetic fields of people using different methods of movement in the Urban Detroit Area

The resulting situations are too complex to be described here in detail. We can only mention two changes that have increased the complexity of life more than anyone still suspects.

The first is that the total growth of everything within our new systems of life has resulted in exposing people to a number of possible alternative combinations of phenomena that are thousands, millions, billions, or even more times greater than ever before in history. New arrivals in the large cities find themselves faced with a bewildering array of new choices, opportunities and experiences — new possibilities for jobs, recreation, education, cultural activities, social contacts. The very magnitude of the selection offered can drive an individual, whose life previously had been organized within a secure framework of tradition in his village, into withdrawal and isolation. The greater the change between his village and the metropolis, the greater his trauma will be. Nonetheless, the much advertized shortcomings of a metropolis, such as its congestion, confusion, pollution and alienation, do not seem to dissuade people in the country from coming into it. Many migrants fail to understand or are not interested in such threats, since they can have no previous experience of anything like it. Even if they do understand, such things are of lesser importance to them than the advantages of the metropolis.

It is not easy to illustrate such a phenomenon, but this next one can be illustrated. It is the fact that Anthropos in his new systems of life is exposed to every possible information and through all his senses. We can illustrate this by the extension which has taken place in Anthropos' vision alone (fig. 54).

When we add the total increase in complexity of life to this incredible increase in information of all sorts, we can begin to see why Society has so many problems. We can also begin to realize our own confusion which has not allowed us to understand some important problems that arise in Society today, such as the change in crime rates, about which we know so little.

Many problems arise in the administration of human settlements today all round the world, though to a reduced extent under communist regimes which have a central authority of greater power. Nowhere has it been realized that the settlements of today are of completely different dimensions to those of the past, and have become dynamic; they are no longer the static cities of the past with walls, but are continuously growing. There are cities today which are controlled by tens or hundreds of different local authorities, and urban systems having thousands of such authorities, all operating without any coordination whatever. In most cases there are far too many hierarchical levels of authority so that it is very difficult to reach solutions on local problems. We found cases, for example, where city authorities had to go through ten stages before they could reach the national government, although the rational need was for only five or six. Local administration belongs to the type of settlements that existed in the past. It is needless to add that from the point of view of a citizen all this

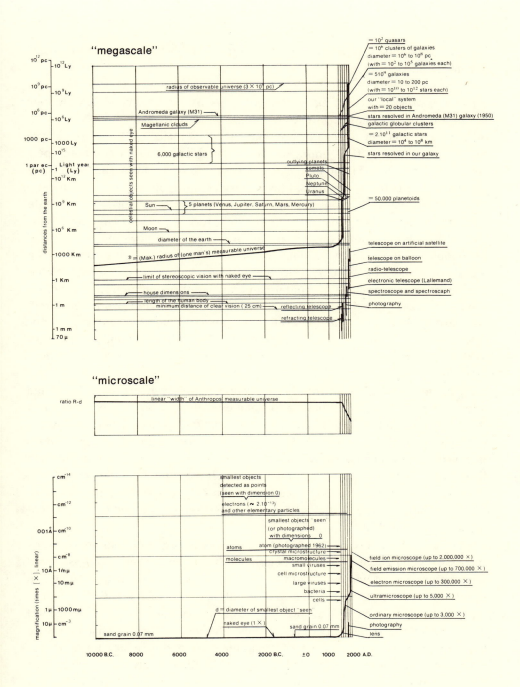

"megascale"

10^{12} pc — 10^{12} Ly

10^9 pc — 10^9 Ly

10^6 pc — 10^6 Ly

1000 pc — 1000 Ly

10^{15}

1 par ec (pc) — 1 Light year (Ly)

10^{12} Km

10^9 Km

10^6 Km

1000 Km

1 Km

1 m

1 m m

70 μ

distances from the earth

celestial objects seen with naked eye

radius of observable universe (3×10^9 pc)

Andromeda galaxy (M31)

Magellanic clouds

6,000 galactic stars

outlying planets

comets

Pluto

Neptune

Uranus

Sun — 5 planets (Venus, Jupiter, Saturn, Mars, Mercury)

Moon

diameter of the earth

⑧ = (Max.) radius of (one man's) measurable universe

limit of stereoscopic vision with naked eye

house dimensions

length of the human body

minimum distance of clear vision (25 cm)

reflecting telescope

refracting telescope

= 10^2 quasars

= 10^6 clusters of galaxies

diameter = 10^6 to 10^8 pc

(with = 10^2 to 10^5 galaxies each)

= 510^9 galaxies

diameter = 10 to 200 pc

(with = 10^{11} to 10^{12} stars each)

our "local" system with = 20 objects

stars resolved in Andromeda (M31) galaxy (1950)

galactic globular clusters

= 2.10^{11} galactic stars

diameter = 10^4 to 10^8 km

stars resolved in our galaxy

= 50,000 planetoids

telescope on artificial satellite

telescope on balloon

radio-telescope

electronic telescope (Lallemand)

spectroscope and spectroscaph

photography

"microscale"

ratio R-d

linear "width" of Anthropos measurable universe

cm^{14}

cm^{12}

$001\overset{\circ}{A}$ — cm^{10}

cm^8

$10\overset{\circ}{A}$ — 1 mμ

10 mμ

1 μ — 1000 mμ

10 μ — cm^{-3}

magnification (times (×), linear)

smallest objects detected as points (seen with dimension 0)

electrons (≈ 2.10^{-13}) and other elementary particles

smallest objects "seen" (or photographed) with dimensions 0

atoms — atom (photographed 1962)

crystal microstructure

molecules — macromolecules

small viruses

cell microstructure

large viruses

bacteria

cells

d = diameter of smallest object "seen"

naked eye (1 ×)

sand grain 0.07 mm

sand grain 0.07 mm

field ion microscope (up to 2,000,000 ×)

field emission microscope (up to 700,000 ×)

electron microscope (up to 300,000 ×)

ultramicroscope (up to 5,000 ×)

ordinary microscope (up to 3,000 ×)

photography

lens

10000 B.C.   8000   6000   4000   2000 B.C.   ±0   1000   2000 A.D.

54. extension of Anthropos' vision through mechanical means (10,000 B.C. to 2000 A.D.)

bureaucracy appears as an overwhelming time and energy consumer that complicates his life enormously.

When we turn to Shells or buildings we find that the new types being created today also present us with many new problems. Although technologically they are of a higher standard than ever before, they are not so satisfactory in many other ways, especially as regards housing. We must realize that Anthropos lives for 67%[12] or more of his entire lifetime in his home, and an additional percentage in educational buildings. Since at least 70% of our lives is spent in these two types of buildings, we should give considerable thought to their planning.

With the advances in modern building techniques, it is now possible to create taller and larger buildings than ever before in history. Enormous buildings tightly packed together do not, however, make for the happiest environment possible for people. It is just such buildings we have created in our cities by allowing the skills of modern technology to be employed purely in the service of the profit-motive in conditions of rapid urban growth. Also, although such buildings can be well constructed and equipped, they are often dark and poorly ventilated, and have no views, as well as subjecting people to all the disadvantages of congested living. The increasing use of standardized prefabricated units in response to the enormous demand for buildings tends to produce a uniformity in their individual design.

Obsolete building codes and the restrictions imposed because of the vested interests of various unions have also hampered those who are trying to meet the rising demand for housing. Rigid construction standards, like that which demands a certain minimum thickness for walls, tend to protect older methods of construction which take longer and need more labor but are not more efficient than those which could be produced much faster using the latest techniques and new materials. If construction standards could be replaced by efficiency standards, it would do away with that time lag between the invention of a new technique and its practical application.

The traditional house of the past was gradually enlarged on and improved by successive generations. It offered people all those things poets have associated with the concept of home — warmth, continuity, involvement, responsibility. In these days of mobility and change we do not place so much emphasis on these aspects of our homes. The average life span of new houses is decreasing, and especially in the higher-income countries. Because of the mechanics of the money-market and the existence of cheap materials and light structures, houses have almost become consumption articles which deteriorate rapidly and must be replaced frequently. The flexibility and adaptability which result are gained at a high price. Even more new houses are needed, not only to supply the needs of a rising population but also to replace existing houses. The process of construction is thus strained even further, and this encourages the use of cheap, fast techniques, often of poor quality. Also, since houses no longer last, the poor are deprived of the exceedingly valuable inheritance of the houses of their ancestors.

Attempts have been made to provide "low-income" houses for the poor, but this has proved not only to be financially impossible, but also creates social stigmatism. Such housing usually deprives people of all responsibility for the design, modification and upkeep of their own homes. The effect of cutting human beings off from any sense of creative involvement with their environment has been catastrophic. In order for a human community to be formed from a collection of individuals, it is essential that each of them should feel personally and creatively involved in their own house and neighborhood, and housing projects which have failed to give the individual a stake in, and therefore a commitment to his environment and its future have always failed to develop as a living and working community.

With the present conditions of unequal incomes, inefficient planning, and lack of resources, the sheer size of the migration to urban centers has led to the formation of vast slum areas, especially around the major urban settlements in Latin America, Asia and Africa. Slums are not automatically bad. They provide temporary low-cost accommodation for unskilled migrants when they first arrive in the city, when the construction industry is unable to provide for such newcomers. It has been repeatedly shown that such migrants improve their own houses and environment as their earning power rises, so long as they are not prevented from doing so by bureaucracy, absentee landlords, or discrimination. The success of self-help "site-and-service" schemes, which supply land, water, drainage, roads and an overall plan, leaving people to build their own houses, has clearly demonstrated that a government program which attempts to build what the citizens can build themselves simply wastes scarce government resources, especially in the lower-income countries. Experience in the favellas of Brazil, the ranchos of Venezuela and the barriadas of Peru, as well as in other Latin American countries, or in the refugee slums around Karachi and the squatter settlements and shanty towns on the outskirts of many large cities all round the globe, confirm these facts about migrant urbanization.

Modern settlements, apart from such exceptional towns as Venice and small towns on islands or in the mountains (which are often in a state of decline), have lost the human scale. That is, they no longer preserve that necessary balance in size and proportion between Anthropos (or the content) and the environment (or his container), which was so important a characteristic of the settlements of the past. The built environment around us is no longer determined by direct relationship to the scale of Anthropos himself and to the small human community. The internal structure of each community, once based solely on pedestrian movement, is being broken up and destroyed by the car. New types of structures make new engineering demands, new transportation devices have new physical requirements, new technologies of construction determine new forms, the system of land ownership limits development to certain areas and certain shapes. Buildings, and the spaces between them, are overwhelmingly big; there is no longer any sense of pleasure at being contained within the streets and squares of a modern city. Builders are rarely given the opportunity to freely create harmonious human spaces through the play of positive and negative elements in a structure. The settlements of today are more and more characterized by sheer visual anarchy — poor proportion, discontinuity between function and structure, meaningless differentiation in size and shape. Urban form, instead of being based on human and esthetic satisfaction, is determined purely by chance, financial greed and the demands of technology.

The Networks, which turned the settlements of the past into the settlements of the present, and in doing so satisfied many of Anthropos' needs, have also created many problems with which we are not at all prepared to deal.

The first is that machines are in control in all the open areas of human settlements and also in those areas needed by machines, from streets and highways to parking places. Anthropos, who should be the master in his own living space, is squeezed between his machines and his buildings. The former master is now the slave so long as he is in the open, but becomes master again when he enters the machines: this is a very serious problem.

The second big problem is that the many great Networks that exist, from those of transportation to those of telecommunication, sprawl through settlements and their surroundings in an uncoordinated way, disfiguring the landscape, destroying the natural environment, and wasting up to five times more land and values than they would if they were rationally coordinated. We can see what could be done by means of the coordination of all Networks in the case of the Northern Ohio Urban System (fig. 55). In most cities today each separate Network is independently conceived, designed, implemented, operated and maintained. As a result, each follows the lines of least resistance for each of its parts in finding its own location, and disregards all the others. The result is endless confusion, a gross waste of land, mutual interference and general inefficiency.

A third problem is that the transportation Networks have tended to disrupt and mutilate the individual communities they were designed to serve by cutting them up into socially meaningless small units; intolerable barriers are created throughout settlements, impeding and contradicting their natural functioning.

Because of the difficulties concerned with Networks today, our settlements no longer operate satisfactorily, even in so far as fulfilling the goals for which technology was invented. There are big cities today, such as Rome and many others, where the automobiles move at an average speed of only 5 or 6 km an hour (3-4 m.p.h.) in the center, that is, at the same speed as a pedestrian. There are many other cities all over the world where the buses move at an average speed of 20 km an hour (12 m.p.h.), that is, at the same speed as the horse-driven carriages of the first decade of this century.

134

- ▬▬▬ national high-speed ground transportation
- ▬▬▬ regional high-speed ground transportation
- ▭▭▭ metropolitan guideways
- - - - - interstate freeways
- _._._ other principal arterials
- • stations

55. future major transportation network in the Northern Ohio Urban System

It is clear that our cities today are suffering from a very severe case of heart failure of the sort which mankind also witnessed in the big cities of the past and, so far as we know, tried to deal with by special regulations for the first time in ancient Rome.

If we add together all the problems concerning Nature, Anthropos, Society, Shells and Networks, even those mentioned here only, we can see how their combination creates difficulties in many other spheres — economic, social, political, administrative, technological and cultural — since no city can cope with these new needs. These problems are now being recognized, even if not properly measured and evaluated.

What we have failed to understand properly, however, is that as a result of all these things we have damaged the quality of human life, of our happiness and our safety within our settlements. By concentrating on the satisfaction of some particular needs, and succeeding in doing so, even if only partially, we have lost that balance in the satisfaction of all human needs that existed in the settlements of the past. This is the great cultural problem of today which must be faced.

20. The new approaches

Since we have now been suffering from the problems of today's human settlements for a century and a half, we have made various different attempts to deal with them. Mayors and city authorities have simply tried to cope with day-to-day problems, such obvious troubles as the lack of water or the totally confused traffic situation. The most far-reaching attempts to deal with things in general have been the remodeling of some parts of the European cities which had been destroyed during the last war; however, even this was done in a most conservative manner and had no real impact on their future. In the U.S.A. a great deal of urban renewal took place which did have an impact on some very small parts of a very few cities, but we doubt that the result in half these cases can be said to have been positive, and for many years the results were negative[13].

Experts in the various professions connected with human settlements have tended to concentrate their attention on projects which were actually under way, and hardly attempted to consider the problem as a whole so as to understand it and work out new solutions.

The main serious attempts to consider what should be done began near the turn of the century in Spain with Soria y Mata's proposal in 1882 for small linear cities, in England in 1898 with Ebenezer Howard's concept of the Garden City, and in France between 1901-4 with Tony Garnier's proposal for industrial cities. These were followed in 1925 by Le Corbusier's proposals for La Ville Radieuse and in 1932 by Frank Lloyd Wright's for The Living City. It took more than two generations after the birth of the new settlements for the first group of these proposals to be made, and more than three generations and the occurrence of World War I for the second group.

137

Proposals from people who were not experts on human settlements began earlier, with ideas for utopias like Etienne Cabet's *Voyage en Icarie* in 1840, Edward Bellamy's *Looking Backward* in 1888, William Morris' *News From Nowhere* in 1890. Later came H.G. Wells' *Men Like Gods* in 1926, James Hilton's *Lost Horizon* in 1933, B.F. Skinner's *Walden Two* in 1948, and Aldous Huxley's *Island* in 1962. These are all dreams of escape, since many people are afraid that the world of George Orwell's *Nineteen Eighty-Four* is very close. All these books have drawn the attention of public opinion to the problems and have helped people to think, but in reality they do not lead anywhere practical[14].

So it took mankind more than two generations after the birth of the new settlements to start talking about new approaches to their problems, and another two generations still without taking any action. Then came World War II, causing enormous destruction, and the post-war period with its economic and population explosions to increase the crisis in human settlements.

This post-war period gave rise to many new proposals for human settlements, and new ones are still being made all round the globe. They range from those which suggest that the existing cities should be given new opportunities to those that propose we all move underground and live there. Some concentrate on solving the traffic or housing problems, others propose new types of structures, or ways of dealing with the natural environment. Some suggest new administrative boundaries for our cities, always a bit larger than those of today, but never as large as those of the real cities within which we live.

Some of these solutions are realistic, others are completely unrealistic, but they are all partial solutions, dealing only with this or that one aspect of existing cities.

Since none of the suggestions for saving the cities has led anywhere, there is yet another school of thought concerned with escaping from them.

One of these solutions is the idea of creating entirely new towns, an idea officially born in England and France as a result of government action, and implemented all over the world on various scales both by governments and by private organizations. Three countries have even created new capital cities — India created Chandigarh as capital of the Indian Punjab, Brazil created Brasilia, and Pakistan created Islamabad.

Some people say that such new towns should incorporate many different functions, others that they should only serve some industry, others again that they should simply be dormitories. Some talk of creating "suburbia", that is new settlements only a short distance from the big cities, others of "exurbia" a bit further out, and others of "new towns" even further out. The fact that none of these theories has a sound basis is proved by many things, and especially by discussions concerning the ideal size for such cities which never reach any conclusion. How could they do so in a global situation which is in a state of continual flux?

Then there are various "technological solutions", which are really no more than personal suggestions of a technological nature, since they have little to do with reality. They range from "motopias", in which automobiles will run on the roofs of our houses, to the idea of covering our cities with special domes, or even of building great pyramids in the deserts, not for the dead this time but for all of us. The ultimate extreme is a concept of monster mechanical cities moving around crushing everything in their way — the dinosaurs were more human!

Humanity certainly cannot be proud of the efforts so far made, nor of many of the ideas for saving our settlements. The main reasons for failure are as follows:

We have concentrated on thinking about the cities and trying to solve problems, forgetting that half of mankind still lives in villages and that people in villages are suffering much more than city-dwellers.

We still insist in thinking about a city of today as if it was confined to those sections under the jurisdiction of a mayor. We never think about the real cities in which we actually live, that is, the urban systems of linked settlements.

We never deal with the whole system of our life: instead, we try to deal with each small part in isolation from the rest.

We think about the five elements that go to make up human settlements one at a time, now about highways, then about the problems of the destruction of Nature, without recognizing that the real settlement includes all of these elements simultaneously.

We concentrate on the symptoms of a disease, never on the causes. We make the same mistake made by many specialists in medicine of examining a patient without asking the guidance of the family doctor who has known him personally for a long time as a living human being.

Our personal conclusion is that all the approaches made so far are partial, unrealistic, and lead nowhere. In order to keep the promise we made in Part One, we shall not present our personal solution here, but merely say that any reasonable solution must take into account the accumulated evidence of Anthropos' settlements in the past as presented briefly in Part Two. It must consider, too, the basic principles that have always been the driving force behind Anthropos in his formation of his settlements, and it must understand what made those settlements successful, what made Anthropos feel happy and safe, and what helped create a harmonious balance between all those elements that make up the system of his life.

21. The global situation

In order that we can see more clearly what the total global situation is today, we have prepared two maps, the first of which shows the distribution of the metropolitan areas with over 1,000,000 inhabitants in 1960 (fig. 56) and the second the megalopolitan areas between 1966 and 2000 (fig. 57).

We can now see that during the last 150 years Anthropos has been creating a totally new system of life, which naturally has resulted in many revolutionary changes in his settlements. He was not aware of the big change that was taking place around him, since it began in a slow and imperceptible way; therefore he was unable to think of solutions for his whole new system, but only for parts of it. Also, since he could not suddenly abandon the millions of human settlements which existed on earth, he continued to live in them, while superimposing on them the new needs of the settlements of the present.

Anthropos today is therefore living in two types of settlements simultaneously: those of the past which were born 10,000 or more years ago; and those of the present — still in a primitive stage of their development — which were born 150 years ago, and which are quite often superimposed on those of the past. The patterns of these two very different types of settlements are confused, and Anthropos himself is even more confused. It was not possible for him to have understood or changed this situation — which is a stage of transition to a totally new way of life — in such a short time. History shows us that all such major changes do take time to be understood. It may have taken hundreds or even thousands of years for Anthropos to understand the change from nomadic life to the life of villages and towns.

The total population of the earth at the beginning of our era — that is, in 1825 — was one billion, from which it has increased until it is expected to reach almost four billion by 1975, representing an average rate of increase of about 1% per year over these 150 years (fig. 58). This is still lower than the five billion which we estimated the earth could have supported at the level of cities in the settlements of the past (fig. 16). Why is it, then, that we are having problems today?

There are two reasons: first, we are no longer living at the economic level of the settlements of the past, nor with the limits of past technology and invention, so our demands are greater; second, we are not evenly spread over the globe, so that while the Amazon region of Brazil has none of the problems of the modern era, many European regions have, and in places like Bangladesh and Bengal the problems of the past are mixed to a critical degree with those of the present.

Since there are areas in which there is a crisis regarding the human container and its contents, we must now ask how the capacity of the container has been changed by the recent enormous technological revolution. It is because we do not really understand this that our confusion is increasing over the entire world today, and therefore we shall devote the next Part to this very important subject. What can be said at this point is that in the future the container will be able to absorb many more people than at present, as we shall show; the fact that some areas do have a capacity crisis at present does not mean that such a crisis exists in other areas such as Africa or Latin America.

The distribution of population between rural and urban settlements has changed to such an important extent that now for the first time the urban population is more than at any previous time, forming 45.2% of the total population of the earth in 1960 and now over 58% according to Athens Center of Ekistics studies (fig. 59).

For many millennia the rate at which the total population of the earth grew was infinitesimally small (fig. 60). As late in human history as 8000 or 10,000 B.C., the yearly growth rate was only about 0.01%. Around 1500 A.D., this rate of growth increased to about 0.1%. By 1800 it had grown to 0.46%, by 1900 to 0.75%, and just before World War II it passed 1%. After the war it surged up to reach just under 2.0% (between 1.90% and 1.95%) during the 1960's. For just over a decade the rate of growth has remained stable at that level, possibly indicating a forthcoming slow reduction in the near future.

We can get a better image of the relationship between the container and its contents when we realize that the total surface of the usable part of the land of the earth, that is, 73.9 million sq. km (28.5 million sq. mi.), is divided as follows[15]:

built-up areas of human settlements	0.4 million sq. km			0.15 million sq. mi.		0.55%
arable land	13.0	»	»	5.0	»	17.60%
pastures	21.3	»	»	8.2	»	»	28.80%
forests	35.3	»	»	13.6	»	»	47.77%
areas potentially usable for cultivation	3.9	»	»	1.5	»	»	5.28%

When we turn to the actual numbers of individual human settlements which exist at this phase of history we can clearly state that the total number of settlements has not changed at all. A few new ones have been created, but their numbers have not increased the total. In fact, since villages are continually being eliminated, and minor settlements being absorbed by the growing urban systems, there are probably fewer settlements today than there were in 1825. Since there is, however, no data which could allow us to make an objective estimate as to how many villages have actually died, we can only say that about the same number of settlements exist today as in 1825, that is, about 14 million.

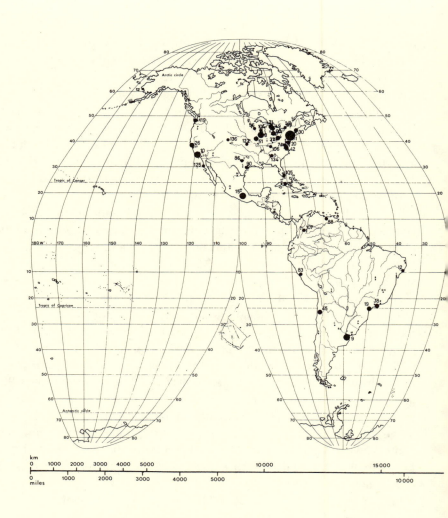

56. distribution of metropolitan areas with over 1,000,000 inhabitants in 1960

● 10 million inhabitants and over
● 5 - 10 million inhabitants
• 2 - 5 million inhabitants
. 1 - 2 million inhabitants

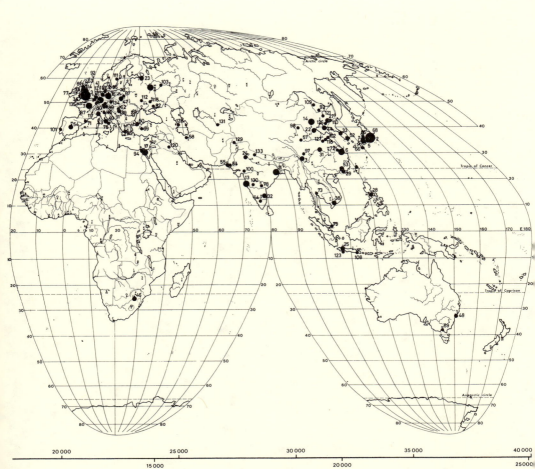

RANK	NAME	POPULATION	RANK	NAME	POPULATION	RANK	NAME	POPULATION	RANK	NAME	POPULATION
1.	New York, N.Y.	16.000.000	36.	Chungking, Ch.	2.420.000	71.	Barcelona, Sp.	1.750.000	106.	Cincinnati, Ohio	1.203.000
2.	Tokyo, Jap.	14.000.000	37.	Pittsburgh, Pa.	2.405.000	72.	Nanking, Ch.	1.725.000	107.	Bogota, Col.	1.200.000
3.	London, Eng.	10.680.000	38.	Saigon-Cholon, Viet.	2.400.000	73.	Bangkok, Thai	1.715.000	108.	Surabaya, Indon.	1.200.000
4.	Moscow, Sov.	7.800.000	39.	Budapest, Hung.	2.400.000	74.	Baltimore, Md.	1.707.000	109.	Tsitsihar, Ch.	1.200.000
5.	Osaka Kobe, Jap.	7.730.000	40.	Milano, It.	2.315.000	75.	Napoli, It.	1.673.000	110.	Fushun, Ch.	1.190.000
6.	Shanghai, Ch.	7.500.000	41.	Hamburg, Ger.	2.262.000	76.	Havana, Cuba	1.650.000	111.	Stockholm, Swe.	1.180.000
7.	Paris, Fr.	7.390.000	42.	Washington, D.C.	2.230.000	77.	Liverpool, Eng.	1.644.000	112.	Kiev, Sov.	1.174.000
8.	Chicago, Ill.	7.281.000	43.	Roma (Rome), It.	2.150.000	78.	Hyderabad, Ind.	1.619.000	113.	Amsterdam, Neth.	1.150.000
9.	Buenos Aires, Arg.	6.950.000	44.	Port Arthur, Dairen, Ch.	2.150.000	79.	Singapore, Sing.	1.600.000	114.	Newcastle-on-Tyne, Eng.	1.144.000
10.	Los Angeles, Calif.	6.743.000	45.	Santiago, Chile	2.130.000	80.	Stuttgart, Ger.	1.575.000	115.	Torino, It.	1.130.000
11.	Calcutta, Ind.	6.570.000	46.	Johannesburg, S. Afr.	2.130.000	81.	Bucharest, Rom.	1.571.000	116.	Kharkov, Sov.	1.125.000
12.	Essen-Dortmund-Duisburg, Ger.	6.250.000	47.	Katowice, Pol.	2.110.000	82.	Stalino, Sov.	1.525.000	117.	Dusseldorf, Ger.	1.102.000
13.	Bombay, Ind.	6.220.000	48.	Sydney, Austl.	2.105.000	83.	Lima-Callao, Peru	1.500.000	118.	Tsinan (Chinan), Ch.	1.100.000
14.	Peking, Ch.	5.400.000	49.	Cleveland, Ohio	2.091.000	84.	Hyderabad, Pak.	1.500.000	119.	Seattle, Wash.	1.098.000
15.	Mexico, Mex.	5.200.000	50.	Instanbul, Tur.	2.080.000	85.	Kyoto, Jap.	1.496.000	120.	Baghdad, Iraq	1.090.000
16.	Berlin, Ger.	5.100.000	51.	St. Louis, Mo.	2.060.000	86.	Dallas-Fort Worth, Tex.	1.491.000	121.	Ch'angch'un, Ch.	1.075.000
17.	Cairo, Eg.	5.000.000	52.	Pusan, Kor.	2.050.000	87.	Cologne, Ger.	1.465.000	122.	Kansas City, Mo.	1.075.000
18.	Rio de Janeiro, Braz.	4.600.000	53.	Canton, Ch.	2.050.000	88.	Caracas, Ven.	1.450.000	123.	Bandung, Indon.	1.075.000
19.	São Paulo, Braz.	4.450.000	54.	Madrid, Sp.	2.030.000	89.	Munich, Ger.	1.450.000	124.	Recife, Braz.	1.070.000
20.	Philadelphia, Pa.	4.400.000	55.	Karachi, Pak.	1.980.000	90.	Houston, Tex.	1.428.000	125.	San Diego, Calif.	1.070.000
21.	Detroit, Mich.	3.995.000	56.	Minneapolis-St. Paul, Minn.	1.950.000	91.	Mannheim - Heidelberg, Ger.	1.422.000	126.	Anshan, Ch.	1.065.000
22.	Tientsin, Ch.	3.680.000	57.	Sian (Hsian), Ch.	1.940.000	92.	Brussels, Bel.	1.410.000	127.	Suchow, Ch.	1.060.000
23.	Leningrad, Sov.	3.675.000	58.	Teheran, Iran	1.940.000	93.	Harbin, Ch.	1.400.000	128.	Baku, Sov.	1.060.000
24.	Delhi, Ind.	3.620.000	59.	Montreal, Can.	1.940.000	94.	Alexandria, Eg.	1.400.000	129.	Lahore, Pak.	1.040.000
25.	Djakarta, Indon.	3.570.000	60.	Toronto, Can.	1.940.000	95.	Copenhagen, Dan.	1.370.000	130.	Poona, Ind.	1.033.000
26.	San Francisco-Oakland, Calif.	3.275.000	61.	Glasgow, Scot.	1.915.000	96.	Buffalo, N.Y.	1.335.000	131.	Tashkent, Sov.	1.025.000
27.	Shenyang (Mukden), Ch.	3.260.000	62.	Vienna, Aus.	1.900.000	97.	Ch'eng-Tu, Ch.	1.325.000	132.	T'apei, Tai.	1.015.000
28.	Manila, Phil.	3.140.000	63.	Leeds-Bradford, Eng.	1.893.000	98.	T'aik'ang, Ch.	1.325.000	133.	Kanpur, Ind.	1.015.000
29.	Hong-Kong, H.K.	3.040.000	64.	Bangalore, Ind.	1.880.000	99.	Ankara, Tur.	1.317.000	134.	Atlanta, Ga.	1.011.000
30.	Boston-Laurence-Lowell, Mass.	3.026.000	65.	Athens, Gr.	1.853.000	100.	Ahmedabad, Ind.	1.315.000	135.	Prague, Cz.	1.009.000
31.	Wuhan (Hankou), Ch.	2.910.000	66.	Yahata - Kokura, Jap.	1.850.000	101.	Lisbon, Port.	1.308.000	136.	Rotterdam, Neth.	1.005.000
32.	Madras, Ind.	2.800.000	67.	Warsaw, Pol.	1.830.000	102.	Tsingtao, Ch.	1.300.000	137.	Denver, Colo.	1.000.000
33.	Seoul, Kor.	2.645.000	68.	Nagoya, Jap.	1.830.000	103.	Gorky, Sov.	1.250.000			
34.	Birmingham, Eng.	2.620.000	69.	Melbourne, Austl.	1.827.000	104.	Milwaukee, Wis.	1.241.000			
35.	Manchester, Eng.	2.491.000	70.	Frankfurt am M., Ger.	1.775.000	105.	Miami, Fla.	1.212.000			

57. world distribution of megalopolitan areas in second half of 20th century

144

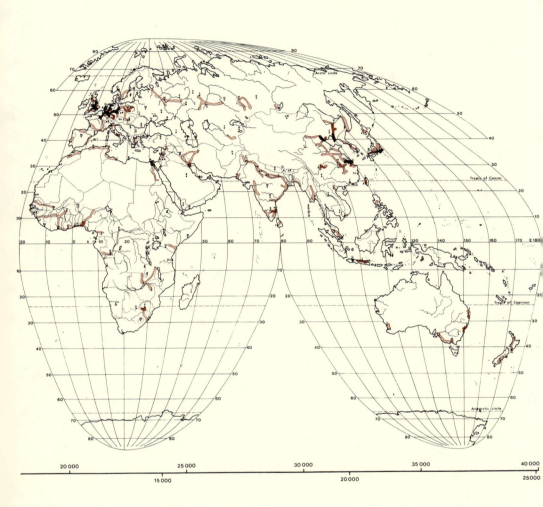

megalopolises:

■ 1970

■ 1980

▨ 2000

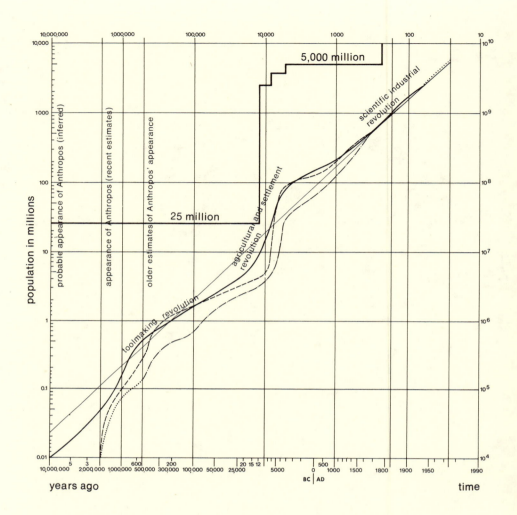

population in millions

years ago

time

- ▬▬ capacity line
- ─── H. v. Foerster
- ▬▬ C.O.F. Standard Curve
- ---- E.S. Deevey (even)
- —·— older estimates

58.   historical evolution of global population
      doubly logarithmic graph

146

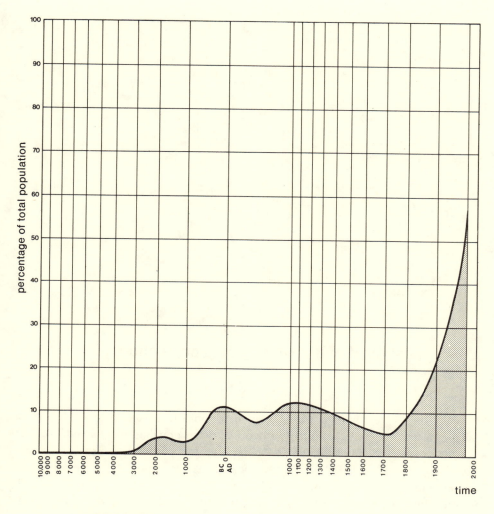

59.   percentage of global population in settlements of
        more than 2,000 inhabitants

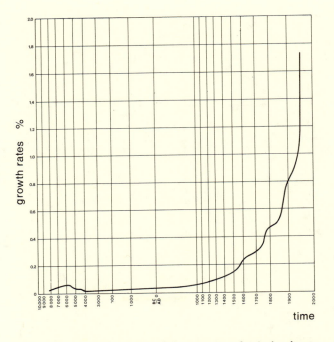

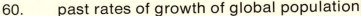

60.   past rates of growth of global population

Theoretically, we have a container which could have supported 3.5 million villages as the only type of human settlement, or fewer villages and an addition of 600,000 towns and 100,000 cities. Moving up in the same relative scale, it could then have supported 15,000 small metropolises (ekistic unit 9), 3,000 metropolises (ekistic unit 10), 500 small megalopolises or urban systems (ekistic unit 11) and 90 megalopolises (ekistic unit 12). This could have had meaning if the whole earth had been filled by all these different types of settlements with a proper relationship between them, but as we have seen, this has never been the case either in the past or the present.

We can say in general that the evolution of the population in the different types of settlements has moved as shown in figs. 61 and 62. This evolution is very different from the sort that took place in the settlements of the past. This does not mean that cities of the past, such as Paris, London, Angkor-Wat, and many others, did not pass through dynamic phases of much more important growth and decline, nor face the same sort of crisis as do the dynapolises of the present. The big difference is that in the past the dynamic phase happened in all the cities of the world at different times, whereas now it is happening in all cities at the same time. Therefore the phenomenon of dynapolis, with its continual growth and change, has for the first time become one of global importance.

148

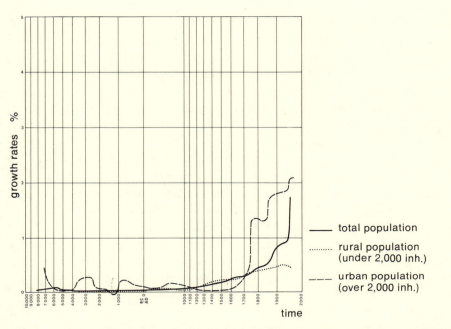

61.   growth rates of urban and rural settlement populations

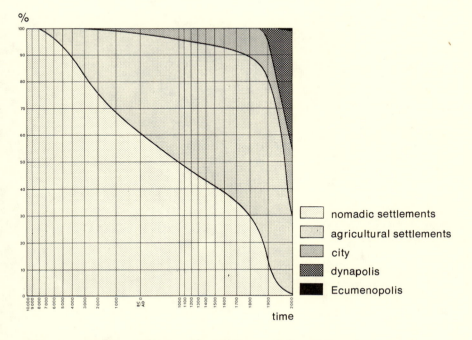

62.   the evolution of human settlements

This then is the situation today: the appearance for the first time in history of a global crisis in human settlements. The crisis in terms of population began before 1825, but this was mostly of local importance concerning northwest Europe alone. By 1825, the revolution in transportation had been added to the industrial revolution and the population explosion.

What would have happened if trains had not been invented? Would London, Shanghai and Peking have passed through the stages of crisis and decline experienced by ancient Rome? We do not know. We can only say that because of an almost simultaneous — at least in historical terms — explosion in terms of population, scientific discovery, industry and transportation systems, mankind has abandoned one stage of the systems of his life, and entered a totally new one.

We do not know whether population pressure precipitates intellectual development, or vice-versa, but the fact is that on this occasion both things happened, and they are still happening all over the earth. Some people speak of a second industrial revolution which occurred in the middle of the 20th century[16]. Whether history will recognize such a revolution we do not know; we can only say that the revolution for human settlements began in 1825 with the development of trains, and then spread as trains and automobiles competed with one another and improved their technologies, and so turned the old type of settlements into the new ones.

22. Conclusions

The settlements of the present, then, were born in 1825 and are still developing into new types, with more people, rising incomes, decreasing differences in income levels between urban and rural people, rising energy consumption, expanding territories and much more complex functions. They are thus creating completely new systems of life. We do not properly understand the changes that are taking place, and, by necessity, we superimpose the new types of settlements on the old ones. Settlements always have changed, but the changes which are taking place today are the result of completely new forces that make these changes much more extensive and abrupt. It is because the resulting patterns are superimposed on those of the past that we have become so confused.

We are in a period of transition towards a new era of human settlements, and we have moved from the period of static cities into that of dynapolis. We can see what is happening more clearly by taking an example, such as the city of Athens, which existed for a period of over 3,000 years within almost the same boundaries (fig. 63). For the last 150 years Athens, which is now close to world averages for many of its features, has been growing with every day that passes at a rate close to 3% per year for population, and much faster for other aspects (fig. 41), and we still do not understand where it is going.

We lose courage — but why? Did the hunters lose courage during the transition in their way of life that led to the creation of villages? Did the farmers lose courage when they moved on to the creation of cities? Certainly not, although they did do a lot of crying and complaining, and Aristotle was obliged to defend the city as a natural phenomenon[17].

Despite the present confusion, the global trends, which are repeating themselves everywhere as new forces enter the scene, lead us to one conclusion: what is happening today is not simply the result of local changes, such as those in organizational capacity which led to the creation of cities in certain limited areas in the past — it is a new phase of global evolution.

If we now look at those five principles that, as we have seen, have always guided Anthropos in the formation of his settlements up to 1825 when this new stage began, we can state the following: The first principle, Anthropos' need to maximize his potential contacts, is still valid. If this were not so he could per-

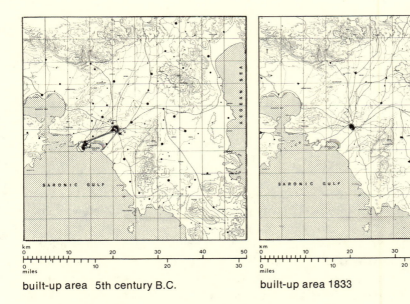

built-up area 5th century B.C.

built-up area 1833

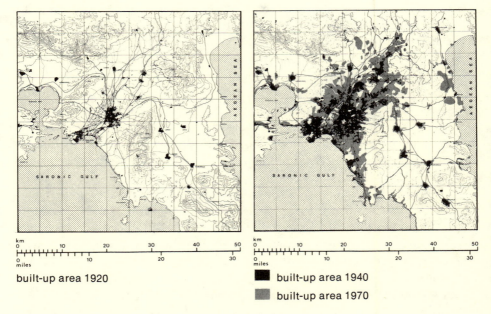

built-up area 1920

■ built-up area 1940

▨ built-up area 1970

63.   evolution of the city of Athens, Greece

fectly well have continued to live in the system of life represented by interlinked villages, towns and cities. Instead, he is abandoning them and merging them into larger types of settlements. The second principle, the minimization of the effort needed for all his efforts, is valid also; otherwise he could perfectly well live far out and still increase his contacts by using the new technological means at his disposal, but instead of doing so he still moves in close in order to save his energy.

Things are different when we turn to the third principle, since at present Anthropos has not managed to satisfy his desire to optimize his protective space. He did manage to satisfy his first two principles with the use of his machines, but he then found himself squeezed up too closely with other people. Therefore he is now beginning to move out again to the suburbs — not, let us note, back to villages or to small towns. This is the new synthesis of Anthropos' first three principles which is taking place.

Anthropos has therefore achieved the satisfaction of his first two principles, although not yet for everyone, but the clash with his third principle, though it is beginning to be overcome, explains why we have a lack of satisfaction at present in the fourth principle, that of a satisfactory balance between the five elements of Nature, Anthropos, Society, Shells and Networks, and also in the fifth, of balance between the first four principles. It is early still in this new stage of development, and Anthropos has not yet managed to respect and conserve Nature as he learned to do at earlier stages after he had burned the forests in order to hunt animals or make fields and found that there was a limit to the amount of forests he could destroy without detriment to himself. Nor has he yet learned to respect other values of the past and so create a balance in everything he tries to do.

We therefore reach a second conclusion: Anthropos has not changed at all, he is still guided by the same five principles. He has satisfied some of them, but not in a balanced way. He enjoys the satisfaction of his first two, or even three principles in some cases, and he is still crying and complaining about the lack of satisfaction of the others.

Settlements are biological organisms which take in energy and raw materials and, overcoming internal resistances, transform them into useful products, generating unwanted by-products and wastes in the process. As a result of recent technological progress and economic development, the flow of materials and energy through the arteries of human settlements has become much more rapid. Goods, energy, people, information and services now pass though the system in unprecedented quantities, varieties, and speeds. The Networks have been of central importance to this tremendous growth.

As a result of this unbalanced development, waste disposal systems have become overloaded, transport and communication systems have grown too complex for efficient action, and the matrix of social relationships within human communities has suffered and dissolved under repeated stress. Because of the increasing interdependence of each part of the total system, any disruption or failure in one section becomes dangerous for the whole urban organism.

The crisis in human settlements today therefore arises from explosive growth pitted against stiffening resistance. Population needs and technological capacity expand at an alarming pace; everyone wants more of everything, and for the moment this remains possible. However, the explosive growth is resisted, first by the inertia of physical structures and Networks, and next by the rapid deterioration of the environment, the threatened exhaustion of resources, and the imbalances that have been generated. Finally, it is resisted by the vested interests of bureaucracies with their obsolete rules, and the persistence in political life of archaic ideologies which cannot yet accept a global psychology.

The contents have been expanding wildly, and the container is unable to accommodate such a sudden pressure. It strains and resists, producing conflict and spreading crisis. Anthropos is only at the beginning of this time of troubles; undoubtedly matters will get far worse before they get any better.

Yet it is in these difficult circumstances that mankind is laying the foundations for the City of the Future. There is no choice: whether by action or inaction, decisions are now being made daily which will have a significant impact on the quality of human life one hundred years from now.

We are completely confused as to what is actually happening today. Some people talk of a big crisis in our resources, and publish their conclusions in *The Limits to Growth*[18], others respond by saying that this crisis is not so great and publish *Thinking about the Future*[19]. No one manages to convince us.

People have come forward with completely irresponsible proposals for the cities of the future, which might be all right if they were accepted as being simply the expression of personal desires. However, important museums have presented them in special exhibitions using models, as if they are serious proposals, which is like presenting an artist's vision as a practical proposal of how our cardiovascular system could be radically transformed. Again, it has been officially stated that cities are growing beyond what is permissible, when we have not explained what we believe this limit is or how we have measured it.

Let us try to be more accurate. The settlements of the present are just as natural as were the cities of ancient Greece, but at present they are only in a transitional stage of development. They are the result of Anthropos' invention of new machines for transportation and new forms of energy. The settlements have succeeded in absorbing the machines, but at the expense of losing human values of the past. Since the machines are not going to be eliminated, Anthropos must open his eyes and see what their real importance is, and what impact they are having on his settlements. He must find out how to deal with them by new approaches, and by the organization of new institutions. It is time for us to understand that what we are suffering from is the transitional phase of our changing dynapolis.

Part four:

Looking into the future

23. How can it be done?

We can see the problems of the present all around us and hear the screaming and complaining that is going on because of them. It is time not simply to recognize the present crisis for what it is, but to try and find out where we are heading and what the actual possibilities for our future are. We know that no one can ever be completely certain about what the future will be, but we can at least make a start by trying to be realistic about it. It is time to take the realistic approach and look at our future with open eyes.

It is now clear that during the last few generations none of us had recognized we were entering a totally new stage in the history of human settlements for which we would have to prepare ourselves. While these changes were in the process of happening it was difficult for anyone to work out what was going on and to see that we are in fact in a period of transition and of dynamic settlements — even now we tend to think and talk as if we still lived in the static cities of the past. When we recognize how hard it is for us to understand the present and what is actually taking place around us, we will see that it must be even more difficult to try and predict our future. We must accept from the start, therefore, that in many ways this excursion into the future is a mental exercise. However, it is an exercise that will at least train us in the actual process of foretelling, and that is something we must learn to do if we are to deal successfully with the affairs of settlements, just as we have to learn to do it in dealing with the affairs of our own lives. Indeed, if we want to find out, for example, what the economic evolution of humanity is likely to be, we must work out what the future of settlements is likely to be, since it is in them our greatest economic investment takes place.

Although it is very difficult to foretell the future of settlements, there is one thing about them which helps us a great deal: this is the fact that humanity has invested so much in them in every way that, even should present trends change completely and we should set ourselves entirely new goals, we would be forced to go on living with the settlements we have today for a certain period and would only be able to change them slowly (fig. 3). This enables us to be sure about some things for the next century or so. Human settlements are not like clothes, to be thrown away as soon as the fashion changes — and indeed we often hang on to our old clothes for several years until they are completely worn out. When we are trying to think about changing and improving our settlements, these forces of inertia from the past can be a great handicap; but when we are trying to foretell their future, they are a help to us, and act as a brake which ensures that extreme changes will not happen suddenly.

In trying to achieve this new ability to look into the future, our best way is to explore many different roads, then try and pick out the one which seems to present the best solution and follow it to see how we can work on it. Nonetheless, we must use a flexible technique which will enable us to keep on changing our forecasts according to the experience we gain on the way. This is the method we ourselves have used during the 15 years of this project, and we would like to emphasize again that the value of all such work increases when the findings are reviewed almost every year. We must recognize that we are involved in a continuously developing process.

We must approach this study with a completely open mind and be prepared to consider every possibility, even the most remote and improbable ones. However, every projection must be properly connected with what is actually happening today, so that we do not produce abstract possibilities, but ideas that can actually help us in a practical way to move from today into tomorrow. We must be free to set ourselves any and every question, and then, having seen what the results of following up these ideas will be, gradually work out which of them is actually the most probable one.

Right at the beginning we are forced to recognize two things. The first is that there is no precedent for what we are attempting to do as every other attempt to look into the future of human settlements has been an attempt to work out someone's personal prediction or vision. We are not doing that at all, but trying to work out what is actually going to take place. The second is even more difficult, and that is that we must make this unprecedented attempt, in the best way we can, at a time when the changes we are trying to analyze are actually taking place. We cannot, for example, wait for another century to go by in order to see what is going to become of the megalopolises that are taking shape today before discussing them; we have to do it now. We know that it is very difficult to make projections about the future, and we can never be certain they will be correct, but it is better to try than to do nothing at all. Unless we try, we face at least the danger that we shall go on making the same mistakes about settlements as we are making today — and that will certainly be disastrous.

When we are afraid to go on, we should remember that there is always the constant future to be relied on (fig. 2). There is also that part of the future that can be predicted quite reasonably, such as the fact that our children will continue growing up at the same speed as they do today, and that their parents are going to go on loving them and so ensure continuity.

All we need in order to go forward is courage — the courage to do the best we can, using whatever knowledge and experience we have, and whatever creative imagination we can summon.

It might be argued that with the growing size and complexity of settlements new and unprecedented problems might arise that could be more difficult than any Anthropos has had to deal with in the past. However, we think this will not be the case and that such problems cannot be proportionately more difficult to solve than those Anthropos faced and overcame in the past without the help of modern science, technology, and organizational ability.

Now it has become quite common to try and forecast the future, although when our project began in 1960 this was a new concept. Scientists and writers have tried to think about the future. The weakness of fiction writers is that they tend to predict too many impossible things, and the weakness of scientists is that each one tends to concentrate on those parts of the future his particular discipline knows best. Fiction writers (and here, of course, we are talking about serious ones) take us so far into the future that we cannot connect their theories with the present at all, while most scientists hold us so closely to one point of view we are unable to check their conclusions against others in order to see how accurate they are. Lately, scientists have given some projections in broader fields, or in systems of interconnected fields, but not specifically about human settlements.

Having considered the achievements of other studies, our conclusion was that the only proper approach is the ekistic one of considering the system of human life as a whole. However, since it was very difficult for us to make projections for all sectors of the system, as we explained in Part One, we have had to concentrate on the container, the people who fill it, and some of their basic activities, but always keeping clearly in mind that no element of a human settlement develops independently of any other. The growth of population and the increase of pollution are not independent phenomena; we must consider what effects the growth of the economy or developments in technology may have on both, and vice versa.

So the road we follow in this study is that of dealing with human settlements as the expression of Anthropos' total system of life. We begin with a discussion on the container of that system, the whole globe on which we all depend, since it forms the basic framework of our life. We can measure its dimensions much more easily than some of the other factors with which we shall have to deal later.

After looking at the dimensions of our container, we then go on to try and understand four basic things: Anthropos' technology, economy, social organization, and the evolution of his population, because as the examination of our past has shown us, our evolution depends on their interrelation.

When we have reached the point of understanding as much as we can about these four things, we go on to interrelate them, and to see what the probable balance between them is likely to be, since without such a balance no long-term progress would be possible. It is clear that before we can do this we must try to work out the evolution of each of the things involved by interrelating them bit by bit. We could call our method the step-by-step approach, since we gradually interrelate the various phenomena more and more completely. So what we are really trying to do is to examine the whole system of our life by first looking at several of the various elements of it, and then by trying to fit them together so that we can see what their overall balance is. To do the opposite, and try to discuss each part without attempting to connect it with the others, would make no sense at all.

Since we must try to describe our whole system of life, how big an area must we cover to do so?

If we had wanted to describe Anthropos' life system 20,000 years ago, we would have been dealing with the period of the hunters and could have limited ourselves to the territory covered by a few bands — let us say an area in the order of 1,000 sq. km (390 sq. mi.). Eight thousand years ago we would have been dealing with the territory of the villages, and could have come down to an area for a few villages of approximately 100 sq. km (39 sq. mi.). Three thousand years ago we would have had to deal with the area included in the territory of a few city-states, say of an area of 1,000 sq. km (390 sq. mi.) or more. If we had wanted to understand the life system of the Roman or Aztec empires, we would have had to consider an area of tens of millions of square kilometers, and even more than that for the Mongol empire[1].

Today we cannot consider less than the area of the entire globe, that is, 510 million sq. km (196.9 million sq. mi.). This is because many of today's cities — whether they have very large territories of their own, or very small ones, such as

Hong Kong — owe their livelihood and continued existence to a global system of Networks. The fact that these interwoven Networks (for trade, transport and information) exist today means that there is a new global framework which must be the basis for our study of the life-system of Anthropos today.

We will now try to describe the methods and forecasting techniques which we used in trying to find out what the future of human settlements will be.

We can begin by saying that a number of possible alternative futures exist. The only way to limit ourselves to describing some out of these innumerable possible alternatives is by developing the ability to select a reasonable number that will enable us to create the framework for the most probable future. "To proceed by elimination", says Stravinsky, "to know how to discard, as the gambler says, that is the great technique of selection. And here again we find the search for the One out of the Many."[2]

How do we decide what to discard? Many methods exist, but we will describe the one we ourselves conceived and successfully applied in working out a model for the various possible alternative solutions for the ekistic development of the Urban Detroit Area[3].

First we grade the various possible alternatives according to their probability, feasibility and desirability.

The relative probability of the alternatives can be decided by first working out what the most likely behavior of the system will be if it is left to develop in response to the operation of the forces at work within it today without any human interference.

We can then decide how far it is feasible that this (most probable) development can be influenced by human action, so that a different — and from the human point of view more desirable — state of affairs will occur.

In deciding how 'desirable' an alternative is, we must introduce a value system extraneous to the model itself. The question arises: whose value system? In our work we tried to make sure it was the value system adhered to by Anthropos himself during the history of human settlements, and which is based on the principles and laws that derive from the ekistic study of these settlements, and never from the values of any individual person or group trying to impose an abstract theory from outside.

Since the ekistic approach always looks at human settlements as total systems, any evaluative technique based on a single criterion is inadequate. Techniques which involve the balancing of several variables become increasingly important, and several such techniques of considerable importance already exist, such as the network or graph theory, and the probability and classification theory. In fields where such techniques do not yet exist, decisions have to be made by the only method that does achieve such balancing — that is, human intuition based on human experience.

There are two ways of working out alternatives for the future. The first is by the use of mathematical models, and the second is the development of descriptive evolutionary 'scenarios' in the sense that Herman Kahn qualified them as: "attempts to describe in some detail a hypothetical sequence of events that could lead plausibly to the situation envisaged"[4].

In order to build a mathematical model, a manageable number of critical variables are selected — that is, factors involved in the situation which may change in quantity — and these represent the behavior of the system we are trying to predict. If the system is a village, we might select such critical variables as the things which would most affect its future development: the fertility of its territory, its technology, and its population. We would then develop a set of mathematical formulae to represent the behavior of each of these variables in a simplified form, the relationships between them, and the effects of whatever restraints may exist on them (such as, for example, climate, geographical limitations, supply of essential resources) which might limit the development of the total system. We can then find out what would happen to it in various possible future conditions by trying out different quantities for each of the critical variables and working out the corresponding equations.

Some situations, however, cannot be dealt with by numbers alone, and here we must adopt the more descriptive-intuitive approach, working out a 'scenario' which will try to show the probable evolution of any situation as accurately and logically as can be done without internal inconsistencies.

It may be useful here for us to describe briefly the different classes of forecasting techniques which have been used to project the form of the future.

The simplest of all forecasting techniques is extrapolation, which is based on the fundamental assumption that things will go on behaving in the future more or less as they have in the past. Its basic assumption greatly resembles the principles of Newton's laws of motion, particularly the first:

"A body will remain in its state of rest or of uniform motion in a straight line unless compelled by some force to change that state."

"The change of motion will be proportional to the force applied and in the direction of its application."

"For every action there is an equal and opposite reaction."

To use extrapolation, we must have enough facts about how something has behaved in the past, and the more facts we have, especially for the distant past or for a given period and for different conditions, the more reliable our forecast will be. We should also know all the factors which have influenced the behavior of the thing we are dealing with, especially if they are likely to change during the projected period. Indeed, one of the most useful things extrapolation can do for us is to show how the expected future behavior of something may change if conditions change.

The determination of the sensitivity of the projected behavior of one variable to the changes in related variables is called "sensitivity analysis".

The reliability of forecasts by extrapolation decreases with the length of time covered (fig. 64). It is therefore not much use for long-range forecasting. When dealing with units of space, its reliability increases with the size of the spatial units (fig. 65). It is more reliable when dealing with physical rather than social phenomena: political events may be impossible to predict, although the exact movement of the earth may be predicted (fig. 66).

A special family of extrapolative techniques has been developed to deal with things that happen cyclically, such as tidal water levels or daily temperature changes. The S-shaped patterns of biological growth are sometimes well suited to cyclic extrapolation when such patterns occur repetitively, and they are also used for economic forecasting.

It is very useful to be able to relate the behavior of one thing to the behavior of another. For example, we know that there is a correlation between the use of seat belts in cars and the death rate in accidents, so if we know what the trends are in the use of seat belts, we will have more knowledge about the future death rates in accidents. Thus the knowledge of correlation between two variables is extremely useful in the development of reliable extrapolations.

When several variables have to be included, as they do in human affairs, we

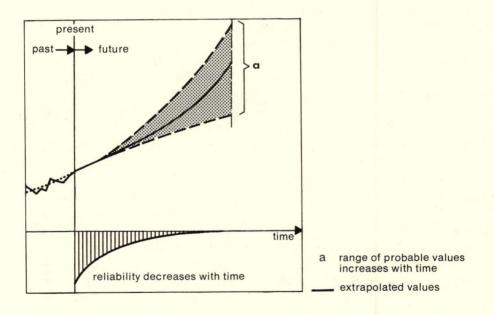

64.   typical reliability of extrapolations

162

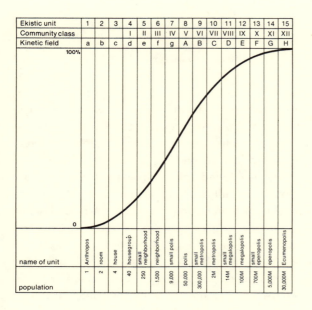

Ekistic unit	1	2	3	4	5	6	7	8	9	10	11	12	13	14	15
Community class				I	II	III	IV	V	VI	VII	VIII	IX	X	XI	XII
Kinetic field	a	b	c	d	e	f	g	A	B	C	D	E	F	G	H
name of unit	Anthropos	room	house	housegroup	small neighborhood	neighborhood	small polis	polis	small metropolis	metropolis	small megalopolis	megalopolis	small eperopolis	eperopolis	Ecumenopolis
population	1	2	4	40	250	1,500	9,000	50,000	300,000	2M	14M	100M	700M	5,000M	30,000M

65.   chances of foreseeing developments in accordance with ekistic units

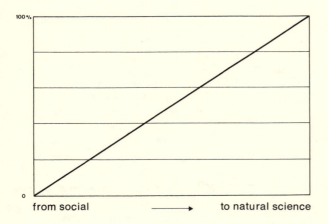

from social   ⟶   to natural science

66.   chances of foreseeing developments in accordance with natural and social sciences

163

turn to the techniques of multivariate analysis, to which the greatest amount of ingenuity and inventiveness has been applied.

There are two main categories of multivariate analysis. In the first and most difficult variety, all the variables must be treated as equally important. In the second, some variables can be taken as dominant, while others can be seen as only capable of qualifying, perturbing or modifying in some way. When calculating artillery projections, for example, the direction of the gun barrel and the size of the explosive charge may be treated as primary variables, whereas wind speed and direction can be regarded as secondary.

Most of the techniques recently developed for multivariate forecasting are "multi-stage", that is, when a tentative result has been achieved by relating one set of variables together, it is used to determine the next stage. A new variable, or set of variables, may be added to produce a second tentative result. This process continues, with the elimination of anything seen to be irrelevant or redundant, until a satisfactory picture is achieved. At any stage, something which has been left out may be reintroduced and kept, or again rejected, depending on whether or not it proves useful. The human brain, drawing on the experience of a lifetime to provide an intuitive value system for making decisions, is one of the most efficient machines known for carrying out this process.

An alternative and quite different approach is called "prognostication" (fig.

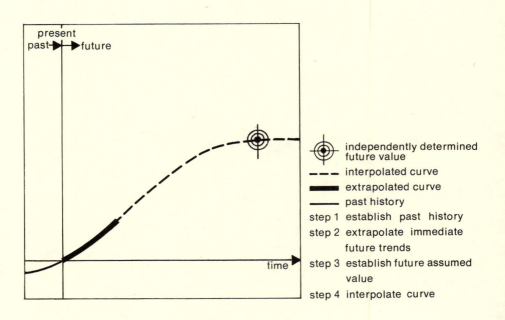

67.   prognostication method

67). In this method we try to see if there are any overriding factors which must limit the number of possible future states of a variable. For example, if a man dives into the sea, it might be impossible for us to work out what his movements and direction are likely to be while he is underwater, whereas the one overriding factor we can be sure of is that he must come up for air after a certain period of time. Once we know such constraints we will not need to trace out the developments of the intervening period in a laborious way.

Extrapolative techniques link present to future, while prognosticative ones attempt to make an independent assessment of future conditions. We have found the two techniques to be complementary. Extrapolation is more useful in the analysis of the near future, and prognostication of the remote future, while the intermediate future is best attacked by both methods, especially by aiming at consistency and continuity from the extrapolated near future to the prognosticated remote future.

Some of the things we try to measure become less and less certain over a period of time. Others remain predictable to the same degree. A third category becomes more easily predicted as time goes on. Variables that go on increasing in indeterminacy are called "open-ended" (fig. 68), while those which tend asymptotically towards some ceiling are called "closed" variables (fig. 69). Income per capita, energy per capita, or the number of satellites that will be

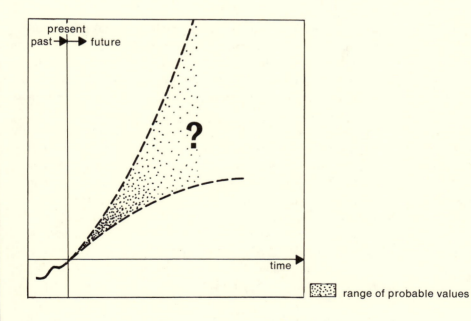

 range of probable values

68. typical open-ended variable

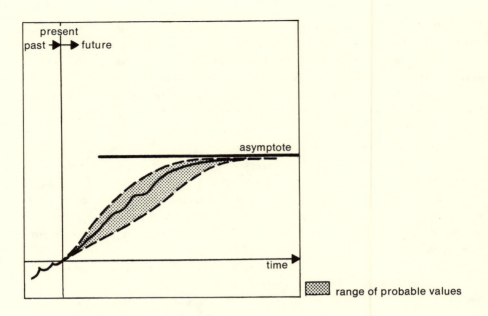

range of probable values

69. typical closed variable: asymptotic

launched, for example, are "open-ended" variables, while the total population of the earth, harmless quantities of pollutants, and the productivity of a cultivated field are closed ones when projected into the future. It is clear that the existence of such "closed" variables is very important for future research, since the reliability of a prediction can be greatly increased if they can be included in the forecasting model.

As time goes on it becomes less easy to be certain about the future of most things, so we say that most variables have a "projection cone" (or "horn") of future values, as in fig. 70. The two extremities of this cone represent the most extreme values considered plausible, and the most likely predictions will lie somewhere between them. Weather forecasting, for example, usually involves bounded projection cones, such as the one shown in fig. 71. Over a short period of time there is only a small range in the plausible variations in atmospheric pressure which may be expected. Over a longer period, as the influence of present conditions declines, the range of possible variations increases, but only up to certain limits, after which they remain stable or at least somewhere in between these limits.

For some things it may be possible to establish only one such boundary, yet even that can be useful in narrowing down the range of possible futures.

It is sometimes possible to take a cross-section at some point through a horn

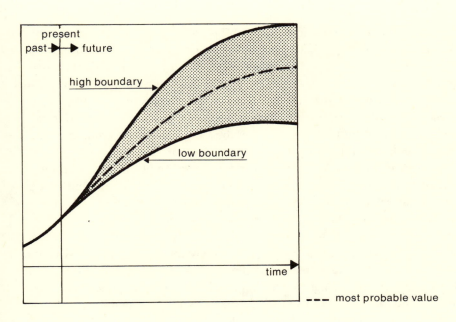

present
past → ← future

high boundary

low boundary

time

- - - most probable value

70.   bounded projection cone

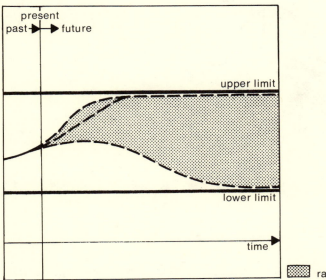

present
past → ← future

upper limit

lower limit

time

range of probable values

71.   typical bounded projection cone: atmospheric pressure

of projections, as has been done in fig. 72. This will represent the relative prob-
abilities of the variables at that point. In other cases we simply do not know
which of a limited number of variables is most likely to occur. We then have
two alternatives: it may be possible to replace the troublesome variable with
another, or transform it in a way that reduces the number of possible values;
or we may arbitrarily divide the possible values into high, middle and low zones,
as in fig. 73. Each of these zones may then be assigned its own crude probability and one central value chosen as a reference point for each of them.

This second method has been much used in the "City of the Future" project.
It does not eliminate the indeterminacy of the troublesome variable, but it does
give us central values for the various zones of variation which we can use as
inputs for future projections and so reduce the number of values we must
consider.

The final outcome found by these methods may then be combined with the
chances of foreseeing phenomena according to the spatial unit with which we
are dealing (as we saw in fig. 65, the larger the unit of space, the greater the
reliability of the forecast). We can then go on to combine several things, such as
the evolution of the urban system as a whole with the evolution of the problem
areas (fig. 74), and make the necessary interrelationships between them.

In these ways we were able to establish a "stable core" for the project, a core

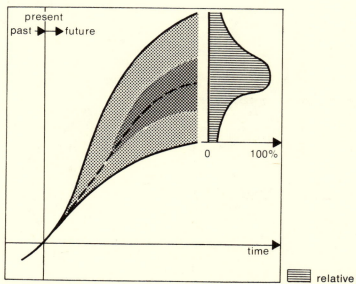

relative probability of values

72.   probability distribution within a cone of projections

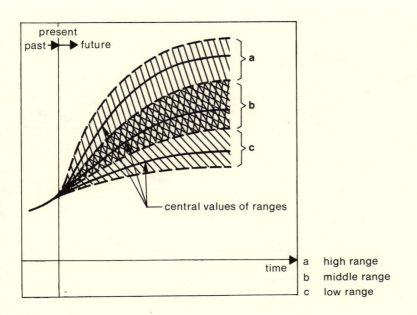

73.   division of projection cone into zones

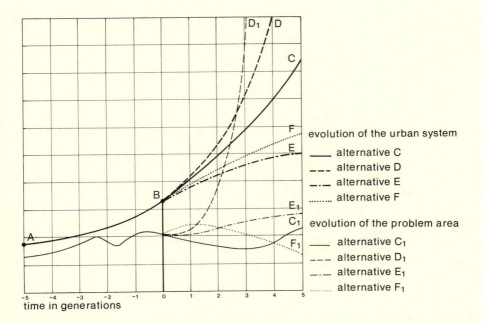

74.   alternative roads for the future

which is not affected by the behavior of highly unpredictable things, and which gives us the essential and unvarying elements in our picture of the future of human settlements.

The greater the number of independent methods one can develop which lead to similar results, the more accurate those results may be considered to be. In Part One (pages 29 ff.) we described briefly the several analytical approaches used during the "City of the Future" project which converged to form the concept of Ecumenopolis. At least three of these — saturation, resources and evolutionary approaches (fig. 75) — could, after careful checking, be considered to be independent. Their existence could therefore be taken as strong confirmation of the validity of the evolving vision of Ecumenopolis. No result blatantly contradicting the concept of Ecumenopolis was produced by any of our approaches.

We will now describe these vital approaches in some more detail. First, the saturation approach. The first set of figures was produced by considering the globe as a container which could be completely filled, and by trying to work out how many people could live in it before it was completely "saturated". A second set of figures was worked out based on the limitations of all resources, and a third on the present evolutionary trends in human settlements.

The saturation approach was the one we used most exhaustively. We can

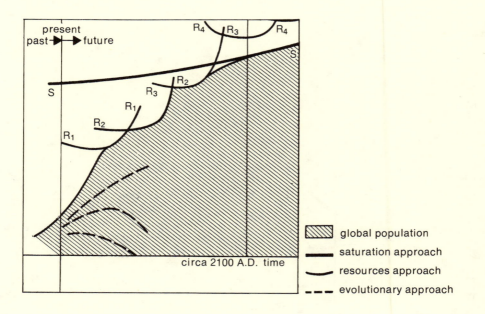

75.   three of the main approaches taken by the "City of the Future" project

make prognostications in this way by accepting that the habitable area of our planet is a closed variable, which must act as a constraint on the expansion of population independent of any other constraining factors. Once this can be taken as true then:
— The population curve can be considered to be a closed variable.
— The maximum population capacity of the earth can be determined.
— Rough limits can be given for other key factors linked to population, such as social and technological aspects, economy and so on.
— It is plausible to assume that these variables will follow logistic curves like those of population as they approach their stable state.

The first step in deciding the capacity of the earth to accept further population is to work out how many people can live in each of its different types of land — mountains, plains, deserts; in other words, what the "habitability" of each area is. We considered a number of factors — the climate, the availability of water, the ruggedness or elevation of the topography, the presence of undesirable features such as desert, frozen areas, swamps, or the frequent occurrence of volcanoes, earthquakes, floods, tornadoes. From these we selected climate, topography and water supply as being of absolute primary importance.

We then defined a scale of habitability for each land area according to each of these three things. We gave each specific area of the whole globe a grade for human habitability according to the three criteria of climate, water supply and topography, and drew global maps representing this.

We know that advances in technology, economics and organization change the habitability of each area, so we took into account our projections of the likely developments in each of these fields and prepared adjusted maps showing the future habitability of the globe by approximately 2100. Maps based on each single criterion of habitability were then combined, assigning different weights to each of the single criterion scales, and combining them to produce a composite grading for each area. Finally, habitability maps were prepared for both 1960 and 2100.

We had now decided how suitable each area of the globe was for supporting people, but in order to find how many people were likely to live there we still had to decide how densely they would live together. We began by considering the densities of population that exist today at all levels of the ekistic scale. Then we considered how human densities tend to evolve by studying how they have done so in the past. We took into account the information we have on what determines the densities people find acceptable in various conditions and we applied these acceptable densities to the areas we had already defined according to habitability. The totals reached gave us a first indication of the maximum population capacity of the earth according to the saturation approach.

This, however, was the maximum "saturated" population, and we know that factors exist making it unlikely such a maximum will be reached; all biological populations tend to stabilize at less than the absolute maximum capacity of their habitat, and there are cultural limitations on what densities can be tolerated. We therefore estimated a lower "optimum" ceiling, which left a margin between the projected population level and the fully saturated state. This approach not only yielded global figures of population, economy and so on; it also gave a picture of the configuration of inhabited areas and their densities as a result of the "habitability plus densities" study — that is, it gave a picture of the world "City of the Future" or "Ecumenopolis" on the map of the earth.

The population ceiling obtained through the saturation method had been worked out on the basis of habitability and densities alone; it had not taken into account the potential restrictions on population that might be imposed by limitations of resources of all kinds. At the same time, therefore, we proceeded with prognostications as to what levels of population might be supported by the estimated stocks of global resources. We also made assumptions as to how technological progress, including entirely non-traditional methods of food production, might improve agricultural productivity and enable Anthropos to discover more raw materials, or extract and transport them in new ways. We took into consideration the fact that rising demand would probably intensify the search for new sources, the development of substitutes, and the use of more low-grade mineral deposits and better organized recycling methods. We included still untapped resources and a proportion of those already in circulation which might be reclaimed and recycled.

We made similar detailed forecasts for food, water, energy and certain minerals. We also estimated how the increasing population might be influenced by increased levels of pollution and a possible deterioration in the environment and, though this was difficult to estimate, we considered how the increasing desire to preserve stretches of beautiful landscape and areas of wilderness might impose further limitations on available space.

In all cases, this second "resources" approach led to the toleration of a usually much higher population figure than that obtained by the first "saturation" approach. This means that the resource approach simply confirms the population levels reached by the saturation approach.

The third, or "evolutionary" approach proceeded with an analysis of the dynamics of urban change. We identified and projected recent developments in the structure of human settlements at all scales. In a second branch of this approach, we tried to define the general evolutionary sequence of human settlements in order to determine which patterns of organization had proved particularly successful in the past and how these were likely to evolve in the near, middle and remote future. The configuration for Ecumenopolis which resulted from this "evolutionary" approach proved to be fully consistent with that obtained by the "saturation" method. Arrived at by two entirely different and independent methods, this was a powerful confirmation of the accuracy of the results as far as the pattern of Ecumenopolis was concerned and therefore justified both of them.

Furthermore, we used the indications of future population behavior as given by the saturation and resource approaches to develop an internally consistent set of projections for such things as population, income, investment, water, energy, and so on. This gave us a multi-variable core of projections which we believe contains the actual future path of each projected variable during the next century.

The crucial finding from the point of view of methodology was that three demonstrably independent approaches to the Ecumenopolis concept clearly converged towards one and the same image, be it for population, income, energy or other resource levels, or as a configuration of the ekistic development on the map of the globe. In this way, the three approaches reinforce each other as valid methods for tackling the problem of Ecumenopolis and provide a conclusive confirmation of the Ecumenopolis image reached through them as far as its basic global dimensions, population, income, and geographic pattern on the map of the earth are concerned. Moreover, this convergence justifies all three approaches used and provides a solid foundation for the whole methodology of the project.

Before we give the results reached by each of these methods, we must here below describe the three major assumptions which underlie all our work and which therefore affect every estimate we make. We cannot prove nor disprove these assumptions; we take these truths to be self-evident, although history may prove us wrong.

First assumption: The majority of humanity will continue to live on this earth during the coming centuries.

We believe that colonization of outer space on a significant scale is highly unlikely. Earth is paradise for Anthropos compared to the solar systems; even its polar regions and burning deserts and the surface of its oceans are far more habitable than any other planet or artificial satellite. It is naturally impracticable to consider the possibility of reaching beyond our own solar system for the next few centuries, which is the period of the future we are studying.

Second assumption: No devastating catastrophe affecting the majority of humanity will occur during the next two centuries.

A major disaster, such as a nuclear war, the accidental sterilization of the oceans, or the appearance of a new and devastating disease, may occur. If it does, such a disaster is unlikely to destory more than a fraction of the human race and not the majority, and mankind's response to such an event will be based on contingency planning. We can reach a comprehensive understanding of our total framework only when we can assess the long-term global relationship between human settlements and Nature.

Third assumption: 'We have a profound faith in the adaptive capabilities and creative ingenuity of Anthropos.

History has given ample demonstration of the astonishing power of mankind's ability of adaptation. Given sufficient time, human beings do discover ways to adapt to great and unexpected changes, and they adapt more easily when many of them face the same difficulties together. During the 21st century these abilities will be helped by a decline in the rate of population growth, a rise in incomes, improvements in technology, better communication of all sorts, and improvement in organizational and planning techniques. New knowledge will be shared more willingly. All that Anthropos needs is greater public awareness of what needs to be done, and a more efficient global organization to help him achieve his goals.

Such, then, are our three fundamental assumptions. We stand midway between the prophets of doom and the incurable optimists; we believe that those who foresee total disaster underestimate technology, and those who believe that technology can solve everything underestimate the size of the problem in terms of quantities and the time dimension.

We do not advocate any "absolute" solution to our problems, such as "environmental purity at all costs" or "zero population growth". We believe that persistence in such limited aims could destroy the delicate balance between Anthropos and his natural environment. The doors which hinder the progress of mankind cannot be opened by brute force: Anthropos must forge complex and multi-dimensional keys of great cunning, and develop sufficiently clever plans for the benefit of humanity as a whole and which respect all the environmental systems.

24. The container

For the future as we have defined it — that is, the next 250 years — the earth will certainly be Anthropos' only container and it will probably remain so for a much more distant future. René Dubos put this clearly by saying: "Science fiction writers and a few scientists notwithstanding, Man will never be able actually to settle anywhere in the cosmos other than on or near the surface of the earth. At most, he will make hit-and-run raids on the moon, Mars, and perhaps other planets; he may also establish some stations for specialized purposes under ocean waters. But he is earthbound forever, because his life is completely dependent on fresh water and especially on the earth's atmosphere".[5]

There may be some doubts about the validity of this statement as far as the very distant future is concerned, but it is certainly valid for the coming centuries pertinent to this study. There are people who insist that we should be prepared to settle on other planets; it is much more practicable to limit ourselves to our own earth.

So our container is this earth. The next question is: what are its dimensions? As far as the biosphere is concerned, that is, the whole surface of the earth consisting of land and water as well as the air surrounding it, we are now able to answer this question with greater certainty than ever before. It is highly unlikely, though of course not totally impossible, that the physical size and configuration of the earth will change in the course of the next two or three centuries. The distribution of land, ocean, air and mountains is likely to remain close to, if not exactly the same as it is today. Anthropos could change even the shape and size of the earth with large-scale nuclear explosions, but if this happens it is only likely to do so after the 250 years of our defined future has passed. So it is the biosphere as we know it today which forms the frame of the world of Anthropos and conditions all his life; we have called it the Anthropocosmos. We can now form an exact picture of the surface of the earth itself of which 29.1% is covered with the continents or land, and 70.9% with the oceans or water (fig. 76).

When we say we know the structure of the biosphere, we should qualify that statement by saying that although we know its dimensions and the amount of oxygen it contains, we do not yet know really very much about it as a total system. We do not know, for example, what is the result of the reduction of oxygen through its use by animals and industry and its replacement over the globe as a whole. Although we discover more about this every day, we cannot yet measure the total process of the ecological system and so cannot be certain about the global results of many processes, such as pollution.

Lately it has become fashionable to say that the earth is shrinking. In some drawings the globe is shown as becoming literally smaller in relationship to the increasing speeds of transportation and communication. The earth has been called a village, but this is quite wrong. We must emphasize here that the earth is not shrinking at all; Anthropos is expanding and that is quite different.

The actual dimensions of the globe do not change, but the capacity of the globe to sustain Anthropos changes continuously. Sometimes it is reduced by such things as pollution, which is one of today's most fashionable subjects, but more often its capacity is increased. As we have seen, in the past the capacity of the earth increased from an ability to support 25 million people to an ability to support five billion. We know that its capacity to support Anthropos is still steadily increasing, although we cannot hope to estimate exactly by how much, any more than the people could work out exactly how much the earth's capacity was increasing during that other great transitional period when the

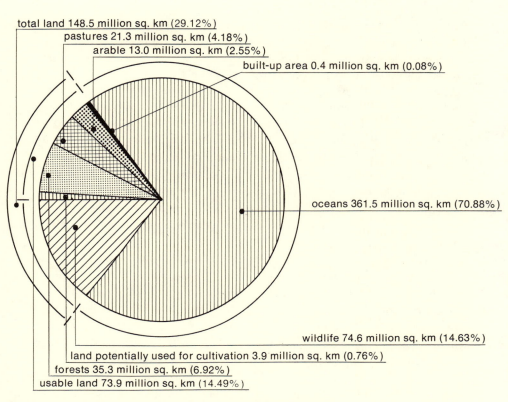

total land 148.5 million sq. km (29.12%)
pastures 21.3 million sq. km (4.18%)
arable 13.0 million sq. km (2.55%)
built-up area 0.4 million sq. km (0.08%)
oceans 361.5 million sq. km (70.88%)
wildlife 74.6 million sq. km (14.63%)
land potentially used for cultivation 3.9 million sq. km (0.76%)
forests 35.3 million sq. km (6.92%)
usable land 73.9 million sq. km (14.49%)

76.   breakdown of the surface of the earth

first irrigation channels were being dug on the plains of Babylon or by the Nile[6]. So we cannot hope to estimate with any degree of exactness what the capacity of the globe will be at this point of time while the changes are actually happening around us, but we can risk making some estimate of the effects of these changes.

How many people can our globe support? Some people think we have already gone beyond the permissible limits. Others say we can do no more than double our present global population — that is, reach 7.5 billion. Others speak of reaching 30, 50 or 100 billion. One even speaks of a possible future population a thousand times larger than the present one, of 3,000 billion, although he adds: "Heaven forbid!"[7]

We cannot hope to discover how many people this globe can support in the future unless we make some attempt to understand developments in technology and how they are likely to affect its capacity. We begin, therefore, by looking at what we possess in our container today, and then go on to see how this may be altered by future technological advances. Next we look at our economy and its development, and at our organizational ability, and only then, by balancing the relationships between these various factors, try to draw some conclusions about the population that could be supported.

When we look at the total land area and the way it is being used today, we see that we are really only using part of it, as table 1 shows.

Theoretically, we use up to 47.2% of the total land available to us. It is questionable, however, whether we use the pastures and forests, which cover 38.1% of the total area, in the best possible way. If we can assume that we do not use more than half this land properly, then in fact we are using only 28.0% (or less than a third) of the total land available. This is shown in table 2.

It is reasonable, then, to say that Anthropos only makes full use of less than one third of the total available land. We can then proceed to make the following assumptions: the habitable space on earth is being increased by human action and will increase even more, and those areas already occupied will become more habitable.

When we talk about the "habitability" of an area, we mean its capacity to sustain human life in the broadest sense. During the next two centuries it is certain that Anthropos will be able to live in some of the areas which are un-inhabitable today, and that some difficult areas will become much easier to live in. Even really difficult places, such as the polar zones and the deserts, will be used more than they are today for several reasons, so the capacity of the earth to support Anthropos can in fact be expected to increase sub-stantially in the next century. As long as unused or underused areas exist, it is inconceivable that Anthropos will not work out ways to use them, though because he is now aware of the dangers, with a more careful eye to the main-tenance of a right balance with his environment than in the past.

There is one important way in which Anthropos misuses land resources as he never did in the past, and that is by allowing his cities to spread so far over the land area around them. Anthropos' movements used to be limited by his own energy and that of his horses, camels or donkeys, so his use of space with-in his cities was restricted and economical. Now with the use of machines, people have energy at their disposal out of all proportion to their actual phy-sical abilities and land is being misused more than at any other period. This is a natural result of the era of explosion of forces we are living through. Urban densities are dropping all over the world as Anthropos, with the increased energy he possesses for transportation, spreads his living areas further and further outwards. We have seen from the analysis of past and present trends that Anthropos prefers to live at lower densities when he can. Since, however, such increasingly low densities are uneconomic from every point of view, we can assume that urban densities will eventually level off and become no less than half of what they are at present.

We wanted to work out what Anthropos' future use and settlement of the total land area of the container would be. This was not easy, since there is

		land	million sq. km	million sq. mi.	%	%	%
usable	used completely	human settlements	0.4	0.2	0.3	9.1	47.2
usable	used completely	arable	13.0	5.0	8.8	9.1	47.2
usable	partially used	pastures	21.3	8.3	14.3	38.1	47.2
usable	partially used	forests	35.3	13.7	23.8	38.1	47.2
unused	usable but with no practical use		3.9	1.5	2.6	2.6	52.8
unused	unused	waste, deserts, mountains	62.1	24.2	41.8	50.2	52.8
unused	unused	uninhabited islands and polar areas	12.5	4.9	8.4	50.2	52.8
		total	148.5	57.7	100.0	100.0	100.0

table 1.   total land area and its use

type of land	million sq. km	million sq. mi.	% of total land
human settlements	0.4	0.2	0.3
arable	13.0	5.0	8.8
pastures	10.6	4.1	7.1
forests	17.6	6.8	11.8
total	41.6	16.1	28.0

table 2.   the land we really use

much confusion as to what the relationship of Anthropos to space really means. We decided to work step-by-step, adding one criterion at a time which would bring us closer and closer to the truth.

The first criterion we used was the amount of land needed by Anthropos at the average global density for built-up areas of 90 persons per ha (35 per acre), not taking into account, for the moment, how much of this land would have to be set aside for agriculture, wildlife, recreation, production of minerals, or any other purpose. We produced table 3 which shows the whole range of alternatives for using from 5% to 100% of the land surface. Alternative A would give us a possible population of 66.6 billion, and alternative T, 1,336.5 billion.

Clearly we would not want to fill the entire land area of the globe with a built-up urban settlement. The next step then is to decide what proportion of land Anthropos should leave quite untouched so that a right balance is maintained between Anthropos and Nature.

We examined as many cases as we could of the past and came to the conclusion that during the last 10,000 years of life in villages and towns Anthropos survived and developed civilizations while living in areas of which up to 50% was untouched. He might use such untouched areas incidentally, by fleeing to the mountains whenever the plains were invaded, or using them for hunting or as a source of timber. We have established that today Anthropos still does not fully use more than 28% of the total land surface including his built-up areas. We can safely say, therefore, that Anthropos can use between 28% and 50% of the land area today and still keep a balance with Nature. This would give us a possible population of between 400 billion (Alternative F) and 668 billion (Alternative J).

So far, we have made assumptions concerning only built-up urban areas and untouched landscape; we have not considered land needed to produce food or used for recreation. Without this land Anthropos would have to live within his city walls and import his food from other planets or produce it entirely in factories.

We know that Anthropos cannot remain within walls — otherwise he would never have abandoned the Garden of Eden. In all his past behavior he has demonstrated that he needs much larger areas outside his built-up environment for entertainment and recreation.

We also have to consider possible alternative densities at which Anthropos can live within his built-up areas. We have said that the average global density is now 90 persons per ha (35 per acre), and though the future average may well be lower than this, it cannot decrease indefinitely because that would be totally uneconomic. Far more space will be needed for recreation, in its broadest sense, than required at present. In order to allow a reasonable increase in such recreational space, we calculated that the built-up areas should be multiplied by two. Anthropos will then need three times the space we have al-

alternative	percentage of total land to be used by Anthropos	corresponding surface in:		possible population in billions
		million sq. km	million sq. mi.	
A	5	7.4	2.9	66.6
B	10	14.8	5.7	133.2
C	15	22.3	8.7	200.7
D	20	29.6	11.5	266.4
E	25	37.1	14.4	333.9
F	30	44.5	17.3	400.5
G	35	52.0	20.2	468.0
H	40	59.4	23.1	534.6
I	45	66.8	26.0	601.2
J	50	74.2	28.9	667.8
K	55	81.7	31.8	735.3
L	60	89.1	34.7	801.9
M	65	96.5	37.5	868.5
N	70	103.9	40.4	935.1
O	75	111.4	43.3	1,002.6
P	80	118.8	46.2	1,069.2
Q	85	126.2	49.1	1,135.8
R	90	133.6	52.0	1,202.4
S	95	141.1	54.9	1,269.9
T	100	148.5	57.7	1,336.5

table 3. . alternatives for the use of land surface

alternative	within the built-up area		within total land needed by Anthropos to live in and for recreation	
	inh./ha	inh./acre	inh./ha	inh./acre
A	10	4	3.3	1.3
B	20	8	6.6	2.6
C	30	12	10.0	4.0
D	40	16	13.3	5.3
E	50	20	16.6	6.7
F	60	24	20.0	8.1
G	70	28	23.3	9.4
H	80	32	26.6	10.7
I	90	36	30.0	12.1
J	100	40	33.3	13.4
K	110	44	36.6	14.8
L	120	48	40.0	16.2
M	130	52	43.3	17.5
N	140	56	46.6	18.8
O	150	60	50.0	20.2
P	160	64	53.3	21.5
Q	170	68	56.6	22.9
R	180	72	60.0	24.3
S	190	76	63.3	25.6
T	200	80	66.6	26.9

table 4.   alternative densities

lowed for built-up areas alone and the densities will drop to one-third of those we allowed if he were to live "within walls". We are left with table 4 of alternative densities.

The lowest reasonable combination of use of land for built-up areas and densities would give us the possibility of 44.44 billion people (Alternative F), and the highest, 173 billion (Alternative J).

We have still made no allowance for the area of land needed for the production of food.

Factors which limit the available land

Water supply

We have now discovered the amount of land Anthropos will need to live on. We must next try to work out some of the factors which limit Anthropos' possibility to live on the land that exists, such things as the availability of water, the climate, the general habitability of the various areas of the globe, and developments in Anthropos' technology that may change not only the habitability of many areas but also our idea about the amount of space needed for food production.

Since human settlements cannot exist without water, the first thing to deal with is water resources. It cannot be said of the whole cosmos that "in the beginning there was water", but it is true as far as our life on earth is concerned. For Anthropos, in the beginning there was water. Over 300 million years ago some strange snouts dared to emerge from the water, thereby starting a process that led, two and a half million years ago, to a few standing primates, and some 200,000 years ago, to an animal called *Homo sapiens*[8]. The blood and tissues of this animal have a calcium and· potassium content quite similar to that of the oceans. In our beginning, there was water.

Seventy-one percent of the total surface of the globe is covered by water. This is our hydrosphere — oceans, seas, bodies of fresh water and ice masses. The volume of water is much smaller than the volume of the earth, but the quantity of life in it is enormously greater, especially in the oceans, in both biomass and numbers, but strangely enough not in the number of species.

Water is also found in the atmosphere, which contains 0.25% water vapor. Molecules of water are more numerous than any other molecules on the surface of the earth.

In spite of this, it is difficult for Anthropos to live close to usable water. This is because 97.2% of the total volume of water is saline, 2.15% is frozen, leaving only 0.65% in the form of fresh water on land (fig 77a). If all this fresh water could be collected on the surface of the non-frozen area of the earth it would reach a height of 73.16 meters, but in fact only 1.08 meters of this total is contained in lakes, rivers and streams; the rest is made up of underground water

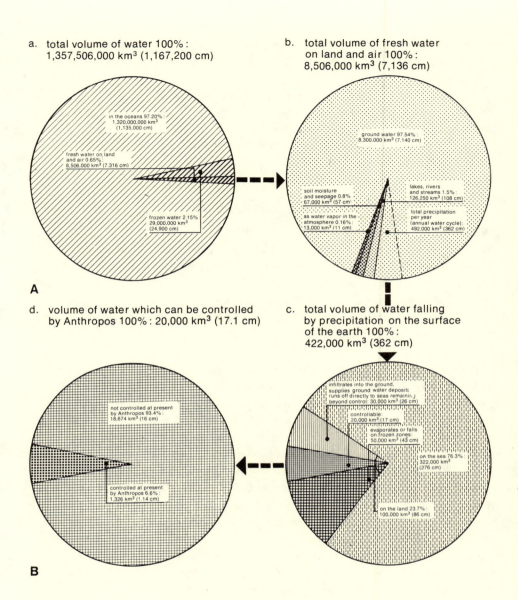

a. total volume of water 100% :
    1,357,506,000 km³ (1,167,200 cm)

b. total volume of fresh water
    on land and air 100% :
    8,506,000 km³ (7,136 cm)

in the oceans 97.20% :
1,320,000,000 km³
(1,135,000 cm)

fresh water on land
and air 0.65% :
8,506,000 km³ (7.316 cm)

frozen water 2.15% :
29,000,000 km³
(24,900 cm)

ground water 97.54% :
8,300,000 km³ (7,140 cm)

soil moisture
and seepage 0.8% :
67,000 km³ (57 cm)

lakes, rivers
and streams 1.5% :
126,250 km³ (108 cm)

as water vapor in the
atmosphere 0.16% :
13,000 km³ (11 cm)

total precipitation
per year
(annual water cycle):
492,000 km³ (362 cm)

A

d. volume of water which can be controlled
    by Anthropos 100% : 20,000 km³ (17.1 cm)

c. total volume of water falling
    by precipitation on the surface
    of the earth 100% :
    422,000 km³ (362 cm)

not controlled at present
by Anthropos 93.4% :
18,674 km³ (16 cm)

controlled at present
by Anthropos 6.6% :
1,326 km³ (1.14 cm)

infiltrates into the ground,
supplies ground water deposit,
runs off directly to seas remaining
beyond control: 30,000 km³ (26 cm)

controllable:
20,000 km³ (17 cm)

evaporates or falls
on frozen zones:
50,000 km³ (43 cm)

on the sea 76.3% :
322,000 km³
(276 cm)

on the land 23.7% :
100,000 km³ (86 cm)

B

figures in brackets indicate the height that the relevant quantities of water would reach if
they were placed on the whole non-frozen land area of the earth which is 116,400,000 km²

A annual water cycle
B breakdown of usable water

77.   water on our earth

reserves and water in the atmosphere. The water easily available to Anthropos is only one ten-thousandth of the total volume of water that exists.

In order to make use of this limited fresh water, Anthropos had to settle close to springs, rivers or lakes. He therefore had to live more densely in certain areas of the earth's surface, and this was one reason why he had to learn to live with other people and create human communities, which led to the development of civilization. Anthropos has always followed water, from the mountains to the plains to the sea; it formed the blood-stream of his life's system and drew him with it along its own course.

As time went on Anthropos could no longer depend on "hunting" water, he had to begin "mining" it from the depths, and then he had to "domesticate" it. He brought it closer in canals and pipes and collected it in dams and ponds. He began to play his own part in the relationship with water. As he needed more water, he replaced canals by pipes or lined his canals, he covered his water tanks and began irrigating by spraying or more elaborate techniques.

The more water he had, the more he used, and he was attracted to places of lower elevation, to great lakes, rivers and sea shores. Today, 92% of the population which live in cities of more than 200,000 people are below the 500 m (1,650 ft) level and 70% of these are near lakes, rivers or seas.

As Anthropos became involved with increasingly greater volumes of water, he had to transport it over increasingly greater distances at higher cost. Having increased the flow of the lifeblood of his system, he began to build systems to get rid of the liquid refuse which resulted. He began to be active instead of passive in his relationship to water.

We can now try to calculate the total amount of water Anthropos needs to live today. The need for water increases with every year that passes. It is calculated that per capita needs may double within a century, and may level off at about 1,100 m³ (242,300 imp. gallons)[9], which means there is enough water available to supply a population of about 19 billion people. Available water resources show that Anthropos cannot draw more fresh water than the annual water cycle allows. The total volume of water that evaporates and falls back onto the total land surface is 86 cm (34 in.). Of this, Anthropos can potentially control 17 cm (6.7 in.) and now controls only 1.14 cm (0.45 in). Anthropos therefore now controls only 6.6% of the water he could actually control (fig. 77b). The most important category of techniques for control of water in the future lies in the development of the rational control of run-off, and if we can assume that a century from now Anthropos will control the entire possible total of 17 cm (6.7 in.), then this quantity of water could support a population of approximately 19 billion allowing 1,070 m³ (236,000 imp. gallons) per person per year. If the population should be more than this, then amongst the more promising other new sources of water are diversion of precipitation from the oceans to the land and the desalination of the oceans. Both methods are likely to be used in the 21st century, especially in arid areas where run-off is not plentiful.

If we think that the average person in order to live needs 1,070 m³ or tons (236,00 imp. gallons) of water a year, compared to only about five tons of all other solid and liquid materials, we will understand why it is more important to devise ways to produce and transport water than any other resource.

We can now reach some practical conclusions as to how the supply of water limits the globe as a container for Anthropos. If we want simply to "hunt" for water, we can cover a big part of our needs with rational use of run-off. If we "mine" it from the depths and domesticate it by modern technology, then according to our researches on other restraints we will have a sufficient amount to supply the number of people we suppose can exist. There is no problem of quantity as regards water; it is simply a problem of economics and technology, and in the future we will have increased incomes and better technology at our disposal, if we want to use them. If we are prepared to pay the price for the desalination of sea water, we can supply as many people as we want with almost no limit at all.

A big problem remains over the pollution of water. We are turning "our waterways into rivers of death" as Rachel Carson aptly expressed it some time ago[10], and the pollution of the oceans has reached dramatic proportions. However, it is now clearly understood that water pollution can be overcome through the proper use of scientific technology and the proper mobilization of organized effort and economic resources, but that effort does need to be very much more serious than the one being made at present. So pollution should not be a limiting factor, no matter how many people live on the earth.

The atmosphere

As far as the atmosphere itself is concerned, there are no limiting factors so long as Anthropos does not live too high up where there is not enough oxygen. Today, however, there is a problem connected with the pollution of the air by automobiles, industry, agriculture, domestic sources and power plants. We can make optimistic forecasts that no limits will be imposed on Anthropos' development because of this, providing pollution is first controlled and then reduced to a point at which no danger exists. Our optimism is greater now than when our study began in 1960, and is based on such achievements as that of the London area where pollution from chimneys has been so much reduced, new policies and regulations enforced in agreement with decisions reached at the United Nations, the passing of legislation in many industrialized countries for the control of industrial pollution, and regulations for stringent antipollution standards of all future automobiles. The problems are still very serious, but the solutions can be seen, and are possible, and need only new organization and the determination of Anthropos to achieve results.

Radioactivity from nuclear tests will remain for centuries perhaps, but present-day international agreements allow us to hope that it will not create unsurpassable limitations on the capacity of our container to sustain life. Recent discoveries show that the checking of this difficult problem may be achieved earlier than was previously thought if public opinion can be sufficiently alerted and energized, and sufficient funds diverted to it.

Concerning the climate, we can say there are enough areas on land and water to sustain life and Anthropos. We think it unlikely that Anthropos' physiological capacity to adapt to different conditions will increase substantially, despite proposals that have been made for totally new ways of life for him, such as under water. The question then arises whether man can, or should adapt the climate to better suit his needs; here the experts are divided in their attitudes. When we consider that big problems would be created for a great many living creatures if Anthropos did manage to change the climate, it would be better to proceed with the assumption that the climate should not be substantially changed, even if Anthropos should discover ways of doing it. This, of course, refers to the overall distribution of climatic zones over the globe. Local control of climate may develop to a considerable extent. Already we are air conditioning the insides of our buildings and are starting, if only moderately, to control the climate inside whole settlements. In 50 or 100 years from now we may be able to control the climate around our settlements to a considerable degree, and if so, that will greatly increase the habitability of usable land areas.

Several problems have arisen over the "pollution of the climate", the longest existing one being the fact that the climate inside large cities becomes warmer. So long as cities are in cold climates this is a good thing, but in hot climates like the Mediterranean, where cool breezes are badly needed, it is bad. The same is true of relative humidity, which also increases within cities.

The climate is also being changed because of industrial and power plants and air pollution, plus a "mushroom cloud" covering cities at greater heights, and may be changed by the use of supersonic airplanes such as the S.S.T. (Supersonic Transportation). It is possible that all these changes may affect some human settlements during some periods of the year or day, but Anthropos is already aware they exist and will certainly solve these problems. One of the reasons why the S.S.T. is not operating today is the awareness of its possible bad effects on climate.

Land, water, air and climate all affect the biosphere and all the micro-organisms, plants and animals that live in it. Anthropos must preserve a right balance with all such living things. We must remember that: "the plants of the earth combine about 150 billion tons of carbon with 25 billion tons of hydrogen, and set free 400 billion tons of oxygen"[11]. This means that the plants produce more than 100 tons of oxygen for every man alive, so we must take good care of them. We do not yet know the exact balance we need, but we know that Anthropos does destroy trees and other plant and animal species by his actions, and we must remain aware of the dangers this creates.

However, we are now becoming far more conscious of all these problems, so we can hope that present negative trends can be controlled and reversed to a considerable extent. If we may assume that we will save a proper proportion of the earth's land and water from the destructive actions of Anthropos, then we can hope that all living things which have survived in them will also be saved. If things follow their normal evolution without major disasters, as is our basic assumption, then we do not think Anthropos will face major problems in connection with the preservation of plants and animals — but he must begin to take the right action to preserve them now.

Habitability

We have said that Anthropos can allow himself to take over from 28% to 50% of the land area of the globe. We must now decide in more detail how much of this is actually fit for him to live on.

Earlier in this section (page 171 ff.) we gave a short description of how we rated the various areas of the globe for habitability, taking three factors — climate, topography and water supply — as being of absolutely primary importance for this rating. Some areas of the globe's surface are also particularly important for the production of new materials of various kinds, so these cannot be used for human settlements. In the future, however, big improvements in transportation are likely to make location of human settlements near such sites of less importance. It is also expected that food production will be less dependent on specific soils and climates, so that its location will be less restricted than it is today.

By taking into account and combining all the factors we have mentioned, we were able to estimate the composite total habitability of the globe in 1960 (fig. 78) and to project changes and also estimate habitability for 2100 (fig. 79). We should point out that we have marked the borders dividing one zone from another on these maps according to the extreme value of each criterion. It is clear that no such strict boundaries actually exist, so we had to use two over-simplifications: a generalized zoning for habitability, and the use of absolute values which were selected to mark the differentiation between the zones.

We must now define how we used each criterion.

Elevation: We are concerned with absolute elevation above sea level and consider conditions become unlivable at 3,000 m (9,850 ft). Five percent of the total area of the earth is at altitudes over 3,000 m (9,850 ft), mainly in the Andean range and on the Tibetan plateau. We selected 3,000 m as our limit because of Anthropos' need for oxygen. In fact today more than five million people live above this altitude, but this is only 1.5% of the world's population and we think it unlikely that a significant proportion of the population will be forced to do so, even in the remote future. Areas between 3,000 m and 1,000 m (9,850 ft and 3,280 ft) are less difficult to settle densely, although quite difficult and expensive to maintain.

The map showing the habitability of the globe according to the criterion of elevation alone is shown in fig. 80. Three contour lines are shown, for 1,000, 1,500, and 3,000 m (3,280, 4,920 and 9,850 ft). We also show a contour line for 200 m (656 ft) indicating the position of the continental shelf which may prove an important factor in influencing the future location of settlements to be built on the ocean surface. When a certain level of population is reached, it may be less expensive to build settlements on the surface of the sea than in difficult areas like deserts, high mountains or polar regions. They will have the advantages of access to food, energy and mineral resources, and might serve as centers for the large-scale photosynthesis of food in warmer climates, or for new forms of recreation and nodal points for Networks connecting the continents.

Climate: We have used Köppen's climatic classification, adjusted to include more information. Extreme climates, i.e. deserts and polar regions, were given the lowest ratings. Other climatic zones were classified into five categories.

When considering future conditions for the year 2100, we took into account such future possibilities as artificially-controlled urbanized areas. The main differences in the maps showing present habitability according to the criterion of climate alone (fig. 81) and that showing projections for 2100 in terms of climate alone (fig. 82) are the following:
— The 'attractive' zones have been somewhat extended.
— Areas with a 'fair' climate today have been extended to include most of those now considered 'bearable' by 2100.
— The remaining 'negative' areas have each been upgraded, so that the 'very difficult' have become 'difficult', and 'difficult' have become 'rigorous'. The 'very difficult' category has therefore been eliminated for 2100, leaving three negative categories and a total of six categories instead of seven.

The conditions Anthropos finds comfortable to live in climatically remain the same, so the cost of making an area comfortable artificially will be higher for 'difficult' than for 'bearable' zones. If ways can be found of making it possible to live in deserts and polar zones, the expense of doing so would probably limit habitation there to the exploitation and conservation of resources, research and experiment, as well as tourism.

Water supply: We assumed that future water supply will remain the same as today so far as adequately rechargeable sources are concerned. When we consider future water sources, we only include those that clearly can be renewed, such as underground streams, storage dams fed from run-off precipitation, and the desalination of sea water. We do not include such things as lakes, since apart from the fact that they become polluted easily they may quickly be exhausted (unless they can certainly be recharged).

189

78.   composite habitability of the globe in 1960

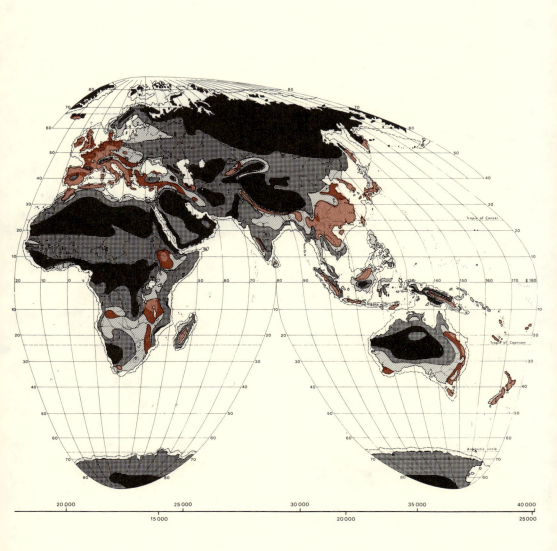

habitability zones:

- E   non-habitable
- D   not suitable for extensive habitation
- C   difficult for extensive habitation
- B   no significant limitations
- A   no limitations

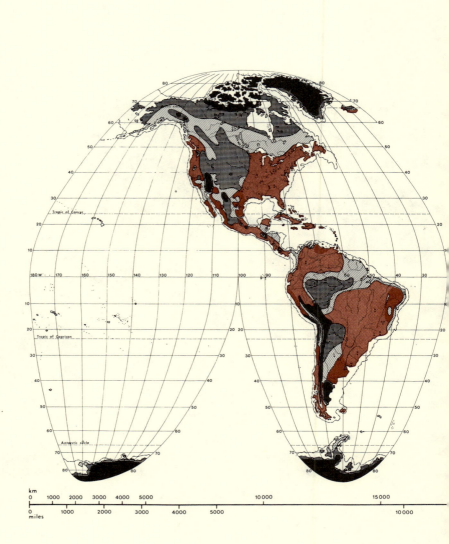

79.   composite habitability of the globe in 2100

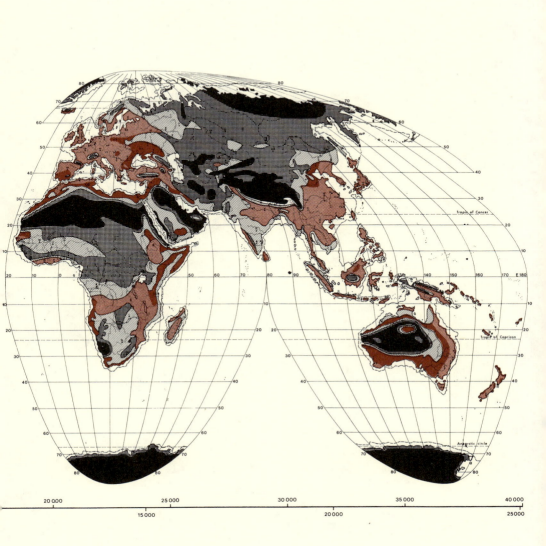

habitability zones:

■	E	non-habitable
▦	D	not suitable for extensive habitation
░	C	difficult for extensive habitation
■	B	no significant limitations
▨	A	no limitations

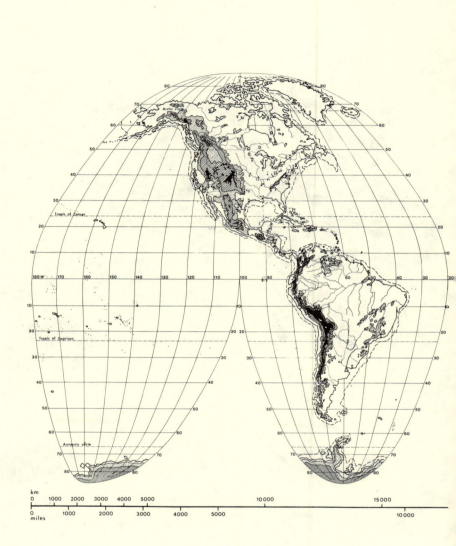

80.   habitability of the globe according to elevation

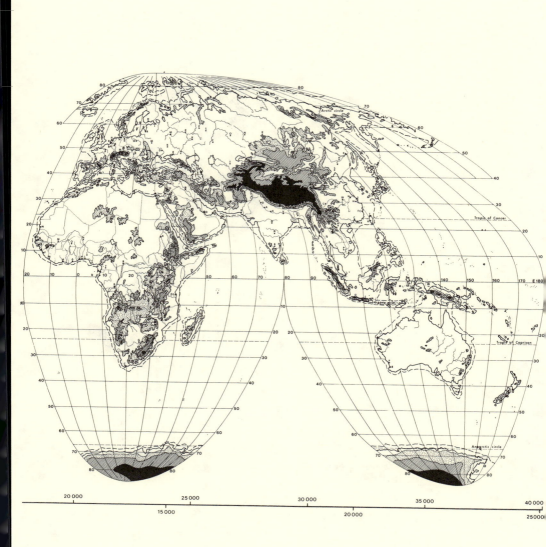

20 000   25 000   30 000   35 000   40 000

15 000   20 000   25 000

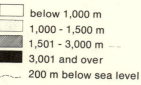

☐ below 1,000 m

▨ 1,000 - 1,500 m

▨ 1,501 - 3,000 m --

■ 3,001 and over

-..-.. 200 m below sea level

195

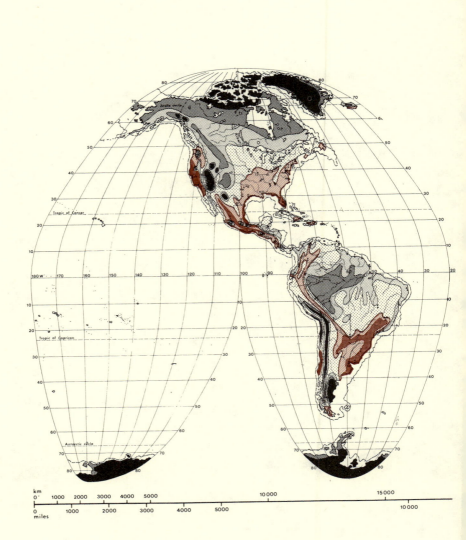

81.   habitability of the globe in 1960 according to climate

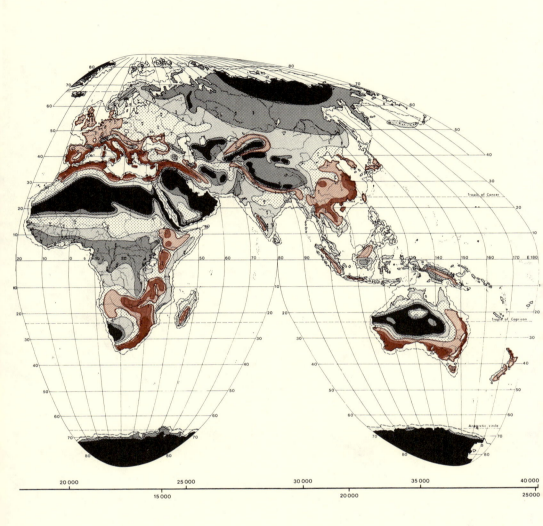

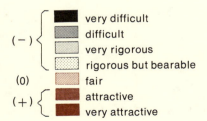

climate

(−) { ■ very difficult
      ■ difficult
      ▨ very rigorous
      ▨ rigorous but bearable
(0)   ▨ fair
(+) { ■ attractive
      ■ very attractive

197

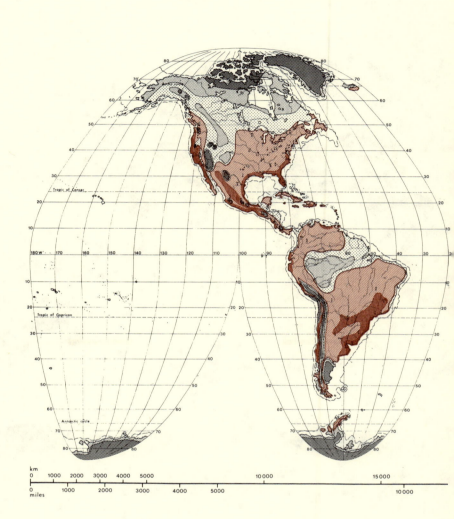

82.   habitability of the globe in 2100 according to climate

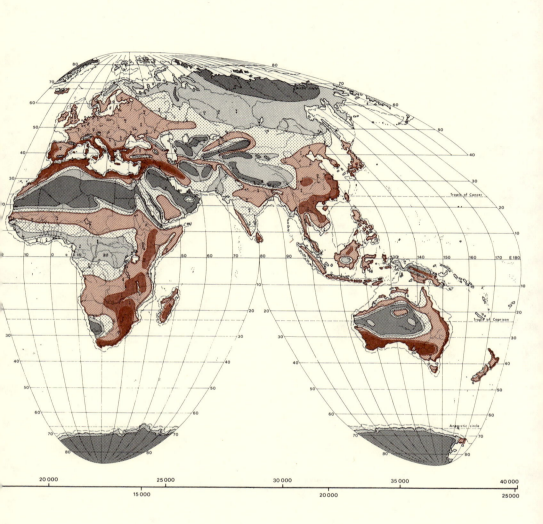

climate

(−) { very difficult
      difficult
      very rigorous
      rigorous but bearable
(0)   fair
(+) { attractive
      very attractive

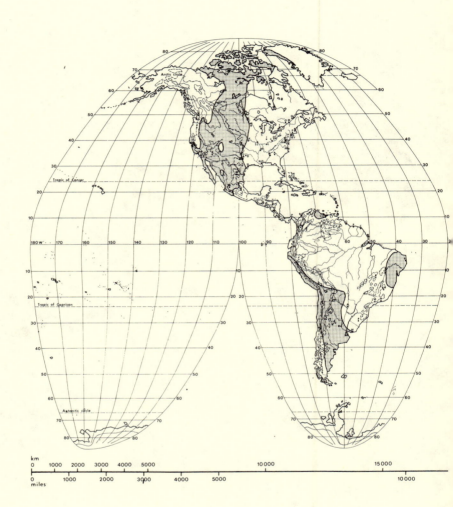

83. habitability of the globe in 1960 according to water scarcity

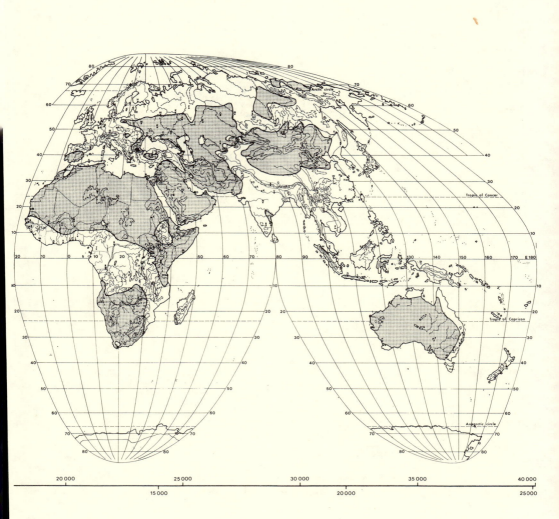

20 000	25 000	30 000	35 000	40 000
15 000		20 000		25 000

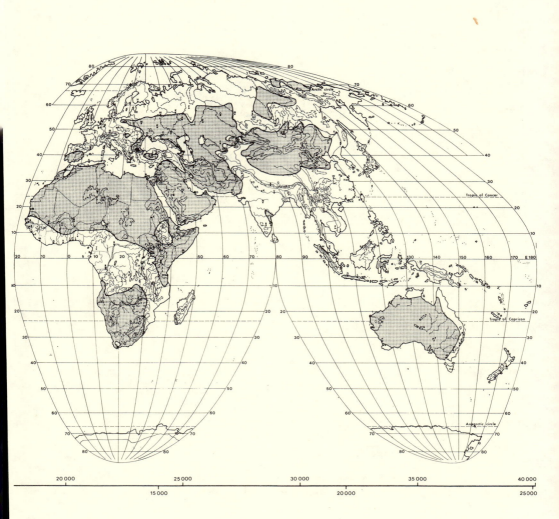 < 5 lit./sec./km²

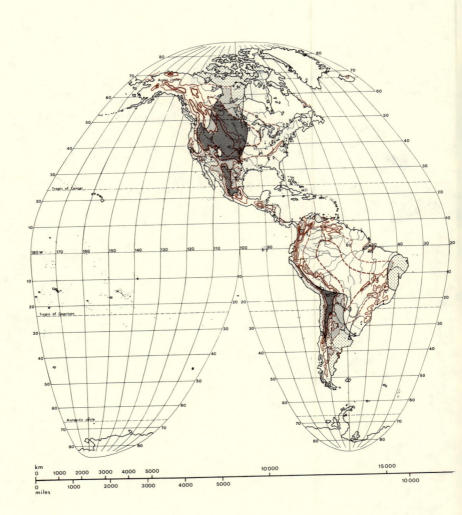

84.   habitability of the globe in 2100 according to water
        supply

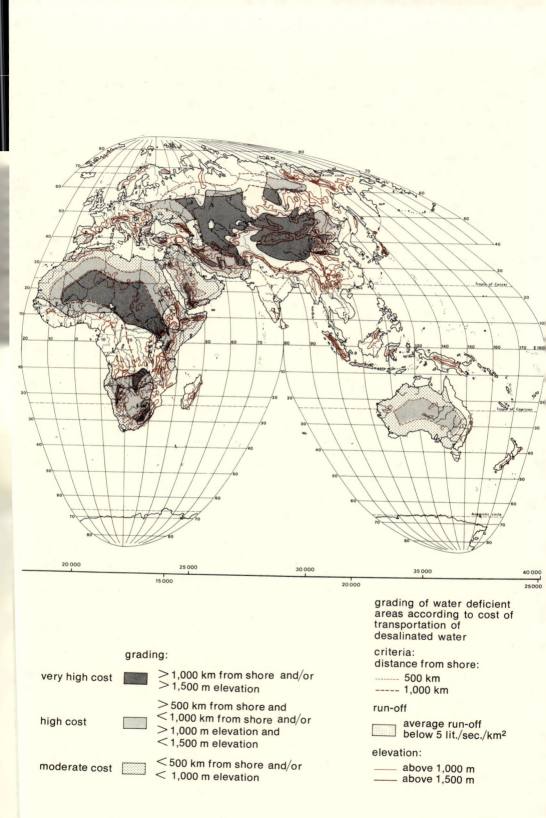

| 20 000 | 25 000 | 30 000 | 35 000 | 40 000 |
| 15 000 | | 20 000 | | 25 000 |

grading of water deficient
areas according to cost of
transportation of
desalinated water

criteria:
distance from shore:

------- 500 km
----- 1,000 km

run-off

average run-off
below 5 lit./sec./km²

elevation:

——— above 1,000 m
——— above 1,500 m

grading:

very high cost >1,000 km from shore and/or
>1,500 m elevation

high cost >500 km from shore and
<1,000 km from shore and/or
>1,000 m elevation and
<1,500 m elevation

moderate cost <500 km from shore and/or
<1,000 m elevation

The limit we have set to discriminate between areas with sufficient water supply and those without is 5 liters/second/km² (1.1 imp. gallon/second/km²). We assume that water-deficient areas will be supplied with desalinated water, and that will become more expensive according to how far inland and how high up the settlements are.

Any future alterations there might be in the assumptions we have made about future water sources would, of course, result in a different zoning according to water supply. Recycling of water has not, for example, been taken into account, and this is a basic concept for the future which can increase available water very considerably. Already several industries are reusing their water more than once.

Maps of the habitability of the earth according to the criterion of water supply alone are shown in figs. 83 and 84.

25. Technology

Next we try to examine what developments are happening in technology. It is very difficult to predict future trends here, but since technology will play such a big part in shaping the City of the Future we must at least try to understand what developments are likely to take place.

Technological forecasting has clarified some issues for the near and middle future, and it is here also that the only existing, serious, really long-range forecasts — such as those for energy — have been attempted by appropriate expert bodies. The Delphic method of research was used to summarize the opinions of leaders in many fields of technology, and a first glimpse of future possibilities is now available. Anyhow, the subject is vast, and here we must concentrate only on those aspects that have a particular relevance for us. These are production (which conditions future economic growth), energy (the key element in changing production and mobility), and transport and communication systems (which define our territorial system of life).

Some recent trends in technology have already developed sufficiently for us to be fairly certain about them — for instance, automation. We are certainly tending towards the most complete automation possible, not to imitate Anthropos, but to do all the things he dislikes doing and so leave him more time to be creative himself. Automation will replace people in the kind of job that is an 'emotional hazard', such as that described in a study on why waitresses cry: "caught as they are between irascible customers and even more irascible cooks"[12]. We are unlikely to see the realization of all the concepts of the "prophets of science", but many of them will be there, just so long as they do not try to replace Anthropos in sectors of his life, such as the arts, in which he needs to express himself.

There is great difficulty in predicting what discoveries will be made, because they would not be discoveries unless they were unexpected. It is not even possible for us to predict the interval between the discovery of a new process and its application, although in the last two and a half centuries there has been a trend towards reducing this interval. Recently, the average interval has been in the order of 10 to 20 years. This, however, only applies to small things, like inventions in electronics. More time is needed for large-scale inventions, such as the supersonic place (S.S.T.), where many commercial risks are involved.

In some sectors technological invention is progressing at a better and better rate, often at twice the speed that was predicted. Developments in agricultural technology, for instance, which it was thought would take 30 years, have been realized in only 15 years. Other things which 20 years ago were thought impossible, such as global telephone dialing, are now in operation and expanding at a high rate. We must take into account Anthropos' enormous ability to communicate and develop any technology which promises him direct personal benefit. We must also recognize that development has not been as fast as it could have been in some areas because courage and resources were not mobilized.

Where is the present explosive development in technology leading? Some people say to an even greater development; others, especially in the physical sciences, predict a slow-down. Personally we do not think we can take a position on this point. The predictions of a slow-down are based mainly on the fact that our container is facing a crisis, but we do not think this is any reason to believe technological invention will stop. On the contrary, because of this crisis we are more likely to see progress in new techniques, such as new ways of recycling materials and resources, which are in a very primitive stage at present.

Our conclusion is that we must be prepared to see a continuation in the present trend of technological development and also the possibility of new explosive advances — at least in some sectors — in response to a greater understanding of urgent human needs.

We can make the following assumption: there is no reason to suppose that progress will not continue in the fields of science in general and technology in particular so long as it continues to be both desirable and possible. It seems out of the question that it should ever become either desirable or possible to halt technological progress. On the contrary, experience has shown that, on average, technological progress has been faster than the rate predicted by any forecaster. There is every reason to believe this will continue, so that much more will be invented and applied in the future than any serious technological forecaster of today has predicted. We know this will happen; we cannot know what will be invented, nor how, nor when.

Technological invention is always valuable and important, although at times — as when the first atomic explosions were made — it can be dangerous. We cannot blame technological inventions for the problems of mankind today; indeed, the problems of many people at this crisis of explosive growth and change would be far worse without them. The real problem is that the changes brought about by technology have happened too fast for Anthropos to adapt to them. There are so many inventions that some are implemented without proper understanding or testing for possible side-effects — as in the tragic affair of thalidomide. We now accept, however, that governments should protect the consumer by checking the content of food, drugs and chemicals, and such things are likely to come under increasingly strict control and legislation. Another example of a useful invention that can have bad effects is of course the private car: when too many people use it as a commuting device it can choke city centers and destroy the quality of human life there. However, it is likely that more control will be exercised over the use of the private car in urban areas, and especially in newly constructed ones where low-income countries may learn from the disastrous experience of high-income ones.

Energy

We now try to examine in more detail those technological developments which will have most impact on the City of the Future, and begin with energy.

The production of energy in commercial form began around 1800, one generation before the birth of the city of the present, when the steam engine was first used for practical purposes. This was a great revolution, because until this time Anthropos had relied on using his own energy, which corresponded to about 2,500 calories a day, the use of horses (in some civilizations and for some classes) which usually provided about the same amount of additional calories (although sometimes considerably more) per day.

From this point on, the consumption of energy, which had remained almost stable, began to grow at increasing rates. Between 1860 and 1950, the annual growth in consumption of energy was 2.2%. Between 1935 and 1950 it had risen to 3%, and between 1953 and 1966 to 5.3% (fig. 85). If we adjust the growth in consumption during this last period to allow for population growth, it means that the per capita consumption grew at 3.4% per year.

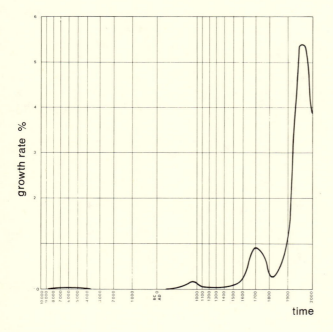

85.   rate of growth of total world energy consumption

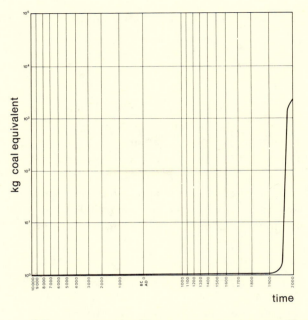

86.   per capita energy consumption

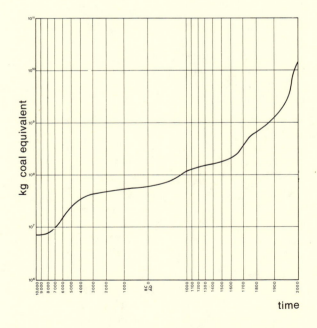

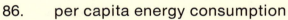

87.   total world energy consumption

As traditional sources of energy are depleted, nuclear energy seems to promise to maintain this growth if not to accelerate it, at least in the near future. The large-scale application of such things as fusion power and solar energy is not impossible, and many other ones may be added during the middle or the remote future.

The amount of energy consumed by each person has grown in an explosive way (fig. 86). The growth of total global energy consumption has increased even more (fig. 87). In high-income countries like the U.S.A., more than 50% of the total energy produced is consumed for space heating and automobile transportation[13]. The rate of consumption differs enormously from country to country, so that the difference between a high-income country like the U.S.A. and a low-income one like India is as much as 50 to 1[14]. This is a greater proportional difference than the one between the two income-levels, which is about 35 to 1 ($3,500 in the U.S.A. and $100 in India).

We can see the same greater increase in growth of energy production than in growth of incomes happening in urban systems. A comparative study made in Athens and Detroit for the period between 1870 and 1970 revealed that growth in the commercial production of energy from such things as fossil fuels, hydroelectric plants and nuclear reactors — which has become a main indicator of material development — was even more rapid than the growth of per capita incomes (fig. 88). In Detroit, production of commercial energy was 11.63 times greater at the end of the hundred-year period, which is the equivalent of an annual growth rate of 2.49%. In Athens the growth was 16.53 times greater, an average yearly rate of 2.84%.

There is no question that it is both desirable and possible for energy consumption to increase on a global scale, as is presented simply in fig. 89. Present estimates for the year 2000[15] suggest a total 2.5 times higher than the present one[16], and for the year 2070, 13 to 30 times higher — let us say an average of 23 times higher than at present (fig. 87). Many people are pessimistic about these predictions, and many others optimistic, and there is no way of being certain that either attitude is right. We can only trust in our belief in Anthropos, and in his ability to overcome the problems of pollution which threaten him because of this growth in some places. We can certainly overcome them; it is only a matter of how much we are prepared to spend on it.

The fact that sources of energy are going to change in the future will influence human settlements in many ways. In the near future, let us say ten years from now, world energy consumption will be based partly on fossil fuels, as now, and more and more on nuclear energy. The total consumption could be divided into percentages as follow: liquid fuels 35%; solid fuels 30%; natural gas 23%; hydroelectric projects 8%; and nuclear projects 4%[17].

This situation will gradually change because of the limitations of global resources. Within one or two generations we shall be relying much more on

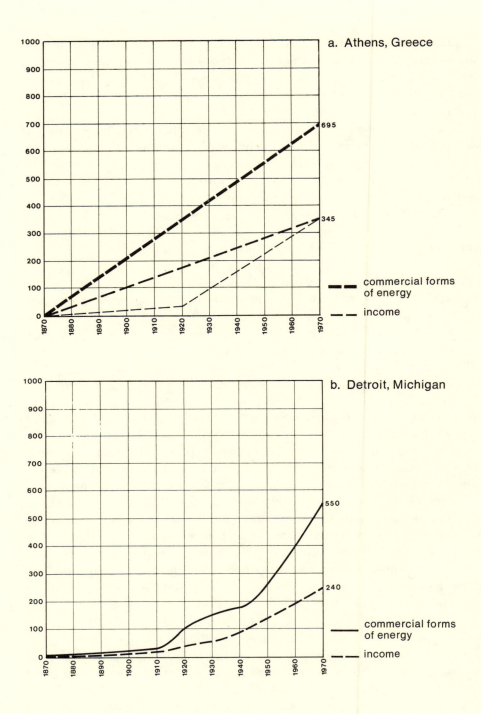

88.   growth of commercial production of energy and per
        capita incomes in Athens and the Urban Detroit Area

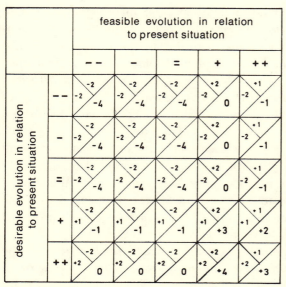

the figures in every small triangle correspond to the *degree of probability* of every feasible or desirable type of evolution and range from −2 (very improbable) to +2 (very probable)

the figures in every large triangle correspond to the *attention* that must be given to it and range from the highest degree of +4 to the lowest of −4

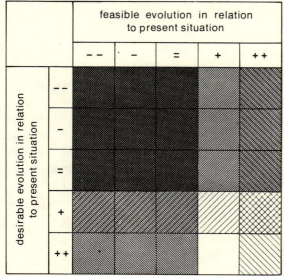

the shades in every square correspond to the attention that must be given to it and range from the highest degree of +4 □ to the lowest of −4 ■

89.   desirable and feasible energy consumption in the future

such sources as nuclear fission and later fusion. This may happen in stages, beginning with light water reactors which utilize only about 2% of the potential energy in natural uranium, and moving on to fast breeder reactors which can produce more new fuel in the form of fissionable plutonium than they consume in the course of operation. This may happen within 15 to 20 years. We may then move on to the use of fusion power, which is still at the stage of laboratory experiment. This will happen probably around the year 2000[18] and will give us huge opportunities for the wide use of energy. It is also possible that other sources of energy may be used, such as geothermal heat, wind power, and solar radiation (only 0.05% of the energy provided by the sun is used today)[19]. Also there may be totally new solutions, such as the idea of underwater dams which will create the possibility of producing energy from the natural movement of water, and many other ideas which have been proposed and could become reality one or two generations from now.

Many more spectacular suggestions have been made. They range from the attempt to reduce the impact of energy on Nature to zero by the creation of projects based on more developed and expensive installations and the organization of global Networks to even the idea of some day creating a more advanced civilization, one that could compete with others in the cosmos by means of those huge increases in energy consumption discussed by Shklovskii and Sagan in their book *Intelligent Life in the Universe*[20].

We cannot say exactly what will happen, or when; we can say that many of these optimistic suggestions do make sense, and that we are heading towards an increase in energy production that will help the progress of mankind and, more especially, lift the level of low-income peoples. A widespread objection to forecasts of increasing energy production has been the threat of thermal pollution on a planetary scale. Since, however, such increase will be gradual, there will be time to invent and apply appropriate counter-measures. The need to allow increased energy consumption is so basic that even if no other means were invented — which is unlikely — the harmful excess of thermal energy could, as leading astronomers and other nuclear experts have suggested, be radiated out into space.

Production

Since technology will go on improving, and the production of energy therefore must increase if we follow those proper policies we are now beginning to formulate through understanding, production of all sorts will increase also.

Nature's own production will be increased through the development of natural processes; there will be more animals, more plants, more algae. Moreover, it is highly likely that many of the products now obtained directly from Nature, like foodstuffs, will be produced by methods far more closely resembling industrial production. Meanwhile, there will also be increases in the production of all man-made products of industry.

The systems Anthropos creates will become larger and more elaborate. Take the water system, for example, which began about 500,000 years ago[21] with the simple collection of water by one man or his family. In the future we will move on to projects concerned with the better use of the total annual water cycle over large regions, and the proper use of the resources of the oceans, perhaps through developing models of oceanic circulation, or the transfer of icebergs in order to use their water. Anthropos will use water in a creative way for his own purposes.

In the same way, with the development and expansion of recycling techniques, Anthropos will take over the management of solid waste (that until now has been left to Nature alone). Such developments will provide the answer to the excess mineral and chemical deposits that have begun to appear in our diminishing resources. Several studies have indicated that solid waste may well double in 15 years, so until recycling is achieved there will be increasing problems of land and water pollution.

There is no problem, however, that cannot be faced. The role played by industry is increasing and becoming wider than is usually thought. We must make proper use of natural and man-made resources and of our rising incomes, which means that wealth should not always be used for further expansion but for the organization of existing facilities and the production of a higher quality of life in general.

Transportation

Advances in technology and increasing production of all sorts will be most clearly expressed in the further development of transportation systems. There will be a need to transport more people, more goods, and more energy itself.

The transportation system created the city; it exists, and will always exist, as an expression of Anthropos' kinetic fields, that is, his ability to move away from his dwelling place and back to it. The transportation system decides how many people can afford to participate in urban life, and how far away from the center their participation can continue. The greatest successes, as well as the greatest problems in human settlements are connected with the organization of human movement. The human community created by Anthropos within the balanced cities of the past, where all movement was on foot and urban architecture and design remained within the human scale, was one of his greatest achievements. Today, however, Anthropos is experiencing one of his greatest failures in moving to the larger scale of the huge roadways and other modern Networks, which waste land and resources as well as time and energy, and cause extensive pollution.

It is certainly a waste of resources to use a car for transporting one or two passengers when only five percent of the car's energy is expended[22]. Yet more people use the car because they prefer to have freedom to decide their own movements and can use cars on old roads without waiting for highways to be built; this is why cars appear before railways in low-income countries.

However, Anthropos is now clearly recognizing the problems produced by cars and their Networks. Car engines which do not produce harmful exhausts are already being made, and will be manufactured in increasing numbers and improved quality. Highways will be turned into deepways — that is, underground tunnels — which will help preserve the human values and quality of life within cities as well as being more economic. These changes will be accomplished within a few decades.

Such developments will not solve all the problems of urban transportation; they will be expensive, and still will not give freedom of movement to those under 16, the old, the crippled and the sick, which accounts for at least half the population. Nor will they provide the much higher speeds currently demanded, as they were able to do at the beginning of the 19th century, that other point of revolutionary change in speeds.

A solution now exists to the problem of increased speeds which did not exist ten years ago, and that is the high-speed tube line which can travel at hundreds of kilometers an hour. The Tokaido railway between Tokyo and Osaka can travel at over 200 km.p.h. (120 m.p.h.). Experimental projects indicate that far higher speeds are possible, and before the end of this century speeds of many hundreds of km.p.h. are likely[23]. Systems of bubbles will operate in deep tubes in order to make use of gravity, and there will be other methods for producing speeds of some say up to tens of thousands of kilometers an hour, which would mean that the distance from Los Angeles to New York could be covered in 21 minutes[24]. Such solutions are only at the conceptual or experimental stages now, but they are being improved and developed, and we can be certain that in the next two generations there will be progress from present train speeds of 100 or 200 km.p.h. (60 or 120 m.p.h.) to speeds of over 1,000 km.p.h. (600 m.p.h.), and later to tens of thousands of kilometers an hour.

Another development which is certainly coming, and not just an idea created by people like ourselves, is a combination of the freedom now given by cars with the economy, speed, and equality between people offered by trains. This concept has been accepted by several research groups, like the one in the Transport Department of the U.S.A.[25]. It is probable that when trains moving at over a thousand kilometers an hour have been developed, private automated bubbles will be invented which will move in the same way.

Revolutionary changes are also expected in sea transportation, which will be used largely for the movement of goods. People will use sea travel for long trips far less, and for short trips they will use new types of boats currently being developed with high enough speeds to serve daily urban systems, such as those using electromagnetic flight (attractive or repulsive magnetic levitation combined with superconductivity) close to the surface of either ordinary roads or water. This has many advantages, such as speed, economy and flexibility. Some day such boats may be replaced by tunnels, such as the one being built to connect England with the continent of Europe.

The revolution that has taken place in the transportation of goods by sea is very big. We are already moving from fuel tankers with a load capacity of tens of thousands of tons to containers with a capacity of hundreds of thousands, or even one million tons. They are called mammoth tankers or sea giants, but they may be small in comparison to those of the future. For human settlements, it will mean that ports of a new type and of increasing economic importance will come into existence having an increasing attraction for Anthropos.

Airplanes are also going to increase their speeds and cross the Atlantic and the Pacific much faster. The first direct jump across the Atlantic was made in 33 hours and 32 minutes by Lindbergh in 1927. His time was cut to 14 hours by 1949, and to 6 hours 30 minutes by 1963. The fastest recorded crossing up to now was made by the Concorde when it flew in 3 hours 9 minutes from Paris to Boston in June 1974, and although environmentalists are protesting the introduction of supersonic flight, it seems that the Concorde will go into regular operation in the not too distant future.

Because of the increasing speeds on land, sea, and in the air, planes will be used more and more for longer distances, and for shorter ones be replaced by high-speed underground or underwater connections until, in a few generations, planes may be eliminated or used only for special surveys and emergencies.

We must expect that many more materials, including solids, will be moved through pipelines and so solve many problems, from technical to biological, within human settlements. This means that many of our Networks will move underground, and those who doubt this should remember what happened in the past with water and sewers. It is, in the end, a matter of economics.

On the subject of transportation, therefore, our conclusions are that speeds, which have a direct influence on the development of human settlements, will go on increasing in the future in continuation of the trends we have seen developing ever since the birth of the city of the present (fig. 90).

Communications

Next to transportation, the technological developments which will have most influence on the development of human settlements are those connected with communication and with the processing of information.

The growth of communications and acceleration in the means of gathering, transferring, storing, processing and disseminating information of all sorts will

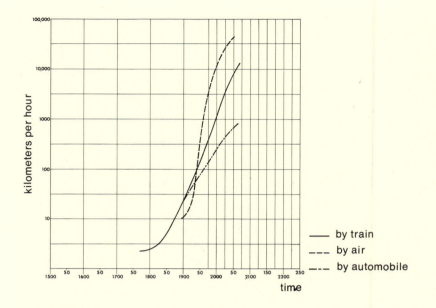

kilometers per hour

| 100,000 |
| 10,000 |
| 1000 |
| 100 |
| 10 |

1500　50　1600　50　1700　50　1800　50　1900　50　2000　50　2100　150　2200　250

time

—— by train
--- by air
-·-· by automobile

90.　past and future evolution of speeds influencing human settlements

continue to be some of the most important factors in welding larger and larger systems into integrated units. This growth will be expressed in many ways, from space communication or the simultaneous printing of a newspaper over the globe in one or more languages to the use of small portable radiotelephones and television sets, as well as the spread of social services, such as education and medicine, to the home.

So far as human settlements are concerned, some of these developments will have the effect of helping people to live further apart from each other, while others may lead them to decide to live closer together. Both trends must be expected to continue as they are at present. It is therefore reasonable to conclude that although advances in communication techniques will add services and quality to human settlements, they will neither spread them further apart nor bring them closer together any more than those other factors we have already mentioned.

26. The economy

We have looked at the container as it is at present, and have seen that developments in technology look very promising. We can now go on to look at likely developments in the economy, since the progress of the economy in general depends not only on Anthropos himself but also on the development of his technology. This has always been so, especially for the last 10,000 years at least.

It is easier for us to speak about the economy now than it was when we began this project. For example, we can calculate future food production more accurately, since when we started we made assumptions as to what it was likely to be and have continued to do so in the intervening period, so now we are in a better position to speak about the validity of our assumptions.

In the early stages of the project we devoted considerable attention to an analysis of how much the future growth of population was likely to be limited by a shortage of resources such as food, water, energy and minerals. As the project developed we were able to take into account new developments and new techniques, and found that the constraints, which we had assumed would be imposed at the beginning, were being weakened by new advances. Many developments which people then thought quite utopian have now become quite feasible and give us a far more optimistic picture of the maximum population which could be sustained in the future as we have defined it.

This is not to say that during the near and middle futures resource shortages might not touch off some major crises; shortages of many resources will undoubtedly arise between now and the end of the 20th century and in the beginning of the 21st. Nonetheless, it does seem safe to assume that in the long run the situation will ease as the anticipated new technologies and better international organization appear, and rising incomes all over the world make it possible to afford such new methods and materials.

Incomes

Incomes are rising and this is the first time in history that they have increased at such a high rate all over the world. It is not true that every individual person's income is rising, however, and in many countries there is still a very low average income of between $70 and $200 per capita per year, which is at the same level as before the industrial revolution. The average global national income (not the Gross National Product) was $950 per capita per year when we worked it out on a global base and is increasing at a rate of 4.1% per annum.

Growth must certainly continue for the low-income areas. High-income areas will certainly go on fighting their competitor nations to achieve better growth rates, and must also give higher incomes to their own poorer classes. Normally we would make projections for the same growth rates to continue for the future. However, since we are not making projections only for the next few decades, but for 250 years ahead, we must take into account that economic growth may be limited by the constraints of a limited container and so consider human capacity to face the problems such growth will create.

There is no doubt that growth has had limitations imposed on it throughout human history. This must have been clear to people who lived in those villages and city-states of the past which survived for thousands of years. Plato, in his concept of the ideal, static city-state, presented the case for such limitations and the philosophy of it very well, and the oracle at Delphi guided the city-states towards colonization so as to avoid wars because of the expanding human population and its needs. Malthus also clearly described the limitations imposed on constant human expansion. The fact remains, however, that despite all these warnings, the economy continued to grow and still is growing. Therefore we do not accept recent pessimistic prophecies of zero growth as reasonable; on the other hand, neither can we prove, as some people believe and we all hope, that growth can go on increasing at its present high rate.

Economic growth can be expected to continue during the next century measured by per capita income at the global scale at a minimum rate of 1% per annum. Based on the estimated rate of technological progress alone, this is the minimum growth possible. It is also the minimum necessary to insure the sustained general development and spread of our present technological civilization, including rising consumption of energy and material goods, rationally increasing incomes, spreading education, improving general health and nutrition, and urbanization. We believe that the actual growth is more likely to be between 2% and 3%, as at present, and that it can be even higher if international organization develops more efficiently.

To remain as objective as possible, we prepared three sets of assumptions on future growth rates: low, medium and high. We combined them with the three population growth assumptions (as discussed later in this Part), also low, medium and high, in order to obtain nine models for economic growth (fig. 91). We assumed that a higher rate of population growth might reasonably be correlated with a lower rate of economic growth. We then correlated the estimated levels of per capita income with estimated levels of essential future

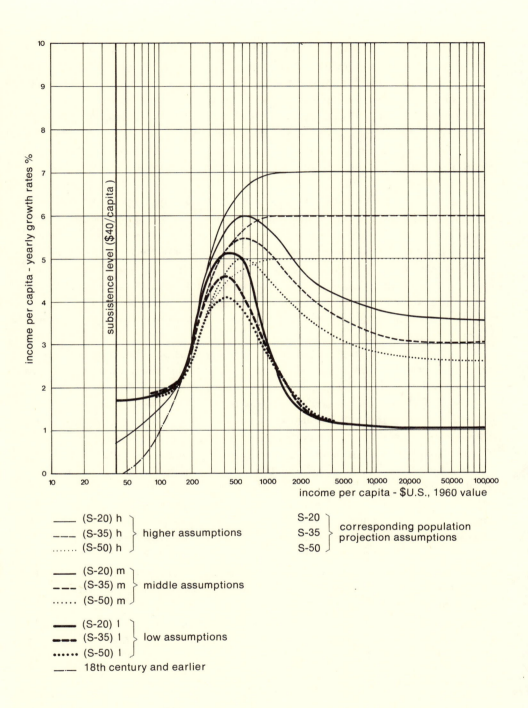

91.　assumed growth rate curves for global per capita
income (the 9 "development curves")

expenditure on such things as energy, education, public health, environmental control and basic applied research, thus obtaining a range of probable future orders of magnitude for these variables. From earlier projections made independently in the earlier phases of the project, we looked for single variables out of these ones and saw that we could now bring these projections into a state of mutual interdependence and overall consistency. We also checked and compared our findings with those of other projects — though naturally we had to limit ourselves basically to those which shared the three basic assumptions we listed earlier.

We found that the results achieved in the field of technological forecasting — which are among the most reliable in our opinion — are generally compatible with ours. We also found that the majority of eminent economists — of whom a considerable number were asked to give their reactions to our views — agreed with us that the medium growth rates were more likely than either zero economic growth (or extremely low, say 1% or less) or the indefinite maintenance of present high rates (such as the 3-7% average of the higher-income countries).

Here are the characteristics of the three assumptions about economic growth in some detail (see fig. 91):

The High (h) long-range economic growth model is based on the assumption that the present average growth rates of technologically-advanced countries (5-7%) will be maintained forever.

The Low (l) long-range economic growth model is based on the assumption that in the long run growth rates of per capita income will tend asymptotically towards 1%, i.e. the rate sustained by technological progress alone, all the other factors that could contribute to economic growth having practically vanished.

The Middle (m) long-range economic growth model assumes an intermediate situation, with per capita income growth rates tending asymptotically towards a value between 2.5% and 3%. This is the assumption regarded as most likely by the majority of economists.

The global income rates which correspond to each of these three projections are shown in fig. 92 and the global investment levels in fig. 93. We cannot predict which of these three should become the basis for our calculations until the factors of food production, mineral resources and population have been considered further.

The fact that all three of our assumptions speak of economic growth should not, as we said, make us think that what happens on average all over the world also happens to each individual or nation. More than 50% and less than 66% of all the people in the world today still live in poverty — that is, in countries where the average income is less than $300 a year. If this is poverty by today's standards, we must also remember that at least half of these people definitely have less than $150 a year, which is poverty even by the standards of the pre-industrial era.

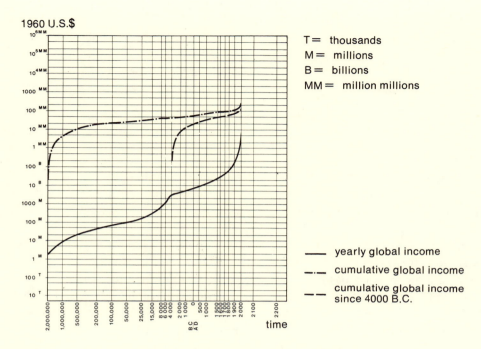

1960 U.S.$

T = thousands
M = millions
B = billions
MM = million millions

—— yearly global income
—·— cumulative global income
– – cumulative global income since 4000 B.C.

92.   projections of global world income

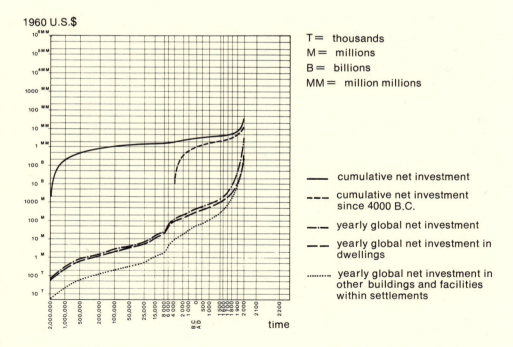

1960 U.S.$

T = thousands
M = millions
B = billions
MM = million millions

—— cumulative net investment
– – – cumulative net investment since 4000 B.C.
—·— yearly global net investment
– – yearly global net investment in dwellings
······· yearly global net investment in other buildings and facilities within settlements

93.   projections of global world investment

We try to face the problem of these inequalities and its implications for overall growth later on. We would like to say here, however, that there are international organizations like F.A.O., and individual people like Gunnar Myrdal in his book *The Challenge of World Poverty*[26], who are not simply concerned, but are proposing plans for action.

Food

Food is the most important sector of the economy; problems of food supply have certainly been of the greatest concern for mankind in the past, as they are today. Everyone speaks of the food crisis, but we must point out that although a considerable proportion of mankind is still starving, the situation is improving with every year that passes. Although world population is increasing by 2.5% a year, food production is increasing by at least 3% a year on average, and in Southeast Asia the increase has been even higher in spite of single years of low yield leading to temporary famine. Since the people in high-income countries, or high-income people in low-income countries, are not consuming any more food per person, the increase in food is being consumed by those people who need it. We are still in a period of crisis, but the crisis is not new: it was certainly worse before World War II in some countries like Bangladesh, and the problem is gradually decreasing.

The big question is not whether food production is going to increase, but if the increase will relate properly to the growth of population, and how it will be distributed amongst people. To deal with this question we must look at the factors which influence food production, such as the availability of labor, land and energy.

In terms of the amount of labor used for food production, recent experience in northern America showed that, whereas in 1800 one person produced enough food for five people, by 1910 he was producing enough for eight, and by 1970 enough for 38 (fig. 94). As other countries are showing the same trends, and as we know that the countryside is being abandoned because of, among other reasons, the high productivity per person, we have no reason to think we will have any problems connected with lack of labor for food production in the foreseeable future. We assume that mankind will recognize the need to pay and treat its farmers better, and if so, we need not fear any problems at all as regards labor.

This great increase in food production per head "has been achieved one-third by mechanization, and two-thirds by increased productivity brought about basically by application of biological and biochemical research to agriculture"[27].

Next to labor comes the land needed for agriculture, that is, mainly for food production. At present, global use of land for agriculture is 1.3 billion ha (3.2 billion acres), or 8.75% of the usable land area of the earth. Calculations made

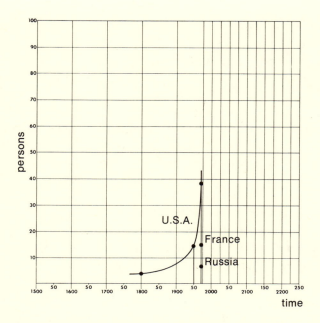

indicative sketch

the vertical axis represents the number of people fed by food produced by one farmer

94. agricultural production: number of people fed by food produced by one farmer

by the United Nations as well as ourselves estimate that there are also 395 million ha (975 million acres) that could be used for production which is not being used, that is, another 2.65% of the usable land area. Although there are estimates which speak of doubling the amount of land used for agriculture[28], meaning the use of 2.6 billion ha (6.42 billion acres), or 17.5% of the total land area, we limit our assumption of the amount that will be used to 1.69 billion ha (3.93 billion acres) made up by the present 1.3 billion ha (3.2 billion acres) plus an additional 395 million ha (975 million acres), or 11.41% of the total land. We do this for the reason we stated earlier, that we know so little about the basic balances of land use and the possible effects of changing these balances that it would not be reasonable for us to change them unduly.

Whether or not we can use more than this area for food production depends on how much land we are going to use up for the built-up parts of settlements, and this in turn depends on the increase in population and on the densities at which people are going to live. We deal with this later in this Part. What we must say at this point is that there is no agreement on a global, or even on a national scale as to how far we will be able to occupy areas like the Amazon basin, which are not being used for production at all at present. Leading experts, like the Brazilian geographer Hilgard O'Reilly Sternberg, believe that low-income countries play "ecological roulette" by destroying natural vegetation in an often unnecessary quest for more land[29]. On the other hand, we know that civilization developed when Anthropos managed to make fields from the forest areas, and that several countries, especially in Africa, need more land for cultivation. It therefore remains an open question how far and by what processes we can take over land not yet touched by Anthropos, both for food production and for the building of settlements.

Since we have no positive facts as yet with which to answer these questions, we assume that there will be changes within regions and within countries, but we take it that the present situation will continue almost as it is so far as the total proportion of land used for food production in the foreseeable future is concerned, and until a full model of ecosystems is developed.

Our assumption of the division of land areas is therefore as in table 5.

This table does not yet take into account the forecasts which have been made for the future area which will be covered by built-up areas of human settlements, but assumes for the moment that they will not grow beyond their present boundaries.

The question is, what is the capacity of the container to produce food, granted that no more than 11.41% of the total land area is used for agriculture, and 14.34% for pastures (that is, that no more than 25.75% of the total land area is used for food production of all sorts)?

land	million ha	million acres	%
to remain without direct impact from Anthropos	7,095	17,518	47.78
used for cultivation	1,695	4,185	11.41
covered by pastures	2,130	5,259	14.34
covered by forests	3,530	8,716	23.78
covered by human settlements	400	987	2.69
total	14,850	36,665	100.00

table 5.   division of land areas

Several estimates have been made of how great the increase in food production can be. They lead us to believe that we can support a population ranging from four times higher than the 1965 one, that is, 12 billion people[30], to 90 billion if we all maintain a Japanese standard of diet[31]. Many independent predictions lead us to similar optimistic conclusions[32], although there are also several pessimistic ones.

Despite the fact that it has recently become fashionable to be pessimistic, our research has made us more and more optimistic about the future possibilities of food production. At the time when we made our first estimates, algae cultures in tanks seemed to offer the most promising supplements to traditional sources of protein. However, as a result of progress in microbiology, chemistry and other branches of science and technology, a considerable number of new alternative methods of protein production have appeared during the past decade, such as production from petrochemical by-products, from a variety of sources related to microbiology and a variety of algae to be industrially cultivated, from the prospects of ocean farming, and special surface cultures in the tropical oceans exploiting photosynthesis to the maximum, and from direct physiochemical synthesis, and so on. It seems almost certain that more novel methods of protein production will be invented in the next few decades, and that some at least will prove feasible for large-scale production. Progress in the production of protein has been more or less paralleled by progress in the production of all other basic foods, although the application of new methods may take longer in some cases. When we made estimates for future food production in 1961 assuming a combination of novel and traditional methods, we decided that a world population of 40-50 billion could probably be sustained in the remote future. The calculations we make now, taking into account the appearance of new methods of food production, and even allowing for improved standards of food consumption in the future, suggest that even higher levels of global population could be sustained than our initial estimate indicated.

The big question is at what speed and under what conditions of technology, economy and organization can food production be increased? It is not clear, for example, when we can expect food production to begin in the oceans, although there are forecasts that this will be done, and that from about the year 2000 we can expect 20% of our total food needs to be supplied in this way[33]. There can be no exact estimate because no proper models exist or can now be developed relating advances in technology to the additional energy that will be required to apply them, and both these to the cost. However, we can be quite certain that under normal conditions food production is going to increase at a higher rate than the increase in population, since the majority of agriculturists are optimistic about increasing the yield per hectare through the progress of biological technology, and the prospects for the large-scale introduction of novel methods of food production are quite encouraging. Although this may not reduce the amount of labor required, progress in mechanical technology will continue to do so.

We therefore proceed on this basis, believing as René Dubos says that: "the future of land management is intimately bound to the development of new sources of energy, as are all other aspects of human life"[34]. As we have already said, we believe that these developments in energy production are in the process of realization.

We can conclude, then, that for the foreseeable future the production of food will not impose limits on population growth. Food production, however, is likely to create pressing problems in the near future, and many experts do foresee large-scale famine over large areas during the next 10 or 20 years, resulting in world-wide crises. Later, however, the situation will begin to improve slowly as new methods of food production reach practical feasibility and as organization, storage and distribution improves. Eventually, the problem of food production may be one of quality rather than quantity.

Since the process involved in producing food will change, and since we will move towards agricultural methods closer to those of industry with a need for higher levels of training and efficiency, human settlements are bound to be affected. Peasants will continue to abandon their farms for the big cities, not only for the social reasons of the past, but also for new economic reasons. It is needless to say that the last hunters and isolated nomads will disappear, even before the isolated farmers do.

It is probable that within a few generations a large proportion of the food needed by Anthropos will be produced by techniques needing far less space, so that much less land will be needed to produce sufficient food for each person. Also, since more food will probably be produced from the sea, the pressure on scarce agricultural land is likely to be eased and settlements built close to the sea will become even more important.

Minerals and metals

After food production, we must look at the next most important resources of minerals and metals, and consider the problems of the extraction and primary conversion of raw materials for industrial processes.

For many thousands of years, and up until a few centuries ago, Anthropos made use of only seven metals: copper, gold, silver, iron, tin, lead and mercury. Today he uses more than fifty. He is also using them in such increased quantities that the supply of some is becoming critical, and we are receiving warnings about the dangers involved.

On the other hand, it is certain that reserves exist which cannot be used at present, for example the manganese nodules in the ocean bed (not to mention the enormous quantities in "poor" minerals, the exploitation of which may gradually become economical in the future with improving technologies). "One study of reserves in the Pacific Ocean alone came up with an estimate that the nodules contained 358 billion tons of manganese equivalent, at present rates of consumption, to reserves for 400,000 years, compared to known land reserves of only 100 years. The nodules contain equally staggering amounts of aluminum, nickel, cobalt, and other metals. Most of these resources exist at great depths of 5,000 to more than 15,000 feet, yet within five to ten years the technology will exist for commercial mining operations, a development that will open to exploitation virtually unlimited metal reserves."[35] The situation with coal, oil and gas, for which offshore drilling has already started, is of a similar nature in this respect but the quantities are not at all unlimited. Although pressing problems are likely to crop up in the near future, later, with new technologies, alternative sources of energy will replace traditional fuels more and more. So in spite of all the problems which exist, it does not seem that scarcities of minerals will limit the growth of global population to a level lower than that already imposed by the density and habitability of the various land areas. Although there may be crises and bottlenecks in the supply of certain raw materials in the near future, we do not think they will continue to happen in the remote future. This may seem paradoxical, but is defensible for a number of reasons. The main ones are rising levels of energy production, the rising economy, and the continuing developments in science and technology which are leading to greater efficiency in everything relating to the extraction and conversion of resources. In the long run, more thorough and systematic prospecting is expected to reveal new deposits of many minerals. With new technological developments it should also become possible to satisfy rising demands by the exploitation of lower quality or less easily accessible deposits, such as those on the ocean floor and those at greater distances below the surface of the earth, or by the extraction of highly diffused minerals and chemicals from sea water. Increased recycling of materials should also help greatly to reduce demand for new production, and when and if resources become scarcer and more expensive, the development of substitutes is bound to be encouraged, including the invention of synthetic and composite materials, which hold out unexpectedly encouraging and far-reaching promise even now.

Such developments have created, and are creating big problems for the environment, which are very dangerous indeed in some areas. However, on the global scale, it is fairly certain that neither the production of minerals, energy or manufactured products is likely to be uncontrollably space-consuming or environment-polluting, and therefore there is no need to make special estimates for this aspect of the problem at this stage of our study.

27. The capacity of the container

At the beginning of this section we explained how little we really know about our total system of life or about the ecosystem of which it is a part. Despite this, the time has now come for us to try and estimate the total capacity of our container to sustain Anthropos on the basis of what we do know, and where we do not know, what we can assume. If Plato was able to do this 24 centuries ago and estimated the capacity of his ideal city-state, then we at least must have as much courage to try and estimate the capacity of our city-state of the future — that is, the whole globe as a container.

Such an estimate can only be based on general human experience, which makes it quite clear that balance between all the elements of our life is a necessity. We know that many different civilizations reached the same conclusion: that what is necessary to save Anthropos' life is balance. The Chinese in the "classical" Tung period held that the concept of the ruler's task was to unify heaven, earth and man"[36]. The ancient Greeks had the ideal of harmony personified in the god Apollo.

It is natural to ask how we can hope to reach such a state of balance in today's world of growing and expanding forces, without apparently enough energy or resources. There is only one thing to do, and that is to remember that if the hunters and farmers had made estimates of their future resources of energy based only on the wood contained in the forests of their day, they would also have been very pessimistic about the future of mankind. It is lucky for us that either they did not make such estimates, or else they confined them to the area of their particular village, and left their children to discover new sources of energy and create civilization and the City of Anthropos.

In order to work out what a balanced estimate might be, we first worked out many individual estimates. Some of these have already been described, others, especially those concerning population, are to follow.

Many of our earlier estimates, some made as early as 1963, and others which have been published in various forms, have now been compared with the results of other projects. It has also been possible for us to repeat a number of the calculations made during the early phases of the project in greater detail, in particular those dealing with the restraints that might be imposed on the expansion of global population by the shortage of single resources. The very fact that this has resulted in such a marked relaxation in the degree of restraint, which we then calculated might be imposed by shortages, corroborates still further the central conclusion of this entire project that it is the habitable area of the land together with acceptable regional densities of habitation that will impose crucial and binding constraints on global population expansion.

We have made all our estimates for the future as we have already defined it, that is, for the period of the next 250 years. Here, however, we face our greatest difficulty, because the accuracy of the estimates depends on the exact definition of time and space. How time will affect things, however, will be different according to the rate at which things operating in time change their force. The population is increasing all over the earth, but to an unpredictable degree. Some countries are already suffering from the pressure of population because of economic limitations mostly imposed by lack of space, but also because of cultural, social, biological, and other factors. However, such limitations may be entirely changed in the future and then the habitable area of land should be increased. Then again, present population trends in certain areas may change and even be reversed. The population of Europe, for instance, could increase as a result of the influx of so many workers from other continents instead of tending to remain stable as at present. Things could also happen faster with future advances in technology. We are used to a certain rate of progress in such things as economic development and urbanization, but if we achieve a much higher rate of productivity in the future, the same stretch of time might result in a much greater advance, so the effects of the unit of time involved could be enormously greater.

Limitation from space is going to become more acute because in some areas the population is reaching the limits of its container. It may reach the limits of space on land, and if it does we may create some settlements on the water, and even put other solutions into operation that may sound strange or ridiculous today — but it is too early for us to talk about such solutions. The fact is that with humanity filling the earth, space will once more come to play the limiting role it played for the ancient and medieval city-states, and for many other cultures of the past within their own areas. The City of the Future may become an urban settlement which will find itself to be in the same relationship to the whole space of the earth as the ancient Greek city-state was to the space in the surrounding narrow valley in which it grew.

We must keep such considerations in mind and recognize that all the estimates which follow are based on assumptions which may be completely altered by events in the five generations to come. All our calculations must be considered to be the best estimates we can make on the basis of what we know today. They will have to be revised continually, since even one change in any of the many factors involved — such, for instance, as the earlier achievement of energy production by fusion — would entirely change the prospects of the globe in every way, so that every estimated development would take place at a different speed.

Summing-up

The conclusions achieved by the many studies we have made with the use of models and computers are presented here in a clear and simple summary, so that they be understood by anyone interested in the City of the Future, even if he is not a specialist in one of the many fields involved in the project.

The capacity of the container to support Anthropos and all his interests is as follows:

One: If the container (that is, the total land area of the globe) is covered by a continuous urban settlement at a reasonable density of 60 people per ha (25 per acre), which is two-thirds of the present average density within urban built-up areas, then it can hold 891 billion people (see page 180 ff.).

Two: If, as already agreed, we should leave 50% of the total land area untouched by Anthropos so as not to invade this part of Nature, and the remaining 50% of land surface were covered by a built-up settlement, then it could hold 668 billion people (see page 181).

Three: If we also leave aside enough land to enable people to move outside their urban settlements into the countryside and have life and entertainment there, then the container could hold 223 billion people.

Four: Since there are no signs of forthcoming food imports from other planets, and since the time when all food production might take place within factories is too distant, enough land must also be reserved for the production of food and other goods. When this is done the container can hold 22 billion people, that is, only one tenth of the numbers that can be supported without land for food production.

Five: This means that the container can support 22 billion people in normal and desirable conditions of urban life as we see it today in terms of Anthropos' need for space and production capacity, and that this number of people can be satisfied so long as the production of energy, the progress of technology and the economy develop in the proper way, as may reasonably be expected. This figure can be taken as the capacity of the normal container 150 years from now.

Six: There are no limitations imposed on the achievement of this population figure by the availability of water. We already have enough water for 19 billion, and the remaining 3 billion can very easily be supplied if we collect more of the annual rainfall on land (see page 185).

Seven: There are no other limitations on the achievement of such a figure, provided we assume that Anthropos, as he has in the past, does solve practically all the problems connected with pollution and environmental conservation.

For those who worry about Anthropos' impact on Nature, we should explain that although Anthropos will infiltrate 50% of the total land surface, he will only have direct influence on 7.55% of the total land area (table 6).

Table 6 is based on various assumptions, such as that Anthropos will not interfere at all with the zones reserved for wildlife, although this does not mean that he will not visit them or establish research stations there. We are also making assumptions about the probable degree of Anthropos' impact on the ecological systems within each type of land, since it will not be equal throughout each zone. For example, it is doubtful if Anthropos changes the system more than 10% to 15% in the areas used as pastures, while even in the built-up areas of settlements, so long as his density of habitation remains at no more than 90 persons per ha (35 per acre), 30% of the land remains as green areas in the form of parks or private gardens, so even there Anthropos has only direct impact on 70% of the land area.

We can see from such calculations that the area affected by Anthropos' total impact can be as little as 7.55% of the whole. As far as the open green areas are concerned the situation is even better than it seems, because a percentage of the outlying areas of human settlements (type 5.1 in table 6) is also going to consist of forest and pasture, so that there will actually be 22% of the whole land area under forest (the 20% already shown in 2.1, 2.2, and 2.3, plus 40% of the 5% of the built-up section 5.1 of human settlements) and pastures will represent 14% of the whole (the 12% already shown plus 40% of the 5% in section 5.1 of human settlements).

The division of land into its various uses can be seen as a whole in fig. 95, which also includes the possible variation in which totally built-up areas of settlements may cover 3.5% rather than 2.5% of the 7.5% allowed for human settlements as a whole, if the average density drops below 90 persons per ha (35 per acre).

When we compare this division with the one existing at present (fig. 76), we can see that because of conditions of habitability and other factors, the overall situation will probably not change in any important degree except in the case of the percentage covered by built-up areas. As the total land covered by built-up areas changes from 0.27% to 2.5%, the actual area covered will increase from 40 million ha (99 million acres) to 371 million ha (916 million acres), but this alteration will not really change the overall balance of land distribution according to uses on the global level.

general categories				zones				impact of Anthropos	
No.	type	surface	%	No.	type	surface	%	% by zone	% of total
1	wildlife	7,425	50.0	1.1	wildlife	7,425	50.0	0	0.00
2	forests	2,970	20.0	2.1	no intervention	1,484	10.0	1	0.10
				2.2	very low intervention	743	5.0	3	0.15
				2.3	low intervention	743	5.0	5	0.25
3	pastures	1,782	12.0	3.1	no intervention	1,039	7.0	10	0.70
				3.2	low intervention	743	5.0	15	0.75
4	cultivated	1,559	10.5	4.1	natural cultivation	816	5.5	20	1.10
				4.2	covered cultivation	743	5.0	25	1.25
5	human settlements	1,114	7.5	5.1	open development	743	5.0	30	1.50
				5.2	built-up areas	371	2.5	70	1.75
	total	14,850	100.0		total	14,850	100.0		7.55

table 6.   probable global land uses and direct impact of Anthropos on land in million hectares

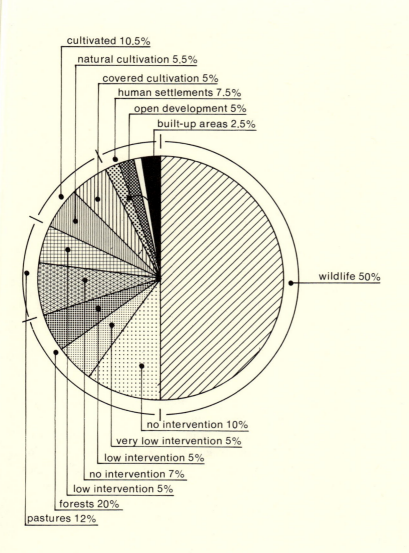

cultivated 10.5%
natural cultivation 5.5%
covered cultivation 5%
human settlements 7.5%
open development 5%
built-up areas 2.5%

wildlife 50%

no intervention 10%
very low intervention 5%
low intervention 5%
no intervention 7%
low intervention 5%
forests 20%
pastures 12%

95.   probable division of land uses in Ecumenopolis

28. Organization

We have already seen that many of the problems concerned with organization today are due to our failure to mobilize human courage and resources.

We mentioned the example of the inequalities in incomes, and although average income levels are expected to rise on the global scale, this by no means indicates that people in every area of the world are going to become richer. This in itself is not something new; never in history has there been equality between people all over the globe, whether in the days of hunters, farmers, city-states or empires. There were always some areas with a high density of habitation in which the human container was filled to capacity, such as Greece in classical times, or Italy and Spain during the Renaissance, and other areas with low densities or even no people at all, such as much of America or Australia at that time. There were always big differences between different peoples in terms of incomes, degree of technological achievement, and organizational capacity, and that is why there were always difficulties leading to colonization, conflicts and wars.

We can see the overall image of this situation in fig. 16. At each stage, the earth was never entirely filled by the number of people that theoretically would have been possible had those people who had reached the most advanced stage of technology and organizational capacity occupied it all according to their way of life. The whole earth was never covered by Anthropos living according to one system of life, since Society always developed in different ways under different conditions and in different areas.

Today the situation is the same, but there are even greater extremes. In ancient days there might have been only one man as rich as King Croesus, and many poor men; today there are many whole nations with much higher incomes and more land and resources than other nations, and within the same nation there are many men richer than Croesus while many are still as poor as the poorest citizens of the past. The gaps between people are increasing in every way, in every field and at all levels, from gaps between nations to gaps between individuals within nations. Never before has there been such a variety of differences on our globe in all scales and within all the different expressions of life.

Because such enormous gaps exist, there is a general imbalance in the conditions of life between different people. The most important and critical imbalance concerns the supply of food, but some of the world's people also have a far greater supply of energy, land or capital, and a higher degree of technology and education than others. Even when we look at the densities of population and see how people are distributed over the globe (fig. 96), we can see a great lack of balance there also. There is an equivalent lack of balance in the distribution of areas of habitability and many other things.

We must therefore ask ourselves, what is going to happen because of the existence of these enormous inequalities and crises of poverty? We know that in the past, stronger nations solved their own problems by the colonization of unoccupied land, by the invasion of weaker areas, or by struggle and warfare. It is unlikely that such solutions can be resorted to today, since there is no longer any unoccupied land that is not already owned by some nation, nor are wars and invasions any longer a probable method for the real solution of problems of even one nation only. We have said that this study of the City of the Future assumes a normal process of development without the outbreak of global wars, so if such outbreaks do occur the situation will change in many ways and fall outside our present discussion; therefore we do not work on such alternatives here.

Throughout human history there has been a constant ideal of peace and stability in many cultures and many parts of the world. It might have been achieved under Alexander as Arnold Toynbee says[37]. Indian myths developed the idea of "a worldwide empire of enduring tranquility"[38]. The Romans created such conditions in the Mediterranean during the period of the *pax Romana*. We have this worldwide dream of peace again today, and for the first time in history it does seem humanly possible to realize it; the question is, how and when?

It is possible that with the widespread realization of the unique advantages of peace today, and the genuine efforts that are being made towards it, a state of peace — allowing perhaps for only local and eventually controllable wars — could be achieved. This could happen precisely at the time the increasing differences of today begin to stabilize and decrease, towards the end of the near future or the beginning of the middle future. As people's income levels start to become more equal and the gaps between their education and social position

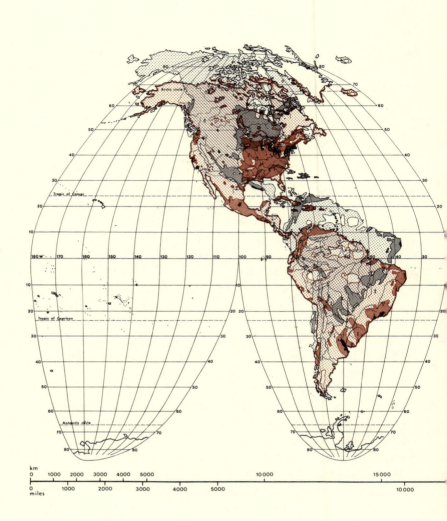

96.　global distribution of population densities in 1960

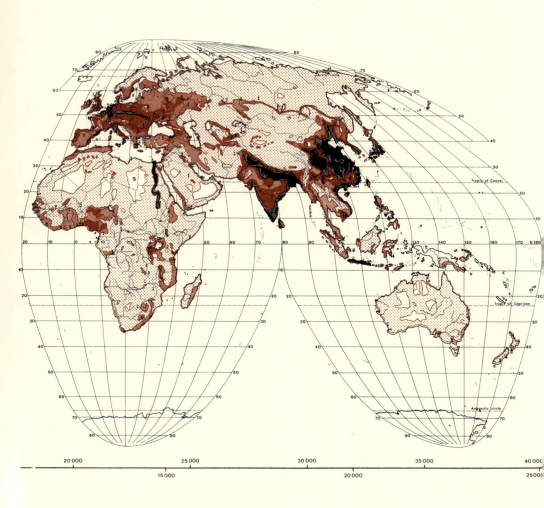

population densities:

☐	uninhabited	
⠿	1 - 9	persons per sq. km
▨	10 - 49	persons per sq. km
▨	50 - 99	persons per sq. km
▨	100 - 199	persons per sq. km
■	200 and over	persons per sq. km

disappear, we may expect them to become conscious of a state of overall balance in the world, and aware of the more equitable distribution of wealth and power. It is precisely such a feeling that would make the attainment of world peace seem genuinely realistic.

One solution to the problem of inequalities between people is the movement of poor people towards areas with better resources. This is already happening, but mostly within the same nation, as we can now see in the movement of people from the south of Italy and Spain towards the north of their countries, and as it happened in the U.S.A. when people moved towards their northern, western, and richer areas. People with lower incomes move to places with better opportunities and, after struggling hard, manage to reduce the gap which exists between themselves and others. This type of movement can be seen within the area of the European Common Market, again from the south to the northwest, and in other places also.

Such movements, however, are only important between villages and cities, or between poor and rich areas of countries, provided people do not cross political boundaries. It is true, as shown by a 1971 opinion poll[39] (16 million adults in the U.S.A. said they would like to emigrate), that many people express a desire to emigrate; but either they do not do so when they belong to high-income countries or else they are not easily absorbed by other countries. As was shown by the 1970 Swiss vote on expelling 300,000 foreign workers, which was only narrowly defeated and followed by restrictions[40], trans-national movements of people are not permitted beyond a certain level. It is needless to elaborate here on the huge difficulties experienced by Asians and Africans immigrating into high-income countries, or even by Asians in East Africa.

It is clear, therefore, that movement of people is not an immediately feasible answer to the lack of balance that exists between people in such areas as southern Asia or Africa. The fact that more than 15 million refugees already exist within two dozen countries of the world[41], and are suffering a lot because they cannot easily be absorbed there, proves that this is not a solution for the immediate future. If it can be done in a few decades or generations, then it will be a great victory for mankind in solving its own problems.

With the large increases in population that are expected, and the increasing gaps and maldistributions of all sorts, the pressure for redistribution will greatly increase. At this point, conditions for the acceptance of immigrants will have to be revised by the receiving countries, and certainly by persuasion in order to avoid a crisis — but we cannot exclude the possible use of force or even local wars. Redistribution may have to be imposed by future conditions to some degree beyond the willingness of receiving countries who wish to preserve their ethnic integrity by excluding immigrants or refugees. Those countries with low overall densities, large available areas, and good prospects for development will some day have to revise their policies concerning the acceptance of immigrants, or withstand terrible pressures from all sides against their autonomy to which they would have to succumb eventually.

It does not seem likely that people will be able to move to other countries in large enough numbers to correct completely the imbalances which exist between them today, yet there is hope that this could be achieved by international collaboration of various sorts. We believe, and proceed on the assumption, that *internationalization of many types of activities will continue and intensify during the next century.*

It is becoming increasingly apparent to everyone today that Anthropos is living within a single closed system. Attitudes and ideologies which fail to reflect this enormously important fact will come to be seen as provincial and out of date. The global community comes ever closer to reality as all nations recognize that they are part of the same threatened earth. Although we cannot say that a unified world government will definitely be established during the period covered by this study, it is fully justifiable to assume at least a movement in that direction. It is reasonable to believe that in the long run humanity will become aware of the sinister consequences of any movement away from increasing internationalization. Many signs do point in this direction: the rapidly increasing number of international organizations, the broadening of their jurisdiction, the expanding network of worldwide communications, and the increasingly easy and rapid movement of people around the world. Our own conclusions, however, lead us to include a cautionary note. Since the period between now and the turn of the century is expected to be a particularly difficult time all over the world, it is quite possible that the movement towards internationalization may suffer severe setbacks during the next 25 years, and may not begin to gain real momentum until after the anticipated crises have begun to die down — which is expected to be sometime in the early decades of the 21st century.

One very important factor is the physical systems of transportation and communication which by necessity bring people closer together. Since it is unlikely that the progress of science and technology will be repressed, and since a worldwide intensification of communication in all fields must inevitably result from such progress, and in spite of a possible increase in the number of countries with totalitarian forms of government during the next generation or so, it is likely that in more and more fields there will be a move towards international cooperation. As international organizations in all fields grow in number, size, sophistication and coverage, they will link more individuals and groups all over the globe and serve as a focal point at which needs can be translated into responses.

The success of such economic international organizations as the Common Market, the increase in international associations and publications, the growth in trade even between areas in total ideological opposition, such as the U.S. and Red China, or across the Iron Curtain, can all be seen as foreshadowing the global trend towards internationalization. Despite the fact that some governments show isolationist or nationalistic tendencies, and the failure of some programs of international cooperation, internationalization has been steadily growing in many fields during recent decades. With the increasing degree of connectivity in transportation and communication that is postulated for the future, we expect this trend to continue, if not to be strengthened.

Since such internationalization will increase the number of people and organizations having a personal stake in the maintenance of world peace and order, it is likely that international tension will begin to reduce somewhere near the beginning of the next century. Many long-standing sources of international, ethnic, and racial tensions are also likely to be reduced by the substantial narrowing of inequalities in income levels which are predicted.

It is indeed probable that by the next century the units of government administration and political power will evolve into much larger units than they are at present within nation-states. It is impossible to predict whether or not they will be united under a world government, or will operate independently. It would be logical to expect that the large units will correspond roughly to the natural cultural and geographic regions. The physical structure of the globe must have a major influence on the boundaries of such large units and on their hierarchical relationship so that the most tightly integrated segments of human settlements will form a natural skeleton for the evolution of major political units. It is probable that the existing national boundaries of the 20th century will have faded by the 21st into a more rational and continuous hierarchical political division over the earth's surface, or that they will be at least weakened in their present form.

We live in a global system and some aspects of its organization, such as the management of the oceans and the atmosphere, can only be done on a global scale. Other activities, nonetheless, will still give individual people and groups the chance to participate in local government.

All political systems during the next century — regardless of their underlying ideologies — will undoubtedly make more use of such sophisticated techniques of planning and management as systems theory, cybernetics, and control and decision theories. Many important advances are expected as a result of improved technology, such as two-way communication between government and citizens and the provision of a much better basis for governmental decisions with quantified data, expert advice, and the greater possibility of contact with public opinion. Much administrative work should be done faster and more efficiently. Citizens may also be expected to take an increasing part in the management and evolution of their own settlements, since they will have more money, less working time and therefore more free time, and a higher level of education and more information than they ever did in the past. It is probable that people in the future will value personal involvement in constructive social and political action far more highly than being simply a rubberstamp voter.

We therefore consider it very likely that several states will become unified into well-operating systems. This may begin with the countries of the European Common Market, whose members, from the Scottish islands, which have a new role, to the Mediterranean countries, are already being given new opportunities.

There is hope that through such means the imbalances which exist at present between resources and people will be gradually corrected. In other places, however, the solution is neither so easy — for example, in South Africa where a segregationist nation has the technology of the 20th century and the social system of the Middle Ages — nor complete in terms of solving such problems as the exploitation of African mineral resources by other nations. Such big problems may need a real crisis, an uprising by the people or local wars, in order for a solution to be reached. However, the example of a country such as Zambia, and the way in which it managed to become independent, does give great hope that even these problems may be solved.

If all these natural optimistic predictions are fulfilled, then we may hope that Anthropos will go on using both the capacity of the globe and its resources in a rational way, with the elimination of as many of the imbalances between people as possible. If the problems of imbalance can be eliminated, then the capacity of the global container will be 22 billion people.

Taking the globe as a whole, we can see that 10,000 years ago Anthropos reached a population that was 64% of the earth's actual capacity to support him, and by 1825 he had reached 20% of the capacity existing at that time (fig. 16). In fact, within individual village territories, many city-states and national states, Anthropos did reach the total capacity of his container to support him. The conclusion is that within his organized spatial units Anthropos did reach the limit of the capacity of his container, and then went beyond this limit by means of colonizing other areas and strengthening his centers.

In our case we cannot colonize any other areas, and the big question is how quickly can Anthropos organize the space and resources he has when he is using the whole globe as his spatial unit? As soon as he does this, the globe will achieve its natural capacity of about 22 billion people. If Anthropos does not achieve such global organization then the population will remain below capacity level, as it did in the past — although not as low as 20% of the total capacity, since in those days many parts of the world were not in contact with one another.

The reasonable assumption is that Anthropos will achieve much more in the way of organization than he did in 8000 B.C. or in 1825 A.D. A similar situation was that of the area of the ancient Mediterranean world where, even when it was not unified, Anthropos may well have achieved population levels between 50% and 100% of the local capacity.

On this basis we proceed with the assumption that if Anthropos does manage to organize himself on a global scale, he may reach a population level of 22 billion, and if he does not manage to organize himself, then his population will probably not reach more than 15 billion.

29. Population

We have looked at the globe as Anthropos' container and at some of the things, like developments in technology, economy and the supply of energy, that are likely to affect its capacity in the future. We can now make some attempt to estimate the future evolution of the population. We have discussed things in this order simply because it is better to begin with the stable elements in a situation, such as the container itself, follow on with things which can be more accurately measured and predicted, such as technology and the supply of energy, and only lastly deal with more unpredictable things such as Anthropos himself. This does not mean we believe growth of population is followed by technological development: it is Anthropos who creates such things, they do not create Anthropos. During history there have been instances after a crisis in terms of numbers when Anthropos invented new technologies — as he did after the crisis described by Malthus — but there were also times of population pressure when he did not deal with it by means of new technology, such as the crisis presented in Plato's ideas.

As we described in Part One on method, we know that Anthropos' economic behavior is more predictable than his biological or psychological behavior; most post-war predictions of economic activity have been shown to be in the right direction, while many predictions made about what the future birth rates would be in various nations have been completely contradicted by events.

At present we are in a phase of talking about the growth of population in terms of an explosion. We say that this is the world's biggest problem, that it will be overpopulated in one generation's time, that there will be 7.5 billion people on earth in the year 2000. We talk of this great danger for the year 2000, of the rabbit-power of Anthropos, the biological time-bomb, standing room only on earth, doomsday 2026 A.D., of death by squeezing and of collective death.

What we do not so often remember is that this explosion really began some time ago (fig. 59). It is simply that we have only recently opened our eyes to see it. This is why we are suddenly screaming and crying and trying to work out what to do about the future in such an excess of nervousness. We are told that families should not be allowed to have three babies because this will lead to overcrowding in countries like the U.S.A., and hear pleas for more birth-control and for all sorts of self-controls. We begin to see results in dropping fertility rates, and then, in some cases, we begin worrying about that.

What we do not hear enough about is any discussion of the problems that may result from hasty actions taken in such an emotional way, and how sudden changes in fertility rates may affect us socially and economically. What about the relationship between the many old people now alive and the few young people to be born? What about future productivity, or the relationships between nations which have different fertility rates and different attitudes towards these rates?

We think we may say that we are behaving in such a nervous way because we were so long in recognizing the population explosion, but that when, as is expected, this explosion begins to slow down, our nervousness will disappear and the evolution of the global population will follow more normal trends.

We now consider what the future growth of population is likely to be. We begin with the assumptions we have already made concerning the increase in the capacity of the container to sustain Anthropos. We do not accept the supposition that the existing trends of enormous population growth will continue unchanged, because we know from history that such trends cannot go on for ever. Nor do we accept the statements of the pessimists that population growth must be stopped completely, since this is simply not desirable nor realistic.

The assumption which we consider very probable and which is based on the biological and human experience of the past is this:

The cyclic nature of global expansion of human populations has not in the past, and will not in the foreseeable future, depart significantly from that cyclic pattern of stability-acceleration-deceleration-stability which is characteristic of plant and animal populations growing within a closed environment.

Animal and plant populations growing within a limited or closed environment usually expand according to rather well-known S-shaped evolutionary curves, such as the curve in fig. 97. The many populations in one ecosystem begin in a state of relatively stable balance. One species gains an advantage and enters a stage of accelerating growth until the limits of the advantage are reached, when the growth rate declines — this is the decelerating phase. Eventually a new, final phase of relative stability and balance is reached, in which the population tends more or less asymptotically towards a steady state ceiling or a condition of very slow growth.

Such considerations are also related to studies like those of Dr. Baade who speaks of the population law of the industrial age as being:

a. "High birth and death rates, almost equal, yield a static or slowly increasing population through many centuries.

b. A rapid decline in death rate occurs as food, medicine and sanitation are improved. With a continued high birth rate, the net population growth spurts upward.

c. The mortality rate continues to decline, but the birth rate also falls off drastically, and so the rate of population growth is sharply curtailed.

d. As education and standards of living continue to improve, parents learn to regulate the size of their families. Individuals are healthier and live longer with better food, housing, water and medical care. In this final stage, both the birth and mortality rates stabilize at low levels. The differential remains small so that the total number of people increases very slowly, if at all."[42]

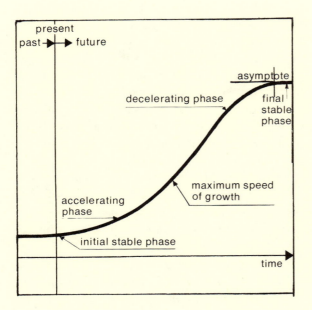

97.   a typical logistic or sigmoid curve

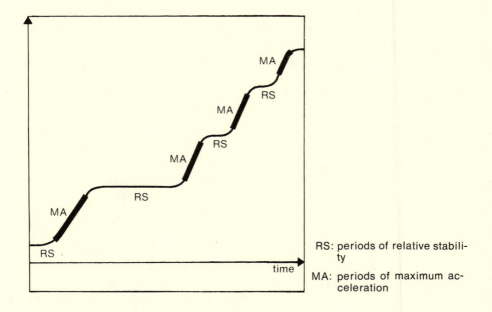

RS: periods of relative stability

MA: periods of maximum acceleration

98.   a succession of logistic or sigmoid curves

When we speak of the stabilization of population, we must remember that experts like P.B. Medawar state: "Stability can be achieved only if the same age-specific rates of mortality and fertility have been in force for something like 100 years. No large population has ever achieved such a stability, and it is not at all likely that it ever will. This is why students of populations wear a censorious frown when people talk, as they so often do, of 'stabilizing' the population of the world or of one country or another at any particular figure they may have in mind; for, short of tyranny, it is not at all clear how any such stability could be achieved."[43]

Statements like this confirm our belief that we cannot speak in terms of a stability imposed by tyranny; however, we can consider stability as probable when it is the result of natural trends, and takes place in its normal time and scale. In our case, when we reach the phase of global unification, which has never happened before in the whole of Anthropos' history, it is probable that stability may be achieved, because then the container on a global scale will act on the total population, as in the past a small territory acted to contain a small population.

In the case of plants and animals, when a population growth, after levelling off, does begin to accelerate again, it is usually because of a fairly sudden increase in the available space, or improvement in environmental conditions, which may mean an increase in food supply. The population expands to take advantage of the opportunities offered. Obviously, this cannot happen suddenly; the population curve only turns up gradually. As the growth of population exhausts the new possibilities and approaches the limit which can be sustained by a particular habitat, a reduction in fertility rate sets in, either because of reduction in the birth rate or an increase in the death rate, or from a combination of both. If the acceleration has been too fast and produced overcrowding, there may be a violent situation in which animals attack one another, or existing plant populations choke off new growth. Eventually, however, the population stabilizes itself at a new level of dynamic equilibrium. This pattern of movement between relatively stable states is repeated through the entire biosphere. It is a scenario which may be repeated often within a single species. There are successive equilibrium levels, each one forming a semi-permanent balance between the habitat and its inhabitant (fig. 98).

It seems most probable then, that human population has also followed such a series of S-shaped transitional curves between periods of relative stability and slow growth during its evolution to present levels, comparable to those typical of plant and animal populations.

Several scholars have attempted to reconstruct the evolution of human population since prehistory. We made a comparative study of some of the more reliable of these during the "City of the Future" project and produced a generalized curve to represent, as accurately as was possible, the demographic development of human populations from the appearance of Anthropos until the present day (figs. 16, 58). The overall form of these curves indicate a close approximation to constant fertility; that is, the population growth curve is approximately a straight line on a logarithmic graph, while four cyclic S-shaped deviations of the growth rate appear as distortions of the general trend.

Each of these distortions corresponds to a specific innovation which gave Anthropos greater control over his environment (tool-making, agriculture, industry), and resulted in his conquest of new possibilities which previously had been beyond his reach (figs. 60, 61).

The first of these innovations was the "tool-making revolution" of perhaps 500,000 years ago, and the decelerating phase was followed by a long period of stability in paleolithic times. The second leap in growth was made possible by the "agricultural revolution", which began about 10,000 B.C., and also gave Anthropos many of his first permanent settlements. Rates of population growth decelerated to a stable constant-fertility state during late antiquity and the Middle Ages, until they accelerated once again in response to the "industrial revolution", which was really three simultaneous revolutions — in techniques of industrial production, in agricultural production, and in transportation. The effects of these last changes began to be seen some time after 1600.

Since the first decades of the present century, mankind has entered yet another such cycle of expansion, and it appears that we are now in the middle of its accelerating phase. The final stage of this last population explosion, however, must be different from those of each of the three earlier cycles. For the first time in human history the growth rate of human population must show a strong deviation downwards from the state of constant fertility, because for the first time Anthropos will totally fill his container. Otherwise, as has been theoretically demonstrated by mathematics[44], the human population of the earth would be infinite by the year 2026. Since this is completely impossible, it is assumed that the terminal phases of the latest cycle of growth will involve a substantial decline in growth rates of population, whether by choice or necessity, or simply by the adjustments which nature seems to make naturally between birth and death rates.

The three previous periods of cyclic growth connected levels of relatively stable growth rates, not stable population sizes, but they still belong to the same family of S-shaped curves which connect stable levels of animal and plant populations. It should be noted that the overall four-cycle curve shown in fig. 56 is a very general representation of the broad phases of human demographic evolution. In reality, each major cycle of growth must have contained a much greater number of many smaller local conquests, each of which would result in an S-shaped surge and decline in population growth rates, and each of which would correspond to some local modification in the balance between a local population and its environment.

The importance for us of these repeated S-shaped cycles should be obvious. They suggest that similar patterns will occur in the future. We are already in the middle of a tremendous surge of acceleration in population growth and it is unlikely that the rest of this cycle will deviate very markedly from the general pattern. We have already seen that an upward deviation sufficient to produce a sustained high growth leads rather rapidly to unlimited increase, which is impossible. A downward deviation sufficient to negate the S-shape of the cycle would imply a major catastrophe on a global scale. Although such a catastrophe is not impossible, any treatment of such a disastrous turn of events lies beyond the scope of this present project and, as we said, we ruled it out in our second basic assumption.

Out of the many calculations and models we made for the probable future evolution of the global population we retained six based on a series of different assumptions, and from those we selected and calculated three ultimate ceilings for the population — a "low", a "middle", and a "high" ceiling of 20, 35 and 50 billion people respectively. These three are keyed as 20, 35 and 50 in the figures and tables. The point at which each ceiling level was reached and the period of stabilization that would therefore begin was taken as the point at which the formation of Ecumenopolis would be completed.

For each of these ceiling levels we evolved two models of population growth, one based on a slower rate of growth (which is keyed with an 'S' prefix in figures and tables) and the second based on a faster rate of growth (keyed with an 'F' prefix). We therefore had a total of six assumptions, two for each ceiling level. We prepared a fully worked-out model for each of these assumptions, giving global population figures at intervals of approximately one generation until the middle of the 22nd or the beginning of the 23rd centuries (fig. 99). These models were also broken down by types of ekistic formation, sizes and types of settlement units, types of habitation (urban, rural and nomadic), and by geographic distribution into large regions. In addition, two and three-way tabulations for these parameters were worked out, as well as growth rates and cumulative population figures. All figures for the six models were checked for continuity and consistency from model to model, and were adjusted where necessary.

These models form smooth extensions of the estimated curve for the historical evolution of the population of the earth, which is shown as the pre-1960 part of the curve in fig. 59. A continuous set of curves is therefore now available, extending from the first appearance of Anthropos some two million years ago to the end of the 22nd century.

The yearly growth rate curves for global population corresponding to each of the six assumptions are shown in fig. 100. These are among the most important graphs since they lie at the heart of any type of population projection. As can be seen, the population had been increasing for many centuries before

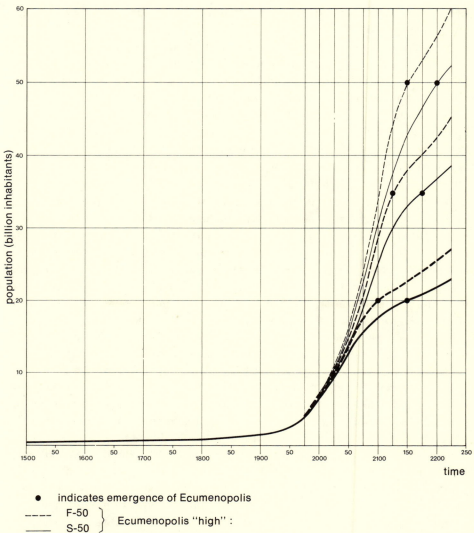

● indicates emergence of Ecumenopolis

- - - - F-50 ⎫
———— S-50 ⎬ Ecumenopolis "high" :
- - - F-35 ⎫
———— S-35 ⎬ Ecumenopolis "middle" :
▬ ▬ ▬ F-20 ⎫
▬▬▬ S-20 ⎬ Ecumenopolis "low" :

99.   global populations projected by the six models

248

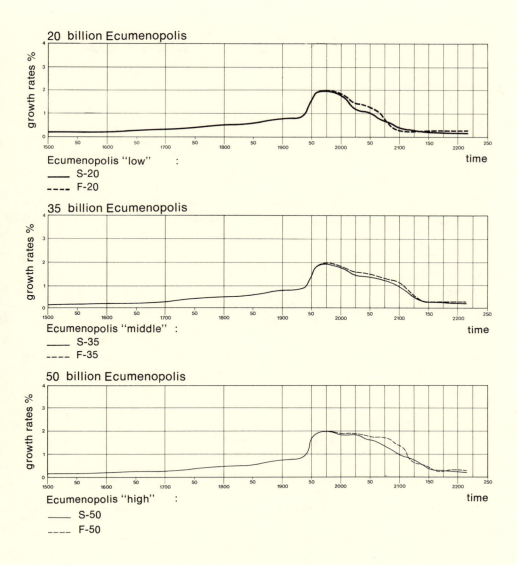

100.   assumed growth rate curves for global population

the early 20th century, but it had been doing so at a very slow rate. Then some-time between the two world wars this rate of growth turned abruptly upwards. Roughly within the span of one generation the growth rate of the total world population rose from below 1% to around 2%.

The growth rate curves shown in fig. 100 were worked out in the early 1960's and first published in the July 1965 issue of the journal EKISTICS[45]. At that time it was felt that some further increase in growth rate was probable, and that even if this increase did not continue for long, an abrupt decrease in the rate of growth was not likely unless a major catastrophe occurred. It was assumed, therefore, that the growth would remain at approximately the same level of the late 1960's (or at slightly higher levels in the case of the faster growth models) for a period of at least one or two generations because it appears that birth control campaigns can only give significant results after a relatively long period of time, and because important changes do not happen overnight. This is specially so in lower-income countries, since effective birth control is dependent on a certain level of general education which cannot possibly be reached within less than a generation.

Even if a precipitous decrease in fertility rates was assumed, it would take some time for the results to be seen. During the first generation or so, the les-sening of world population would be negligible because of the also decreasing death-rates, and it would be still small even after two generations. It takes periods of the order of a century for a sudden drop in fertility to result in a real diminution of total population — although of course the age structures within societies change much earlier.

It is less difficult to predict rates of mortality. We assumed in forming the growth curves of fig. 100 that mortality decreases steadily as incomes rise and public health services improve. Changes here will be more dramatic in the low-income countries during the next century, since in the higher-income countries the revolution in public health has already brought mortality rates to low and fairly stable levels.

Since 1960 the growth rates of world population in fact appear to have stabilized at around 2% per annum. All six of the growth curves developed from our projections at that time therefore imply a more rapid expansion of global population than has actually been the case during the last ten years. At the time when these population projections were worked out on the basis of preliminary studies of resource-availability and habitability, we estimated that the '35' models represented the most likely stabilization figure at which Ecumenopolis would begin. Yet completion of the habitability study has now required a shift in the probability distribution, so that a final population level of between 15 and 25 billion, and hence the '20' model, now seems more likely.

The new estimated probability diagram for the six models is shown in fig.

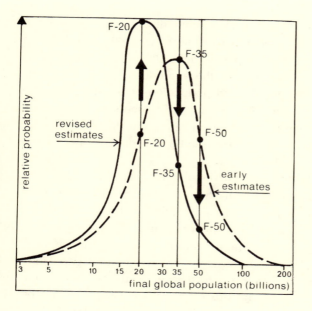

101. revised probability diagram based on population models

101. It is regarded as equally improbable that the final figures will be either as low as 10 billion, or as high as 50 billion, so a final figure of around 20 billion has been given a 70% relative probability.

The fact that population growth has stabilized during the 1960's at levels lower than those predicted confirms our conclusions that the models indicating a slower rate of growth were more likely than other series indicating a faster rate of growth. This conclusion is close to the findings of demographers who showed that it is probable that: "If the developed peoples reach an average family size of two children by the year 2020 and the developing nations by the year 2040, total world population would level off at just under 16 billion. If 20 years could be taken off this adjustment, total population might stabilize at just over 11 billion — or about three times its present level."[46]

It should be pointed out that the change in relative probability assigned to the different models in no way affects the internal validity of the six models since it has no bearing on either the parameters going into them or the methodology of their derivation, and this shows the importance of continuous readjustments as already stated.

The moment at which rapid increase of global population stops (indicated on fig. 100), leaving only a limited margin for further population increase, has been taken as the moment at which the formation of Ecumenopolis will have been completed. The date when this will happen differs according to the various assumptions. It will be reached at earliest by 2100 (according to model F-20) and at latest by 2200 (according to model S-50).

We feel that the most likely figures are those produced by model F-20. According to this there will be a total world population of no more than 6.4 billion people by the year 2000, and the point when Ecumenopolis begins will be reached by the year 2100 when there will be a world population of 20 billion. After this, the population will continue to grow, but at a very slow rate, so that it will reach 22 billion by the year 2150 A.D.

In dealing with our predictions for Ecumenopolis, we worked out how the population would be distributed between the various land-zones, built-up areas, rural areas, difficult areas and so on, and tried to determine what the probable evolution of population would be within each one.

We first used three criteria to define the urbanized "core" of Ecumenopolis within which it was estimated 85% to 95% of the projected world population would live, the percentage varying according to the figures of the six different models. Our first criterion to define the urbanized area (which must not be confused with the built-up area) of human settlements was that of density. We reckoned that density of habitation in an urbanized area is higher than 5 persons per ha (2 per acre), that is, 500 per inhabited sq. km or 1,300 per inhabited sq. mi. The second criterion was that of connectivity, which must be at least of megalopolitan strength. This is explained in Part Five. Areas which do not fulfill this stipulation are defined in the figures as areas of "middle density". The third criterion used to define such urbanized areas is that they contain more than 500 million inhabitants within their whole extended system. Places in which people live at a density of over five per hectare and with a megalopolitan degree of connectivity, but in which there are less than 500 million people within the whole system, are defined as "isolated megalopolises".

We worked out projections for the expected population in each of the traditional forms of settlements, and also for the nomads existing today. In addition, we included two new categories: the "new rural" and the "new nomads". The new rural settlements are those which are expected to be formed outside the megalopolitan areas by people who want to achieve isolation and seclusion, or for purposes of recreation and tourism, for scientific exploration, or for technological or economic development. The emphasis in defining this category is not on conventionally "rural" conditions, but on the small size of the settlement and its relative isolation from large urbanized areas. The new nomads are those people not closely connected to one place of residence, that is, those with several alternative homes, or those who are entirely mobile with no fixed place of residence. It is expected that the class of people who are entirely mobile and constantly on the move may increase.

If we make a proportional division of the expected population according to

total world population: 20	main habitable areas: 19.00	Ecumenopolis core I (on habitable areas): 16.80		total Ecumenopolis core: 17.30
		isolated megalopolises: 1.00	total complement: 2.70	
		middle density areas: 0.80		
		low density areas: 0.40		
	difficult areas: 1.00	other areas: oceans : 0.25 land : 0.25		
		Ecumenopolis core II (on difficult areas): 0.50		

population figures given in billions

table 7. breakdown of global population in 2100 into the core and complement areas of Ecumenopolis

these zones, we find that out of the 20 billion people projected for the year 2100 by model F-20, 17.30 billion (or 86,5%) will live in the core and 2.70 billion in the complement area outside this zone (table 7).

The complement area outside the core's urbanized zone has been further broken down into categories in table 8 and fig. 102 which show trends in developments in the different categories between 1960 and the remote future.

Using a different breakdown of the total population in 2100, 18.5 billion, or 92.5%, will live in urban areas, if these are defined as settlements with a population of more than 2,000 people, and 1.2 billion will live in rural areas, if these are defined as settlements with populations of under 2,000 (table 9). These assumptions are not based on precise calculations, but simply given as an image of a possible distribution based on the opinions of the authors. We would like to emphasize that no matter how isolated and small any individual human settlement may look, because of communication and transportation systems it will still be a cell of the whole global settlement of Ecumenopolis.

We can see what the projected geographic distribution of population is expected to be in the various continents and geographic regions according to the F-20 model in fig. 103. We considered a number of different assumptions about the evolution of global density patterns, and finally retained one which was a compromise, because the projections were carried out independently of

type of complement		old rural	old nomads	new rural	new nomads	other urban	total
isolated megalopolises		—	—	—	0.025	0.975	1.000
middle density		0.550	0.001	0.150	0.050	0.049	0.800
low density areas		0.150	0.003	0.150	0.025	0.072	0.400
difficult areas	land	—	—	0.100	0.100	0.050	0.250
	oceans	—	—	0.100	0.100	0.050	0.250
total		0.700	0.004	0.500	0.300	1.196	2.700

population in billions

table 8.   further breakdown of population in complement area in 2100 (model F-20)

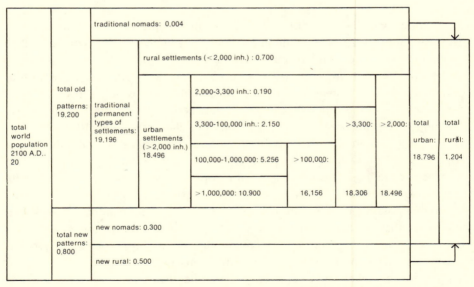

population figures given in billions

table 9.   breakdown of global population in 2100 by types of settlements (model F-20)

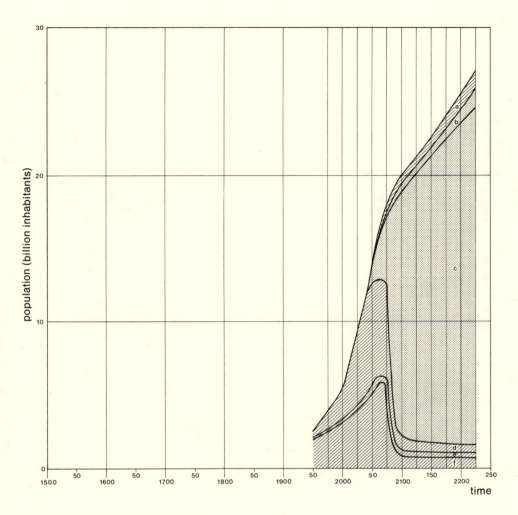

a difficult areas (complement)
b difficult areas (Ecumenopolis core II)
c main habitable areas
d isolated megalopolitan areas
e low density areas
f middle density areas

core of Ecumenopolis
complement of Ecumenopolis

102. formation of global population: distribution into core
and complement of Ecumenopolis (model F-20)

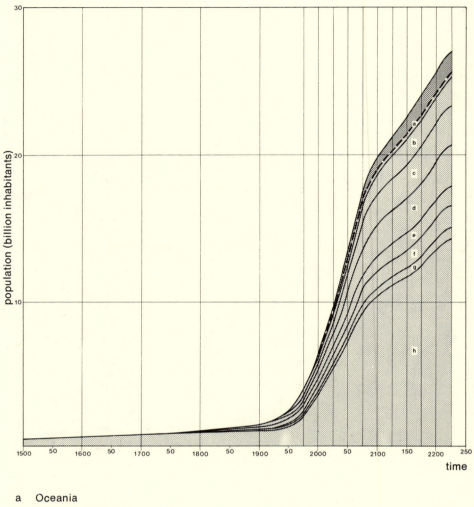

a Oceania
b N. and C. America
c S. America
d Africa
e Europe
f U.S.S.R.
g S.W. Asia
h S.. S.E., and E. Asia
▓ difficult areas
▒ main habitable areas

**103. formation of global population: geographic distribution
        (model F-20)**

the habitability study so that the geographic distribution of population calculated here differs somewhat from the optimal density patterns determined on the basis of the habitability study.

The first hypothesis we rejected was that the present densities of people all over the globe would continue with the same relative distribution, so that population growth would simply mean that places all over the world would go on growing in the same relative proportions. This idea proved unacceptable, since as the highest density areas existing in 1965 would then have reached such intensely high levels of density by the time of Ecumenopolis, population pressure would make it almost inevitable that some form of redistribution would take place, whether by migration or by territorial conquest. It would be quite unreasonable to assume that densities in Southeast Asia will continue to increase to such an inordinate level, while vast areas of the globe, such as parts of north and south America and Africa, remain relatively empty and fully habitable. If some form of massive population redistribution did not take place, then it would have to be assumed that some other factor — such as acceptable density limits within habitable areas — would slow growth within the high-density areas before that in low-density areas, so that in fact the high-density areas would reach the point of stabilization of population growth, which is consistent with the formation of Ecumenopolis, before the low-density areas did so.

A second hypothesis about the future distribution of densities that we rejected was that by 2100 the population of the earth would be evenly distributed across the area of Ecumenopolis. This also was unacceptable, since it would mean that areas which have a comparatively low density of population today, such as the U.S.A. and Oceania, would have to accept an enormous influx of people from the low-income areas during the next century. Not only would there be tremendous social difficulties involved in such a process, but it would also be extremely expensive. In reality, a substantial part of the resources available for the development of the low-income areas would have to be used up in simply transferring so many of their people to the richer areas rather than in solving their problems where they are living at present.

The compromise hypothesis we accepted, therefore, assumes that the present pattern of world densities will continue, but that slowly it will be modified towards greater equalization. According to this, our projections allow for a lesser increase of densities in the Far East and a higher increase in North America and other relatively under-populated continents, such as S. America, Africa, Australia, than those postulated by our first assumption, but to a far less revolutionary degree than would be called for by our second assumption of complete overall equalization of densities. It does, however, still assume that several of the high-income areas will have to accept a considerable influx of population from the lower-income areas.

The projected changes in structure of world population according to settlement sizes for the F-20 model are shown in fig. 104 and the projected changes within the various types of settlements in fig. 105.

We have assumed that the movement towards greater urbanization is likely to continue growing for about one generation, and to remain stable at a high level of growth for at least another generation. We therefore take it that the continuing growth of cities can be shown by extrapolation of present trends. We grouped the world's settlements according to their size, as well as by their geographic regions and other variables, and determined what were the present growth rates and trends for each of these categories. We assumed that as each settlement grows and passes into the next category size, its rate of growth will also change and become that of the average for its new category size. After a number of checks, the curves of growth for each settlement size were adopted nearly unchanged until almost 2020. After this date their rates of growth were assumed to slow down to reflect the projected slowing of growth required by the approach to stabilization levels (fig. 106).

Although we believe that the remaining five models we made for the projection of future population are less likely than the F-20 one, we retained them, and some of the data in them are summarized in Appendix 1. These other models require longer to reach the point of stabilization at the higher figures assumed for them. They also assume that the proportion of urban population to rural will be higher by the time Ecumenopolis begins, and that there will be a higher proportion of people living in the core and in the complement area.

These six models have proved useful in working out many aspects of demographic forecasting, especially since they allow for interpolation and (up to a certain degree) for extrapolation, too. Unfortunately, they do not include the possibility that the population may stabilize at levels of much less than 20 billion, although it is possible to extrapolate downwards from the '20' series models in order to work things out for stabilization levels of between 15 and 20 billion.

Density

We must now consider in detail the factors which limit density. Our calculations up to now have taken several factors into consideration, one of which was the density of human settlements, and so far as we could without knowing what would be the results of another revolution in food production, especially the density of habitation.

On this we proceeded with the following assumption:

In the long run, average human densities will tend asymptotically towards the maxima consistent with the maintenance of a sustainable balance between Anthropos and his global environment.

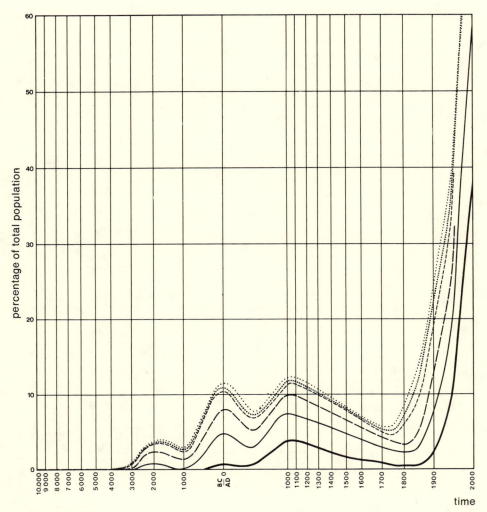

settlements with:

.... over   2,000 inhabitants

.... over   3,300 inhabitants

----- over   5,000 inhabitants

— — over   20,000 inhabitants

——— over   100,000 inhabitants

——— over 1,000,000 inhabitants

104.   formation of global population: distribution by settlement size (model F-20)

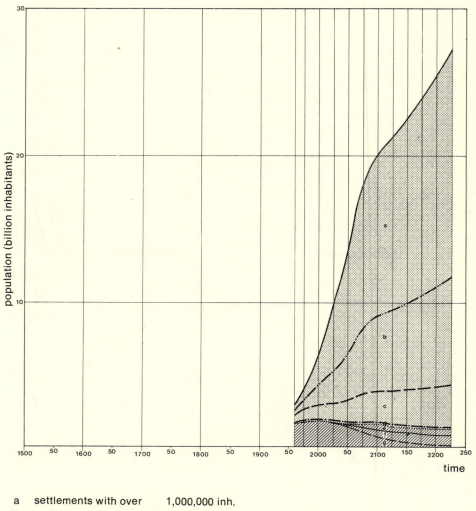

a settlements with over   1,000,000 inh.
b settlements with 100,000 - 1,000,000 inh.
c settlements with   3,300 -   100,000 inh.
d settlements with   2,000 -   3,300 inh.
e new nomads
f new rural
g old rural
   rural
   urban

105.   formation of global population: distribution by types
       of settlement (model F-20)

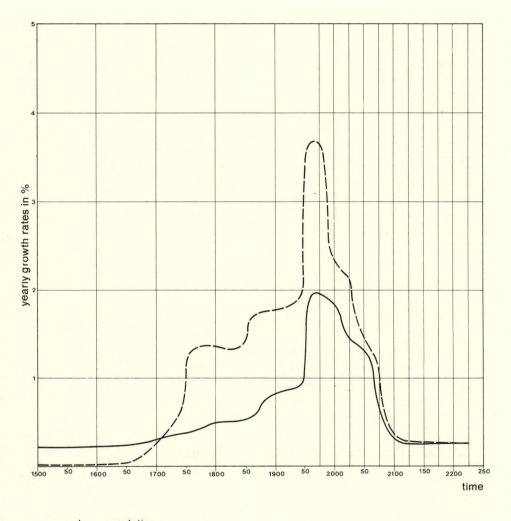

yearly growth rates in %

time

1500 50 1600 50 1700 50 1800 50 1900 50 2000 50 2100 150 2200 250

_ _ urban population

___ global population

**106.   yearly population growth rates by settlement sizes
(model F-20)**

261

Anthropos is expected, like other biological populations, to breed to fill his environment until negative repercussions are bad enough to stabilize his numbers. However, since Anthropos' advancing technology and increasing wealth will lessen the degree to which he is restricted by his environment, we assume that in general the human population will maintain an impetus for growth. Population will continue to expand wherever and whenever Anthropos gains a new leverage over his environment. Individual awareness of the negative effects of such growth will be one of several factors likely to restrain it, and such awareness will automatically increase as Anthropos approaches closer to saturation of his whole global environment.

Our study of densities, then, begins with these two important concepts: first, that densities will tend to expand until constrained; and second, that maximum densities do exist which can be approached and even reached, but cannot be exceeded without grave repercussions. These are laws which govern the general relationship of all living organisms with their environments where a natural ecological equilibrium exists. This is demonstrated in the characteristic S-shaped curves taken by the growth patterns of biological populations.

Since human population is still growing rapidly, we deduce that its density at present still lies well below global limits. Several questions arise. What are the factors which determine such limits of density? Can we estimate what the saturation densities will be for the future? Is there a relationship between the density which is most satisfactory and the greatest density which Anthropos can tolerate, and how does this relationship vary?

When we speak of what density is tolerable, we must recognize that the figures will differ in areas with different degrees of habitability, and with different cultural and social backgrounds or different types of technology. It will also be very different according to the ekistic scale of the unit we are considering — the larger the area, the lower the density that can be sustained. Exceedingly high densities, for example, have been created and may be maintained for quite some time in some limited areas, such as Hong Kong with its high-rise, low-income blocks of housing giving densities as high as 8,000 persons per inhabited hectare (3,240 per inhabited acre) or New York with densities of 3,000 per inhabited hectare (1,215 per inhabited acre). Yet, when we talk about a big metropolitan area, the densities are invariably much lower — between 30 and 120 per inhabited hectare (12 and 48 per inhabited acre) — and if we talk about a whole region, they are lower still.

In large cities and metropolises the tolerable maximum density under present conditions seems to be about 200 to 300 persons per inhabited hectare (80 to 120 per inhabited acre). In Moscow, for example, it is 245 per inhabited hectare (100 per inhabited acre). The upper limit within an urbanized region seems to be only several tens per inhabited hectare even for the future. The most densely populated megalopolises of the present day barely reach 10 per inhabited hectare (4 per inhabited acre) and existing non-megalopolitan regions with comparable areas of around 30,000 sq. km (11,680 sq. mi.) scarcely reach 5 per inhabited hectare (2 per inhabited acre), but we should not forget that these are not normal densities because these areas only now are beginning to be formed. The Dacca region in Bangladesh, Java, Holland, Kerala (India), Belgium, Taiwan, and two or three dozen other major units of similar size defined by national or regional boundaries, have densities falling between 2 and 5 per inhabited hectare. In larger regions densities are even lower. India and some areas of Pakistan are the only regions of over 1,000,000 sq. km (390,000 sq. mi.) in area which have a present density of over one inhabitant per hectare.

It seems, then, that the greater the area under consideration, the less the maximum reasonable density. As the size of the spatial unit we are talking about increases, so the proportion of land covered by built-up settlements falls, since inevitably more land must be included which is either uninhabitable, such as high mountains or deserts, or else is devoted to other uses. There is a very high percentage of human habitation in Hong Kong and a much smaller percentage in the entire Indian subcontinent with its many uninhabitable areas. It is therefore necessary to think about the total mixture of land uses necessary to support settlements in any region when trying to work out the maximum possible densities for a large-scale area.

Densities are also strongly related to the habitability of the area. A place that is easy and pleasant to live in will naturally be able to support much higher densities than an unpleasant and difficult one. By the time of Ecumenopolis it is probable that many areas of the world that are now considered difficult to live in will have been much improved by technological advances, and will therefore be able to sustain far higher densities, but nonetheless, areas of higher natural habitability will probably still continue to have the highest densities.

People with different cultures and social traditions and different stages of economic development seem to have very different ideas about how close to one another they want to live. Those living in Southeast Asia, for example, seem capable of tolerating extremely high densities of habitation, while those in some parts of Britain, Scandinavia and Australia find it difficult to accept densities that, by global standards, are quite low. However, even in such countries we must remember that the central part of Stockholm on the island of Städsholmen must have had a density of several hundred, and the walled city of London must also have had a density in the hundreds. People will also accept different densities at different periods of their history, but the variation over time is not clear nor characteristic enough for us to make projections for the future. It is clear, too, that the layout, the Network system and the methods of building construction used in settlements of various scales can have a big effect on how many people can live comfortably within it.

It is sufficient for our purposes that we should accept that limits to tolerable densities do exist. If given the choice, people will not continue to squeeze them-selves into an area at greater densities than they find pleasant for the style of life they like to live. This will continue to be so even if time is allowed for a possible adaptation to changing conditions. We know that future life-styles and future technologies may be very different from ours, but nonetheless it has been possible to make estimates for maximum tolerable density levels in different types and sizes of area on the basis of studies of historical and of present densities. These estimates may include an acceptable margin of error of as much as 50% to allow for their wide possible range and for the fact that Anthropos may consciously intervene to change them by such means as education, propaganda, economic inducements or sanctions. Advanced technology will make it possible to build very massive urban structures in the future so that high densities could be possible in some limit-ed areas — but this fact has little bearing on the consideration of densities at the larger scale.

In the remote future, then, it seems likely that the maximum density at the city scale will be about a few hundred per inhabited hectare. On the metropolitan scale the maximum may be one or two hundred per inhabited hectare (40 or 80 per inhabited acre). On the regional scale the maximum will probably not exceed 100 persons per inhabited hectare (40 per inhabited acre) and on the continental scale the maximum will not exceed 10 per inhabited hectare (4 per inhabited acre). The global average could very probably be around 90 per inhabited hectare (35 per inhabited acre). When we do not consider any of the other factors that may limit the population of the earth, these limits to tolerable densities on their own suggest an aggregate maximum population for the earth of between 7 and 15 times larger than the present population, that is, between 20 and 50 billion people.

When we look at the way densities are changing today in response to urban-ization and increasing incomes, it looks as though these estimates of max-imum densities are in fact higher than those that will actually be achieved if existing trends persist in the future. Studies made by the Athens Center of Ekistics on hundreds of settlements have shown conclusively that the growth of large settlements all over the world (with exceedingly few exceptions) fol-lows the same pattern; area grows more rapidly than population (fig. 32), therefore the average density of large settlements drops continually. Other studies have shown that as people become richer they demand more space in which to live, so as incomes rise, densities drop. Therefore, if these trends continue and if, as is expected, the future is a time of increased urbaniza-tion and increased incomes, then the total and average density levels ac-ceptable by that time may be lower than the present ones.

If we wonder whether it is in fact reasonable for Anthropos to follow such trends towards lower densities, we should remember that throughout human history, whenever there was enough security to allow it as there was in ancient Rome and at times in ancient Athens, people moved out of the cities into the outlying areas where they could live at lower densities. This movement is being repeated in the settlements of the present and this is one reason for increase of energy and cost. It may simply reflect Anthropos' desire for more open space; however, it could also be a much more important and serious attempt to assure the survival of the human race. We know that at all periods the population of big cities continuously declined and was replaced by newcomers from the countryside. Is not the permanent aristocracy of any country always based in the countryside?

Densities are expected to stabilize within each area of the globe at levels which form a balance between population expansion and the rising forces of repression. We therefore anticipate that regional densities will stabilize somewhat below their saturation levels. Relatively large fluctuations may take place in small areas without disturbing the stable average optimum level for the larger regions to which they belong. If densities become too high, we anticipate that the resultant pressures will drive them down again, and if they become low, the natural tendencies towards population growth will drive them up.

We take the "optimum levels of density" to be those which would allow a balanced and continuing relationship between Anthropos, his settlements and the global environment. Higher densities would disturb the complex balance of Ecumenopolis, while substantially lower ones would not allow a sufficient degree of contact and inter-communication between all its parts, which we believe will be one of the most desirable things about the City of the Future.

On the basis of an assumed population of 20 billion for Ecumenopolis, the average global densities will be as in table 10.

density	inh./ha	inh./acre
total surface	0.39	0.16
total land	1.35	0.55
cultivated and inhabited land	4-5	1.62-2.00
land directly related to human settlements	15-20	6-8
built-up area of settlements	50-60	20-25

table 10. future average global densities

30. Conclusions

When we look into the future, trying always to emulate the two-headed eagle who looks back as well as forwards, we know that we cannot see too far ahead. We are entitled, however, to speak about the most probable evolution during the next few generations.

We are at present in the middle of an explosion of many forces. We did not become aware of this until recently, and now that we have begun to open our eyes and see what is going on we have become frightened and have begun to scream and cry. There is, however, no reason for pessimism. This is simply a transitional phase we are in; our problems are the problems of growth, not of disease — we are suffering from growing pains.

We can say that our life in this transitional phase began in 1825 and that it may last for another 150 years, that is, up to 2125. That may sound like a very long time, but it is not really so. It must have taken Anthropos much longer to change his way of life from that of a hunter to that of a cultivator and producer. Once this transitional period is over, we will enter a period of stabilization and the formation of Ecumenopolis.

The only thing that could prevent Ecumenopolis being realized is the development of technology in quite unforeseen ways, creating such a revolution in natural and human settlement laws that we cannot foresee the result. But this is very improbable.

It was during this transitional phase that global population began to grow so fast. It began at the start of the transitional period in 1825 with just over one billion, has now reached 3.7 billion, and will continue to rise until it reaches between 15 and 20 billion. The reason for this growth is the change in the capacity of the globe as a container to support Anthropos. It could have supported five billion people in 1825, and it will be able to support 20 billion in 2100. This is a four-fold increase, but it is a much smaller increase than the one which occurred 10,000 years ago when the capacity of the container increased 200 times. We are in the middle of a revolution which in terms of global capacity is 50 times smaller than the last one.

It is quite probable that our global population will become about 15 billion if we are able to adjust the organization of resources and our settlements to increasing needs on a global scale. However, if we do solve such problems of organization, then we may well reach a total population of 20 billion.

When we look objectively at all the estimates and forecasts which have been made, we see that scarcities of resources such as food, water, energy and minerals — although they may create problems for the near future — will not impose limitations on the remote future greater than those already imposed by the available habitable area of land and acceptable human densities. It should be entirely possible with the advanced technologies and high incomes anticipated for the period of Ecumenopolis to produce adequate supplies of these resources to sustain a larger global population than that which Anthropos may desire to have for reasons of the habitability of various areas and acceptable levels of density within them. In the long run, therefore, it will probably not be lack of material resources, but lack of habitable space on earth that is most likely to play the dominant role in determining both maximum and optimum levels of global population.

Since we need not worry now about forecasts for the distant future, we must concentrate on the transitional phase we are in at this time, so as to get a better understanding of it and see how it develops into Ecumenopolis.

Part five

The immediate future:
the next three generations

31. The continuation of present trends: the end of the transition crisis

The human settlements with which we personally will be concerned.

Having made many assumptions* about the container and its contents, we now turn to the real subject of our study: the human settlements of the future. First we must see what is going to happen during the rest of the transitional period immediately ahead which will precede the establishment of Ecumenopolis. We have reckoned that Ecumenopolis should be completely established not earlier than 2100, and if some trends, such as the increase of population, slow it down, then at the latest by 2200. The transitional period should therefore continue for another five to nine generations from now.

In dealing with the human settlements of this transitional period we are discussing the settlements of our own personal future. Babies born today will live at least until the year 2045, and their children will live until 2070. Young parents today with a vital interest in the lives of their children and grandchildren have a direct commitment to the events of this whole transitional period.

In this Part we shall concentrate on this period of time which is of direct interest to ourselves, and in the following Part we shall try to describe the period of Ecumenopolis which will follow.

Many of the buildings we are now creating will still be there when this period ends, and they, together with the decisions we are now making, will affect and condition what happens in Ecumenopolis.

The four divisions of the future

When we consider the future, we must always remember that we are trying to deal with a dynamic and changing system about which we can only make general statements. We must speak of global trends and never of specific dates or particular countries.

Our main goal was to find out what are the inevitable trends which will shape our immediate future. There are forces and constraints which, by their interaction, will largely determine the development of human settlements within the next few generations. Our conclusions were both pessimistic and optimistic — pessimistic, since we were forced to recognize that we are entering a period of trial and deepening crisis in human settlements which will last until at least the year 2000; optimistic, because we have good reason to believe that Anthropos' settlements will survive this time of trial, perhaps their greatest in history, and will then enter a period of steady improvement, both in standards of living and in quality of the human environment.

In order to discuss the future, we divided it into four parts, which we called the Near, Middle and Remote Futures (fig. 107), followed by the Unknown Future.

The divisions we made were as follows:

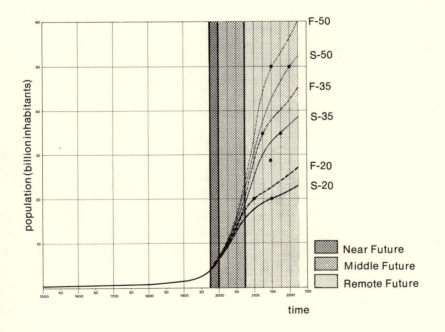

107.   Near, Middle and Remote Futures

The Near Future: This extends from the present day until the year 2000 A.D. It will be the period of peak growth rates for all the factors we have been discussing — urbanization, pollution, rise in incomes and the increasing gaps between incomes, shortages of food, water, energy and other resources. As this acceleration outstrips Anthropos' adaptive capacities, conditions of human life will grow progressively worse in settlements of all sizes. It is true that definite improvements can and are expected to occur in parts of some settlements during the 1980's and 1990's, but they will take time to spread on the global scale. Despite Anthropos' best efforts, we will probably see spectacular crises up to the year 2000. By a global mobilization of human effort it may be possible to reduce the speed of deterioration, but not to avoid it totally.

The Middle Future: Between about 2000 and 2075 a gradual easing of the crises is expected to take place. The habitable area of the earth is a limited system, so a reduction in population growth is inevitable. The general trend towards deterioration will be reversed, although crises will certainly continue to occur, and especially during the first half of this period.

The Remote Future: After 2075 there will be a period of relative stability of at least several generations during which it is anticipated that human settlements will gradually consolidate into a functional unity. Ecumenopolis will emerge towards the end of this period as a unified global system of settlements, and this brings us to the last limit of our research.

Since the reduction in acceleration of forces will be gradual and uneven, the final date for the appearance of Ecumenopolis cannot be definitely predicted. It could be as late as 2200. The period we qualified as the Near Future may extend for one or two decades beyond the year 2000. Transitions between the various periods will be imperceptible, and naturally will take place at different times in different areas. Exact dates are less important than the finding that the evolution of human settlements does seem to tend towards a stable state.

The Unknown Future: When Ecumenopolis takes shape (which will certainly be by 2200) humanity will enter a completely new phase of its history and a system of life with completely new dimensions. This system is predictable only in certain physical terms — as was described in Part Four — and only in its first phase. It is totally unpredictable in other ways. For us to try and make predictions about what will happen in the time of Ecumenopolis would be as reasonable — and as possible — as for a citizen living in the feudal estates of Attica in the 7th century B.C. to have made predictions about what would happen during the time of classical Athens in the 5th century B.C. without knowing that Cleisthenes would be born and later would organize a democracy.

32. New dimensions

The new and larger human settlements

The transitional period in which we are presently involved has already seen the development of new dimensions in everything concerning human settlements. So far as whole settlements are concerned, we have already seen the appearance of the metropolis (ekistic unit 10, community class VII) and its spread from just a few to many hundreds. Next we have seen the appearance of the small megalopolis (ekistic unit 11, community class VIII) which now exists on a global scale. We are just beginning to notice and to understand the emergence of the next unit, the megalopolis (ekistic unit 12, community class IX).

In the Near Future — that is, the period until 2000 — the megalopolis is going to be established in many places all over the globe. We are next going to become aware of the emergence of larger units, small eperopolises (ekistic unit 13, community class X). These will become completely established in the Middle Future, and eperopolises (ekistic unit 14, community class XI) will then begin to emerge.

The whole transitional period of human life in terms of human settlements can therefore be summarized as follows:

1. The transitional period began in 1825 with the appearance of the first metropolis.
2. Metropolises spread and became completely established by 1900.
3. Small megalopolises emerged and are now completely established (1975). These are our present daily urban systems.
4. Megalopolises emerge and will be completely established by the first quarter of the 21st century.
5. Small eperopolises emerge and will be completely established by the middle of the 21st century.
6. Eperopolises emerge and will be completely established by the last quarter of the 21st century.
7. Ecumenopolis begins to form and will be completely established sometime between 2100 and 2200.

It can be seen from this time scale that whereas at first it took about three generations for a new ekistic unit of a higher class to emerge, as the transitional phase went on one generation became long enough for a larger ekistic unit to take shape.

The conclusion is clear. Anthropos has already laid the foundations for completely new dimensions in his life-systems. He himself is not changing, but everything in his system of life is in a stage of continually changing dimensions. Each new and larger life-system appears without mankind in general, or any individual man having prior conception of it; each individual man is simply following the five principles in pursuance of his own ends that have always resulted in the formation of human settlements, and these growing and changing systems of settlements are natural and inevitable.

The population

Of all the things which are increasing in dimensions, the thing we notice most is population. We are aware of the results of this growth all around us every day, so it is about the growth of population we complain most.

Our calculations in the previous Part led us to assume a population in Ecumenopolis of about 20 billion. We should therefore reach a population of about 6.43 billion in the Near Future (by the year 2000), and 9.60 billion in the Middle Future (by the year 2025). The level of urban population — which now in 1975 is 2.30 billion — will have reached 4.60 billion by 2000. It will have increased at an average annual rate of 2.7% and will have absorbed 71.5% of the global population.

Urban population is now growing at a global rate of 3.7% annually, although the total growth rate for all population, including rural settlements, is only 2%. Population growth rates within the built-up areas existing today are expected to decrease gradually to 2.8% by the latter part of the 20th century, and to 2.2% during the beginning of the 21st century. The real growth will be due to the growth in total areas covered by the new settlements, which we will discuss in the following chapters.

The general trend towards urbanization all over the world has meant that recently the metropolis has become the most important and characteristic type of human settlement. Soon, however, it will be supplanted by the small megalopolis. While smaller settlements, such as villages with less than 3,000 inhabitants, will become progressively less important, and small urban settlements will also decrease, although to a lesser degree, medium-sized settlements will remain static in population size and the larger cities and metropolises will continue to fuse into ever larger multinuclear regional units.

It does seem that the mononuclear settlement of today has limits beyond which it cannot grow without signs of malfunctioning. Urban densities beyond the metropolis on the ekistic logarithmic scale are decreasing rather abruptly at present because of this functional limitation of size. Regional settlements, such as the small megalopolis and the megalopolis, are larger in area but much less densely populated, and are structured as a nodal system of centers and interconnecting axes.

To give a clearer image of what this sort of growth in population will mean in the case of some specific towns, we give the figures produced in some of our research projects for certain large cities in several different continents. We have the data to justify these predictions, although naturally we cannot guarantee them absolutely because of the big question of the changing limits of human settlements (table 11).

We are entitled to reach the conclusion that in general by the year 2000 the average growth of large urban settlements will lead to an urban population of more than twice the present one. Large cities in high-income areas may not grow so much, but only a few of the cities under consideration belong to high-income countries; on a global scale, therefore, we must think in terms of a doubling of the urban population.

area	date		% of increase 1970-2000
	c. 1970	c. 2000	
Great Lakes Megalopolis	27.000	85.000	215
Urban Detroit Area	7.693	15.000	94
Northern Ohio Urban System	5.674	7.107	50
Barcelona (province), Spain	3.929	7.800	99
Rio de Janeiro (Greater Rio), Brazil	6.686	18.200	172
Athens, Greece	2.733	4.300	57
Teheran, Iran	3.900	10.500	167
Lusaka, Zambia	0.350	1.500	230
Mediterranean region, France	4.976	11.000	121
Lagos, Nigeria	1.589	7.540	270

table 11. estimated growth of large settlements

Incomes

Another very important increase for the future of human settlements will be the increase of income levels. The average annual per capita income is expected to rise from $550 in 1975 to $1,400 in 2000, an average growth of 3.8% per year. The combination of population growth with per capita income growth will lead to an increase in global gross national production, from $2,200 billion in 1975 to $8,900 billion in 2000, an annual growth rate of 5.80% (this is estimated on the value of the purchasing power of U.S. dollar in 1960, see Appendix 2).

There will be increased investment in all urban building as a result of this growth in wealth. Over one and a half billion new homes are expected to be built between 1975 and 2000 in order to house the expected increase in population and replace existing old buildings. Vast numbers of new Networks and all other sorts of urban structures will have to be created in the same period. No way has yet been found in low-income countries by which governments can raise enough money to build houses and amenities for the expected growth of their urban population. Their only resource not in short supply will be the population itself, so their only hope may be in helping their people to build and improve their own houses.

The growth in income levels is expected to be different in low and high-income countries. While low-income countries — after a period of relative stagnation in the immediate future — are expected to have a growth of per capita income rates until the end of this century, growth rates in the high-income countries are expected to show a progressive decline from their present high level. Average urban incomes all over the world will then continue to rise during the Near Future, but perhaps more slowly than at present.

The social aspects

Changes in the numbers of the population and in the economy create changes in social patterns.

One big change will be in the distribution of people between agricultural and non-agricultural occupations. The 8,000-year-old distinction between urban and rural dwellers is going to vanish. Our society no longer needs hunters or peasants; for the first time in history agriculture is starting to depend on farmer-citizens, who are urban dwellers taking care of the farming interests of the community, not as social outcasts, but as equal citizens, and in future this will be more and more the case. One problem that will vanish will be the social inequality which has always existed between people simply because of where they live and what they do — so far as town and country are concerned. The problem that will arise instead will be that of the far greater numbers of people who will have to live together in social harmony within the same settlement. It is here that we may well face social disturbances in the Near Future, and we shall deal with this problem in more detail elsewhere.

The increasing growth of urbanization will result in an increase in all those tendencies linked with it — changes in the age-structure of populations, in life-expectancy, a fall in birth rates, a further fall in death rates (especially in lower income areas), a spectacular swelling of the older age-groups, and a moderate increase of the labor force. The increase in life-expectancy has already resulted in a substantial increase in the proportion of old people in the population, especially in areas where the population growth is beginning to level off. The patterns of family and social life are having to be changed to accommodate these increasing numbers of old people. Although the recent breakdown of the traditional family has tended to obscure it, the fact is once more beginning to be recognized that the old have always played an indispensable role in building and passing on the structure of the healthy human community. We can only assume that present trends towards over-fragmentation of family life will tend to be corrected.

The spread of education goes on, but within the high-income countries its rate of growth, especially at the secondary school level, is expected to slow down or decline, since it will have reached all those who can benefit from it in the Near Future. In lower-income countries the numbers of people are growing too fast for the schools and universities to accommodate them, so it is probable that in the Near Future the proportional numbers of educated people in these countries will tend to drop, but will rise again by the turn of the century as incomes rise and new teaching aids and techniques are found.

An important aspect of the new trends in human life today is that Anthropos is beginning to have more time to develop during his childhood, and more time for leisure and the expression of all types of creativity. Exact figures cannot be obtained, but it does seem probable that in high-income countries Anthropos can now spend 38% of his time in leisure and therefore, hopefully, in creativity. When he was a farmer he could spend only 22% of his time in this way, and when he was a primitive hunter only 17% of it. Today, therefore, Anthropos is beginning to have the same opportunities for creativity as he did in classical Athens, where many citizens had the leisure for the proper education that is termed *paideia*[1], and which led to so many new concepts in art, science, and philosophy.

Let us now look at some of the changes that are taking place in individual man's physical condition. A more serious concern is developing for health in general; diseases that were overlooked are being studied, and people who could not be helped at all in the past are now seen to be suffering from diseases that can be understood and possibly prevented. The situation for the new-born looks better all over the world than it has at any previous time.

Higher incomes are producing changes in average human characteristics and health. It is probable that "health for all from the cradle to the grave", which is already proposed as a target for the U.S. health service, may be well on the way to world-wide realization by the time of Ecumenopolis. Better nutrition and living conditions are already producing taller and broader human beings. Many basic dimensional standards will therefore have to be changed — as the Japanese and others are already experiencing.

We do not yet know if larger people are better people. We do know, however, that excessive food consumption — especially in the earliest years — can bring on permanent debilitating obesity and other "civilized" malfunctions, especially when combined with inadequate exercise. Unless Anthropos lives a more balanced life than the residents of high-income countries do today, it may well be that the average man will be increasingly bald, with a softer skin and a weaker heart and muscles.

It is also possible that if all infants survive regardless of malformations, genetic damage, or the presence of hereditary diseases, then genetic abnormality and hereditary diseases may spread. However, if the causes of such problems are faced, we may have far healthier people.

Improvements in agricultural productivity, the introduction of new techniques and rising incomes will lead to the elimination of famine as a widespread phenomenon within one or two generations. General health will also improve, and many of the major illnesses and diseases which currently trouble mankind will be eradicated or reduced to minimal levels. This does not rule out the possibility that new or rare diseases may spread during the next century as a result of greatly changed conditions, such as environmental pollution, the slow accumulation of poisons in the tissues, or lack of exercise. Such things should be brought under control more quickly, however, as a result of improved research techniques, increased funds, and continuously improving methods in both preventive and curative medicine.

Life-expectancy has already been raised as a result of better food and medical advances. While the average primitive person had a life-expectancy of only 18 years, this had risen to 33.5 years by 1600, was 49.2 years in 1900, and is today over 70 years. We are reaching the point when people in low-income countries have a life-expectancy equal to that of those in high-income countries now, and when life-expectancy in the high-income countries will probably rise even slightly higher.

33. New systems of life

The big change

The present systems are going to go on changing for two main reasons: people will continue to flow into the cities because of the greater advantages they can obtain there, combined with the decreased need for agricultural labor (fig. 94); and the increased mobility of the ordinary human being will continue to enlarge the radius of his daily system of movement to and from his city.

There is a third important reason why this flow to urban centers will go on increasing, and that is that the largest proportion of energy is consumed within big settlements and this continues to rise. In earlier periods of human history most people were engaged in "primary" economic activities, such as agriculture and the extraction of natural resources. Since the industrial revolution, "secondary" activities — the processing of raw materials and so on — have become more important. Lately, the "tertiary" section — organization, administration, transport and entertainment, with professional and domestic services — has shown rapid growth. Most recently of all, the "quaternary" section — information processing and communications — is expanding most. This is another reason for the gravitation towards big urban centers, since primary industries are tied to one area only, whereas higher-order industries can settle anywhere and will choose the big urban centers with concentrations of both consumers and big resident labor forces. Types of industry which used to be thought unpleasant are now accepted, since they pay attention to appearance and emission controls, and cooperate with local education authorities, and research and other institutions.

The great migration from rural to urban areas is therefore sure to continue in the Near and Middle Future. Not all small settlements will vanish: many will continue to exist, but will become functionally integrated into a larger system by means of more efficient Networks. Smaller settlements which mediate between agricultural areas and major centers may gain in importance. These trends will continue all over the world, until by the time of Ecumenopolis 95% of the total world population — or even more — will participate in some form of urban life.

We do not see such urbanization as the threat it is often taken to be. It is a process which promises to improve the quality of human life; the acute poverty which now characterizes most small rural settlements today will be replaced by the much higher standards of an urban environment, which can be purged of its current failings if only Anthropos can decide to take an active part in the control and guidance of what happens.

If, because of some recent official statistics, we have doubts about the accuracy of these predictions, we must remember, as we have emphasized before, the basic weakness of such statistics: they describe growth only within a limited built-up area that exists today. We estimate that while the urban population is expected to reach 71.5% of the total by 2000, in reality the real proportion — including farmers, who today live as much as 160 km (100 mi.) outside cities in high-income countries such as the U.S.A., but still participate in urban life — is more likely to be 99% (fig. 108). The urban population increases

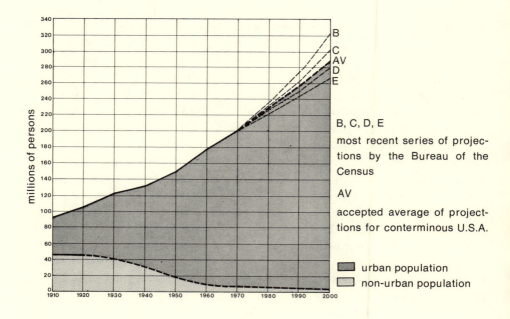

B, C, D, E

most recent series of projections by the Bureau of the Census

AV

accepted average of projections for conterminous U.S.A.

■ urban population
☐ non-urban population

108.   the expected urban and non-urban population for the U.S.A., 2000

far more than we realize, because not only do more people flow into the city, but the city flows out to embrace them.

Let us try to see what the form, dimensions and locations of these new systems of life are going to be. In order to understand what they are really going to be like, we must understand where people are going to live and how they are going to live, because only by trying to understand their systems of life as a whole can we hope to see what their dimensions and complexities will be.

The size of the city

The next question is: just how far out is the city going to flow? We can answer that by making estimates of expanding daily systems of movement. In 1960 in the U.S.A. they had reached a maximum area of 26,200 sq. km (10,200 sq. mi.) (fig. 31) with an average radius of 90 km (56 mi.). Even in the lowest-income urban areas the radius was 30 km (19 mi.), so in 1960 the global average radius of daily systems of movement could be considered as being 60 km (37.5 mi.).

By 2000 this radius will certainly be more than three times larger, so the global average radius will be around 200 km (120 mi.) and will range from between 600 km (370 mi.) for high-income areas to 100 km (60 mi.) for low-income areas (fig. 109). We can see from such figures how far present urban systems will expand outwards. In the Near Future they will cover an area ten times larger than today and contain populations three times larger than those existing today.

In the Middle Future, trends towards increasing areas will continue. By then the average maximum radii of high-income settlements will be well over 1,000 km (620 mi.) with a minimum of several hundred kilometers, which may well mean an overall average radius of 1,000 km (620 mi.). The areas of the urban systems of the Middle Future will then be several tens of times larger than they were in 2000, and their population could well be one hundred times larger. These settlements will not, of course, be totally built-up areas; they will take the form of a grid of linked built-up areas with open countryside in between.

It is natural to wonder if such trends can and will really continue. We have already seen that trends in technology and in economics do make it perfectly possible for them to continue (Part Four). We have also discovered that the past history of human settlements shows that Anthropos has always spread his settlements as far outwards as he could whenever it was possible for him to do so. We have no reason to think that machines will be eliminated; and as long as Anthropos has machines, then he will use them to move as far out as he can. He will continue to follow the first principle we discovered from our study of human settlements of the past: his desire to maximize his potential contacts.

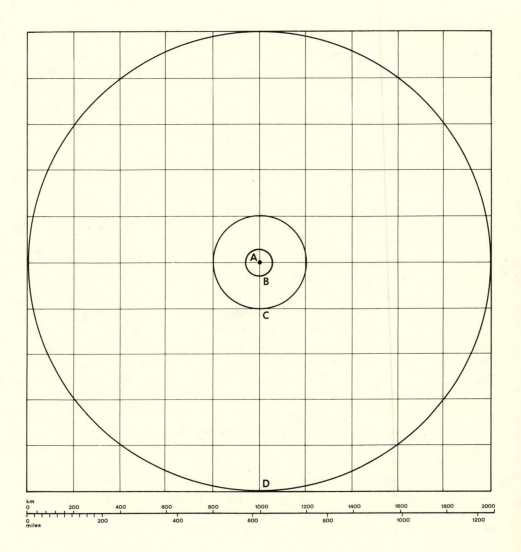

A past radius
B present radius — 60 km
C Near Future radius — 200 km
D Middle Future radius — 1,000 km

109. commuting fields of an average daily urban system (DUS) in the past, at present, in the Near Future and in the Middle Future

Density

Having seen how large settlements are likely to be, we must now try to decide how densely they will be inhabited. Here we must be careful to avoid the usual confusion that has existed about densities since the birth of the cities of the present. We have seen (fig. 32) that densities within urban systems as a whole continually decrease. If we look at the territories of urban systems as they exist today, then it is probable that densities will drop in the central and over-congested areas but increase within the territory of the systems as a whole, since many of the gaps which exist in the fabric today will become built-up. However, when we consider the new territory of the expanding daily urban systems, then once again the densities may decrease. This is only natural in a transitional phase in which all dimensions must change in structure also[2].

The problem of densities is very complex, and differs very much according to the spatial unit and the stage of evolution in which it is. We must limit ourselves to estimates of average global densities as we did in the last Part. We must also remember that there can be no problem of densities on a global scale as long as we keep within the limits of the container; there will be local difficulties only which will be overcome gradually — at least in those settlements where action is taken in time.

The daily urban systems

When we consider present trends in the changing systems of life today, the most spectacular phenomenon has been the emergence of the megalopolis in the northeast of the U.S.A. This began to form in the 1950's but only began to be seriously understood with the publication of Jean Gottmann's research. This book clarified former vague concepts, such as that of corridor-cities, which referred only to forms. The Northeastern Megalopolis of the U.S.A. is not a megalopolitan community, but as Gottmann himself says: "Even though we do not feel justified in considering this region as one community, much less, of course, as one city, we have found enough integration in the whole and enough interplay between its various parts to indicate strongly that all those thirty-seven million inhabitants counted in Megalopolis by the 1960 Census are close neighbors."[3]

We can see, then, that a megalopolis is not yet a daily system of life, nor a daily urban system, but only an agglomeration of daily urban systems that will eventually merge together. They will do this for the same reason that the superimposed daily systems of movement of metropolises (fig. 33) have led to the formation of small megalopolises which are the present daily urban systems (figs. 34, 35). It is the scale that has changed, and that will go on changing. When we move upwards from the 500 km (300 mi.) scale of previous

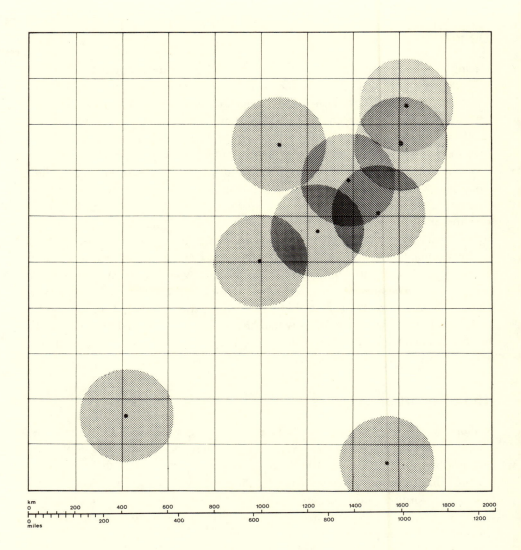

km
0   200   400   600   800   1000   1200   1400   1600   1800   2000

0
miles   200   400   600   800   1000   1200

daily urban systems
superimposed daily urban systems

110.   the emerging megalopolis

284

figures to the 2,000 km (1,200 mi.) scale of fig. 110, we can see how the daily systems of movement of several daily urban systems with an average radius of 200 km (120 mi.) overlap and form a megalopolis of superimposed fields. By the first quarter of the 21st century, such a megalopolis with daily systems of movement of average radii reaching up to 500 km (300 mi.) will become one daily urban system.

The megalopolis of today, then, is at a comparable stage of its development to the London of 1800 seen as metropolis. At that time London was thought of as an agglomeration of villages; it did not turn into a unified daily urban system until the underground was built. Megalopolises can be expected to become integrated daily urban systems in the same way by the first half of the 21st century.

We are seeing the same process take place today that in the past gave rise to the formation of the metropolis and even the polis[4]. We are led to the conclusion that all human settlements, past, present and future, irrespective of their scale, follow the same process — which depends on Anthropos' mobility and which has the following stages:

a. formation and isolation of separate life-systems;
b. contacts between those life-systems;
c. overlapping or superimposition of some life-systems;
d. unification by fusion of life-systems (fig. 111).

This analysis helps us to understand what is happening to the development of human settlements today. We already know enough about metropolises, since there are several hundreds of them in existence all over the globe. We cannot be certain how many, since different countries use different definitions, but in the U.S.A. alone there are said to be 500 metropolitan areas.

Let us then concentrate on the most recent units larger than the metropolis, the small megalopolises. The small megalopolis consists of several distinct metropolises which form a closely-knit system of centers interrelated to a degree never before found in the history of human settlements. They began to appear in the late 1930's and 1940's but have only recently become the characteristic form of large settlements. They are expected to remain the dominant form up until almost the year 2000. As urbanization increases and neighboring metropolises and smaller settlements become functionally integrated, more small megalopolises will emerge. They will grow both in average size and in total number.

After a while they will begin to merge together into the next largest ekistic unit, the megalopolis, and they will do this at a faster pace. The coalescence of some small megalopolises into megalopolises can already be observed, and the process will accelerate until the megalopolis in turn will become more important as the leading regional settlement.

During the period from 1980 or 1990 to about 2040, the megalopolis will

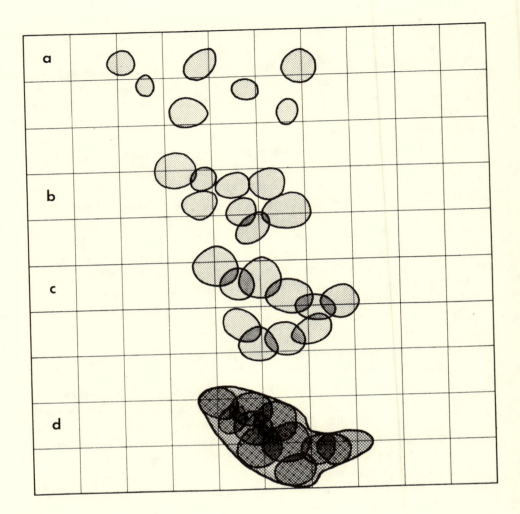

a formation and isolation of separate life-systems
b contacts between those life-systems
c overlapping or superimposition of some life-systems
d unification by fusion of life-systems

111.   the stages of the creation of human settlements

remain the characteristic large settlement of the earth. After this date it will be superseded by the next largest ekistic unit — the small eperopolis. The succession by fusion of ekistic units during the Near and Middle Future is shown schematically in fig. 112.

In form, the small megalopolis tends to become more linear as it becomes larger. Small megalopolises with a "blob" shape exist all over the world, but a megalopolis with a population of over 10 or 15 million will always tend towards the formation of a linear system. Many small megalopolises with populations of between three and ten million sometimes show a tendency towards this linear system, but not always, since the structure depends on the local topography and on the position of pre-existing human settlements in the area. This finding lends strong support to our earlier contention that functional limitations in size do exist for compact, non-linear settlements.

In trying to discuss the megalopolis we are hindered by the fact that so few exist, and even those that do are so unlike they cannot be validly compared. Their sheer size and complexity, and the absence of any authority which could supply data for the whole megalopolitan scale, add to our difficulties. We can predict that by the end of this century megalopolises will be multinuclear regional systems of settlements tending to a linear structure, with average populations of 100 million, an average area of 80,000 sq. km (31,100 sq. mi.), and an

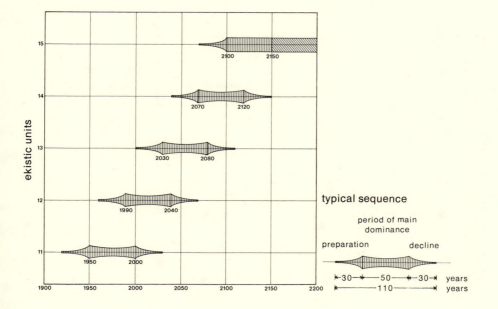

112.   emergence and dominance of ekistic units in the Near, Middle and Remote Future

average density of habitation of about 12.5 inh. per ha (5 inh. per acre), which will be as low as this because the total area will include open spaces for recreation and food production.

As yet, no existing megalopolis has become as large as this, although the Japanese megalopolis has already exceeded 70 million inhabitants, and the Northeastern Megalopolis of the U.S. has — on a certain assumption — exceeded 140,000 sq. km (54,400 sq. mi.). Eleven megalopolises in 1960 and 19 in 1970 had already reached dimensions which, according to our definition[5], qualify them as fully-fledged megalopolises, and their number will reach 30 in 1975.

We give average data for the 19 megalopolitan systems of settlements in 1970 with projections for the year 2000 in table 12. It can be seen that in 1970 the population of the average megalopolis is still only one quarter of what is predicted for its maturity, with only one half the predicted overall density in about six-tenths of the predicted final area. The megalopolis of today is therefore clearly in a very rudimentary stage of its development by comparison with its fully-developed form.

In the Middle Future the complex networks of megalopolises, small epero-polises, and eperopolises will coalesce into star-like formations that will extend their tentacles into the surrounding regions to establish contact with other similar super-systems. Such small eperopolises have begun to appear already,

	1970 megalopolises	2000 megalopolises
average population	26,000,000	100,000,000
average area (sq. km)	50,000	80,000
average density (inh./ha)	5.2	12.5

table 12. average data of megalopolises in 1970 and 2000

if only in rudimentary form. A small, but true, small eperopolis (over 80 million inhabitants) consisting of five interconnected megalopolises emerged in the Rhine area of northwest Europe in the early 1960's, and two more, the Japanese one reaching over Kyushu island and the Great Lakes one in the U.S. and Canada, are also emerging now.

As the world becomes increasingly interdependent — which it cannot help doing — no settlement can remain isolated from others for long unless it is cut off by insurmountable physical barriers. Sooner or later all other settlements will be brought into contact with one another by the development of transport and communication channels surrounded by an urbanized zone at the organizational level of a megalopolitan axial link. By the 21st century we expect this gradual process of unification to have led to the almost complete functional interconnection of all the major settlements in the habitable areas of the globe, in other words to Ecumenopolis. We describe Ecumenopolis itself in the next Part.

Our final conclusion about the systems of human life in the Near and Middle Future is this. The systems of the present day are clearly urban in character, and we are therefore justified in calling them daily urban systems. (This is dealt with in Part Three, fig. 21, and page 88 ff.). In the Near and Middle Future these systems will grow and change their basic character so much that it will no longer be accurate to call them urban systems. They will no longer contain only built-up sections, but also fields, pastures, mountains and even oceans within the texture of their total system. We should find a new term to describe them more accurately, and this could perhaps be daily life systems.

Location

Before we discuss the future of each type of settlement, we must decide whereabouts these daily life systems will appear.

The habitability of the various parts of the world will naturally set their individual limits on settlement. The formation of settlements will also continue to be guided by the same five principles which have always guided Anthropos, and their location will be determined by the same three forces of attraction.

In the Near and Middle Future, therefore, we can predict that human settlements will continue to spread around existing major centers, along main transportation corridors, and close to areas with more opportunities for work or greater esthetic and cultural values.

Both the major transportation axes and the sea coasts are likely to exert an even greater attraction in the future than they have in the past. It is very likely that food production will depend more than it does now on highly space-preserving techniques and therefore is more likely to be concentrated near transportation axes. More food is also going to be produced in the sea, so for this reason the coast will attract settlements, as well as for ease of transportation, recreation, and esthetic values.

Another new development which will affect the form and location of future settlements is that many ordinary people, not just feudal lords as was the case from ancient Rome until quite recently, are going to have a second home. Many people will choose outlying areas for such a second home, and may, as increasing mobility makes it possible, come to use it all the year round as their only home. This trend is intensified by the increasing numbers of people who are able to take vacations. In 1969, 61% of people in the Netherlands, 45% of people in France, and 21% of people in Italy took a vacation[6]. The formation of the daily life system will certainly be affected by this shift from the ownership of only one home, the location of which was chosen as a satisfactory habitat for an entire lifetime, to the ownership of two homes chosen to serve differing needs.

For all these reasons the human settlements of the Near, Middle and Remote Future will be much more widespread and much more complex in their structure than we tend to think when we make oversimplified projections about them.

34. Evolution of the different categories of settlements

The new trends

We have seen that the major changes which characterize the present transitional phase of development will spread through the settlements of more countries and will continue to create problems. Not least amongst the new problems will be that the ever-expanding settlements will use up more and more of the available land area.

Since urban flow (the movement of people from the smaller to the larger settlements) will be the primary force in the Near Future, small and isolated settlements will tend to disappear, and larger settlements to become larger. Nonetheless, we expect this movement to be balanced by the strengthening of units of the size of the natural human community within these larger urban settlements. We have had the opportunity to do research on the meaning of human dimensions, and to study the formation of the human community in many countries amongst people of many races, incomes and habits, and have come to the conclusion that this unit — based in size on the daily movements of people on foot — has always existed, and although it has been broken up and destroyed in many places it still has great significance for human life today. We have termed this unit community class IV in the ekistic scale, and believe that increasingly it will become the basic cell, or sub-unit of the large urban settlements — an area built to the natural human scale within which people may carry on their daily life, children may play, where there can be open spaces, shops and cafés, all undisturbed by traffic of any sort. Highways will surround these basic cells, but never cross them.

We believe that the present dissolution of the natural unit of the human community has been due to the unbalanced development of technology, but that as people become richer and more aware of what can be achieved by planning, as well as what sort of life they really want to lead as human beings within their settlements, they will demand the re-establishment of such simple and long-tried standards and the architectural background for a satisfactory way to live and work in a human community.

Another factor which will affect the development of settlements in the future is that land will become scarcer, so there is bound to be competition for what land remains between the forces of conservation, production, and urban expansion. However, as developments in technology make settlements easier to construct, service and administer, and new communication systems make more areas accessible, it will be possible to live in places that today are considered unsatisfactory. In general, some settlements will move slightly upwards to higher altitudes. Because of this more money will have to be spent on energy for transportation, but a lot will be saved by the availability of soil with good fertility and easily accessible water, making it possible to produce more faster and with less labor.

When we turn to the probable future of each category of settlement we begin by saying that hunters and nomadic bands will disappear within one or two generations; all our own studies have led us to this conclusion, as have those of other people, such as R.K. Nelson, who concluded that the "death of hunting" is inevitable[7].

Villages will not disappear entirely, but there will be fewer and their character will change. If they are close to large settlements, they may be drawn into their sphere. New techniques for better production, such as inexpensive resource conserving techniques (like hydroponics) and combined production cycles, have been developed but they cannot be expected to save the villages entirely. Some will survive because they are located in areas of special value, or because of their esthetic and cultural traditions. Villages will survive, but not as we know them today; they will become parts of urban systems of settlements, and their houses may be either first or second homes for their inhabitants.

The fate of small towns and cities, which live today by supplying services to a number of surrounding villages, will be linked with the fate of the villages themselves. If those villages survive, then the central towns or cities will grow in income and activities; if the villages die, then the towns and cities will die with them.

New types of small settlements, however, will develop. They will be built for special purposes, like scientific exploration in difficult areas — deserts, mountains, or areas permanently covered with ice — and they will grow in number. Small settlements will also develop on the oceans. It is likely that groups of people who prefer isolation, or have a back-to-nature philosophy, will choose to avoid urbanization and create secluded havens for themselves in the untouched parts of Nature. Settlements of these types are being created already and will become more numerous, but never so numerous as the villages which will vanish. The transitional period will therefore see the end of the small isolated settlement as the prevailing type of settlement in the world.

Larger settlements, as we have seen, will increase in numbers and in dimensions. We made detailed studies of settlements chosen for their different regional characteristics: two from the high-income and highly-industrialized Midwest of the U.S.A. (East Michigan and Northern Ohio)[8], and three in middle-income areas in the Mediterranean (Southern France, Catalonia, and Greater Athens)[9]. Our results show clearly that the continuing present trend is towards the depletion on the peripheries of small megalopolises (ekistic unit 11) and the increase of population in their middle sections — which does not, of course, mean the central part of their cities (figs. 113, 114). The trend will be the same even in cities where there are not so many cars. Calcutta and Shanghai continue to grow enormously, although there are not many motor vehicles there as each has a big port and railway. No matter what the income level of the city may be, growth is clearly going to continue for a long time.

We will therefore see the appearance and growth of more major small megalopolises and megalopolises. There are now no more than 45 megalopolises under formation, and there will probably be 163 of them by the year 2000 (Appendix 3, table 2). The number of eperopolises will depend on whether or not we consider Europe to be separated from Asia, America to be one or two continents, and Oceania to be a continent (ekistic unit 14) or urbanized region (ekistic unit 13).

As these major ekistic units form, a pronounced change will take place in the distribution of settlements by category of size, as can be seen in figs. 115 and 116. Here we can see the decrease in numbers of small isolated settlements and the total population living in them, and the fastest growth in the larger settlements and systems of settlements with an accelerated merging into larger units at about the level of the metropolis. It is to be noted that there will always be some examples of each category of settlement left, and that each class will be replenished as the smaller ones grow up into the next class.

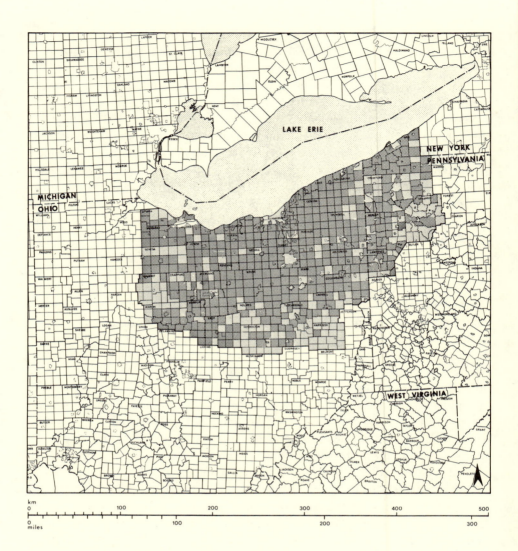

population

▓ increase
░ decrease

113. areas of depletion and increase of population in the
     Northern Ohio Urban System, 1950-1970

294

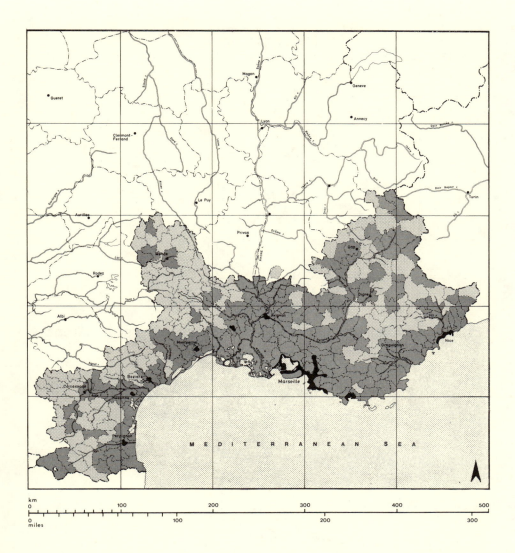

population
 increase
decrease

114.   areas of depletion and increase of population in southern France, 1962-1968

295

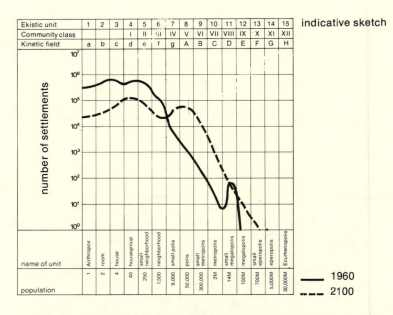

Ekistic unit	1	2	3	4	5	6	7	8	9	10	11	12	13	14	15
Community class				I	II	III	IV	V	VI	VII	VIII	IX	X	XI	XII
Kinetic field	a	b	c	d	e	f	g	A	B	C	D	E	F	G	H

number of settlements

name of unit	Anthropos	room	house	housegroup	small neighborhood	neighborhood	small polis	polis	small metropolis	metropolis	small megalopolis	megalopolis	small eperopolis	eperopolis	Ecumenopolis
population	1	2	4	40	250	1,500	9,000	50,000	300,000	2M	14M	100M	700M	5,000M	30,000M

——— 1960
--- 2100

115. change in number of settlements by size category: 1960, 2100

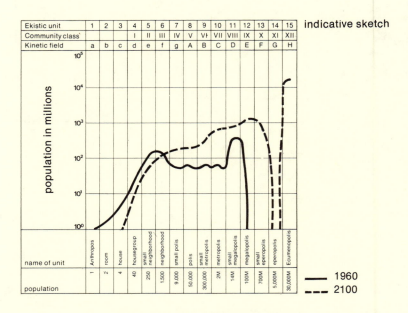

Ekistic unit	1	2	3	4	5	6	7	8	9	10	11	12	13	14	15
Community class				I	II	III	IV	V	VI	VII	VIII	IX	X	XI	XII
Kinetic field	a	b	c	d	e	f	g	A	B	C	D	E	F	G	H

population in millions

name of unit	Anthropos	room	house	housegroup	small neighborhood	neighborhood	small polis	polis	small metropolis	metropolis	small megalopolis	megalopolis	small eperopolis	eperopolis	Ecumenopolis
population	1	2	4	40	250	1,500	9,000	50,000	300,000	2M	14M	100M	700M	5,000M	30,000M

——— 1960
--- 2100

116. change in total population of settlements by size categories: 1960, 2100

The new systems of life

The location of settlements, as we have said, will be determined by the three main forces of attraction which have always determined them, but there will be some new forces, and some of the old ones may have much more effect.

Transportation systems have always had a very strong effect on settlements, but the very high-speed systems of the future will allow places 300 km (185 mi.) or more from the centers to become parts of daily urban systems. Scarcity of land will become a newly important factor, and settlements will have to develop at slightly higher altitudes or in areas of only fair habitability.

Forces which could cause the creation of completely new settlements could be political redivision or regional replanning. New capitals may have to be built, as happened with Ankara in Turkey, Islamabad in Pakistan, Brasilia in Brazil, or Chandigarh in the Indian Punjab.

The question of defense might have a big influence on the location of settlements because of the great range of today's missiles, except that Anthropos now believes there is a probability of world peace. A map drawn in 1972 showing how far China could strike across the world with a new missile showed that a city today would need a safety zone of 4,000 km (2,500 mi.) radius (fig. 117), that is 800 times larger than the safety zone of 5 km (3 mi.) radius required by a city in 1825. The change in the radius needed for defense is much larger than the change in radius for daily movement made possible by advances in transportation, which has increased from 5 km (3 mi.) to 2,000 km (1,200 mi.), that is 400 times larger.

Whether or not connected with the technology of war, for new scientific, technological or economic reasons there is now a tendency for the creation of new settlements completely outside existing systems. Such is the case with the Clear Lake Manned Spacecraft Center near Houston in Texas which was built for space exploration, and new cities and settlements in Siberia and Antarctica.

Because some places will change in importance, systems of settlements will develop in new areas. The development of a new small eperopolis can be seen at a primitive stage in the region of the Rhine in Europe (fig. 118). In 1960 this consisted of five integrated megalopolises with a population of about 60 million. By 1980 it is expected to grow to include seven megalopolises and a population of nearly 110 million.

By the year 2000 about a dozen such supersystems will have emerged as functionally coherent units. Between them they will involve about 50 to 55 megalopolises with a population of between 1.4 and 1.5 billion people. By the turn of the century the average size of these immature small eperopolises is expected to be about 120 million people, which is just larger than the predicted population of 100 million of the mature megalopolis. By that time the largest of them is expected to have reached a population of some 250 to 300 million. The main development of the small eperopolis is therefore expected to take place in the Middle Future (fig. 119).

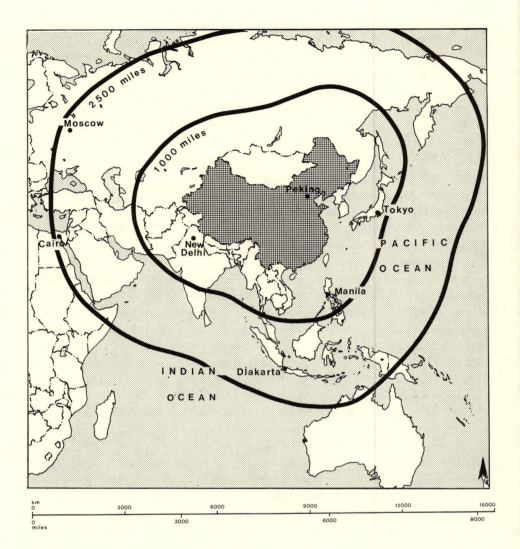

the new Chinese missile has a range of up to 2,500 miles, compared to the previous range of 1,000 miles

map shows areas covered by the two missiles measured from the Chinese borders

117.   safety zone required by a city today

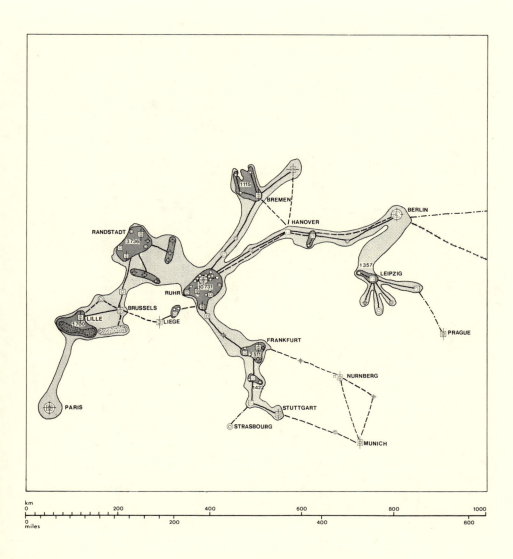

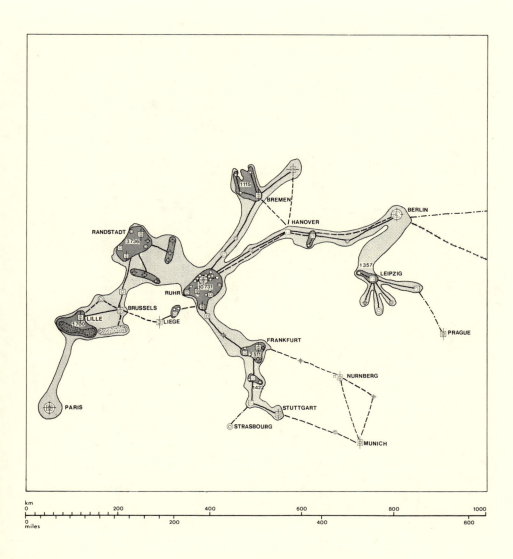 composite settlements and their populations (in thousands, 1960)

 dispersal area

date when strength (S) ≥ 4.00:

---- to 1980

-..-..- to 2000

++++ after 2000

118. development of a small eperopolis in the Rhine region

119.   distribution of small eperopolises, end of first half of
        21st century

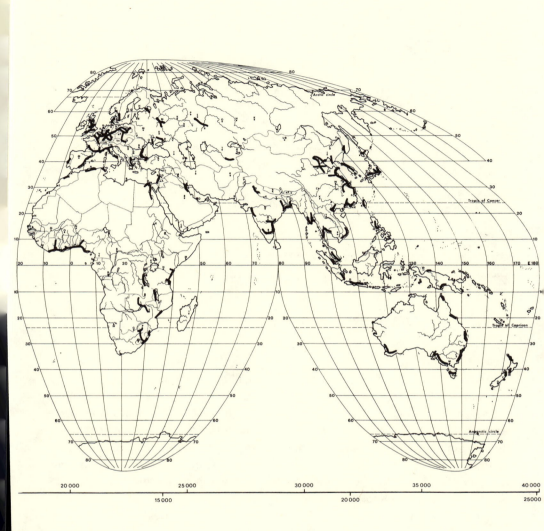

schematic presentation

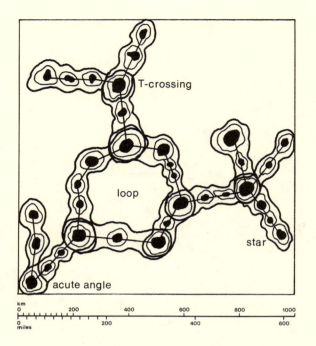

T-crossing

loop

star

acute angle

```
km
0        200        400        600        800       1000
├┼┼┼┼┼┼┼┼┼┼┤    ┤          ┤          ┤          ┤
0                200                 400               600
miles
```

120.   schematic evolution of small eperopolises

Around the first half of the 21st century small eperopolises of much larger dimensions will appear (fig. 120). Megalopolitan axes will have developed more and more extensions and interconnections, and have spread over available space so that they form systems of a higher order with the necessary connectivity between the megalopolises that compose them. The built-up parts of the typical mature small eperopolis will attain a size comparable to a medium-sized country of today, with a total area of 0.25 to 2 million sq. km (97,300 to 778,000 sq. mi.) and an average of 800,000 sq. km (310,000 sq. mi.).

We studied many specific cases of emerging megalopolises and small eperopolises in order to try and understand them. Our special studies included the triangle of Scandinavian capitals in the north of Europe[10], the future urban development of New Zealand[11], and many other cases such as the Amritsar-Calcutta axis in India[12], the west African urban system, the southern part of the U.S.A.[13], and megalopolises in Ireland, central Europe, Great Britain, Greece, Egypt, Brazil, Japan, China, Chile and others.

These studies confirmed our initial findings and led us to the point where we could present the forthcoming evolution of small eperopolises in a quite systematic way. We show it both in specific areas such as Europe (fig. 121) and the U.S.A. (fig. 122), and on the global scale where we show the development during

302

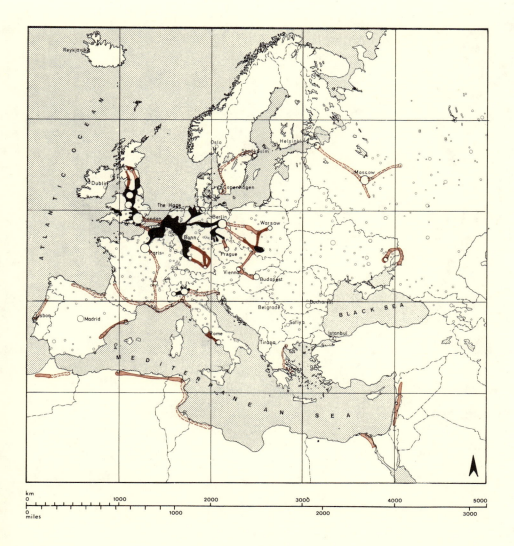

date of formation:

■ (black)	1970
■ (dark red)	1980
■ (light red)	2000
▦ (stippled)	shortly after 2000

121.   megalopolitan system in Europe, 2000

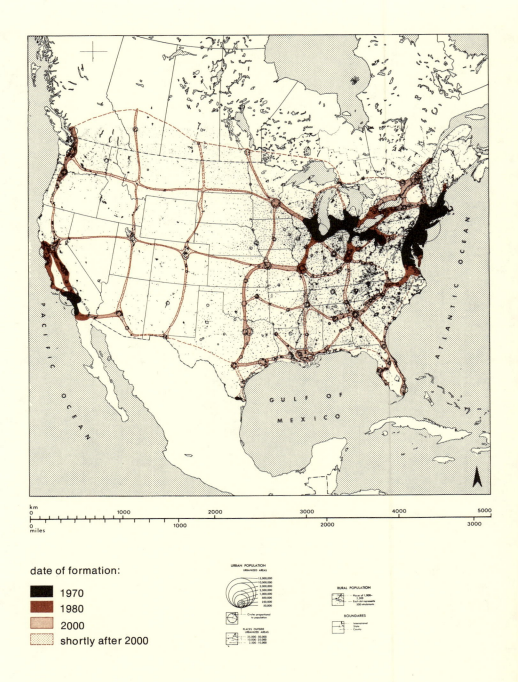

·122.   megalopolitan system in the U.S.A., 2000

three phases, 1960-2000 (fig. 57), the first half of the 21st century (fig. 119), and the second half of the 21st century (fig. 123).

By the middle of the next century many more small eperopolises will exist, and their average size and structural complexity will have grown substantially. As such small eperopolises and the remaining isolated megalopolises fuse together, even larger coherent systems will be generated which will cover areas of continental dimensions. Such areas will include Western Europe, China, the Indian subcontinent, East Africa, the eastern half of North America, Brazil and Argentina, West Africa, and most of Australia.

Since these new units will far transcend in dimensions and in complexity the small eperopolis with an average population of about 3.5 billion, they have been given a separate classification as eperopolis. The population of the mature eperopolis will range from 500 million to 6 billion. Their initial population will be far smaller than this, but it will grow rapidly because of the twin processes of coalescence and population growth.

One possible configuration on the map of the earth of the major regional ekistic units around the second half of the next century is shown in fig. 123. The larger groupings — the eperopolises — are clearly apparent on this map, as are the changes that have taken place since the previous stage shown in fig. 119 about two generations earlier.

The structure of the new settlements

We have tried to see what the size, location and overall formation of the settlements of the Near and Middle Future will be, so let us now try to think about their internal structure. Since this internal structure is largely determined by what Anthropos himself decides to do and what action he does or does not take by means of planning and administration, our comments on what the future structure will be must be more speculative.

One thing we must emphasize, however, is that the popular image of the megalopolis of the future as one vast, depressing, built-up area is completely wrong. Even today, open areas far exceed built-up ones in every megalopolis, although it is true that their distribution could be much improved since they are seldom in places where most people can reach them. At present, the form of major settlements outside the central built-up areas takes the shape of an open network or strips along the transportation corridors linking the centers. An example of this form in the Japanese megalopolis is shown in fig. 37. The major centers themselves retain their clear individuality, but the linking strips have no such importance, since the higher urban functions are still concentrated in the centers. It is probable that, rather than becoming blurred, the identity of these centers is likely to be strengthened in the Near Future by the forces of urbanization.

Although in the Near Future an overall increase in the density in megalopolises

123.   global evolution of eperopolises in the second half of
        21st century

306

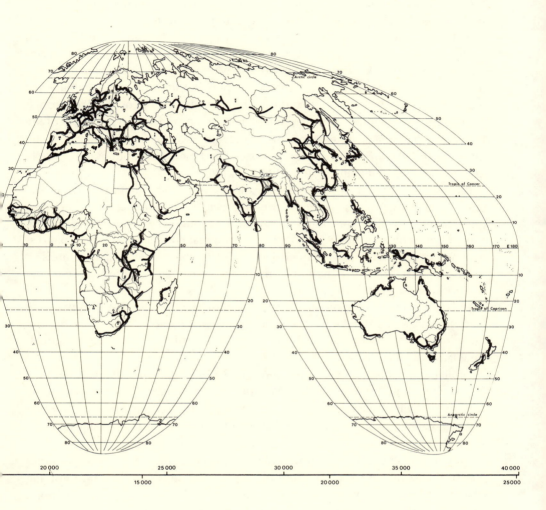

schematic presentation

is expected, it is still predicted that aggregate open spaces will remain considerably larger than built-up areas. Difficulties will certainly be increased because there is no administrative machinery on a large enough scale, and a great deal depends on what action is taken to prevent urban sprawl. If such action is taken, then it will be possible to preserve large units of open space connected by "green bridges" within the built-up texture of the megalopolis. We said at the beginning that in this book we are concerned with what is actually going to happen and not with what we ourselves think should happen, but the general desirability and feasibility of measures is such that it is highly probable that people will choose to take them. We therefore give here the plan for the proposed development of the Urban Detroit Area as an example of what could be realistically achieved in the future in the way of preserving green spaces by timely conception and sensible decision-making and planning (figs. 124, 125, 126).

If we want to provide a variety of accessible green spaces that can serve everyone's recreational needs, we must preserve existing green spaces and connect them together with green bridges. Since no administrative control of land use exists at present, speculative activity has led to great confusion and the rapid disappearance of large tracts of open land close to the megalopolitan centers. It will be far easier to take action now to preserve such land than to restore it later by knocking down buildings.

We have seen an example in the region around Detroit (fig. 46) of how vacant land, forests, and agricultural land tend to decrease rapidly in areas far beyond the urban centers. Nonetheless, a small residual area of highly-productive agricultural land usually remains.

Similar studies made in the Northern Ohio Urban System[14] (fig. 127) and the Great Lakes Megalopolis[15] (fig. 128) have shown that to some degree the spreading settlements will remain interwoven with Nature. The only question is whether realistic planning is going to preserve a right balance between the built-up areas and Nature or not.

There is one important conclusion to be drawn from all such studies: the structure of the settlements of the future on the large scale is going to have nothing whatever to do with anyone's personal and esthetic theories of design; it is going to depend on the laws imposed by Nature, on Anthropos' real needs, and on his ability to organize the use of his technology to serve those needs.

There are three things which we must consider to see if they will have a big influence on the future internal structure of settlements, and these are the need for hierarchical organization, the need to economize resources, and the need for defense.

The need for a hierarchical structure of settlements is not yet clearly recognized, but of necessity it will be imposed. This will lead to the gradual creation of a hierarchical organization for all services, with centers at various levels.

The need to economize resources, to avoid wasting land, to shorten journeys,

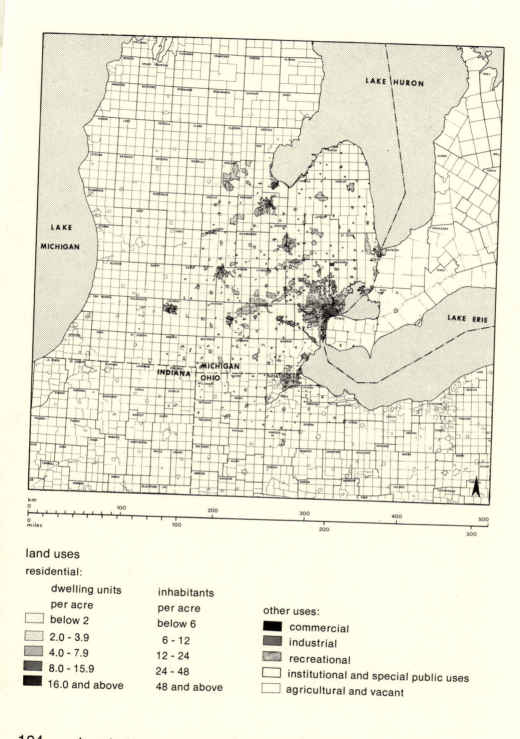

land uses

residential:

dwelling units per acre	inhabitants per acre
below 2	below 6
2.0 - 3.9	6 - 12
4.0 - 7.9	12 - 24
8.0 - 15.9	24 - 48
16.0 and above	48 and above

other uses:

commercial
industrial
recreational
institutional and special public uses
agricultural and vacant

124.   development of a green network: initial phase

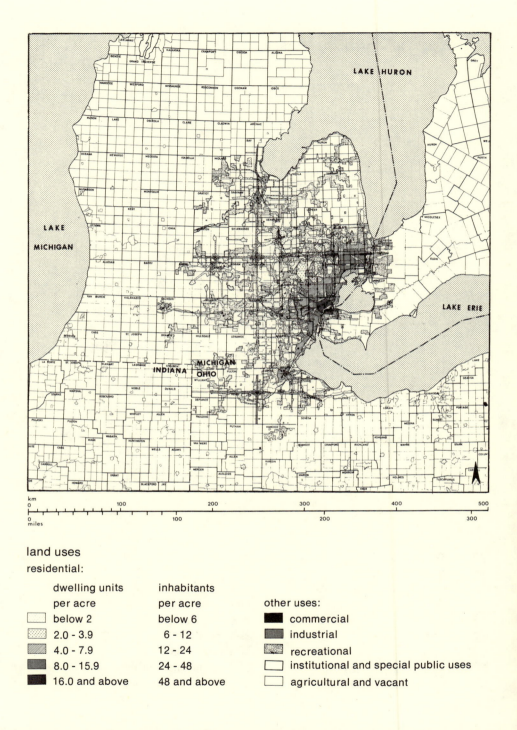

land uses

residential:

dwelling units per acre	inhabitants per acre		other uses:
below 2	below 6	commercial
2.0 - 3.9	6 - 12	industrial
4.0 - 7.9	12 - 24	recreational
8.0 - 15.9	24 - 48	institutional and special public uses
16.0 and above	48 and above	agricultural and vacant

125.   development of a green network: intermediate phase

310

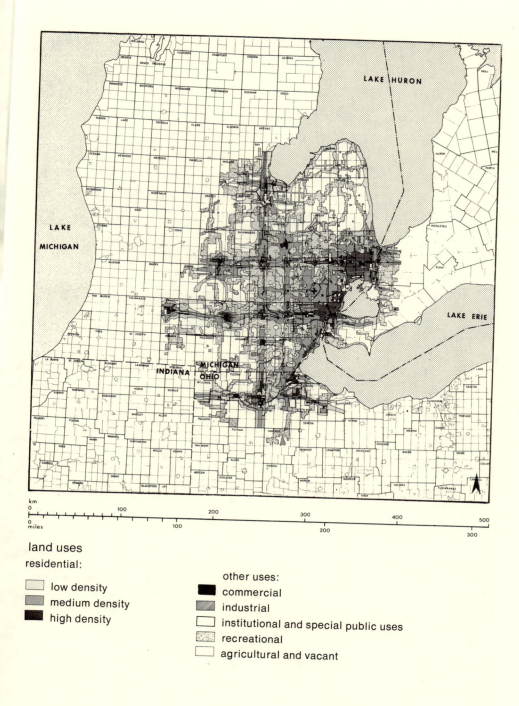

land uses
residential:

	low density
	medium density
	high density

other uses:

	commercial
	industrial
	institutional and special public uses
	recreational
	agricultural and vacant

126.   development of a green network: continuing phase

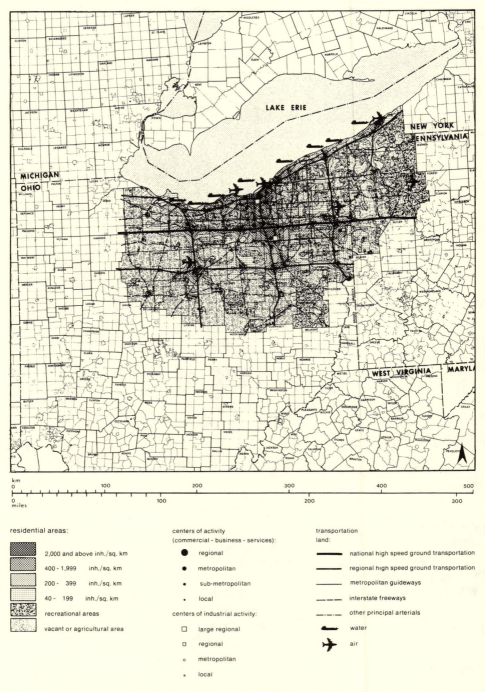

residential areas:

▨ 2,000 and above inh./sq. km
▦ 400 - 1,999 inh./sq. km
⬚ 200 - 399 inh./sq. km
⬚ 40 - 199 inh./sq. km
▨ recreational areas
⬚ vacant or agricultural area

centers of activity
(commercial - business - services):

● regional
● metropolitan
• sub-metropolitan
· local

centers of industrial activity:

□ large regional
▫ regional
▫ metropolitan
▪ local

transportation
land:

━━━ national high speed ground transportation
━━ regional high speed ground transportation
── metropolitan guideways
- - - interstate freeways
-··- other principal arterials
⬥ water
✈ air

127.   relationship of urban development and Nature in the
        Northern Ohio Urban System

312

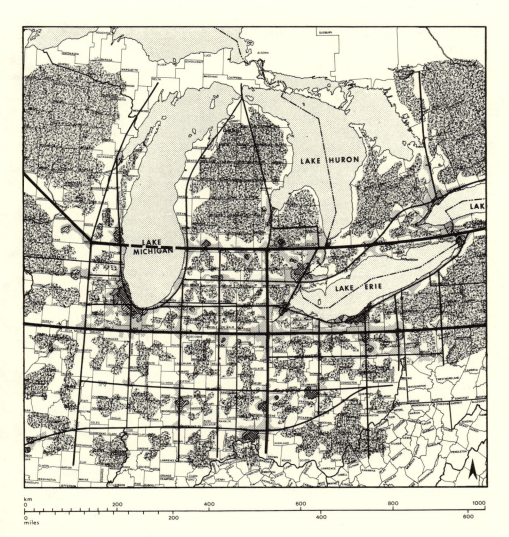

residential areas:

  2,000 and above inh./sq. km
    400 - 1,999   inh./sq. km
    future growth
    recreational areas

transportation (land):

▬▬▬ national high-speed ground transportation
───── regional high-speed ground transportation

128.   relationship of urban development and Nature in the
        Great Lakes Megalopolis

and to save fuel in keeping cities warm or cool (we must not forget that space-heating is the largest fuel consumer[16]) is going to lead to a gradual improvement in the internal structure of the city. The balanced cities of the past which we so admire today must have begun in a completely disorganized way, and then managed to solve their problems by a process of trial and error. Many of the mistakes we have made in building the internal structure of our cities today, such as the construction of high-rise towers and the dispersion of buildings without proper cohesion, will no doubt go on being made in the Near Future, but the experience of history does show that Anthropos eventually learns from his mistakes, and it is to be expected that in the Middle Future his settlements will become increasingly better in their internal structure.

When we come to the question of defense we must realize that it cannot have a great effect on the internal structure of the city although, as we have already said, on the macroscale it does and will continue to influence the location of important centers. However, when we recognize the effect a 50-megaton bomb can have on an area such as Manhattan (fig. 129) we see that there is no way in which the upper levels of a city could be designed to ensure its defense. The only thing that could be done would be the construction of very deep, underground shelters for the protection of selected functions and people, or perhaps for many of them.

The new "city"

It is clear, then, that all human settlements, and especially those with more than 50,000 inhabitants (ekistic unit 8), are going to go on growing in the Near and Middle Futures.

Many people, it is true, and among them some distinguished intellectuals, refuse to accept this and dream of static cities. Many static town plans are produced and solutions proposed — such as New York State's "Change: Challenge: Response" — which devise ways of blocking the interconnection of settlements into broader systems. Whatever the abstract value of such plans, we have just two things to say about them: first, they ignore the principles and laws of the development of human settlements which have been demonstrated by the whole of human history; and second, there is no sign yet whatever that they have ever been made to apply in practice. A characteristic example of the failure of such a static plan has been the overthrowing of the whole principle behind the new town theory in the United Kingdom (where new towns were built in the belief that certain ideal static sizes exist) by the recent decision to double the built-up area of the town of Cumbernauld in Scotland, and to increase its population from the projected 50,000 to an actual 70,000[17].

Other people still hold to the idea of containing the growth of cities within green belts. This fails to recognize that both Anthropos and Society are far better served by Nature if there are open spaces of green for everyone's pleasure and

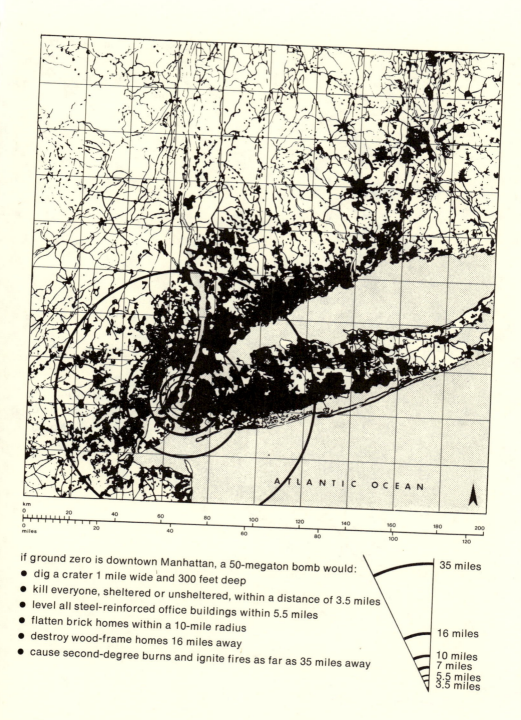

if ground zero is downtown Manhattan, a 50-megaton bomb would:
- dig a crater 1 mile wide and 300 feet deep
- kill everyone, sheltered or unsheltered, within a distance of 3.5 miles
- level all steel-reinforced office buildings within 5.5 miles
- flatten brick homes within a 10-mile radius
- destroy wood-frame homes 16 miles away
- cause second-degree burns and ignite fires as far as 35 miles away

35 miles

16 miles

10 miles
7 miles
5.5 miles
3.5 miles

129.   the effect of a 50-megaton bomb on Manhattan

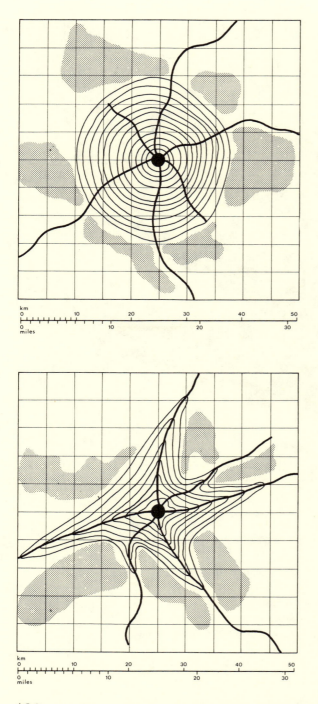

the concentrically grow-
ing city increases the distance of Anthropos from
Nature

maximum distance from non
built-up areas: 15 km

the naturally growing city
decreases the distance of
Anthropos from Nature

maximum distance from non
built-up areas: 8 km

130.   green open space in relation to type of urban devel-
        opment

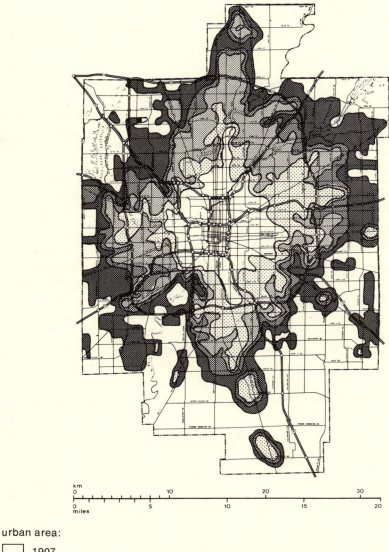

131.   growth of Indianapolis, 1907-1985

recreation throughout the whole texture of the megalopolis rather than just in a green belt far outside a uniform built-up area, where only those with cars can reach it (fig. 130)[18].

All such mistakes arise from thinking in terms of the much smaller scales and static cities of the past. It is certain that in time we shall take a realistic approach to facts as they actually are, and accept growth as inevitable. We have some confirmation for this optimism in the plans of a few cities today, such as Indianapolis (fig. 131), which have begun to take into consideration realistic forecasts about their future growth in a way which would have been quite impossible a decade ago when everyone was tending to ignore the truth.

We ourselves have come up with the conviction that Anthropos will discover the weaknesses of his present settlements and, by the use of more elaborate methods and models, will manage to face the difficulties created by his expanding systems of life. He will use heuristic models at first, and deterministic ones later.

We would like to emphasize again the term daily life systems rather than daily urban systems. In these settlements there will be many people living outside the really urban parts who will feel themselves to be citizens of the megalopolis because of the ease of movement provided by high-speed transportation systems. Not all citizens, by any means, will be urban dwellers; many of them will live in outlying areas of the countryside. These huge new human settlements of the future can indeed be compared in some ways to the small towns of the past (fig. 11) in which the largest number of citizens lived within the city walls and a smaller number lived not more than an hour's traveling time away in the villages and fields. The "polis" of antiquity was a daily life system of equal people, and the human settlements of the future are going to tend in the same direction. Only in scale and in structure will they be different. The new "City" of Anthropos will follow the laws of the past.

35. Problems in the Near and Middle Future

The general situation

We described the problems of the present situation of human settlements in Part Three, and saw in Part Four that these problems are expected to increase. We could end this Part simply by saying that, in the future, an acceleration of all such problems seems inevitable. Such a statement would be pessimistic, and we are glad to be able to say that according to the careful studies we have made, it would also be too simplistic; many problems are indeed increasing, but many others are becoming less acute with every day that passes.

Is the present flow of people from the country to the cities likely to decrease? The answer unequivocally is: no. Urbanization is likely to continue at least at its present rate. It may begin to decline slightly by 2000, but may also increase slightly, depending on many factors. People can still gain many advantages from urban life — improved health, higher incomes, more opportunities. The funds available for putting technological advance into action are still concentrated in the cities. Only one thing could possibly change the present trend towards urbanization, and that is the serious deterioration of the cities themselves, for if present negative trends are not checked, the city and the ideals it embodies could pass through a very serious crisis. The central areas of cities will continue to decay, and the outskirts to spread. Traffic congestion, air pollution and parking problems will worsen in many cities, though they may improve in some parts of some of them. The inevitable increase in traffic simply cannot be dealt with by the automobile and the freeway. Industry will continue to abandon the centers of cities, which will weaken their economic ability to improve their abandoned areas. Even if all necessary measures were taken now, the situation will continue to get worse for many years, although its severity may differ in different places.

New methods of improving the urban environment and new methods of pollution control are constantly being developed. If we demand that technology provide the cure for the ills it has produced, we are fast becoming aware that technology can do so. However, awareness of the problem is not enough in itself; we will have to be prepared to pay handsomely to stop increasing damage to our environment and to provide balanced and satisfactory cities. People are beginning to change their priorities, and rising incomes could provide the financial energy needed to attack all our urban problems; all that is really necessary now is that Anthropos should decide to do so.

In order to understand in detail the problems of the city, we developed a method of estimating the degree of satisfaction of Anthropos' needs in each area and charting this on a grid (fig. 132). When we take Anthropos' first principle, his desire to maximize his potential contacts, we can say that the city does supply this need in general but not equally for all people; indeed, in some ways equality between men decreases within the city. As a total system then, the city is not satisfactory in this respect. Anthropos' second basic need is to minimize the effort he makes in order to make contacts of all sorts, and here again the city does answer this need in many ways: within the city it is easier to make contact for jobs, with other people, and experience opportunities in general — though again, not for everyone. The poor do not have cars, so they cannot take advantage of the same opportunities as the rich.

When we take all these considerations into account, we can use them to evaluate specific aspects of the city, and insert the results into our model of the total urban system. We can see that when we all come together into the city, we do satisfy our first two basic needs to some extent, but as yet we have not managed to build a satisfactory total system. Only by learning to think of the city as a total system in this way can we avoid following any one isolated road in our attempt to solve its problems, a thing which must lead us to disaster. Only when we include a city's problems as a total into a model can we be certain that no single problem will be misunderstood in its relationship to the settlement as a whole.

We can say in general that present trends in problems will continue in the Near Future, with an increase in many of them and a decrease in others.

In the Middle Future the situation will have changed, since new problems will

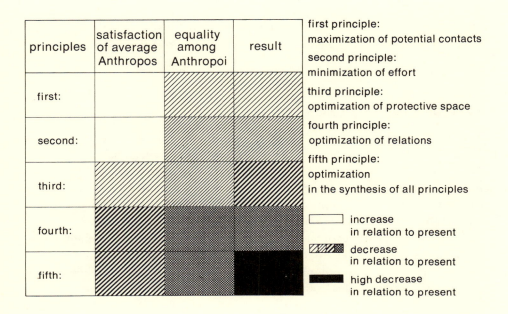

principles	satisfaction of average Anthropos	equality among Anthropoi	result	first principle: maximization of potential contacts
				second principle: minimization of effort
first:				third principle: optimization of protective space
second:				fourth principle: optimization of relations
third:				fifth principle: optimization in the synthesis of all principles
fourth:				increase in relation to present
fifth:				decrease in relation to present / high decrease in relation to present

132. evaluation of human satisfaction in human settlements from several points of view

have been produced by the emergence of such totally new systems as the eperopolis, while some old problems will be eased by the fact that the acceleration of continual change will have slowed down and the many acute scarcities of resources will be less. Moderate crises will continue to affect limited areas for relatively short periods. However, the general trend will be one of slow but steady improvement.

There will certainly be great problems concerned with the organization and administration of vast areas on a scale never before experienced, such as the new small eperopolises and eperopolises will be. Anthropos will need to create completely new methods to deal with them. More and more very different subsystems become increasingly interdependent. However, their problems should be easier than those encountered during the transition from metropolis to megalopolis. Several factors will make things somewhat easier. First, the population increase rate will slow down, so those many other changes dependent on it, such as the rate of urbanization, will also slow down. Settlements will therefore be able to evolve more slowly, giving people time to gain experience in the management and control of the megalopolis. We can reasonably assume advances in such things as cybernetics, systems theory, decision theory, automation, and the extensive use of computers and other information techniques, which will simplify organization. The emergence of the megalopolis in the past few decades as a functionally integrated unit has in fact been due largely to the improvement in communication Networks. During the Middle Future the growth of data banks, documentation centers, and computing facilities will play increasingly important roles.

Problems relating to Nature

There will certainly be problems in the future because of radical changes in the relationship between Anthropos, his settlements and their global environment. The quality of the symbiotic relationship that develops between Anthropos and Nature will depend to a large extent on the action Anthropos himself takes in the Near and Middle Future in preserving balances, conserving resources, and avoiding any changes which cannot be reversed in the biological processes of the earth.

We believe that the general deterioration of the human environment, which will characterize the Near Future, will slowly and fitfully turn to improvement in the Middle Future. This optimism is based on our projections of increasing incomes and investment, the continuation of technological progress, the reduction in the time-lag between the discovery and application of new techniques, and our finding that several of the factors now driving population and settlements to continual expansion will be affected by natural constraints and will therefore slow down. The period of transition will certainly not be easy, and the decades on either side of the turn of the century inevitably will bring crises in the urban environment, but we believe it will be possible to impose order and bring about relative stability. Progress at that time will be hesitant and irresolute, but by the first quarter of the 22nd century progress should be evident, and then will steadily gain in strength.

At the present time, all the problems concerned with Nature around large settlements are getting more acute with increasing concentrations of wastes and undesirable by-products. There is, however, encouraging evidence that badly-polluted rivers and air can be cleaned in between five and twenty years. In Pittsburgh, London, Sheffield and the Ruhr, great strides have been made. For instance, there are now many species of fish in the Thames, although two years ago the river was close to biological death. The Rhine, which for centuries has served as a major sewer for northern Europe, has also been improved considerably, although in this case the choice may well be between a living river and a thriving industry. Those industries which now dump their untreated waste in the Rhine claim that the cost of cleaning it first would put them out of business. This is the kind of choice that will become increasingly frequent in the Near Future; as Anthropos draws nearer to the limits of the habitable area of the earth, a *laissez faire* attitude in environmental policy cannot continue.

Increasing production of energy will add thermal to chemical pollution. Even now we face a dangerous level of deterioration in all forms of pollution, particularly in water, from which it may prove almost impossible to extract highly diffused substances. Increasing concentrations of poisons in water could endanger the highly sensitive micro-organisms which form a critical link in food chains and oxygen production throughout the whole biosphere. Experts say that one major shipping disaster on the scale of the Torrey Canyon could, if the cargo was certain chemicals, sterilize the oceans and threaten life on earth through depletion of oxygen. For the first time in his history Anthropos is gambling daily with the survival of the thin film of living matter on the surface of his planet.

Solid waste presents fewer technical problems for its treatment and disposal than does the control of water or air pollution. Difficulties here lie in separating different types of solid waste so that some can be recycled and the rest disposed of. Generation of solid waste is certain to increase at a rate reflecting the growth of world industrial production. A particularly difficult case is that of radioactive waste, for which only burial at great depths seems effective. In the future other methods of neutralizing such waste may be found, but the problem is likely to remain difficult.

For the natural environment in general then, we must expect things to get worse. Countries in the middle range of economic development will naturally attach first priority to increasing production rather than environmental control. An improvement is likely in higher-income countries during the next decade, since public awareness is higher there and resources and technology capable of improving the situation exist. The lower-income areas, however, are faced with a terrible choice: they are asked to divert resources to prevent environmental deterioration when they need everything they have to raise the standard of life for their increasing populations. They are expected to act altruistically in a world which has shown them remarkably little altruism. However, people are beginning to realize that this is a global problem, for pollution created in low-income areas can spread to affect increasingly large parts of the earth, until it produces a major hazard for the future of the whole world. It is a problem calling for large-scale international cooperation: high-income countries threatened with pollution caused by low-income ones will have to realize that they must pay to avoid such a threat, and it is reasonable to expect that they will allocate the funds necessary for the prevention of further global deterioration of the environment. Wherever pollution arises it will affect all of us, since we all inhabit the same closed system. Richer nations must realize the necessity of providing money and technical help to the poorer nations for prevention of pollution as well as supplying the more conventional aid for economic development. Experts have predicted that, with a global mobilization against pollution, by the year 2000 we could achieve a return to the level of global pollution that existed in 1940. This was the result of a survey using the Delphi forecasting method carried out among the experts participating in the 1967 Oslo First International Future Research Conference organized by Olaf Helmer. According to this survey, the peak period for environmental deterioration will come some time in the 1980's.

Periods at which the various types of pollution are expected to reach their peaks and decline are shown in a tentative way in fig. 133. Conditions are expected to change from deterioration to a gradual improvement around the turn of the century. The actual behavior of these variables will undoubtedly be more irregular and erratic, as shown in fig. 134, but we have simplified and smoothed the curves in order to show the general trends rather than the temporary variations.

Other authors have made predictions for the period of environmental decline which vary from one decade to half a century or more, especially in the case of water pollutants, certain of which seem to need 80 to 100 years in order to be neutralized by natural processes. Deforestation, erosion, and other forms of environmental deterioration, may also require several decades to be halted or cured, but the extermination of endangered species of animals or plants is, of course, irreversible. The short term predictions, however, usually assume that there will be a major environmental catastrophe which will threaten the survival of urban Anthropos.

We have said earlier that our predictions are based, amongst other factors, on the assumption that no such sudden and total disaster will overtake the human race in the period under discussion. We do not take this view simply because we are optimists by nature: we have scientific proof that pollution can be cured and prevented, and reasonable evidence that Anthropos will possess the better technology, higher incomes, and better organization combined with public awareness, that will be needed to make sure that pollution is both cured and prevented in the future. Our findings are quite comparable with those of other authors who share our basic assumption.

Problems related directly to Anthropos

Every problem affects Anthropos indirectly, but let us now turn to the problems which affect him more directly. Some of these, like those involving nutrition and his health for example, are going to become less acute since in these matters the future will certainly be better than the present.

There are two problems which will become worse until the moment they are understood and faced; these are inequalities between people, and the complexity of human life.

Inequalities are arising more frequently from the fact that great advances are being made all the time which benefit only a few people, while others suffer because of them. An example is the increasing use of the automobile. For the owner, the car has obvious advantages, but it also dehumanizes human settlements, and by preventing children from being able to run and play normally around their homes weakens the chances of their growing up normally. A similar case is the use of machinery for agricultural production. Certainly agricultural production is increased, but in many countries great unemployment is created among agricultural laborers. Small landowners are pushed out and more country

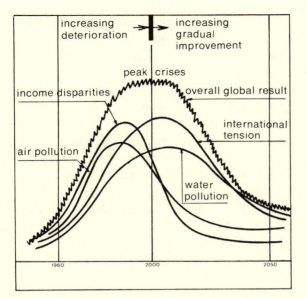

133.   schematic curves of global deterioration

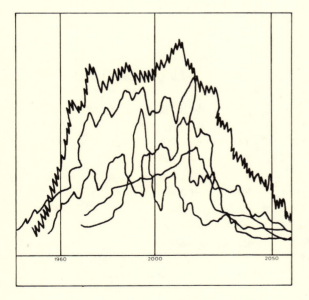

134.   more realistic scenario of global deterioration

dwellers are forced to migrate to the big cities too quickly and therefore without any preparation for such a total change in their way of life.

The increasing complexity of life is a more critical personal problem for Anthropos. We have shown in a simplified way on a graph the increasing complexity of life as it exists in today's settlements (fig. 40). Since such complexity is directly related to the size of a settlement, its population, area, and use of energy, it will clearly become worse as settlements turn into larger and larger systems such as the megalopolis. Certainly such complexity gives benefits like increasing opportunities, but it can become so great that the ordinary citizen is unable to cope with it emotionally, and the administration is not equipped to deal with it. Perhaps the greatest danger of all lies in the lack of organization to administer such large-scale settlements, which could lead to progressive loss of control and dehumanization of the urban environment.

Megalopolis, in fact, presents Anthropos with an entirely new challenge. He cannot hope to prevent its increasing growth and complexity since these are intrinsic to its nature, so that any improvement in the balance between him and his settlements depends on his own skill in working out new methods of organizing such large units. Many small megalopolises of today have over 1,000 separate units of local government, and many megalopolises have more than 5,000. If existing urban organisms can be brought into correspondence with megalopolitan structure instead of being left in the same small units that managed the cities of the past, then Anthropos as an individual will suffer much less.

Problems of Society

Society as a whole is affected by what happens to Anthropos. Economic and social problems will be created by the changes and increasing complexity of life.

One example is the increasing gap which will occur in income levels. Feelings of envy and anger will certainly be aroused in the large numbers of people who will be obliged to live at relatively low levels of consumption while surrounded by others living at an unprecedentedly high level. There will certainly be social, political and psychological repercussions. Relationships between groups living at different levels within the same cities and within different countries will be strained. Unless drastic measures are taken to reduce income gaps, the planet could well face local disturbances, revolutions, even world war. Yet even such drastic measures could only slow down, not reverse the trend.

This problem of income disparities is typical of many other lagged growth processes, that is, processes in which growth in one area follows the same curve as growth in another but begins at a later period. The gaps between the two areas are always greatest at the time of greatest acceleration. An abstract example of such lagged growth curves — they might represent growth of incomes, or of population, or of energy consumption — is shown in fig. 135.

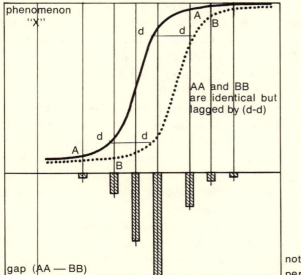

phenomenon "X"

d   d

A
B

AA and BB
are identical but
lagged by (d-d)

d   d

A
B

gap (AA — BB)

note that gap is worst at
period of maximum growth

135.   gap problems inherent in similar but lagged curves

The differential between the two identical curves AA and BB, which follow one another after a lag of five years, is shown at the lower half of the graph. The horizontal distance between the two curves d-d remains constant, but their vertical separation varies according to the steepness of the rise involved and the lag between the points at which acceleration begins.

The Near Future, therefore, which will consist of a wild acceleration of similar but lagged processes of growth in various areas of the world, is certain to produce just such extreme gaps between different peoples. The differences which result, both in income levels and in conditions of life between different groups, drives more and more people to migrate to the cities and increases local and international tensions.

We can therefore predict increased desire of the population to move around the world. The lure of high-income areas will be reinforced by better transportation and reduction in fares. Such migration could be a smooth infiltration of the higher by the lower-income peoples, but it could also become attempts at regional conquest by guerilla activity, or even open warfare.

Many cities, and especially those in high-income areas, may have to assimilate large influxes of people, which will certainly cause problems connected with the acceptance of minority groups. The new high-incomes will be unevenly distributed, so groups of highly affluent people will live in areas where many others live in poverty and squalor — as is already happening in such cities as Rio de Janeiro, São Paolo, Hong Kong and Bangkok. The number of cities containing such striking disparities between rich and poor will undoubtedly increase in the Near Future. It seems inevitable that there will be areas of extreme poverty in most large settlements, and that in smaller settlements increasing gaps will develop between people in terms of their conditions of life.

In general, then, social problems are likely to increase enormously in the Near Future. The physical anarchy and visual ugliness of the majority of settlements is likely to increase, and it is doubtful if enough administrative authority will be mustered to exercise control on them during the period of maximum urban growth.

Some social problems, such as that of racial segregation in some countries, may, it is true, be reduced, but not as fast as problems of other sorts increase. Although we can be optimistic in some areas, we must expect an increase in social problems in general. These disparities are expected to start decreasing, though slowly at first, as we enter the Middle Future, then progressively at a more substantial rate in the more Remote Future. Concomitant with this decrease, an easing of tensions and a more successful handling of connected social problems are expected to characterize this period.

Problems of administration

The problem of administrative organization on the scale of the small megalopolis and megalopolis is a very great and difficult one. These large units have developed very suddenly and we simply do not have the experience or practical machinery for dealing with them. What is worse, existing bureaucracies have a vested interest in preserving things as they are. Individual authorities now tend to proceed by a series of uneasy coalitions in which each one jostles for its own advantage. Even on the metropolitan scale, the achievement of really efficient administrative machinery seems to be beyond our reach for the time being. It could be that we shall need the sort of acute crisis that may well arise in the Near Future to force us to create the kind of consolidated administrative units that are needed.

The period of actual consolidation between two or more metropolitan systems, often very dissimilar, can be especially difficult, and aggravated by lack of such machinery. The new megalopolitan links will be subject to sudden and enormous increases in traffic flow, and everything within the new system will suffer from changes in the scale of all its elements.

Often there will be both natural barriers and man-made political divisions to be overcome — as will be the case when the Eastern Megalopolis and the Great Lakes Megalopolis in the U.S.A. coalesce and join into one system with the Canadian Megalopolis through the Mohawk bridge, as will happen probably around 1990. The Rhine complex of megalopolises has crossed national boundaries, making a bridge between Germany, the Benelux countries and France. Although such new systems will clearly create totally new problems of administration, they will also ease tensions and even remove those divisions between nations which have no rational cause.

We must recognize that we can now predict in some detail the merging together of such systems in the future, so that we can no longer excuse ourselves from making adequate preparation for it by complaining we did not know it was going to happen.

Megalopolis will therefore play an increasingly important role in forming the framework of regional unification. It can provide the means for breaking through national boundaries, and can help us towards internationalism, which is essential if we are to cope with the problems of the new regional scales.

The structure we create now for each megalopolis is laying down the units of the future structure of Ecumenopolis, the global settlement of the future. It is vital, therefore, that we should succeed in devising means to administer these new big units. What we do now cannot easily be undone later, so we are creating the future of Anthropos every day.

The problems of Shells and Networks

Our problems will not of course be limited to those of social structure and administration: there will also be very practical and physical problems concerned with Shells (or buildings) and Networks.

We have not yet developed a clear image of what we want our settlements to look like and what way of life we want them to express, and therefore we do not possess the controls, laws or regulations as to how they should be planned. The existing confusion of buildings in today's cities — huge towers next to tiny old houses, different architectural styles jumbled together, new buildings pushed up against old ones with no regard for appearance or spatial relationship, high densities mixed with low, vast stretches of depressing uniformity, old and beautiful properties unnecessarily destroyed in sudden urban renewal projects — all these terrible things can only become worse in the Near Future because we ourselves have not bothered to formulate a concept of what is right, or the machinery to prevent the situation becoming worse.

New techniques and higher incomes will make it possible for much better buildings to be constructed but, sadly, the contrast between these and the old buildings will be all the greater, so that people will reject the old ones more rapidly than ever. We have no concept of our city as a whole, nor any interest in its old buildings so they are often neglected, and the contrast between different parts of the city increases.

Technology will certainly make spectacular progress in inventing ways to improve all the structures within settlements, although the appearance of a new technique seldom results in its immediate use; however, the time-lag between these two is becoming shorter and is likely to diminish further in the future, especially when dealing with the smaller-sized units. Techniques of constructing the buildings themselves and all household equipment will improve vastly. Methods of laying out Networks and improving the capacity and performance of transport systems will improve. New and more efficient communications and information handling systems, and new planning techniques will be devised. Nonetheless it is a sad fact that other things which hold up the application of inventions, such as traditionalism, vested interests, political implications, shortage of funds and lack of skilled labor, will go on existing as well. It usually takes between one half and one full generation — that is, up to forty years — for a new technological innovation to be widely applied, although this time period does seem to be getting shorter. Innovation in Network systems take the longest time of all to be put into practical effect.

Techniques which belong to several stages of technological evolution are often employed side by side because new methods are accepted only in a patchy way, so difficulties arise in setting standards and codes for building and the supervision of construction work.

Networks of all sorts — the circulatory, digestive, nervous, sensory, respiratory, and regulatory systems of settlements — will increase, and their condition in general is bound to become worse. In telecommunications, and energy and water supply, conditions are becoming better in some cases, but still there is a lack of coordination in the system of Networks as a whole which makes it inevitable that their total condition will worsen, at least in the Near Future.

The picture of the present which we saw in Part Three, then, will definitely become worse in the Near Future. However, gradually it will come to be understood and made better in the Middle Future. The problems we face are undoubtedly great from every point of view, for Nature, for Anthropos himself, and for Society.

36. New approaches

A realistic time-schedule

We have seen that during the past few generations, Anthropos has failed to face several new problems of his settlements, and we have examined why he has not been able to do so. Unfortunately, we have no reason to believe that Anthropos is going to develop any new and revolutionary ways of dealing with these problems immediately.

We ourselves believe that such new methods do exist. There is the science of ekistics itself, and there are new methods which can be very helpful, such as the Isolation of Dimensions and Elimination of Alternatives (IDEA) method[19] which has been evolved for dealing with the total problems of a settlement. However, there are no signs that these can be put into effect simultaneously all over the globe. If someone invents a small thing like a more efficient lighter, it can and is produced all over the globe within three to five years. A larger thing, like a better automobile, will take longer, perhaps ten years, or until the initial investment on current types has long exceeded its value. When we come to new ideas about such large and complex things as human settlements, things take very much longer. Even if new concepts are accepted by a few intelligent and open-minded people, it takes time for them to pass them on to the younger generation, and more time for this younger generation to reach the positions of power from which new ideas can be put into action. It takes one generation to begin a world-wide change in concepts, more time still for them to be developed, and even more for them to be put into action on any significant scale.

We must therefore conclude that new approaches will not begin to have effect tomorrow. Some have already begun to be active, some will start in the Near Future. They will each be tested out, and will gradually spread. The development of new ideas about settlements will take place in the Near Future, but will be applied actively on a world-wide scale only in the Middle Future.

Realistic and non-realistic attempts to deal with problems

New ideas for dealing with the problems of settlements are being put forward all the time, and some of these — such as stopping their growth entirely — we can only call "crazy", if only because they are completely non-realistic. Other solutions are not so much crazy as bad, since they are put forward by those who serve the interests of private landowners and entrepreneurs rather than Anthropos. Such people, in order to increase their own profit by increasing the size of their buildings, often make use of the evidence of so-called "experts" who write articles and arrange exhibitions attempting to justify the alteration of age-old restrictions concerning size, without really explaining, or justifying in any scientific way, why such things really would be better for Anthropos and Society.

Luckily, non-realistic schemes can be put into practice only on a small scale, and so do little large-scale damage. Two examples are the "designs" for pyramid cities in the American desert, and a city on the waters of Tokyo bay.

Conditions in large-scale settlements are not damaged by non-realistic new ideas but by the persistence of old ideas worked out to deal with small-scale settlements; when these are put into effect on the large scale they turn out to be totally unsuited for it.

However, some realistic new proposals for dealing with the problems of new settlements have been made. One of these is the idea of turning highways into deepways by covering them so that pedestrians once again may walk freely within their cities[20]. Total communities have been created in several places, and the first plans for whole megalopolitan areas have appeared.

We can be sure that in the Near Future, Anthropos, by his age-old process of trial and error, will test out all such new ideas to see if they work or not. Anthropos can be taken in by a crazy idea for a short time, but not for long when he has had time to live with its results and find out in a practical way what they mean.

Three specific efforts

There are three new developments in ideas about settlements which we can be certain that Anthropos will be successful in implementing in the Near Future.

The first is the development of the concept of the new town. Until recently, new towns had been built either for private profit or as an expression of one or another personal theory about cities. Anthropos is now beginning to see the weakness of both these approaches, and to understand the principles that lay behind the successful cities of the past. In the Near Future Anthropos will not build new towns and cities for profit, nor as places of escape from larger settlements, but as natural living units of an expanding total system of linked settlements. When this happens these new towns will be able to serve all citizens for ever, rather than a few citizens for a short time. Today, when a satellite town is built without proper consideration for its hierarchical position in the system of settlements as a whole, it is very soon engulfed by the advancing metropolis, and loses its identity and fails to achieve its goals.

The second new approach which shows signs of being successful is that of the coordination of all Network systems. There are signs that professional associations are looking at the present chaotic system of Networks in a systematic way[21]. Up to now they have limited their plans to the unification of all utilities along the same corridors, so they have been termed "utilidors". There is good hope, however, that the trend will lead on to the coordination of all transportation, utility and communication Networks, which might be termed "coordinets". In fact, when we ourselves proposed such a coordination just five years ago there was not the slightest sign of general interest, but now that Walker Cisler and the Detroit Edison Company have mobilized all the representatives of transportation and utilities in the broader Urban Detroit Area — which covers parts of Michigan and Ohio in the U.S.A. and Ontario in Canada — a systematic study has begun[22]. Today, research and discussion about the possibility of realizing the unification of Network corridors are spreading in many places.

Another new concept which really shows signs of realization is the effective organization of larger units. Cooperation at a level which once seemed impossible has already been achieved, like the Columbia river agreement between the U.S.A. and Canada to achieve "the development of an international river". This sort of thing is being made possible not only by physical and technological advances but also by political and administrative ones.

The tasks ahead

We do have reason to believe that new approaches will be found for dealing with the problems of our changing settlements. People who study creativity say that once the right question has been asked, half the problem is solved, and at least we can say that we are now able to classify the problems of settlements so that the correct basic questions about them and their future can be asked.

It is now clear that the next important phase is that of the organization of settlements. A very great deal depends on how successfully we can achieve the coordination and efficient functioning of the huge regional and continental systems which will begin to appear in the Near Future, and which will mature in the Middle Future. Can we control their physical unification and extension during the next hundred years so that the administrative units dealing with them correspond to, or anticipate their actual physical unity? Can we create a clear structural hierarchy of dependent centers from the local community up to the megalopolitan center or even the center of a small eperopolis or eperopolis?

If we can organize things on the big scale, it will also help us to organize the internal structure of settlements. The location of major centers for major functions, and the rational planning of "coordinets" to enable everyone to have access to all services and places of recreation, can help us to work out the logic of our local communities based on the natural sizes of the human scale, and achieve a proper balance between green spaces and built-up areas.

Those small megalopolises and megalopolises which develop later should prove more successful in creating a genuinely human environment since they will be able to learn from the mistakes made by others through the lack of clear concepts as to what we want our settlements to be, and the consequent lack of efficient administration and essential local controls.

We believe that we can close this section on new approaches by saying that we do suffer today and will go on suffering because we are in a transitional period to which we have only just begun to open our eyes and so have not yet had time to develop new concepts to deal with the new situation. The very fact that we have now begun to open our eyes, however, means that we are beginning to cope with the crisis. The end of this transitional phase should definitely mean the end of the expansion of the crisis. The difficulties we are experiencing now will be overcome, first in some parts of some settlements, then in more and more of them, until we reach our final goal of saving all our settlements. This can be achieved with the establishment of Ecumenopolis, the static City of the Future.

37. Conclusions

Our general conclusions are that during the Near and Middle Future, that is, up to the year 2075 or perhaps 2125, the present trends in human settlements will continue. The current crisis, therefore, will expand at first and then gradually decrease. This is inevitable because we are in the middle of the greatest transitional period of the whole of human history, so Anthropos must suffer first, and then go through a natural stage of growing pains.

The greatest change taking place is in the speed of development. It took the entire course of human history until the year 1825 for Anthropos to develop settlements up to the level of the large city, that is, to ekistic unit 9. It took only 150 years from 1825 to the present day for Anthropos to progress through the next three ekistic levels up to the appearance of megalopolis (ekistic unit 12), and it will take only about another 150 years to develop through the next three ekistic units to Ecumenopolis (ekistic unit 15).

This continuous development has led to continual changes in the systems of Anthropos' life, and these changes will accelerate in settlements of all scales and types. Nomads and hunters will disappear, villages will decrease, and those surviving will change their nature; towns and cities will change also and decrease in numbers, while larger and larger urban centers will emerge. Settlements of an entirely new type will evolve which will incorporate other settlements of all types, as well as landscape of all types, within their total structure: we have called these daily life systems.

The Near Future will be the era of greatest crisis, during which we will gradually come to see what is happening and develop new ways of dealing with the situation. In the Middle Future these new solutions will have a real impact all over the world and will lead Anthropos towards an Ecumenopolis which will not be an ideal situation, especially when it begins, but which will certainly be very much better than the conditions which exist now, and will grow better and better as time passes.

This will be the end of what we know as the settlements of the present and the beginning of a new era in human development on the earth.

Part six

Ecumenopolis

38. The end of the changes

The present phase is a transitional one which will continue into the Near and Middle Future but will be followed by an era in which Anthropos achieves a state of balance and harmony with Nature.

Such a sequence of events is not new; it happened at least three times before in human history, at different times, in different parts of the world, and under different cultures. There was a time of extreme difficulty for the hunters, when hundreds of people living close together, eating and producing their wastes in a confined place, created their own pollution, and it was from these intolerable conditions that the first villages were created. Another period of difficulty preceded the creation of the first towns by the farmers. Then the large cities had to survive periods in which disease killed huge percentages of their populations before the balanced cities such as London, Paris and Tokyo of the 1800's came into being. We do not know how long it really took Theseus and the first citizens to make Athens into a balanced city, but we can be sure that it took quite a long time because Aristotle, centuries later than Theseus, still felt the need to defend the *polis* as a natural phenomenon[1].

Each time that Anthropos has shifted from one major phase in his way of life to another, it has taken many centuries of hard work to achieve a successful state of balance. Therefore we should not be surprised if the present transitional period of major changes, which started within the first half of the 19th century, lasts in all for about three centuries, to end — according to our most probable assumption — in 2150.

In continuation of Part Five we can now summarize the findings and assumptions that have emerged from our look into the future which was described in Part Four.

At some point between 2025 and 2100 the rate of population growth all over the world will start declining substantially. At this point the final stable phase of this cycle of expansion will begin — the fourth of the great stages of expansion that have marked the history of Anthropos' conquest of his planet. About then, Ecumenopolis will come into being, binding together all the habitable areas of the globe as one interconnected network of settlements operating as one functional unit.

A schematic summary of the emergence of Ecumenopolis is shown in fig. 136. The exact dates shown in this figure are relatively unimportant — for example, the beginning of Ecumenopolis which is shown as 2150 could actually take place at any time between 2100 and 2200 — but the general proportions of the successive phases are believed to be reasonably accurate. The present period of wildly accelerated changes will be followed by a period of equalization, lasting about half a century, in which the uneven developments and disparities gradually will be substantially reduced. The various factors involved will naturally take different periods of time to become stable, but by the end of this initial period most of them should have steadied considerably.

Our models show the transition to the state of equilibrium as taking place smoothly, but of course this is only a theoretical simplification. In fact there will be many fluctuations; some parts of the globe will experience dramatic

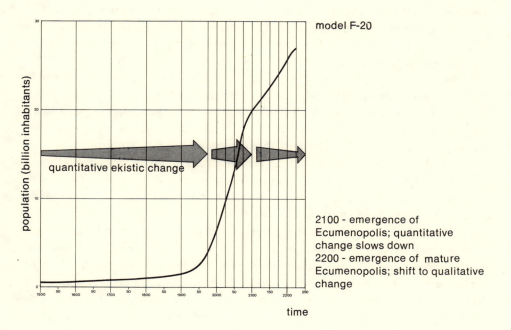

model F-20

quantitative ekistic change

2100 - emergence of Ecumenopolis; quantitative change slows down
2200 - emergence of mature Ecumenopolis; shift to qualitative change

time

136.   diagram of developments leading to Ecumenopolis

advances, while others will suffer agonizing delays. We must think not only about the slowing down of such major things as the rate of population growth, and the speed and degree of urbanization, but also of the progressive reduction in the inequality of incomes. Many social and economic variables are connected with income levels, such as health, nutrition and education.

Population may continue to expand a little during the early stages of Ecumenopolis as global ecological equilibrium is compatible with a small amount of residual growth. Many biological populations that have reached a condition of stability show such residual growth. Fluctuation around the stabilization level may appear during the period of equalization. If technological progress in the future allows Anthropos to conquer areas of the globe thought to be uninhabitable when the point of equalization is reached, then some further minor cycles of expansion could take place, but the increase in population which may result is unlikely to be significant in comparison to the surge in numbers taking place at present.

Once human population reaches the total capacity of the globe to support it, ecological equilibrium must have also been reached if the human race is to survive. Three types of balance must be achieved: firstly, Anthropos must reach a balance with Nature, both within the areas he inhabits and uses and between these areas and the parts of the world he leaves totally untouched; secondly, Anthropos must achieve a right balance in human densities in the relatively scarce areas of the world where he finds it easy and pleasant to live; thirdly, Anthropos must achieve a right balance between the various uses to which he puts his land in the way every successful human settlement of the past which became a functional unit, such as the city-state, has always done.

Anthropos' only long-term hope is to establish a genuine partnership with Nature; his destiny is inextricably linked with that of the biosphere, that fragile and infinitely complex living system which forms the organic skin of our planet. In the past, human settlements have become successful just because they managed to bring the five elements that composed them — Anthropos, Nature, Society, Shells and Networks — into a right balance, but this has always been on a small scale. In the construction of Ecumenopolis, Anthropos is faced with a far more challenging task — to achieve balance at every scale, from the single house with its garden to the entire globe.

We have firmly established the general concept of Ecumenopolis but as yet we cannot be very exact about its basic dimensions. We cannot pick one out of the many images which could result from variations in the combination of factors affecting its formation, and say: 'this is exactly what Ecumenopolis will look like'. In this Part we attempt to produce a "central image" of Ecumenopolis in order to give some picture of it that can be discussed, though we must emphasize it is unlikely to be precisely the image which will emerge eventually. When we mention a specific numerical value it should be taken as representative of a range of possibilities, so that when we say: 'variable A will have a value of one hundred', this is understood to mean: 'one hundred, plus or minus thirty'. The only way we can hope to analyze Ecumenopolis at all is to work with specific models one at a time, and then compare, revise, extend or reject them as proves necessary and according to the particular topic we are discussing.

Precise mathematical formulae can have no real meaning until we find out a great deal more about the relationships between the variables which govern the development of human settlements. Experiment proved that the best way of constructing models was first to determine certain key values for the main variables on the basis of the whole conception of Ecumenopolis, then on an empirical basis, adjust the course of each single variable graphically, and then the graphic models to one another, often by computer, in order to bring them into a state of internal and mutual consistency. Different sets of analytical and graphic models were worked out for different initial assumptions as to the final level of population stabilization, the rate of population growth, and rate of economic development. Sets of curves were drawn for each major variable, checked with other predictions for consistency, and then smoothed. These curves were used to check how meaningfully and how smoothly they evolved, but the main process of model building was analytical, computers often having been used. The curves for second and sometimes even third derivatives of the primary curves were constructed and smoothed. On the basis of the corrected values of the derivative curves, the primary curves were adjusted. Sets of interrelated projections were obtained from the smoothed graphic models, and tables of numerical values for each of the main variables and various further breakdowns were prepared.

The description in this Part of the general equilibrium to be reached in Ecumenopolis is based on such models. Some of the models themselves have already been shown in Part Four, and others are shown in Appendix 2.

39. New dimensions

Ecumenopolis will be ekistic unit 15, which is the largest ekistic unit possible on our globe. In order to create an ekistic unit 16, Anthropos would have to reach beyond our globe and more people would have to live on satellites than on earth; we can therefore quite certainly say that the moon will not become ekistic unit 16, since it is not nearly large enough. A unit 16 would require the space around the earth to be filled with millions of small satellites, thousands of major ones or hundreds of huge ones. Alternatively, Anthropos would have to transform some of the large planets, which are now totally uninhabitable, into habitable ones by operations similar to those described as possible by F. Zwicky[2] at some future time. If it ever does become possible to reach out beyond the solar system to other planetary systems, it will not be possible within the future as we have defined it, that is, within the next few centuries. There is no need for us to go any further with this idea, since for the next three or four centuries it is a "crazy" one; as for the idea of using the moon, it could only become a small satellite settlement for use as a base for the extraction of mineral resources, for scientific exploration, or maybe as an area for the disposal of waste.

The dimensions of everything to do with Ecumenopolis will be new. Its population may be of the order of 20 billion, and all our calculations have been based on the assumption that this population will remain stable for quite some time, as stable, that is, as were the populations of the static cities of the past, within and outside their city walls.

We can predict more about the dimensions of some things in Ecumenopolis — such as the economy, technology, production and use of energy — than we can about others like the exact size of the population. When we were working out how Anthropos could reach a balanced and successful Ecumenopolis, we made assumptions and calculations which took for granted that the economy, production, use of energy and the development of technology would all grow — but we cannot say what will happen in these spheres once Ecumenopolis is established. There are many reasons why we cannot: the distance of time is too great for us to make reliable predictions except about such things as the dimensions of the container and Anthropos' relationship to it; then, more importantly, we know that the long-term future of the economy and the production of energy will depend on what inventions are made in science and technology, and it is impossible for us to hazard any guess as to what these may be. When, for example, a really efficient way of producing power from fusion is discovered, Anthropos will be able to have as much energy as he desires, and it is feasible that he will also be able to develop corresponding methods for dealing with the problem (which will certainly result) of causing danger to the environment through thermal pollution. Then all our present problems may be solved in ways that look utopian today.

The conclusion is clear: Anthropos in Ecumenopolis will achieve a state of balance with Nature. His abilities may lead him to develop a power potential that will enable him to create a static city of continually improving quality. He may even reach a point when the dimensions of his population can once more increase and he can move from this static phase to a further dynamic phase in his history. We need not face here whether — or how — this could be done. If it ever should happen, it will be at a very distant point of time and long beyond the static phase of Ecumenopolis, which is all we can predict with any reasonable certainty at this time.

Although we cannot predict the future dimensions of the economy, technology, or the production of energy within Ecumenopolis, we can say with certainty what its physical dimensions will be, since at that time the unified settlement of Anthropos will cover the entire globe. This does not mean, of course, that one vast built-up area will stretch over the whole earth, although this mistaken concept is one which many people have and which naturally makes them very alarmed. Ecumenopolis will be an interlinked system which will include settlements of every size and landscape of every type, from the intensely cultivated to the completely wild and untouched, within its structure.

This is nothing new: the real village always included an area much greater than its built-up nucleus — fields, pastures, wild forests, rocky mountains, or even deserts. In fact, the built-up part of an average village was usually around only one percent of its total land area, although in irrigated plains the built-up area could be a slightly larger percentage of the whole. In Ecumenopolis only 2.5 percent of the total land surface of the globe will be built-up. This is less than the percentage covered by the built-up area of a village in a rich plain, or the built-up part of one of the rich and successful cities of the past.

The main change will be in total dimensions. A village of the past could be seen from the top of a hill, and a city of the past from a mountain top. We can see a small megalopolis today from an airplane. However, in order to see only one half of Ecumenopolis we would have to ride in a satellite. If we did so in the daytime we would see exactly the same earth as we would today (except that the air would be cleaner), but at night, because the huge energy then available will illuminate it clearly, we would be able to see the real extent of Ecumenopolis.

We would be able to see that up to about 2.5 percent of the land surface is highly illuminated, since this would be where the built-up areas are. Five percent would show very few lights coming from sports clubs and other entertainment areas. About 10 percent would show a few lights from installations for agricultural production in the cultivated open areas. About 15 percent would have very few lights indeed, and these would be spread out over very wide distances where there are some buildings for visitors and inspection stations for the forests. Fifty to seventy percent of the land area would show no lights at all[3].

We may wonder if the need for defense will have any effect on the physical formation of Ecumenopolis. The answer is that Ecumenopolis will hardly be able to exist at all as a balanced city of some 20 billion people unless the population of the world is unified in some way. It may not necessarily become one state, but it must become some kind of a federation of equal people. Defense from nations, therefore, cannot become a dominant consideration in the formation of Ecumenopolis, although defense from criminals will remain a goal. We have no reason to take into serious consideration any danger to our planet from others within or beyond our own solar system. The need to think of defense will therefore continue to have some influence only for a few more decades or generations, and will give rise to the development of some major urban centers in virgin land that will gradually become centers of major importance within Ecumenopolis; but as a whole, Ecumenopolis will not be greatly influenced by considerations of defense. It will develop according to the same rules and principles which have always guided the formation of Anthropos' settlements throughout his history.

40. The ecumenic system of life

It is hardly likely that Anthropos will develop a totally new way of behaving in the short time that remains between now and the establishment of Ecumenopolis; we can safely say, therefore, that he will follow the same course as he has always followed in the development of his settlements. The new unified settlement of Anthropos will spread all over the globe according to the same five principles which Anthropos has demonstrated during the whole course of his history (as we described in Part Two) and which are as valid today as they ever were. Just as the settlements of today and of the past were, Ecumenopolis will be affected by three forces of attraction: towards existing large settlements, towards the main axes of the transportation Networks, and towards areas which possess any special esthetic, historical or cultural values, and especially coastal areas.

The systems of life which already exist will continue to grow following these three forces of attraction until the Network systems of all the megalopolises now appearing, as well as of new ones to come, reach a point of total interconnection on the global scale. The world will not, of course, have become politically or culturally unified by this time, since the adjustments of organizations, institutions, administrative units and cultural values are expected to take at least a few more generations.

The hierarchical structure of both urban axes and urban centers will be stabilized by the end of the period of equalization. After this, megalopolitan Networks will not extend much further, and the main changes that will take place in the physical structure of Ecumenopolis will be in the redistribution of land uses, which will be done so as to achieve a better balance between built-up areas and open land used for all purposes at all scales.

The period which is just ending has been one of extreme change and acceleration of all forces; it will certainly leave behind it a legacy of hostility, crisis and upheaval which will delay functional unification within Ecumenopolis. Change will go on, but gradually the change will be in the quality of human life rather than in dimensions. Ecumenopolis will be static in its spatial structure, but paradoxically dynamic in its internal structure. Not only will increasing amounts of capital, goods and services move throughout the length and breadth of its system of Networks, but also increasing numbers of more educated people, more information, and more ideas. A condition of intellectual and cultural change will exist which will last much longer than the period of the formation of Ecumenopolis around 2200.

The principles, laws[4] and forces which govern the formation of Ecumenopolis will remain the same as those which have always guided the formation of human settlements, but as each area of the globe receives its final evaluation on its position within the global system as a whole and its capacity to sustain Anthropos, several centers of gravity within it will change from those which exist today. Outlying centers, for instance, and especially those with bad climates, are likely to be less important. Cities like Tromsö within the Arctic Circle in Norway cannot expect to maintain proportionately the same numbers of people as they do now, since for two months of the year they are totally without sun. They will be visited by tourists, but otherwise their population is likely to remain minimal. Places with the best climates are also likely to achieve even higher numbers in proportion to their present ones, both because of their inherent attractiveness and because there is a higher concentration of solar energy in such areas which is being wasted at present, but which could be used to supply the needs of greater numbers of people.

The creation of new nodal points on the broader, global ekistic transportation system will certainly be another change in the present physical structure of settlements. We have no means of knowing where these new centers will be, since no study of the global organization of transportation has yet been made, but we will refer to this later in theory. All we can say here is that such new centers will certainly develop in new locations as we move from isolated systems to overlapping ones (fig. 137) and as the final development of the transportation Network of Ecumenopolis takes place.

The daily life system

In Part Five we said that the settlements of the future would be better termed 'daily life systems' than 'daily urban systems', and we defined them as systems through which their citizens could travel easily during the course of one working day. Ecumenopolis will be linked by a system of Networks covering the entire globe, but will not immediately become a unified daily life system. The megalopolises of today are not yet daily life systems, although they are becoming physically unified settlements, because the distances involved are too far for the present speeds of their transport systems. The daily life systems of the past were formed with an average internal traveling time of one hour for an ordinary citizen. Within the Japanese megalopolis, for instance, it still takes four hours to travel from Tokyo to Osaka by the fastest train, and it takes even longer to travel from Boston to Washington

in the past

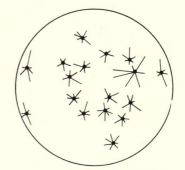

in the present

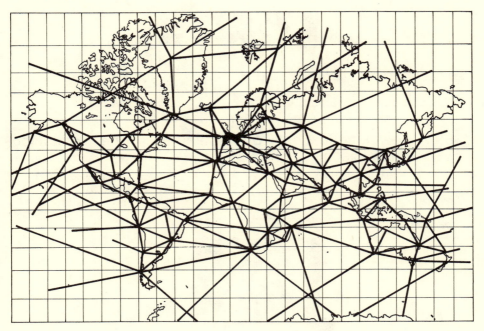

in the future

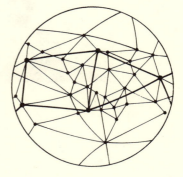

137.   image of global Networks

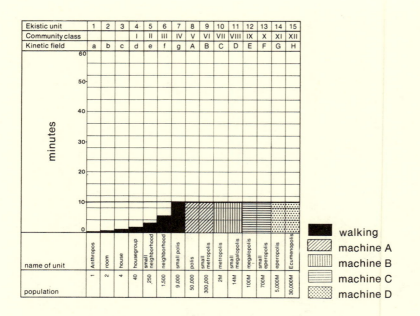

Ekistic unit	1	2	3	4	5	6	7	8	9	10	11	12	13	14	15
Community class				I	II	III	IV	V	VI	VII	VIII	IX	X	XI	XII
Kinetic field	a	b	c	d	e	f	g	A	B	C	D	E	F	G	H

name of unit: Anthropos, room, house, housegroup, small neighborhood, neighborhood, small polis, polis, small metropolis, metropolis, small megalopolis, megalopolis, small eperopolis, eperopolis, Ecumenopolis

population: 1, 2, 4, 40, 250, 1,500, 9,000, 50,000, 300,000, 2M, 14M, 100M, 700M, 5,000M, 30,000M

- ■ walking
- ▨ machine A
- ▥ machine B
- ▤ machine C
- ▦ machine D

138.   ideal kinetic fields of 10 minutes in the ekistic logarithmic scale

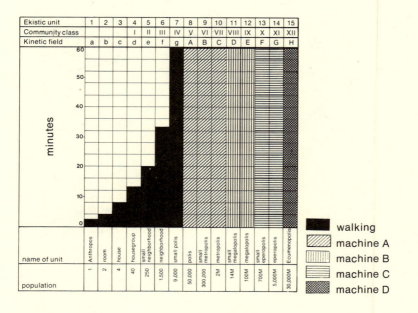

Ekistic unit	1	2	3	4	5	6	7	8	9	10	11	12	13	14	15
Community class				I	II	III	IV	V	VI	VII	VIII	IX	X	XI	XII
Kinetic field	a	b	c	d	e	f	g	A	B	C	D	E	F	G	H

name of unit: Anthropos, room, house, housegroup, small neighborhood, neighborhood, small polis, polis, small metropolis, metropolis, small megalopolis, megalopolis, small eperopolis, eperopolis, Ecumenopolis

population: 1, 2, 4, 40, 250, 1,500, 9,000, 50,000, 300,000, 2M, 14M, 100M, 700M, 5,000M, 30,000M

- ■ walking
- ▨ machine A
- ▥ machine B
- ▤ machine C
- ▦ machine D

139.   kinetic fields of one hour in the ekistic logarithmic scale

348

D.C. in the Northeastern Megalopolis of the U.S.A. Even if we consider the time taken by plane — which is certainly not available to the ordinary citizen and so hardly counts — the actual time taken is far more than two hours when we add the 30 minutes or so waiting in airports at both ends of the journey, as well as the time traveling to and from the airports.

What time-distance becomes the accepted norm within Ecumenopolis will be decided when it does become one daily life system. The ideal city of the past had a maximum walking distance of ten minutes within the walls, and theoretically we might expect ten minutes to become the goal for Ecumenopolis (fig. 138), but this goal remains theoretical, since analysis has shown that although it might be possible to cover half the surface of the earth in ten minutes with the use of more technically advanced satellites, it would still be impossible if we include the time required at the start and end of each trip. However, in practice many citizens of the ideal cities of the past traveled up to one hour each day to reach their city centers, and this leads us to the concept shown in fig. 139.

Here we see that in the past it took one hour to cover the distance from the periphery to the center of a small polis (ekistic unit 7), and that today, with the use of a car, it takes the same amount of time to travel from the periphery to the center of a metropolis (ekistic unit 10). With the development of new underground automatic transportation systems, in the Near Future we should be able to travel the distances within the megalopolis (ekistic unit 12) in the same one hour, because we should reach speeds allowing us to cover 500 km (300 mi.) in 40 minutes, which gives us 20 minutes walking time within that one hour. Such speeds will certainly be reached within some megalopolises by the year 2000, and these conditions will gradually spread to others.

During the Middle Future we can expect to take one hour to travel from the periphery to the center of a small eperopolis (ekistic unit 13) or an eperopolis (ekistic unit 14). The goal will eventually be reached when Anthropos can travel within the whole of Ecumenopolis in 40 to 50 minutes, traveling through tunnels or maybe by satellite for the longest distances between primary centers at 20,000 km (12,400 mi.) per hour. This will probably happen at a later stage of the development of Ecumenopolis.

The evolution of the daily life systems in terms of area can now be seen as follows: hunters needed to move a maximum distance of 11 km (7 mi.) daily; farmers moved a maximum distance of 3 km (2 mi.); citizens in towns moved a maximum of 5.5 km (3.5 mi.); present-day citizens of a metropolis travel a maximum of 100 km (60 mi.) daily. We then look at the future when Anthropos' movement in the daily life systems in small megalopolises and megalopolises will cover distances up to 500 km (300 mi.) (fig. 140), in small eperopolises distances up to 1,500 km (900 mi.), and in eperopolises distances up to 5,000 km (3,000 mi.) (fig. 141), until we reach the point when the whole globe is covered by one daily life system with distances up to 20,000 km (12,400 mi.) (fig. 142).

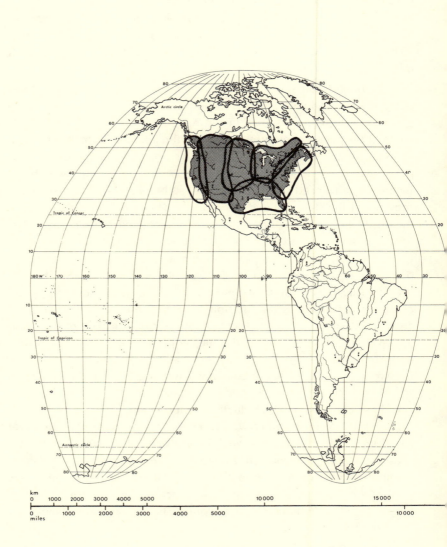

140.   daily life systems in small megalopolises and megalo-
        polises

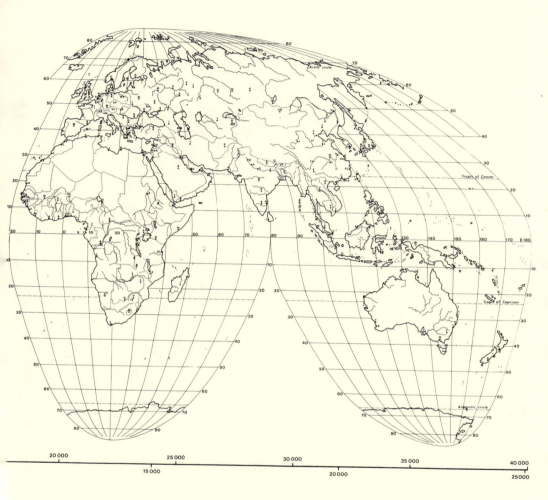

Scale markings (top row): 20 000 25 000 30 000 35 000 40 000

Scale markings (bottom row): 15 000 20 000 25 000

indicative sketch of scale

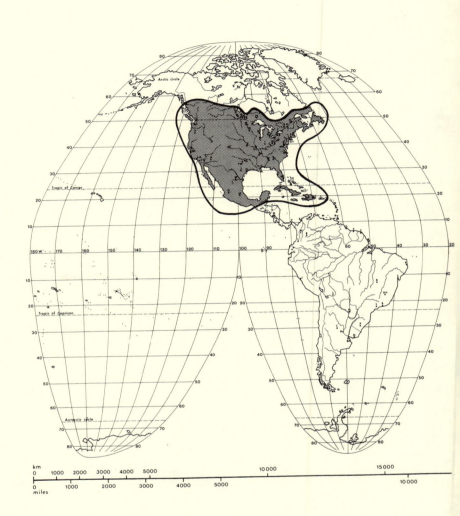

141. daily life systems in small eperopolises and eperopo-
      lises

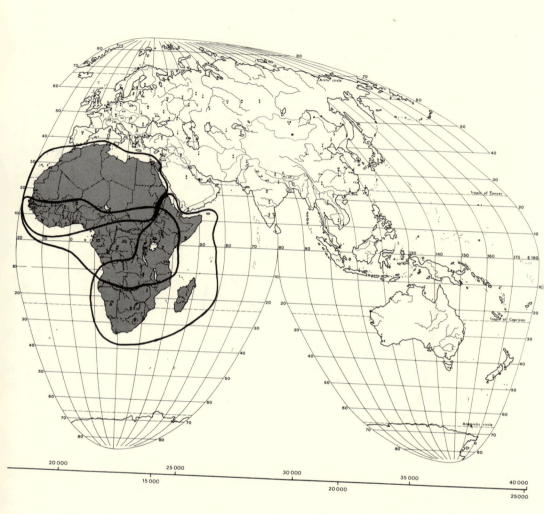

indicative sketch of scale

142.   daily life system in Ecumenopolis

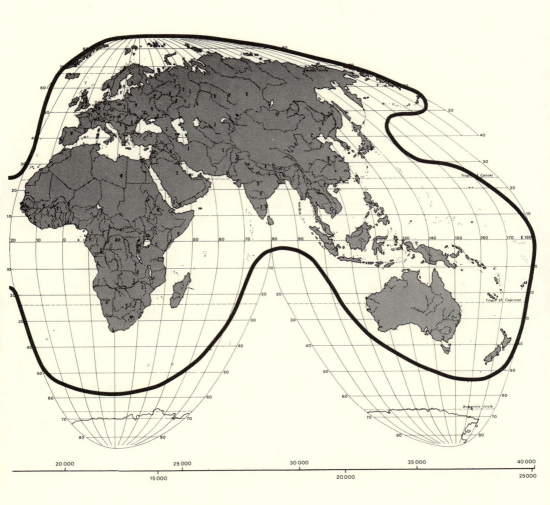

indicative sketch of scale

355

41. The physical configuration of Ecumenopolis

Concept and method

It is now clear that we are dealing with an ecumenic system of life in the dimensions of the whole globe; we can go on to work out what the physical configuration of Ecumenopolis on the surface of the globe will be. It is possible to do this in some detail, and it will help us to understand the problems and potentials of what is going to happen in a clearer way.

As a purely theoretical concept, the ideal City of Anthropos has often been conceived as a circular city somewhere on the earth and concentrically surrounded first by gardens, then by pastures, and then by forests. Perhaps some people who hanker after the idea of cities surrounded by circular green belts of open land are still being influenced by this concept. Of course, even if the world were totally uninhabited and in 2125 were suddenly settled by a population of 20 billion from another planet, the City of Anthropos could not possibly take this form because the physical geography of the earth would not permit it. As things are, the earth is already covered by many established human settlements so, as well as being influenced by the physical structure of the earth, Ecumenopolis will also be strongly influenced by the position and traditions of these settlements, the roots people have put down in certain places, the investments they have made, and their economic and cultural creations during the 20,000 years of history of permanent human settlements.

Of all the work we have done on this project, the most successful has been in working out the location, physical layout and topographical structure of Ecumenopolis. We have described earlier the methods we used in defining the habitability of the globe and the likely distribution of population densities within the habitable areas.

Another important aspect of working out the future configuration of Ecumenopolis was to decide what the pattern of land uses would be, so we introduced various topographical arrangements of land use into our analysis.

There are various major categories of land use, such as for agriculture, for recreation or for industrial production, and each of them has its own best arrangement of shape, size and pattern. These patterns differ when the areas devoted to each category are small or large. We tried to decide what the ideal patterns were for each major category of land use in terms of the area of land needed, and how important it might be for them to be well-connected with other areas.

Areas used for non-agricultural production require only a limited area of land but good connections with transportation systems in order to bring in workers and raw materials and take out finished products. When we show such places on large-scale maps they can be drawn as points, with the Networks serving them as lines. It could be that such individual production points will cluster together for mutual advantage and become major nodes of industrial production.

Agricultural production, when it is mechanized and large-scale, needs bigger areas of land but the same needs for transportation. Special conditions of soil or of climate may mean concentration of production of certain foods in certain belts of land, but these do not need a well-developed hierarchical spatial organization to carry out their functions. It is probable that in the future most foodstuffs will be produced by methods similar to those of industry — in factories, water tanks, automated greenhouses, and so on — that require very little space. Agriculture of the traditional type, which requires a lot of land, will probably be limited to small quantities of high-quality luxury foodstuffs. Land used for animal husbandry will also be reduced by methods like intensive grazing. Land requirements for primary production are expected to be quite manageable.

Areas to be kept for conservation must be large undivided tracts of land, and many will need only minimal connection with other areas. Even on large-scale maps they will appear as large sections.

Recreation will be a more important concept in the future. Recreation in the fullest sense needs a complete range of interconnected land areas of different sizes. Recreation areas, like the various categories of school or university, or the various levels of medical facilities, should serve populations of various sizes. The larger they are, the less frequently they will be used by the average person. Regional recreational centers like the Alps or Mediterranean coast, for example, will be accessible to all citizens, but used only infrequently by the average person. Our assumption is that areas to be used as open spaces will grow larger in proportion to the size of the community being served, and will give everyone the opportunity to relax, contemplate, or do nothing at all, as well as the opportunity to take energetic exercise, face challenging adventure, or come into contact with every form and mood of Nature. This is the all-inclusive concept of recreation which will be built into the physical structure of Ecumenopolis.

We used these assumptions about land uses together with those of habitability and maximum densities to calculate the future configuration of Ecumenopolis.

Our estimated maximum population for the earth was about 25 billion, and optimum population 20 billion. When we take into account the probable structure of Ecumenopolis, and the prior commitment of various areas of the globe to certain land uses which may not be the best possible ones, we must adjust these figures downward by one to two billion. Since these final figures are still somewhat impressive, and are only indicative, we should perhaps adjust downward by some five billion; so the maximum population of the earth of around 25 billion could be given more accurately as between 20 and 30 billion, and the optimum population of around 20 billion as between 15 and 25 billion.

We have said that as the final stage of a series of adaptive processes the population will tend to stabilize at around the optimum size, provided everything goes normally. This is to assume there will be no unanticipated constraints other than those applied by density levels, the habitability of various areas, and the patterns of land use. One such possibility might be the internationally imposed limitation of population by some new type of global tyrant, but it is to be expected that the intellectual development of Anthropos in the future would be able to prevent such an exercise of arbitrary power.

Population distribution

In working out this future image of Ecumenopolis we kept to the rule we had set ourselves of not putting forward what we ourselves believed would be best, but simply working out what Anthropos was going to do in continuing to follow the laws he has always followed in developing his settlements.

Two factors which will have a strong influence on the position of future major areas of habitation are the position of habitable areas in relationship to the rest of the structure of established human settlements, and the economic and cultural condition of existing settlements. If an area with good conditions as far as habitability is concerned is located in an isolated position, somewhere in the Pacific, while another is in West Africa between Ghana and Nigeria, then it is clear the second will attract more people than the first, although both have equally good physical conditions. In the same way, an area which has successful large settlements in it already, or one in which everything is advancing, will attract more people than one with few people and stringent laws against immigration.

We developed models of Ecumenopolis based on several different assumptions as to what the global population would be. In working out how a final balance in the relationship of habitable land to the density at which people lived in it might be reached, we also made several models based on different assumptions as to how much mobility might be allowed between various nations. Out of the many available models, we concentrated on those closest to what we considered the most probable population for Ecumenopolis — that is, 15 to 20 billion people. The conclusions reached according to this model are those we give as the most probable for the image of the City of the Future.

In order to give some idea of the wide range of possibilities actually covered by our research, and to show what a very different picture might emerge if one factor, let us say technology, should develop in an unpredictable way, we also show what the probable structure of Ecumenopolis would be should the population reach 50 billion people (fig. 143). This, according to all our assumptions, would seem very improbable indeed.

We turn now to the calculations based on the most probable assumption — a population of 20 billion — and show first the preliminary model of Ecumenopolis (fig. 144) based on the extrapolation of observable present trends and patterns in urbanization, which shows what might happen in global urban development if relatively little were done to rationalize or channel development in any way. This model also used the geographic distribution of world population worked out in the context of the population projections.

When we looked at these figures we saw that if present trends should continue then there would be a very uneven distribution of densities over places with the same conditions of habitability; some areas would have far too many people for comfort, and others far too few in terms of what they could easily support. We therefore undertook a purely theoretical study of the different ways in which a given world population might be distributed over the given areas of the world according to their degree of habitability for the year 2100 to discover what the optimum distribution might be. We assumed that this optimum distribution should satisfy two criteria:

1.   Land areas having similar conditions of habitability should have people living in them at the same densities.
2.   The densities at which people were living in zones with different ratings for habitability should reflect the qualitative differences between those zones.

In our habitability analysis, the globe was divided into five areas, running from A to E, according to how easy and pleasant each area was to live in. For the purpose of this study we assumed that zones A and B would have people living in them at three times the density of zone C. We also assumed that the great majority of the world population would live in the three best zones, A, B and C, and so did not work out the specific distribution of the remaining population that would live in difficult zones D and E.

The distribution of world population shown in fig. 145 results from taking the population model F-20 (20 billion) and subtracting from it the numbers of people projected in this model who are likely to be living in the difficult areas of the world (1.00 billion, a large figure, but one which had to be tested). The remaining 19.00 billion people were then distributed over world habitability zones A and B at three times the densities of zones C.

The densities taken as normal for zones A and B were 70 persons per inhabited ha (28 per inhabited acre) and for zone C, 23 per inhabited ha (9 per inhabited acre) — a ratio of 3:1. If we were considering any geographic unit on a large scale, considerable local variations in densities would of course be seen because of the influence of local criteria — mountains, deserts, or local conditions generally.

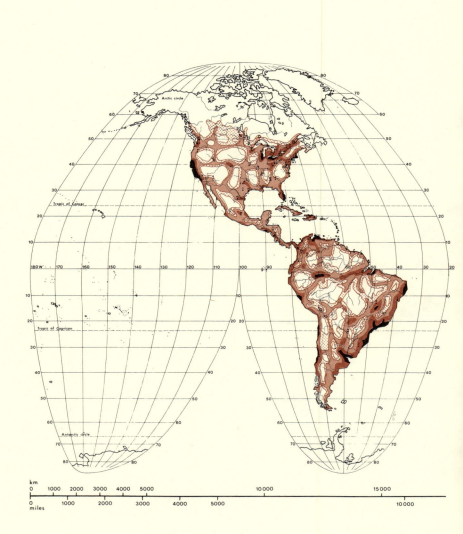

143.　probable structure of Ecumenopolis with 50 billion inhabitants, 2200

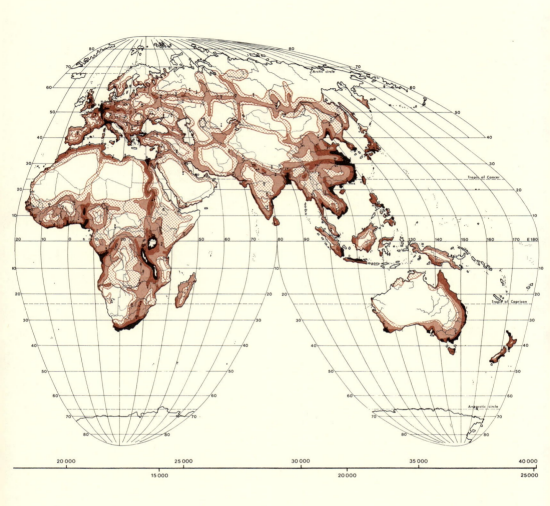

 100 million inh. per 10,000 km²
20 million inh. per 10,000 km²
5 million inh. per 10,000 km²
1 million inh. per 10,000 km²
0.1 million inh. per 10,000 km²

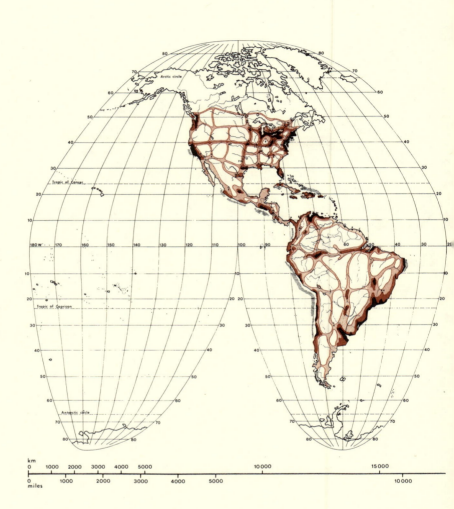

144.   probable structure of Ecumenopolis with 20 billion inhabitants, 2100

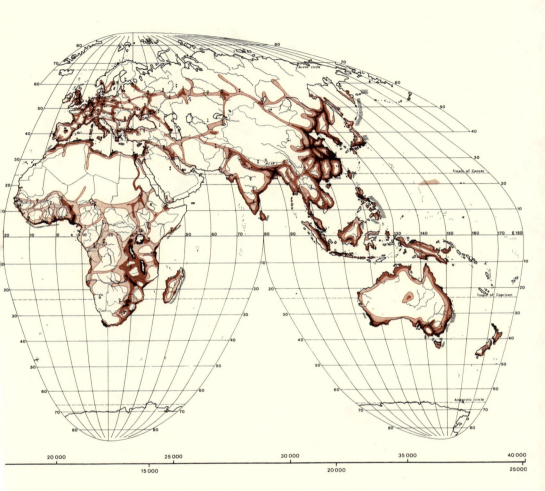

relative degree of elaboration by region (highest = 1)

1. Europe
2. North America
3. Australia, Japan, Egypt
4. Africa south of 0°, S.E. Asia
5. other

 high density
medium density
low density
deep ocean waters (practically no continental shelves)
deep ocean waters (greater depths)

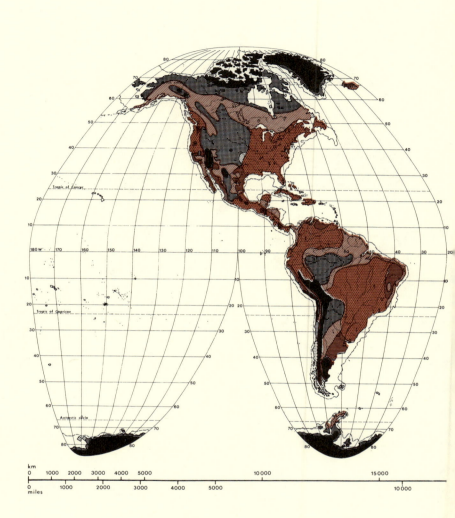

145. probable distribution of a world population of 20
billion, 2100

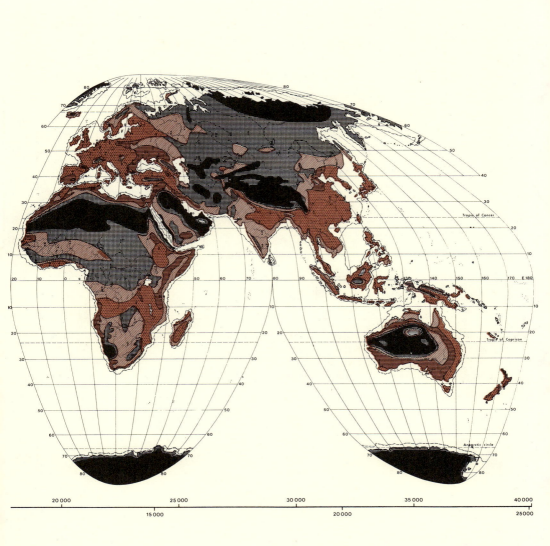

habitability zones:

■ E non-habitable
▓ D not suitable for extensive habitation
▒ C difficult for extensive habitation
▦ B no significant limitations
▓ A no limitations

density 2100 A.D. inh./km^2
■ in habitable zones (A + B) : 370
▒ in habitable zone (C) : 123

population / continental regions	1970	2100			ratio			balance
		first set	second set	third set	(3) : (2)	(4) : (2)	(5) : (2)	(3) - (4)
(1)	(2)	(3)	(4)	(5)	(6)	(7)	(8)	(9)
world	3.632*	18.960**	18.960**	14.200***	5.60	5.60	4.10	—
N. & C. America	0.321	1.750	3.130	2.000	5.45	9.75	6.25	+ 1.380
S. America	0.190	2.640	4.190	3.000	13.90	22.00	15.80	+ 1.550
Africa	0.344	3.210	3.380	2.000	9.30	9.80	5.80	+ 0.170
Europe	0.462	1.090	1.600	1.200	2.40	3.50	2.60	+ 0.510
U.S.S.R.	0.243	1.060	1.040	1.000	4.35	4.30	4.10	− 0.020
Asia	2.056	8.895	3.880	4.500	4.30	1.90	2.20	− 5.015
Oceania	0.019	0.315	1.740	0.500	16.50	91.50	26.30	+ 1.425

*
the figures have to be adjusted to correspond to population in zones A, B and C only.
The total world figure would be approximately 3.300 billion
**
the total world assumption is 20 billion people
***
the total world assumption is 15 billion people

table 13.   comparison between the three sets of population
projections

The relationship between the distributions of population over the globe according to these two projections — the first based purely on a projection of present trends, and the second on a rational distribution of densities according to the habitability of the various areas — is shown in table 13. The most striking difference between the two sets of figures can be seen in the projections for Asia. The last column of table 13 shows what a difference there is between the population which will be produced if present trends go on as they are now and the numbers that should be reached according to a more equalized distribution based on the habitability of the areas. We can see that according to the more equalized distribution projected, Asian population growth by 2075 should be reduced by about five billion, and the population of other areas of the globe should grow more than projected at present.

Several interpretations of these differences are possible. One is that there might be a massive migration out of Asia to other areas in the next century; this is hardly likely, at least on a large enough scale, when we consider the time and resources needed and the enormous difficulties of antagonism and acculturation that would be caused. A second and more realistic interpretation is that the constraining effects of overcrowding and bad living conditions will be felt earlier in Asia, and the populations there will be slowed to stabilization rates of growth before they reach such excessive numbers. It is likely that Asian densities will be higher than theoretical norms because of their present situation and their impulse to growth, and also because Asian populations are accustomed to live at higher densities without any abnormal or anti-social consequences. However, simply because of the restraints that will be applied by conditions of habitability, it seems unlikely that Asian densities will reach the levels projected by the F-20 model within the next century.

In other areas of the world where the projections of the F-20 model show that there will be a relatively sparse population in 2100, it may be that growth of population will continue after that period until numbers achieving a comfortable balance with Nature are reached.

After studying these figures and others based on more extreme assumptions, such as a future world population of 50 billion (fig. 143), we came to the conclusion that we should work out a probable evolution combining the figures based on a projection of existing trends and those based on the acceptable densities in the habitable areas. We therefore produced a third generalized set of figures which was based on the assumption of a future population of 15 billion, and this is shown in fig. 146. We did this, of course, in a very simplified and generalized way, since exact projections for such a distant and unknown future as that of Ecumenopolis, although it is inevitable, can be based only on such indicative general assumptions. All our work, however, and the considerable experience gained by it, allows us to say that fig. 146 gives the most reasonable assumption of what Ecumenopolis will look like in the Remote Future — that is, after 2100.

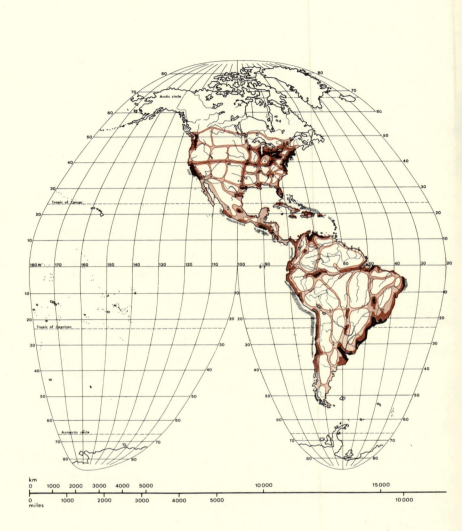

This map is similar to that of 20 billion, pp. 362, 363; the only difference is that densities within the respective areas are supposed to be somewhat lower

146.　probable structure of Ecumenopolis with 15 billion inhabitants, 2100

368

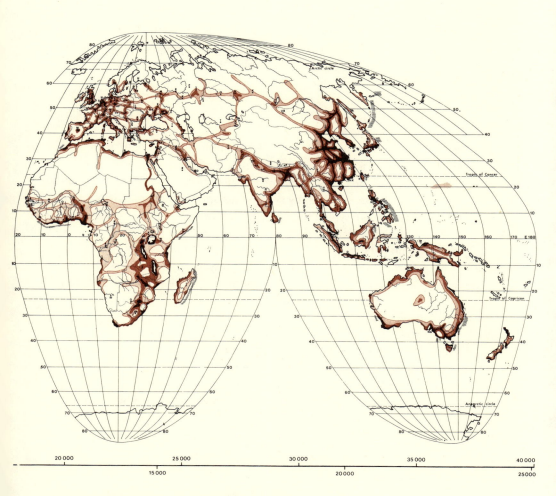

relative degree of elaboration by region (highest = 1)

1. Europe
2. North America
3. Australia, Japan, Egypt
4. Africa south of 0°, S.E. Asia
5. other

 high density
medium density
low density
deep ocean waters (practically no continental shelves)
deep ocean waters (greater depths)

Three specific areas of Ecumenopolis

As it is useful to have some sort of picture of what Ecumenopolis will be like, we have selected, and describe here, three areas (out of the many on which we carried out research) on three continents with very different geographical conditions, numbers of population and stages of development. The work on these three was done at the Athens Center of Ekistics, but the amount of data amassed and the value of each case in general was different because of the differing numbers of experts and length of time spent working on each; we mention, therefore, their relative values as we come to them.

We first look at the European part of Ecumenopolis (fig. 147). Its main center will be London-Paris-Randstadt, and we notice at once that this "looks towards" the eastern seaboard of the U.S.A. A strong link will therefore exist between these two large centers of Ecumenopolis, by sea and air and possibly means of tunnels. The other main center with which the European one will be connected will be the Yang-Tse Delta towards the east, but as it is nearly twice as far away, it is likely that the physical links between it and the European center will be weaker than those between Europe and the eastern U.S.A. However, since the continents of Europe and Asia have a land connection, there will be opportunities for other types of connections between London-Paris-Randstadt and the Yang-Tse Delta.

An important secondary center within Ecumenopolis is likely to develop along the eastern coast of India, and a transportation link will therefore be necessary between it and the European center. The focal point of the important North African branch of Ecumenopolis will be the Nile Delta, from which a vertical branch of Ecumenopolis will extend along the East African Rift Valley, through the plateaux of East and South Africa with their favorable climate, to the southern tip of the African continent. It is clear that a link by air, sea and tunnel will also develop between the European center and this Nile Delta center.

Central Asia has difficult geographic conditions. Europe will therefore be connected to the main Asian centers over two main axes: the first northern one, via Moscow and more or less along the present course of the Trans-Siberian railway to the Far East; and the second, more or less following the Asian Highway from Northern Iran and Turkestan, via Afghanistan, through Western Pakistan and the Ganges Valley, towards the rest of India and Indochina. The European center may be connected with the beginning of this second axis in several possible ways: over the Black Sea and along the western coast of the Caspian; through Istanbul and then either along the south coast of Asia Minor, or diagonally through it towards the Euphrates and Tigris Valley, and again through Iran to the Asian Highway.

These would seem to be the main transportation linkages between the European part of Ecumenopolis and the adjoining continents. They should be kept in mind in order to understand the future pattern of development of Ecumenopo-

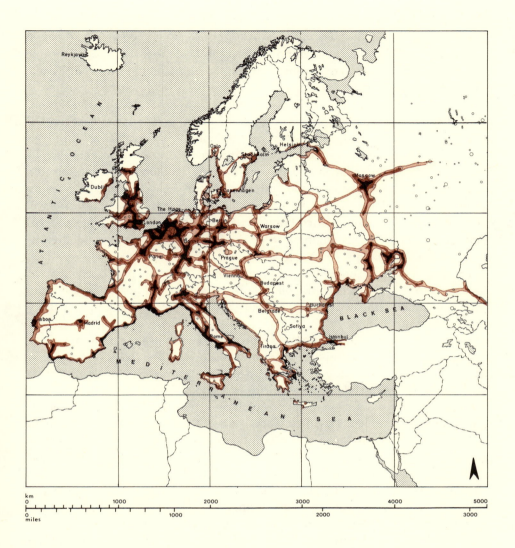

density

high
medium
low

147. Ecumenopolis in Europe after 2100

lis in Europe. As we come nearer to Ecumenopolis, the formation of transportation axes and urban centers within Europe is going to become far less dependent on the internal configuration of Europe itself and far more on the world-wide system of axes we have just described.

The oceans, which are now a dividing factor as far as urban development is concerned, will become a unifying one in the Remote Future. The Mediterranean, the Baltic, and the North and Black Seas in particular are likely to act as areas of connection between the shores around them. The Mediterranean especially, with its particularly favorable climate and its long historic traditions, may develop into a sort of inland lake to connect southern Europe, northern Africa and the western shores of Asia both ekistically and culturally. The North Sea and the Channel will also be of particular importance because of their proximity to the most important future center of Ecumenopolis in Europe — the area around London-Paris-Randstadt and the Rhine.

The gateways from Europe to the Oriental world are likely to develop, as far as the northern branch of Ecumenopolis is concerned, around Moscow and, for the southern branch at the two places which give access to the Asian Highway — Istanbul and Rostov.

Some further connections should be recognized, such as the one from Greece through the Aegean Sea and the islands towards the southern coast of Asia Minor and Cyrenaica; another from Italy through Sicily to Tunisia; and yet another from Gibraltar to Morocco and northwest Africa.

Once the main external connections between the European part of Ecumenopolis and other continents have been recognized, the main axes of development inside the continent itself can be traced. The main grid of axes might be rectangular, but this is theoretical and valid more for small units with complex geography. The regular grid is distorted, both by the complex shapes of the mountains and coasts of Europe, and by the fact that the main center — London-Paris-Randstadt — in fact lies eccentrically to the northeast.

We therefore see a system of horizontal axes fanning out from the London-Paris-Randstadt center towards the east. The northern one connects the center to Berlin, Warsaw and Moscow, and so to southern Siberia and the northern part of Asia. The middle axis runs through Silesia and the south of Poland to Kiev, Rostov and the southern slopes of the Caucasus, to reach the western coast of the Caspian Sea towards the Asian Highway. A third axis starts further south from the main western European center, runs through Bavaria more or less along the course of the Danube down to its delta on the Black Sea. There it bifurcates to pass northwards to join the previously described middle axis near Rostov, and southwards towards Istanbul from which the other connection with the Asian Highway is established. Near Yugoslavia this same axis branches south through the eastern part of Yugoslavia to reach Salonica, so extending along a horizontal branch towards Istanbul, and towards a vertical branch which extends south of

Athens through the Aegean to the south coast of Asia Minor and to Africa. A fourth horizontal axis starts from the south coast of Spain, follows the northern coastline of the Mediterranean along the south of France, passes through northern Italy and northern Yugoslavia, joins the previous axis near the Rumanian border, and proceeds along the course of the Danube. It also bifurcates southwards to Salonica from the Yugoslav-Rumanian border.

This system of four horizontal European axes is crossed, more or less at right angles, by another system of vertical axes. If we begin from the west, the first of these vertical axes follows the west coast of Portugal and the north coast of Spain and from Bordeaux passes diagonally to Paris and the West European center. The next vertical axis coincides with the southern one along the southern and eastern coast of Spain, passes through the Rhone valley to the Rhine towards the Western European center and, in another eastern branch, towards Berlin. A third axis starts from Tunisia and passes via Sicily and Italy to Berlin. A fourth starts from Gdynia, goes directly south to Warsaw, crosses Czechoslovakia near the border between Bohemia and Slovakia, connects with the third and fourth horizontal axes, and proceeds southwards to Salonica, Athens, and so to the south coast of Asia Minor and Africa. A fifth vertical axis starts at Riga, goes southeast through Kiev to reach the Baltic near Odessa and becomes connected with the branches from the third horizontal axis. Finally, a sixth vertical axis connects Leningrad to Moscow, passes on to Rostov, then along the northern slopes of the Caucasus towards the Asian Highway. The main centers of ekistic development will be formed where this system of axes crosses.

This is a picture of the spatial configuration of the axes and centers in Europe at the time of Ecumenopolis at about the end of the next century or a little later. Although this is still a preliminary picture and may have to be modified in its details by further and more thorough research, we believe that it does represent a first and usable image of the conditions in Europe at the time of Ecumenopolis.

A second similar study was made for the North American part of Ecumenopolis, and this is presented in the same scale as the one used for Europe in fig. 148. The difference in this case is that whereas in Europe the geography of the land makes it clear what future formations must be, in the U.S.A. this is only true as far as the eastern third of the country is concerned. What we show for about half the area concerned, therefore, is based on general assumptions and has only an indicative value. The Northeast Megalopolis and the Great Lakes Megalopolis have, however, been studied in detail and therefore the image we give of them is more accurate.

A third study was made of West Africa, and the results are shown in fig. 149. This image is of more general value and since it is based on far less detailed data is important only as an indication of what may happen in the area. We had sufficient data only for Ghana and Nigeria. The West African part of Ecumenopolis is shown here on the same scale as the other two so that we can compare the ex-

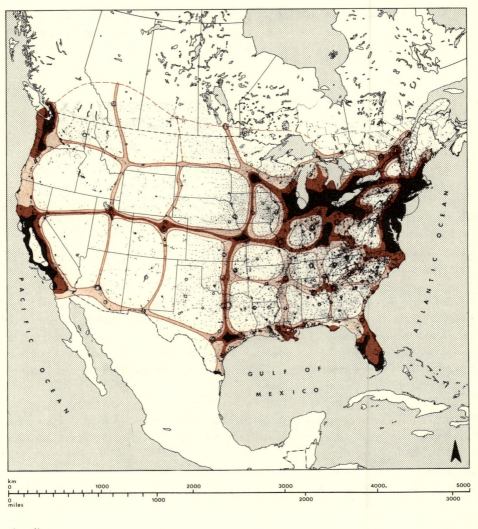

density:

high
medium
low

148.   Ecumenopolis in U.S.A. after 2100

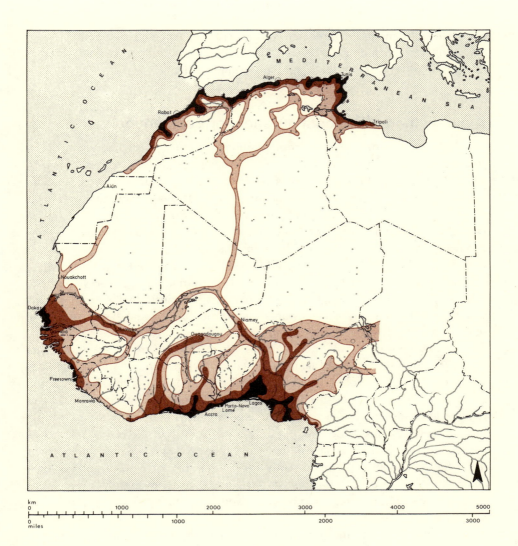

149.   Ecumenopolis in West Africa after 2100

pected developments in three areas, one with an expected population of 1.8 billion (Europe, including European U.S.S.R.), one of 1.2 billion (U.S.A.), and one of 0.8 billion (W. Africa), at the time of Ecumenopolis.

A purely theoretical configuration for Ecumenopolis

One generation from now the configuration of human settlements will be influenced more by the position and condition of those that already exist than by the habitability of the various areas of the globe, but four or five generations hence, at the time of Ecumenopolis, habitability will have the stronger influence, and in a thousand years habitability will be even more important. If we had to consider a totally new plan for Ecumenopolis that did not have to take anything surviving from the past into consideration at all, we could try various global systems to see where each possibility would lead us. We are not yet at the point where we can say what the most desirable or feasible pattern for such systems might be; however, we thought it might be interesting to demonstrate the sort of thing which can be done by taking as an example our orthogonal system from the numerous possible systems and seeing where this would lead[5].

We show here only two of the models which resulted from this study: one (fig. 150) shows the results of taking a purely orthogonal grid and imposing it on the structure of the globe; and the second (fig. 151) adjusts this first structure by allowing for various distorting factors, such as topography, coastlines, habitability, local history and so on. These, we emphasize, are not what we expect the probable systems to be like, but are only examples of the research that was carried out. These models have a theoretical interest only since in fact they could never be implemented — unless Anthropos and all his principles should change completely or the oceans become deserts. We give them merely as examples of the many structures that could be conceived, so that they may be compared to others.

Our team worked on these models purely as an experiment, but another good reason for showing them here is as a demonstration of the sort of thing that can be put forward as a reasonable plan. They may look convincing at first, but they have no practical value at all since they ignore the facts of geography and the real conditions for living in the various parts of our earth. If we want to make better use of our earth, we must take in every aspect of every environment in great detail, as well as many other factors.

Our conclusion is that it is too early to discuss possible new proposals for the configuration of Ecumenopolis. Theoretically, the pattern of its structure could be based on hexagons, or maybe triangles, not on the gridiron. The average distance could be much larger or much smaller, and not about 500 km (about 300 mi.) as in the last two examples. We do not yet understand our whole earth as one total system, so we cannot make any interpretation unless we base it on the realities we do know — of geography, of the conditions for habitation in the various areas, and of the systems Anthropos created in these conditions by following the five principles he has always followed during his history.

150.   Ecumenopolis: theoretical configuration of global axes
        and centers

378

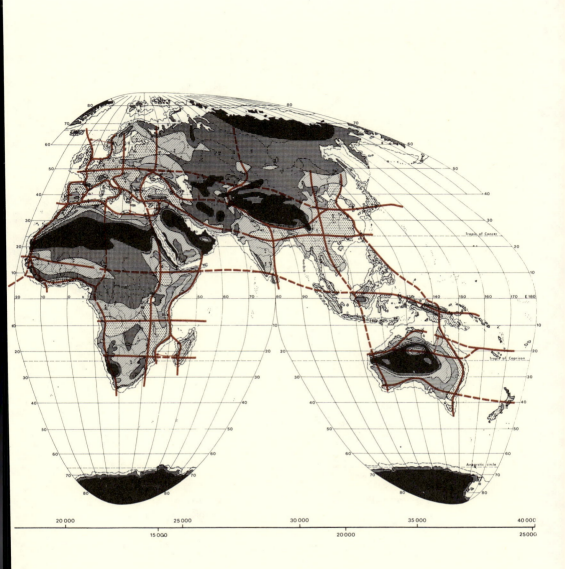

habitability zones:

■ E non-habitable
▨ D not suitable for extensive habitation
▦ C difficult for extensive habitation
▤ B no significant limitations
▥ A no limitations

— major habitability and coastal axes
⊏ alternative or split course
--- parts of axes through difficult areas (land or sea)

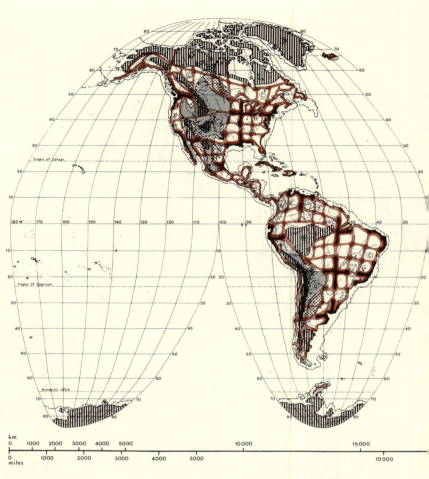

km
0   1000   2000   3000   4000   5000   10 000   15 000
0   1000   2000   3000   4000   5000
miles

negative areas for Ecumenopolis, habitability zones E & D
(only connections and compact points allowed within them)

elevation > 3,000 m, habitability zone E

'difficult' and 'very rigorous' climate 2100, habitability zone D

151.   Ecumenopolis: theoretical configuration of global
        axes and centers adjusted for distorting factors

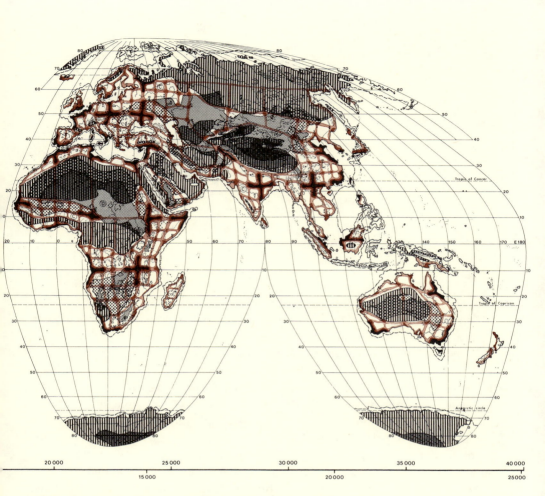

difficult areas for Ecumenopolis, habitability zones E, D & C
(substantial cost involved)

░ water scarcity: very high cost, habitability zone D
░ water scarcity: high cost, habitability zone C

nodes:

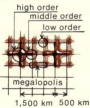

high order
middle order
low order

megalopolis
1,500 km 500 km

zones:
━ high density
〜 middle density
⋈ low density

grids:
major grid
1,500 × 1,500 km = 2,250,000 km²
basic grid
500 × 500 km = 250,000 km²

42. The new balance

When we were discussing the human settlements of the past and present and Near and Middle Futures in other chapters, we spoke of their problems at those particular points in time. We cannot do the same in this section since Ecumenopolis will not be reached at all unless Anthropos manages to solve his problems, or at least is prepared to solve them. In our more optimistic reckoning, we hoped that this would be done during the Middle Future, which will run from 2000 to 2075, or 2100 A.D. Ecumenopolis, in our view, will be either the era in which a real and complete state of balance in Anthropos' system of life is achieved, or at least the point at which Anthropos recognizes that this state of balance is his main goal, so that he will be approaching it and will reach it within a few generations.

According to our most optimistic prognostication, the day celebrating the creation of Ecumenopolis and the establishment of this new state of balance will take place in the year 2075. According to our most pessimistic one, in that year, whoever is then the global leader will deliver a speech declaring that it is the goal of all men to reach such a state of balance and will name the date by which it should be achieved.

We do not say that it is easy to reach such a goal. We do say, however, that it is a natural goal: human achievement in the past shows that Anthropos can reach a state of harmony and balance in his systems of life and has achieved this many times — and it can be done again.

Towards balance

We believe that it will be possible to achieve a state of balance at the time of Ecumenopolis because all the factors which today are changing and growing so fast will have reached a static point. It will be far easier to reach balance then than now, when all the elements of our lives are changing and growing dramatically, each according to its own particular and different rhythm, so that it is almost impossible for us to keep them in harmony with one another. We see the same thing happening in our own lives: it is far easier for an individual to reach a state of balance in his maturity than during the violent changes of his adolescence. Fast growth is always accompanied by errors of judgement, and this is just as true of companies and institutions when they are in a period of fast expansion.

There is another good reason why Ecumenopolis can be the human settlement which achieves an ideal state of balance, and this is because we all learn from our mistakes. Anthropos is making more mistakes about his settlements today, on a much larger scale, than he has ever done before. He is therefore being given the opportunity to learn from his mistakes what he should do to make his settlements successful. He is training himself according to the same process of trial and error he has always used to achieve the far better settlements of the future. This time, however, he is learning far more, and he will have far greater resources to help him, with higher incomes and a more advanced technology than he has ever had before.

In the past, Anthropos succeeded by trial and error in creating such cities as Athens and Florence, but he also lost many cities by the same process. This time he will be dealing with just one human city; he must turn it into a success, and by trial and error he will eventually do so. Unfortunately, at first he may only succeed in some of its parts while others remain far less successful. Balance will not be reached everywhere at the same time but will spread gradually, just as the problems did. They appeared in community after community, spreading from cell to cell throughout the tissue of human life, and the cure has to follow a similar process and spread slowly through the whole organism.

Naturally, the first areas to be saved will be the smaller ones that have suffered less, and the remote and isolated ones. The first settlements to be completely without problems will be the new small units, which will have the opportunity of solving all their difficulties as they are created, and will become the prototypes for others to follow and so achieve their own therapy. Progress will continue in this way until the largest and most severely suffering large centers are cured as well.

Three types of balance to be achieved

What is the balance that we need to achieve? The three most basic and important types of balance are the following:

First, we must achieve a state of balance between the five elements that make up human settlements — Nature, Anthropos, Society, Shells and Networks. At present we are suffering because of the exaggerated growth in Networks of all sorts, from highways to airports, and in the equally exaggerated numbers of Shells, buildings of all sorts, that are being put up without any overall concept. There is a complete lack of balance both with Nature and with Society, and above all Anthropos himself is out of balance with everything. Anthropos is losing the battle for harmony at present, but we do not believe, as the pessimists do, that he will lose the war.

Secondly, we must achieve a good state of balance between all the goals Anthropos sets himself as an individual, and as a Society. We must not follow any one aim — economic, social, political, administrative, technological or cultural — at the expense of any of the others. At present we are overwhelmingly trying to achieve technological and economic goals at the expense of social, political, administrative and, above all, cultural ones.

Thirdly, we must achieve a proper ekistic balance within each unit of space in which Anthropos lives, from Anthropos himself, who is ekistic unit 1, and his room, which is ekistic unit 2, to the house, the neighborhood, the village, the town, until we reach the whole earth or Ecumenopolis itself, which is ekistic unit 15. Today the only places in which really satisfactory human solutions are being found are within the houses and individual rooms of the wealthy classes, and even for these people the solutions only exist inside; when they go out they walk into the chaos and ugliness of modern settlements. When we consider any ekistic units larger than these few favored ones, we observe nothing but disaster.

The goal to be reached by Ecumenopolis must take into account all three of these types of balance. We must therefore find solutions to the relationship between the five elements, from the points of view of the five goals and within all 15 ekistic spatial units. Only then can we hope to reach a total balance which will satisfy genuine long-term human interests, human aims and human dreams.

In the sections which follow we deal with some of the things Anthropos is going to face. We do this not to describe in detail what Ecumenopolis will be like, but to say what balances Anthropos is going to try to achieve and is likely to achieve according to the basis of our present knowledge.

Balance in wealth

We start by considering the economic aspect of life, and look at the possibility of achieving balance in respect to the incomes and possessions of all people. A hope and a dream has always existed among men for the reduction of the inequalities in wealth between people, although now these gaps are increasing and there is no certainty as to what extent they can be reduced. When we know that in communist countries even, there are very large differences in the facilities that are available to different people, such as ownership of cars, we realize that we can speak only of the probability of a future Society with smaller income gaps than our present one, and of an international situation in which there may be less extreme differences between nations and people than there are at present.

We have three main reasons for this hope. First, the clearly expressed desires of people all over the world, and especially of the younger generation in all countries, for a world with fewer gaps in wealth between people. Second, the fact that as information increases there is always a recognition of the gaps which exist between people, and a tendency for these gaps to be reduced. A good example of this is the recognition of the "urban poor" in the U.S.A. which has led to the introduction of policies for producing higher incomes for the lowest groups. Thirdly, countries like China, where the gaps between people seem to be smaller than anywhere else, may prove to be very successful societies, and this will mean that they may have a greater influence internationally.

This reduction of inequalities has been substantiated by our team's economic projections, which were based on models for economic growth reflecting the recent history of economic evolution and trends; these models clearly show a reduction of inequalities — both between large geographic areas like groups of countries, and at a smaller scale within single countries — starting in the Middle Future.

Our conclusion on economics, therefore, is that we can definitely expect much higher average global incomes and many more opportunities for individual persons. It is to be hoped as well that the gaps in wealth which exist between people today, although they will probably never be fully eliminated, will tend to be continuously and substantially reduced.

Balance within Society

Let us now consider Society and the different social balances that are bound to be achieved in Ecumenopolis because of increasing incomes and many other changing factors. Orwell's predictions for Society in 1984 may turn out to be valid for some countries in the Near Future, and even to a lesser extent in the Middle Future, but can hardly be valid for the time when all nations will be interwoven into one system; so the overall situation in Ecumenopolis will be a better one.

Our reasons for saying this are comparable to our reasons for believing that inequalities in wealth will be reduced. The real desires of people all over the globe, and especially of the younger people, are towards less repressive societies and greater equality. As information spreads, so freedom in countries tends to increase. Every individual in Ecumenopolis will have a greater choice and more opportunities, and Society will be better organized, so we can look forward optimistically to the opportunity Anthropos will have for selecting the best characteristics of his present-day systems to help create his future Society.

Pessimistic studies have been made that suggest social conflicts will arise as a result of the much higher densities that will exist. Such studies, however, have been based on what happens to such animals as rats under conditions of extreme overcrowding, but it has now been proved that the extraordinary high densities produced in these laboratory conditions will never occur amongst people on earth in the foreseeable future. Even with extremely high densities, such as those prevailing in some Oriental cities like Hong-Kong or Singapore, no signs of major social misbehavior whatsoever have begun to appear. As for Ecumenopolis, densities of this kind are unlikely on any global scale, and if there are local problems there is very good reason to believe that these will be overcome.

One development which may give rise to social problems, however, will be the great increase in human mobility which is bound to occur. This is a very new factor, and we cannot venture any certain predictions about it, but we can say that if present trends continue, then those citizens who can escape easily from any unpleasant or deteriorating social conditions will tend to do so, and since many more citizens in Ecumenopolis will be able to move if they choose to, then this trend may well lead to the disintegration of communities that for one reason or another have become unpleasant and difficult to live in. A place that is experiencing only mild troubles could therefore be plunged into a rapid spiral of decay by the flight of its richer inhabitants and the people who should be its leaders. Difficulties may be increased by the fact that a great many residents of some communities will be short-term transients, hopping from place to place, severing all connections and tearing up roots with each move. On the other hand, the present trend in the growth of transients with no interest in building up a durable community life anywhere could be changed by the fact that many more people will own several permanent homes in different places instead. Families may move frequently, but they will do so between places in which they own property and have formed ties. One probable development is that the average family will have one primary house in the community in which it has formed the strongest ties, but will also own houses in other areas to which it will move from time to time to satisfy different needs or simply in order to experience different life-styles and other surroundings.

If all goes well, another positive development within Society should be the revival of small community units, the natural units of space within which people can make contact with one another without need of mechanical transport. At present the trend in some richer countries is in the opposite direction; the human scale is being wiped out. Nevertheless, throughout human history the success of small human units — the housegroup, the neighborhood, the small polis — suggests that it is on this scale that a satisfactory social life develops, and that face-to-face contact is of crucial importance in human life. The physical form of these small units of the ekistic scale is vital in establishing stable and self-reinforcing networks of contacts between people, and it is likely that much more attention will be paid to their creation in the future.

The spontaneous growth and future strength of the natural human community will be helped by the improvements that will be made in technology. The home will become easier to run and more pleasant to live in, and will incorporate equipment that will provide all kinds of facilities and opportunities for a multiplicity of functions like education, culture and recreation that are not available in the home today. The layout of a neighborhood will be rationalized in such a way as to provide easier contacts and communication on the local scale, so that the citizen of Ecumenopolis will become aware of his multiple citizenship, his ties to his own home and local community, to his own town, and so on up the scale to his citizenship of the global community of Ecumenopolis, the home of World Anthropos.

People will have to spend far less time earning a living. The rising productivity of human labor will mean that everyone will be able to give more time to other activities. A working day will consist of fewer hours, a working week of fewer days; there will be longer monthly or seasonal vacations, plus various types of "sabbatical" leave lasting for several months at a time, and earlier formal retirement·will become widespread. It seems likely that some form of adult education will become part of the normal conditions of work, reflecting a general concern with the fuller development of human potential. Many more people may choose to take a second or even a third job, which may be concerned less with making money and more with personal interests or creative work of various kinds.

It is clear that our optimistic belief is that many of the problems of our present deteriorating Society will be overcome by the time of Ecumenopolis, and that there will be a reappearance of the age-old human values and recognition of the human scale, but in a new form consistent with the life-patterns at the time of Ecumenopolis. However, we must also add that Anthropos has never had to deal with things on such a large scale before in his entire history, nor has he ever been faced with so many alternative choices. It is clear that there may also be social developments that are quite impossible to foresee.

Political balance

The political organization of Ecumenopolis will be its most difficult aspect, and the most difficult for us to cover now. Humanity has never had to face the problem of organizing an area the size of the whole globe across which messages and the supply of electrical energy can be passed in seconds, and across which people can be transported in a matter of hours or even minutes.

When we think of the great empires of the past it is true to say that they were created by great conquerors rather than being formed by peaceful federation; it is also true that many peace-loving federations did not last as long as many empires. There is, however, no easy or simple comparison between the processes which led to territorial or national federations in the past and the processes which will lead to the formation of Ecumenopolis. It is not only the change in dimensions, but also the change in the reasons for the formation of the new big systems of today and the meaning of these systems for Anthropos that are different; so we cannot make any sure statement as to what the political structure of Ecumenopolis will be.

We can say that a real Ecumenopolis will need a unified global government of some sort, but we cannot say how democratic such a government will be in any phase of its development. We can only say that because of the common dreams of modern Anthropos there is a good hope that it will be sufficiently democratic in form.

No matter what form the government will take, the territorial organization of administration will be much better than it is now; if it is not, Ecumenopolis will be unable to function normally. While it is probable that we will have some malfuctioning in the Near Future, it is very improbable that this will continue into the Remote Future. Human history proves that although Anthropos has difficulties of administration in times of transition, he always discovers and establishes a normally-balanced administrative system during periods when his life-system is in a state of balance or when he makes this his main goal. He did this within small units, such as the classical Greek democratic *polis*, and within enormous autocratic units, such as the Roman Empire which led to the establishment of the *pax Romana*.

Technological balance

We can be both sure and optimistic about the development of one thing in Ecumenopolis, and that is the improvement in technology. Both authors started out as optimistic about this, and as a result of our research we can now state as a fact that the balance that can be created through technology will be able to fulfill the most idealistic dreams of contemporary Anthropos. In fact, since we do not think that contemporary Anthropos has yet really understood or conceived what such a balance could be, we may say that the future can be better than he has ever dreamed possible. We talk today about a loss of balance at the local scale of the neighborhood or city, but we have not yet even considered what a total, overall balance and harmony between Anthropos and Nature all over the world could be like. This concept will develop in the Near Future, and we will begin to put it into effect so that it can be realized in Ecumenopolis.

There will be many different aspects of balance to be achieved. First, the establishment of a biological balance on the global scale must be made. In Part Four we predicted in a simplified way what would be done to bring about such a state of biological balance, and as time goes on this will be worked out in a detailed and scientific way. Anthropos, Nature, and Anthropos' activities within Nature will once again be brought into a state of harmony, as in fact they often have been in the past within small and successfully functioning units such as villages in all parts of the world, or within city-states or the territories of medieval monasteries.

The present war between Anthropos and the machine will be won decisively by Anthropos. Today the machine is in charge, and Anthropos is suffering, but in the future with improved technology and ergonomics Anthropos will become the master of the situation and will be able to make sure that everything that is built will be built only for his benefit, and on the human scale.

Because of this we are certain that Anthropos need not fear the development of industrial processes. They will not turn him into a slave, laboring like one of his own machines in the factories. Full automation of industrial production will mean in fact that Anthropos is no longer involved in the non-human processes of production; instead he will become the creator and the true master of the machine.

Cultural balance

We cannot easily predict what the cultural aspects of Ecumenopolis will be, but if Anthropos continues to follow his present trends then all local and national cultures will tend to be eliminated and a new global culture will develop based on the completely new systems of life that will then exist. Of course, from the point of view of the 25th century such a culture may seem to be ideal, but we as citizens of the 20th century cannot fail to see the great dangers and threats involved in the disappearance of all the existing regional cultures. It would seem to be taking an enormous risk for humanity to wipe out all that has been created with so much skill and care over so many centuries and in so many different, individual ways in the hope that a new culture would be better than them all. This is a great problem for Anthropos, and as cultural diversity is surely desirable we expect that the majority of people are likely to realize this and therefore try and achieve it, even if only in limited ways.

To illustrate the importance of cultural balance and what it means at all scales — the neighborhood, within one nation, or globally — let us consider the esthetic appearance of our human settlements.

Today we are clearly moving from a period in which many thousands of local architectural traditions exist, many different solutions to the problems of construction based on local materials, local methods and local ways of life (even such a small country as Greece has many hundreds of different styles), to a period in which all structures will be in accordance with standardized methods and using the same materials. The forces of necessity are today being expressed by enormous corporations which are becoming international, and spreading their styles and methods of construction in exactly the same forms all over the world.

Modern solutions to architectural problems are very efficient and helpful in many ways, so it is inevitable that they will spread more and more widely. If these solutions are the only ones to prevail, and if economic and technological considerations are the only ones to be taken into account in the construction of buildings, then Ecumenopolis is going to look identical in each of its newly-built parts, and even in those parts which exist already. If such trends do continue, then Ecumenopolis could well become a settlement resembling a larger version of the world depicted in 1984 — though it will come into being closer to 2084 — and which would indeed be an anthill, thus turning Anthropos into nothing but an ant.

43. The big questions

It may be worrying, even frightening, that at the conclusion of a study of the future and one that has tried to be as objective as possible, and has certainly been optimistic in contrast to the present fashion of screaming and crying about what is about to happen, we have just raised the possibility that Anthropos may be turned into nothing but an ant. Indeed, we can give Anthropos a capital A, but we cannot give this ant a capital A, because while Anthropos believes in humanism, no ant believes in antism; to be an ant is to be part of a whole society, never an individual.

The fact that we have been forced to consider such a possibility makes it clear that no matter how optimistic we personally may be by nature, and no matter how objective we have tried to be in this study, we must always remember two things:

1. None of our statements or measurements, as we have said repeatedly, can have any certainty; they can have only a high probability.
2. We cannot be sure that Anthropos will find and put into effect the right solutions to some of the very critical problems of the future in time to save the situation.

It is therefore possible that we may have to face greater crises and greater disasters in the Near and Middle Future than we have predicted, and that there will be a longer delay before a normal, well-balanced and efficiently-operating Ecumenopolis can be established. We must remain aware of these possibilities, and recognize that there is no certainty of a better future for Anthropos, while holding to the faith that it can certainly be better so long as Anthropos takes care of his future in the same way as he has done on similar occasions in his past.

An enormous number of questions remain to be answered before we can be certain about the future and certain about a successful Ecumenopolis, too many by far for us to deal with here. Anthropos must answer all these questions gradually and in a wise and successful way if he is to achieve that future which we know it is possible for him to achieve.

Three big areas of doubt

Where are the remaining areas of greatest doubt? We know there is little to worry about concerning Anthropos' economic and technological future: despite his present screaming and crying Anthropos does know what he wants — higher incomes and improved technology. It is certain that Anthropos will make immense advances in these fields, even if he does make mistakes at first. Eventually he will rectify his mistakes because he does have a clear goal, that his wealth and his machines must be used to serve him.

In three big areas though, considerable doubt remains, and the future will depend on how Anthropos faces these problems:

One: The continuing break-up of the smaller social units, such as the family, the extended family and the neighborhood, and the continuing growth of the larger social units such as multinational corporations.

Two: The continuing disappearance of local cultures in the smaller ekistic units, such as the village, town, or small valley area, and the growth of a global culture based on a shared technology.

Three: The continuing lack of any political or organizational apparatus capable of dealing with the problems and opportunities which will arise on the new global scale.

We do know that throughout human history the idea of creating an organization on a genuinely global scale has often been clearly stated. It was said as early as the 4th century B.C. by Diogenes, who made it clear that he considered himself not an Athenian or a Greek but "a citizen of the world"[6], and it is being said by historians and philosophers of our own time, such as Toynbee and Teilhard de Chardin, who have said that the Age of Nations is past[7].

Such statements are true: but the big question remains whether in creating such large units in order to form the global system, we will allow the smaller units with all their cultural and human values to disappear altogether. This is a very big question that lies behind all the social, political and cultural ones. We are attempting to realize dreams of world unification without knowing how to do so, nor how to save what Anthropos has created during his long history. What is more, it is necessary to save these cultures not as museum exhibits but as vital and living systems of life.

This leads us to another and more practical question: if we want to solve the problems created by the processes that are taking place around us, should we do so by allowing the transition to Ecumenopolis to go on by itself, following the present trends created by the explosion of forces, or should we try to understand what is happening, conceive clearly what we want our future to be, and then guide the forces in that direction?

From civilization to ecumenization

We are not, as Anthropos has been many times in the past, in the process of transition from one stage of civilization to another; we are in the process of transition from civilization to ecumenization.

The first big change in Anthropos' stage of life came when he changed from hunting and food gathering to farming and cattle breeding, that is, from the collection of food to food production. The second change was from natural production alone, with the simple repetition of the processes of Nature, to a mixture of man-made and natural production. This started with the use of pottery for cooking food and ended with the industrial production of food in rapidly expanding human settlements. The third change is one that is still taking place as production becomes more and more automatic, so that Anthropos need no longer concentrate on the processes that ensure his mere survival, but can become both better and happier by giving his attention to the achievement of true human development. In classical Athens this was possible at least for free male citizens; in Ecumenopolis it will be possible for everyone.

Ecumenization inevitably is the next phase for Anthropos. It will give him the opportunity to take the next big step forward in his evolution, but it will also make it possible for him to destroy himself completely unless he opens his eyes to what is taking place.

44. Conclusions

The establishment of Ecumenopolis will mean the end of the changes which create major problems and the beginning of an era in which those problems which still remain will be solved.

The major characteristic of Ecumenopolis will be the completely new scale of its dimensions. Throughout the whole of Anthropos' history until the year 1825, he only managed to move in the dimensions of his settlements from the scale of the human band — ekistic unit 4 — to that of the small metropolis — ekistic unit 9. Within three hundred years, from 1825, he will have moved on from the small metropolis to the scale of Ecumenopolis — ekistic unit 15. He took ten thousand years to climb slowly up five steps in the dimensions of his settlements, and he is now taking three hundred years to climb the next six steps. No wonder he is out of breath, and no wonder we are aware of strain.

The changes which are taking place now will end in a completely new system of life, which will be ecumenic in form and will lead us from civilization to ecumenization. Human settlements will have a completely new physical structure, a total global system of linked units of every size. Their eventual size and form will depend on the geography of each area as well as the developments in technology and in Anthropos' organizational ability.

The establishment of Ecumenopolis will mean a new state of balance between Anthropos, Nature, and human settlements. Conditions, and the quality of life, can be very much better than they are now, and probably better than at any previous time in Anthropos' history.

Not all human problems will be solved, and three big questions remain: what will happen to the smaller social units such as the family and neighborhood; what is to become of threatened local cultures; will we develop organizations capable of running things successfully on such large scales?

We are left with the optimistic belief that ecumenization is extremely probable, and that a happy Ecumenopolis will be achieved. However, we have one big final question. Ecumenopolis is coming; whether we do nothing or whether we take action, it is certain to happen. The question is: should we allow it to happen without any human guidance, or should we take a hand in our own futures by guiding the development of Ecumenopolis towards the form Anthropos most deeply desires? Should we try to make the future City of Anthropos really happy and safe, as Aristotle said it should be? We turn to this question in the Epilogue.

Epilogue

Before closing this book, we feel that we should allow ourselves in this Epilogue to give our personal opinion as to what we think should happen, and say that Anthropos should not allow the process of events to go on by themselves and produce whatever Ecumenopolis comes about by chance, but he should exercise the privilege of Anthropos and take a hand in his own evolution.

We know that it is possible for a good Ecumenopolis to be created that is better than the systems of life which exist at present. We know that we can study the successful settlements of the past in order to find out what factors make Anthropos happy and safe. We know how to ask the right questions in order to find out how to solve the problems of any specific area and create models that will be good rather than bad solutions. We know how to influence the natural development of our settlements so as to reach an Ecumenopolis that will be close to the best model we can create. All that we have to do is to define our goal, realize its importance, and unite in our determination to achieve it.

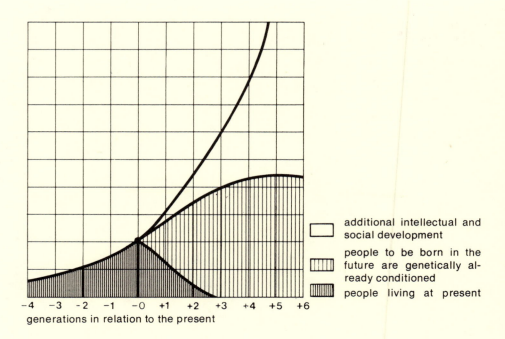

additional intellectual and social development

people to be born in the future are genetically already conditioned

people living at present

generations in relation to the present

152. the total potential of mankind in the future

Where can such guidance have effect? Let us look at the future which can be controlled by Anthropos himself (fig. 152). All the people in power today will have disappeared by the end of the Near Future. Everyone who reads this book will have gone by the middle of the Middle Future. Those people from the Near Future who survive to the Middle Future will decrease in active influence. New ideas and new techniques alien to their experience will be needed to deal with the completely new situation of a static Ecumenopolis.

The vital factors upon which all the necessary changes will depend are the new intellectual and cultural developments of mankind. New ideas, new techniques, new attitudes to life do not depend on Anthropos' food, but on Anthropos' mind. We must concentrate on the mind of Anthropos if we are to achieve the Ecumenopolis that we desire.

We are left with five conclusions:

One: Ecumenopolis will come inevitably, but it will only come in its most desirable form if Anthropos guides events.

Two: We must set our goal as harmony between the five elements that make up human settlements — Anthropos, Nature, Society, Shells and Networks. Growth takes places naturally; harmony can be achieved through the conscious action of Anthropos.

Three: We must use a rational and scientific approach, making a careful study of the complex systems of life in which we live. Our goal cannot be achieved by means of abstract theories, however well-meant, without knowledge of the factors which really make Anthropos happy. Without knowledge, we are relying on blind chance, and it is not right to play games with the future of mankind.

Four: We must find the courage to act on the global scale. Until we can manage to organize plans on this scale, we must act within as large a scale as we can achieve, keeping in mind the first three points.

Five: Our actions must never be based on the desire to show-off — as individuals, groups or corporations — but only on the desire to serve Anthropos. Everything we build now lays the foundations for the Ecumenopolis of the future.

Finally, we must follow these steps towards serious, guided and altruistic action. We must be clear about our priorities and not run-up huge towers in the city to show off our skill or wealth that do nothing to make Anthropos happy and safe. Above all we must take action; screaming and crying about our problems is not enough. We must stop acting like the witch-doctor, screaming and running round his patient in the hope of driving the symptoms away; instead we must become modern scientific practitioners, study our patient carefully as a living human being with a mind and a spirit as well as a body, and learn how to cure and prevent his diseases.

Appendix 1
Selected data on population

In this Appendix some material on various aspects of population, to which there is a more or less frequent reference in the main text of this book, has been assembled.

Tables 1, 2, 3, 4 and 5 give various types of breakdowns for number and size of settlements in the period 8500 B.C. to 1960 A.D., together with the corresponding total population, percent structure of past population, and yearly growth rates (Athens Center of Ekistics estimates, based on a larger number of sources).

Table 6 gives a standardized sequence of past populations of the earth based on a comparative study of several sources by the Athens Center of Ekistics. This "Standard City of the Future Curve" is regarded as the springboard from which projections for future population start.

Table 7 gives the present distribution of settlements by size categories, both in numbers and in population, partial and cumulative, according to estimates made by the Athens Center of Ekistics based on a comparative study of data from a large number of sources.

Table 8 compares growth rates for population and for area for a sample of 15 metropolises studied at the Athens Center of Ekistics for the period 1940 to 1960.

For population projections according to model F-20, from 1960 to 2225 A.D., see tables 1,4 and 5, Appendix 2.

dates	settlement categories						
	over 1 million inh.	over 100,00 inh.	over 20,000 inh.	over 5,000 inh.	c. 3,300-5,000 inh.	over c. 3,300 inh.	2,000-c. 3,300 inh.
				urban 1		urban 2	
8500 B.C.	—	—	—	—	—	—	—
8000	—	—	—	—	—	—	—
7500	—	—	—	—	—	—	.002
7000	—	—	—	.01	.004	.014	.005
6500	—	—	—	.03	.01	.04	.007
6000	—	—	—	.05	.01	.07	.009
5500	—	—	—	.06	.01	.07	.014
5000	—	—	—	.06	.01	.07	.02
4500	—	—	—	.06	.02	.08	.02
4000	—	—	—	.07	.02	.09	.03
3500	—	—	—	.13	.04	.17	.04
3000	—	—	.2	.60	.08	.68	.08
2500	—	.6	2	3	.2	3	.2
2000	—	.9	3	4	.3	4	.3
1500	—	.6	2	4	.4	4	.4
1000	—	.1	2	3	.4	4	.5
500	—	3	6	9	.7	10	.8
B.C./A.D. ± 0	1	8	13	17	1	18	1
A.D. 500	1	6	10	13	1	14	1
1000	9	18	24	28	1	29	1
1500	6	19	25	30	1	31	2
1650	6	18	25	30	2	32	2
1750	4	18	26	33	4	37	6
1800	5	21	29	56	14	70	14
1850	6	34	56	110	25	135	25
1900	35	117	191	290	45	335	45
1950	225	448	604	783	78	861	77
1960	370	702	936	1,164	85	1,250	85

table 1. past global population by broad settlement categories (also urban and rural)

400

settlement categories							
over 2,000 inh.	1,000-2,000 inh.	over 1,000 inh.	under 5,000 inh.	under c. 3,300 inh.	under 2,000 inh.	under 1,000 inh.	total population of the earth
urban 3		urban 4	rural 1	rural 2	rural 3	rural 4	
—	—	—	14.5	14.5	14.5	14.5	14.5
—	.002	.002	16.0	16.0	16.0	15.598	16.0
.002	.01	.012	19.000	19.000	18.998	18.988	19.0
.019	.03	.049	22.990	22.986	22.981	22.951	23.0
.047	.05	.097	28.970	28.960	28.953	28.903	29.0
.079	.06	.139	37.940	37.930	37.921	37.861	38.0
.084	.07	.154	50.940	50.930	50.916	50.846	51.0
.09	.09	.18	61.94	61.93	61.91	61.82	62.0
.10	.12	.22	71.94	71.92	71.90	71.73	72.0
.12	.15	.27	79.93	79.91	79.88	79.73	80.0
.21	.25	.46	85.87	85.83	85.79	85.54	86.0
.76	.5	1	92.40	92.32	92.24	92	93.0
3.2	1	4	98	98	98	97	101
4.3	2	6	106	106	106	104	110
4.4	2	7	116	116	116	114	120
4.5	3	7	129	128	128	125	132
10.8	4	15	137	136	135	131	146
19	5	24	148	147	146	141	165
15	6	21	182	181	180	174	195
30	7	37	217	216	215	208	245
33	9	42	365	364	362	353	395
34	12	46	515	513	511	499	545
43	32	75	697	691	685	653	728
84	75	159	850	836	822	747	906
160	140	300	1,050	1,025	1,000	860	1,160
380	220	600	1,320	1,275	1,230	1,010	1,610
938	320	1,248	1,710	1,632	1,555	1,245	2,493
335	330	1,665	1,796	1,710	1,625	1,295	2,960

population figures in millions

dates	settlement sizes					
	million inhabitants				thousand inhabitants	
	10—20	5—10	2—5	1—2	500—1000	200—500
8000 B.C.	—	—	—	—	—	—
7500	—	—	—	—	—	—
7000	—	—	—	—	—	—
6500	—	—	—	—	—	—
6000	—	—	—	—	—	—
5500	—	—	—	—	—	—
5000	—	—	—	—	—	—
4500	—	—	—	—	—	—
4000	—	—	—	—	—	—
3500	—	—	—	—	—	—
3000	—	—	—	—	—	—
2500	—	—	—	—	—	—
2000	—	—	—	—	—	.3
1500	—	—	—	—	—	.3
1000	—	—	—	—	—	—
500	—	—	—	—	1	1
B.C./A.D. ± 0	—	—	—	1	3	2
A.D. 500	—	—	—	1	1	2
1000	—	—	5	4	3	3
1500	—	—	5	1	4	5
1650	—	—	2	4	3	5
1750	—	—	—	4	5	4
1800	—	—	—	5	5	6
1850	—	—	2	4	10	10
1900	—	5	11	19	23	29
1950	23	62	59	81	69	85
1960	41	97	107	25	96	130

table 2.   past global population by settlement sizes over 5,000 inh. (1:2:5 scale)

settlement sizes					total
thousand inhabitants					over 5,000
100—200	50—100	20—50	10—20	5—10	—
—	—	—	—	—	—
—	—	—	—	—	—
—	—	—	—	.01	.01
—	—	—	.01	.02	.03
—	—	—	.03	.03	.06
—	—	—	.03	.03	.06
—	—	—	.03	.03	.06
—	—	—	.01	.05	.06
—	—	—	.01	.06	.07
—	—	—	.03	.10	.13
—	—	.2	.2	.2	.6
.6	.5	.6	.4	.4	2.5
.6	.6	1	.6	.6	3.7
.3	.7	1	.8	.7	3.8
.1	.6	1	.7	.7	3.1
1	1	2	2	1	9
2	3	2	2	2	17
2	2	2	2	1	13
3	3	3	2	2	28
4	3	3	3	2	30
4	4	3	3	2	30
5	4	4	4	3	33
5	4	4	10	17	56
8	9	13	20	34	110
30	36	38	39	60	290
69	71	85	73	106	783
106	108	126	107	121	1,164

population figures in millions

rates	over 1 million inh.	over 100,000 inh.	over 20,000 inh.	over 5,000 inh. (urban 1)	c. 3,300-5,000 inh.	over 3,000 inh. (urban 2)	2,000-c. 3,300 inh.	over 2,000 inh. (urban 3)	1,000-2,000 inh.	over 1,000 inh. (urban 4)
8500 B.C.	—	—	—	—	—	—	—	—	—	—
8000	—	—	—	—	—	—	—	—	1	1
7500	—	—	—	—	—	—	1	1	3	4
7000	—	—	—	1	1	2	2	4	8	12
6500	—	—	—	4	2	6	4	10	18	28
6000	—	—	—	6	3	9	5	14	22	36
5500	—	—	—	7	4	11	6	17	29	46
5000	—	—	—	7	5	12	7	19	32	51
4500	—	—	—	8	7	15	10	25	37	62
4000	—	—	—	10	9	19	13	32	62	94
3500	—	—	—	16	16	32	24	56	105	161
3000	—	—	6	47	29	76	43	119	215	334
2500	—	4	30	117	53	170	80	250	440	690
2000	—	5	40	170	80	250	110	360	870	1,230
1500	—	3	47	208	90	298	150	448	1,150	1,598
1000	—	1	39	194	110	304	200	504	1,650	2,154
500	—	16	96	388	180	568	300	868	2,500	3,368
B.C./A.D. ± 0	1	27	141	500	215	715	315	1,030	3,300	4,330
A.D. 500	1	26	122	435	250	685	330	1,015	4,300	5,315
1000	5	43	165	551	290	841	420	1,261	5,000	6,261
1500	3	52	210	711	350	1,061	700	1,761	6,500	8,261
1650	4	51	215	731	500	1,231	850	2,081	8,700	10,781
1750	3	57	239	969	1,000	1,969	2,330	4,299	23,000	27,299
1800	4	66	251	3,471	3,500	6,971	5,550	12,521	53,000	65,521
1850	4	113	664	7,114	6,350	13,464	10,200	23,664	97,000	120,664
1900	19	361	2,132	23,762	11,700	25,462	18,800	44,262	150,000	194,262
1950	90	960	4,800	25,600	20,500	46,100	32,500	78,600	210,000	288,600
1960	141	1,460	7,200	32,700	23,000	55,700	36,500	92,200	222,300	314,500

settlement categories

table 3.   past number of settlements by broad categories (also urban and rural)

dates	over 1 million inh.	over 100,000 inh.	over 20,000 inh.	over 5,000 inh.	over c. 3,300 inh.	over 2,000 inh.	over 1,000 inh.	under 5,000 inh.	under c. 3,300 inh.	under 2,000 inh.	under 1,000 inh.
settlement categories											
				urban 1	urban 2	urban 3	urban 4	rural 1	rural 2	rural 3	rural 4
8500 B.C.	—	—	—	—	—	—	—	100	100	100	100
8000	—	—	—	—	—	—	.0125	100	100	100	99.985
7500	—	—	—	—	—	.0105	.063	100	100	99.9895	99.937
7000	—	—	—	.043	.061	.083	.21	99.957	99.939	29.917	99.79
6500	—	—	—	.104	.138	.162	.334	99.896	99.862	99.838	99.666
6000	—	—	—	.158	.185	.208	.392	99.842	99.815	99.792	99.608
5500	—	—	—	.118	.137	.165	.302	99.882	99.863	99.835	99.698
5000	—	—	—	.097	.113	.145	.290	99.903	99.887	99.855	99.710
4500	—	—	—	.083	.111	.139	.306	99.917	99.889	99.861	99.694
4000	—	—	—	.088	.113	.150	.337	99.912	99.887	99.850	99.663
3500	—	—	—	.151	.198	.224	.535	99.849	99.802	99.776	99.465
3000	—	—	.215	.64	.73	.82	1.07	99.36	99.27	99.18	98.93
2500	—	.59	1.68	2.48	2.67	2.87	3.85	97.52	97.33	97.13	96.15
2000	—	.82	2.27	3.36	3.64	3.91	5.72	96.64	96.36	96.09	94.28
1500	—	.50	1.84	3.17	3.50	3.84	5.50	96.83	96.50	96.16	94.50
1000	—	.076	1.29	2.35	2.65	3.03	5.30	97.65	97.35	96.97	94.70
500	—	2.06	4.11	6.17	6.64	7.20	9.93	93.83	93.36	92.80	90.07
B.C. A.D. ∓0	.61	4.85	7.88	10.3	10.9	11.5	14.6	89.7	89.1	88.5	83.4
A.D. 500	.51	3.1	5.1	6.7	7.2	7.7	10.8	93.3	92.8	92.3	89.2
1000	3.7	7.4	9.8	11.4	11.9	12.3	15.1	88.6	88.3	87.7	84.9
1500	1.5	4.8	6.3	7.6	7.9	8.1	10.6	92.4	92.1	91.9	89.4
1650	1.1	3.3	4.6	5.5	5.9	6.2	8.4	94.5	94.1	93.8	91.6
1750	.55	2.5	3.6	4.5	5.1	5.9	10.3	95.5	94.9	94.1	89.7
1800	.55	2.3	3.2	6.2	7.7	9.3	17.6	93.8	92.3	90.7	82.4
1850	.52	2.9	4.8	9.5	11.6	13.8	25.9	90.5	88.4	86.2	74.1
1900	2.2	7.3	11.9	18.0	20.8	23.6	37.2	82.0	79.2	76.4	62.8
1950	9.0	18.0	24.3	31.5	34.7	37.7	50.1	68.5	65.3	62.3	49.9
1960	12.5	23.7	31.7	39.3	42.2	45.1	56.3	60.7	57.8	54.9	43.7

% of the total global population

table 4.   structure of past global population by broad settlement categories (also urban and rural)

405

periods	over 1 mil. inh.	over 100,000 inh.	over 20,000 inh.	over 5,000 inh. urban 1	over c.3,300 inh. urban 2	over 2,000 inh. urban 3	over 1,000 inh. urban 4	under 5,000 inh. rural 1	under c.3,300 inh. rural 2	under 2,000 inh. rural 3	under 1,000 inh. rural 4	total population of the earth
8500 – 8000 B.C.	—	—	—	—	—	—	.000	.020	.020	.020	.020	.020
8000—7500	—	—	—	—	—	.000	.360	.034	.034	.034	.034	.034
7500 – 7000	—	—	—	.000	.000	.450	.280	.038	.038	.038	.038	.038
7000 – 6500	—	—	—	.220	.210	.180	.140	.047	.047	.047	.046	.047
6500 – 6000	—	—	—	.140	.110	.104	.072	.054	.054	.054	.054	.054
6000 – 5500	—	—	—	.000	.000	.012	.025	.056	.056	.056	.056	.056
5500 – 5000	—	—	—	.000	.000	.013	.025	.039	.039	.039	.039	.039
5000 – 4500	—	—	—	.000	.027	.021	.040	.030	.030	.030	.030	.030
4500 – 4000	—	—	—	.031	.023	.037	.041	.021	.021	.021	.021	.021
4000 – 3500	—	—	—	.124	.130	.110	.110	.014	.014	.014	.014	.014
3500 – 3000	—	—	.000	.310	.280	.260	.155	.015	.015	.014	.014	.016
3000 – 2500	—	.00	.460	.320	.300	.270	.280	.012	.012	.012	.011	.017
2500 – 2000	—	.081	.081	.058	.058	.058	.081	.016	.016	.016	.014	.017
2000 – 1500	—	-.081	-.081	.000	.000	.045	.031	.018	.018	.018	.018	.018
1500 – 1000	—	-.350	.000	-.058	.000	-.045	.000	.021	.020	.019	.018	.019
1000 – 500	—	.680	.220	.220	.180	.200	.150	.012	.012	.011	.010	.021
500 – 0	.00	.196	.155	.127	.116	.110	.094	.016	.016	.016	.015	.024
A.D. 0 – 500	.000	-.045	.053	-.055	-.050	.048	-.027	.041	.042	.042	.041	.033
500 – 1000	.440	.220	.176	.154	.145	.138	.114	.035	.035	.036	.036	.0455
1000 – 1500	-.081	.011	.0082	.0137	.0133	.0191	.025	.104	.104	.104	.104	.0955
1500 – 1650	.000	-.036	.000	.000	.0217	.0196	.605	.233	.231	.230	.233	.215
1650 – 1750	-.400	.000	.0392	.096	.147	.239	.501	.304	.299	.293	.268	.290
1750 – 1800	.450	.360	.220	1.067	1.283	1.350	1.515	.405	.388	.378	.278	.437
1800 – 1850	.370	.970	1.32	1.365	1.325	1.300	1.280	.432	.414	.398	.290	.493
1850 – 1900	3.590	2.500	2.49	1.960	1.830	1.740	1.396	.465	.447	.423	.328	.656
1900 – 1950	3.790	2.720	2.33	2.010	1.910	1.830	1.480	.530	.505	.482	.448	.875
1950 – 1960	5.100	4.590	4.50	4.050	3,790	3.580	2.920	.497	.459	.440	.411	1.730

average yearly growth rates for each period in %

table 5. yearly growth rates of past global population by broad settlement categories (also urban and rural)

date years ago B.C. or A.D.	population (billions) at date given	population (billions) average during preceding period	birth rate in % (average during preceding period)	cumulative births (population total) since 2,000,000 years ago (millions)	population growth rate in % (yearly average during the preceding period)
2,000,000	.00005	.000023	50	0	(0.000020)
1,000,000	.00020	.000100	50	5,000	0.000138
(600,000)	.00049	.000315	50	11,300	0.000224
500,000	.00055	.000520	50	13,900	0.000117
300,000	.00086	.000690	50	20,800	0.000225
200,000	.00110	.000970	50	25,650	0.000247
100,000	.00180	.00141	50	32,700	0.00049
50,000	.00280	.00225	50	38,330	0.00089
25,000	.00450	.00355	50	42,770	0.00190
15,000	.010	.00660	50	46,070	0.0080
10,000 – 8000 B.C.	.016	.013	50	49,320	0.0094
6000 B.C.	.037	.024	50	51,720	0.0419
4000 B.C.	.080	.055	50	57,220	0.0386
2000 B.C.	.110	.095	50	66,720	0.0159
1000 B.C.	.132	.121	50	72,770	0.0182
± 0 B.C./A.D.	.165	.147	50	80,120	0.0223
500 A.D.	.195	.180	50	84,620	0.0333
1000 A.D.	.245	.218	50	90,070	0.0455
1500 A.D.	.395	.310	50	97,820	0.0955
1650 A.D.	.545	.463	50	101,290	0.215
1750 A.D.	.728	.630	50	104,440	0.290
1800 A.D.	.906	.815	49	106,440	0.437
1850 A.D.	1.160	1.025	48	108,900	0.493
1900 A.D.	1.610	1.370	45	111,980	0.656
1950 A.D.	2.493	2.000	40.5	116,030	0.875
1960 A.D.	2.960	2.720	38	117,070	1.730

table 6.   the "Standard City of the Future Curve" for past total global population

size categories (inh.)	number of settlements		average population (inh.)	total population	
	estimate by the Athens Center of Ekistics				
	partial	cumulative		partial	cumulative
in millions:			in millions		
10-20	3	3	13.66	41	41
5-10	14	17	6.93	97	138
2-5	38	55	2.82	107	245
1-2	86	141	1.34	125	370
.5-1	142	283	.677	96	456
.2-.5	426	709	.306	130	596
.1-.2	751	1,460	.141	106	702
in thousands:			in thousands		
50-100	1,595	3,055	67.8	108	820
20-50	4,145	7,200	30.4	126	936
10-20	7,750	14,950	13.8	107	1,043
5-10	17,750	32,700	6.82	121	1,164
c. 3.3-5	23,000	55,700	3.74	86	1,250
2-c. 3.3.	36,500	92,200	2.33	85	1,335
1-2.	222,300	314,500	1.35	300	1,635
.5-1	604,500	919,000	.678	410	2,045
.2-.5	1,118,000	2,037,000	.349	390	2,435
.1-.2	1,723,000	3,760,000	.145	250	2,685
in units:			in units		
50-99	1,940,000	5,700,000	74.7	145	2,830
20-49	1,480,000	7,180,000	33.8	50	2,880
10-19	1,050,000	8,230,000	14.3	15	2,895
5-9	2,600,000 ⎫	10,830,000	6.93 ⎫	18	2,913
2-4	1,970,000 ⎬ 5,570,000	12,800,000	3.05 ⎬ 4.49	6	2,919
1	1,000,000 ⎭	13,800,000	1.0 ⎭	1	2,920
nomads	400,000	14,200,000	100	40	2,960
world total		14,200,000			2,960

total populations in million inhabitants

table 7.   present distribution of settlements by size categories (1960), for the entire globe

metropolitan areas	area					
	1940 sq. km		1960 sq km		1940 - 1960 annual rate increase	
	Bu	M	Bu	M	Bu	M
	1	2	3	4	5	6
Athens	215	565	409	1,141	3.28	3.58
Vienna	344	1,227	559	1,951	2.44	2.38
Stockholm	445	1,875	985	3,039	4.02	2.44
Madrid	71	312	190	1,276	5.24	7.30
Paris	1,092	2,775	1,786	5,026	2.50	3.04
London	2,055	5,074	2,467	6,673	0.94	1.40
N. York	3,584	7,540	5,696	13,507	2.38	2.95
Detroit & Windsor	640	1,860	1,241	3,866	3.36	3.72
Toronto	365	1,273	1,195	2,894	6.12	4.18
Rio de Janeiro			1,192	3,633		
Delhi	103	422	284	1,191	5.22	5.34
Karachi	37	108	333	870	11.61	11.00
Bangkok	70	329	206	946	5.56	5.43
Melbourne	404	1,288	1,126	3,263	5.28	4.78
Tokyo	670	1,444	2,192	5,787	6.07	7.18

population in thousands
Bu :   built-up area
M :   metropolitan area

table 8.   1940-1960 trends of growth in the metropolitan areas

metropolitan areas	population					
	1940 in thousands		1960 in thousands		1940 - 1960 annual rate increase	
	Bu	M	Bu	M	Bu	M
	7	8	9	10	11	12
Athens	1,120	165	1,870	1,950	2.60	2.62
Vienna	1,860	2,040	1,747	1,930	−0.32	−0.30
Stockholm	100	850	1,140	1,300	2.47	1.94
Madrid	1,300	1,350	2,245	2,360	2.78	2.84
Paris	5,880	6,020	7,480	7,800	1.20	1.32
London	9,350	9,970	9,370	10,650	—	0.33
N. York	10,850	11,630	14,600	15,600	1.62	1.47
Detroit & Windsor	2,130	2,340	3,170	4,270	2.02	3.04
Toronto	870	920	1,770	1,840	3.78	3.53
Rio de Janeiro	1,600	1,800	4,300	4,600	5.10	4.80
Delhi	760	830	2,350	2,530	5.81	5.74
Karachi	350	365	1,900	1,930	8.80	8.70
Bangkok	700	950	1,900	2,260	5.10	4.47
Melbourne	1,045	1,110	1,840	1,934	2.90	2.80
Tokyo	8,000	8,300	12,300	13,000	2.18	2.21

table 8 cont'd

410

densities				income per capita in metropolitan areas		relationship of annual rates of population & area increase	
1940 inh./ha		1960 inh./ha		in 1960 $			
Bu	M	Bu	M	1940	1960	Bu ($^7/_{15}$)	M ($^8/_{16}$)
13	14	15	16	17	18	19	20
52	21.5	46	19	350	720	1.25	1.37
54	17	26	9	580	1,120	−7.70	−7.90
16	5	12	4	1,450	1,900	1.65	1.26
183	43	115	19	270	550	1.90	2.56
52	22	42	16	380	1,550	2.10	2.32
46	20	37	16	1,150	1,450		4.30
31	16	26	12	1,750	2,800	1.48	2.00
33	13	25	11	1,450	2,200	1.68	1.23
24	7	15	6	1,350	2,600	1.63	1.19
		36	13	250	380		
74	20	97	21	158	145	0.90	0.93
95	34	57	22	156	150	1.33	1.27
100	29	92	24	160	200	1.10	1.23
26	9	16	6	1,300	1,500	1.83	1.70
120	58	56	23	420	750	2.78	3.23

Appendix 2
Selected long-range projections for population, income and energy

Introduction

A set of interconnected long-range projections, reaching into the period of the incipient Ecumenopolis, have been worked out at the Athens Center of Ekistics for various aspects of *population, income* and *energy* (and also partly for certain other variables such as education, research, nutrition, etc.). Retaining a certain number of *basic assumptions* (six for population, nine each for income and energy), an equal number of *models* was developed for each variable which give a coherent picture of its future evolution. Congruent assumptions and models lead to figures that can be *combined, interpolated*, and — within limits — *extrapolated*, without loss of consistency: in this way a much larger number of models can be generated, in total or partially, according to the particular needs for each type of question.

The *six population models* refer to three "ultimate" values for world population at the time of incipient Ecumenopolis: 20, 35 and 50 billion, respectively, the lowest figure being regarded by far as the most probable and the other two as assumptions whose meaning we have to understand. Two types of evolutionary curves leading to these "ultimate" figures were chosen: one "Fast" model (F) and one "Slow" model (S), the slow one leading to the same "ultimate" figure as the fast one, but 50 years later. The six models are: F-20, F-35, F-50; and S-20, S-35· and S-50. Each model provides consistent figures for a variety of types of breakdown of total world population (by size and type of settlements, by geographic areas, etc.) and for future dates at a distance of about one generation from each other. (Initially this distance was 30 years, but in a recent revision it was changed to 25 years). The families of curves graphically representing each model have been smoothed out to at least first differences, often to second and third differences, thus providing for easy interpolations and extrapolations.

Nine models for income and other economic variables corresponding in groups of three to the three "ultimate populations" of 20, 35 and 50 billion were developed. For each of these, three types of economic growth were retained: a high one (h), a middle one (m) and a low one (l) as shown in fig. 91, the resulting models being 20h, 20m, 20l; 35h, 35m, 35l; and 50h, 50m and 50l. Again, the lowest population (20 billion) and an area somewhere between middle (m) and low (l) growth are regarded as the most probable. For each model, several aspects of income and investment, variously broken down, were calculated and presented at the same time intervals (initially 30 years, later revised to 25 years) as for population, also carefully smoothed out in their values.

Similarly, *nine models for energy* were worked out corresponding exactly to the nine models of income on the basis of a relation between per capita income and per capita energy consumption obtained for groups of large numbers of countries at comparable development levels.

Selected presentation

Some representative tables of a small number of models have been selected for presentation in this Appendix.

For *population*, only the Summary tables 1 and 2 give data for all six models. Some more detailed data are shown for *model F-20*, the one considered as more probable. Table 3 refers to urban population, table 4 to types and sizes of settlements, table 5 to geographic distribution.

The initial population projection models were worked out on the basis of actual population data up to 1960, assuming that the growth rate for total world population would continue to grow for a short while before stabilizing and then declining[1]. Recently, these projections were revised, taking into account actual population figures published for the years up to 1972 which show an almost complete stabilization of the world population growth rate since c. 1960. The result of this revision was to *"push back"* into a more remote future the dates at which the "ultimate" (incipient Ecumenopolis) would be reached. It is these *revised projections* that are shown here.

For *income*, the nine models were initially developed for the slow population assumptions (S), but because of the rather small differences between slow and fast assumptions, they are considered as applicable to the fast assumptions (F) as well, following the necessary adjustments. This being so, *two models* (revised as above) were selected for presentation here, so as to give the outer limits of the most probable range: model S-20l which represents the slowest growth assumption (table 6); and model F-20m which represents a middle growth rate assumption (table 7). The most probable projected values are likely to be close to the geometric mean (or thereabouts) of the figures for these two models, according to the prevailing opinion of the largest proportion of experts.

Correspondingly, from the nine models for energy projections, the two models S-20l and F-20m (revised as above) have been retained and are presented here in tables 8 and 9; again, the most probable values may come more or less close to the geometric mean of the figures for these two models.

414

	S-20	F-20	S-35	S-50	F-35	F-50
1950	2.486	2.486	2.486	2.486	2.486	2.486
1960	2.982	2.982	2.982	2.982	2.982	2.982
1975	4.000	4.000	4.000	4.000	4.000	4.000
2000	6.420	6.430	6.400	6.440	6.490	6.500
2025	9.450	9.600	9.700	9.900	10.230	10.380
2050	12.730	13.500	13.850	14.650	15.700	16.300
2075	15.700	17.800	19.150	20.900	22.850	23.600
2100	17.900	20.000	25.250	28.600	30.650	34.600
2125	19.100	21.300	30.300	35.000	37.750	44.200
2150	20.000	22.600	33.100	37.800	43.400	50.000
2175	21.000	24.100	35.000	40.200	46.800	53.300
2200	22.000	25.600	36.800	42.700	50.000	56.600
2225	23.100	27.100	38.600	45.300	52.500	60.200

(population in billions)

table 1.   global population projections, 1950-2225 (revised, March 1974)

	S-20	F-20	S-35	F-35	S-50	F-50
1950-1960	1.84	1.84	1.84	1.84	1.84	1.84
1960-1975	1.97	1.97	1.97	1.97	1.97	1.97
1975-2000	1.91	1.92	1.89	1.92	1.93	1.96
2000-2025	1.56	1.62	1.68	1.74	1.83	1.89
2025-2050	1.20	1.37	1.44	1.57	1.72	1.83
2050-2075	0.83	1.11	1.30	1.44	1.52	1.76
2075-2100	0.52	0.43	1.12	1.26	1.19	1.55
2100-2125	0.32	0.25	0.74	0.84	0.84	0.98
2125-2150	0.21	0.25	0.35	0.31	0.56	0.50
2150-2175	0.20	0.25	0.23	0.25	0.30	0.26
2175-2200	0.20	0.25	0.20	0.25	0.26	0.25
2200-2225	0.20	0.25	0.20	0.25	0.20	0.25

growth rates in %

table 2.   global population projections, 1950-2225 (revised, March 1974)

year		total urban population (billions)	% urban of total global population	% annual growth rate of urban population (average within period)
	1960	1.335	44.7	3.70
	1975	2.300	57.5	2.81
	2000	4.601	71.5	2.21
	2025	7.940	82.8	1.67
	2050	11.991	88.9	1.27
	2075	16.454	92.5	0.55
Ecumenopolis starts	2100	18.796	94.0	0.29
	2125	20.238	94.8	0.28
	2150	21.649	95.9	0.27
	2175	23.210	96.3	0.26
	2200	24.750	96.7	0.25
	2225	26.280	97.0	

table 3.   urban population according to assumption F-20

year	total global population	main habitable areas						
		total	North & Central America	South America	Africa	Europe	U.S.S.R.	S.W. Asia
1960	2.982	2.982	0.264	0.139	0.268	0.425	0.215	0.080
1975	4.000	4.000	0.350	0.216	0.380	0.470	0.281	0.105
2000	6.430	6.425	0.515	0.425	0.670	0.570	0.395	0.160
2025	9.600	9.500	0.760	0.755	0.990	0.695	0.550	0.240
2050	13.500	13.000	1.040	1.280	1.400	0.840	0.760	0.350
2075	17.800	17.050	1.340	1.800	1.850	0.950	1.000	0.480
2100	20.000	19.000	1.500	2.050	2.100	1.050	1.120	0.540
2125	21.300	20.200	1.595	2.180	2.230	1.115	1.190	0.575
2150	22.600	21.400	1.690	2.310	2.360	1.185	1.260	0.620
2175	24.100	22.600	1.785	2.440	2.490	1.250	1.330	0.655
2200	25.600	23.200	1.880	2.570	2.620	1.320	1.400	0.690
2225	27.100	25.600	1.975	2.700	2.750	1.385	1.470	0.725

table 4.   geographic distribution of global population (model F-20)

416

S.E & S.E. Asia	Australia & Ocea- nia	difficult areas			
		total	deserts, moun- tainous and other difficult land areas	Polar areas	Oceans and Lakes
1.574	0.017	—	—	—	—
2.177	0.021	—	—	—	—
3.655	0.035	0.005	.003	.002	—
5.450	0.060	0.100	.060	.040	—
7.230	0.100	0.500	.300	.180	.020
9.475	0.155	0.750	.320	.190	.240
10.440	0.200	1.000	.350	.200	.450
11.100	0.215	1.100	.360	.210	.530
11.745	0.230	1.200	.370	.220	.610
12.605	0.245	1.300	.380	.230	.690
13.460	0.260	1.400	.390	.240	.770
14.320	0.275	1.500	.400	.250	.850

model F-20
population in billion inhabitants

table 4 cont'd

417

	1960	1975	2000	2025
total global	2.982	4.000	6.430	9.600
1. old patterns (total)	2.982	4.000	6.420	9.550
1.1 permanent settlements	2.942	3.965	6.395	9.535
1.1.1 urban settlements incl. Ecumenopolis core	1.335	2.300	4.595	7.915
over 1 million inh.	0.370	0.800	2.175	4.425
100,000 - 1 million inh.	0.332	0.680	1.350	2.200
over 100,000 inh.	0.702	1.480	3.525	6.625
c. 3,300-100,000 inh.	0.548	0.720	0.950	1.150
over c. 3,300 inh.	1.250	2.200	4.475	7.775
2,000 - c. 3,300 inh.	0.085	0.100	0.120	0.140
1.1.2 rural settlements under 2,000 inh.	1.607	1.665	1.800	1.620
1.2 traditional nomads	0.040	0.035	0.025	0.015
2. new patterns (total)	—	—	0.010	0.050
2.1 new rural	—	—	0.004	0.025
2.2 new nomads	—	—	0.006	0.025
3. total urban (1.1.1 + 2.2)	1.335	2.300	4.601	7.940
4. total rural (1.1.2 + 1.2 + 2.1)	1.647	1.700	1.829	1.660
5. rate of growth (annual) of total urban (3)	3.70%	2.81%	2.21%	1.67%

table 5.   total global population by settlement types and sizes
            (model F-20)

418

2050	2075	2100	2125	2150	2175	2200	2225
13.500	17.800	20.000	21.300	22.600	24.100	25.500	27.100
13.300	17.300	19.200	20.400	21.630	23.060	24.490	25.920
13.291	17.294	19.196	20.398	21.629	23.060	24.490	25.920
11.911	16.264	18.496	19.898	21.279	22.810	24.320	25.820
7.100	9.564	10.900	11.763	12.604	13.550	14.480	15.410
3.251	4.600	5.256	5.650	6.050	6.500	6.950	7.400
10.351	14.164	16.156	17.413	18.654	20.050	21.430	22.810
1.400	1.920	2.150	2.300	2.450	2.600	2.750	2.900
11.751	16.084	18.306	19.713	21.104	22.650	24.180	25.710
0.160	0.180	0.190	0.185	0.175	0.160	0.140	0.110
1.380	1.030	0.700	0.500	0.350	0.250	0.170	0.100
0.009	0.006	0.004	0.002	0.001	—	—	—
0.200	0.500	0.800	0.900	0.970	1.040	1.110	1.180
0.120	0.310	0.500	0.560	0.600	0.640	0.680	0.720
0.080	0.190	0.300	0.340	0.370	0.400	0.430	0.460
11.991	16.454	18.796	20.238	21.649	23.210	24.750	26.280
1.509	1.346	1.204	1.062	.951	0.890	0.850	0.820
1.27%	0.55%	0.29%	0.28%	0.27%	0.26%	0.25%	

population in billions

Date A.D.	groups of countries (arranged by income)	average income per capita	population (billions)	total income (billion $)
1960	a. over 575$/cap.	1,150	0.440	0.506
	b. 200-575	350	0.620	0.217
	c. 100-200	140	0.257	0.036
	d. under 100 (S.E. Asia)	80	1.444	0.116
	e. under 100 (Africa, etc.)	80	0.222	0.018
	habitable areas	300	2.982	0.893
1975	a. over 575$/cap.	1,579	0.506	0.799
	b. 200-575	726	0.796	0.578
	c. 100-200	201	0.370	0.074
	d. under 100 (S.E. Asia)	105	2.011	0.211
	e. under 100 (Africa, etc.)	98	0.316	0.031
	habitable areas	—	—	—
	difficult areas	—	—	—
	total world	423	4.000	1.693
2000	a. over 575$/cap.	2,320	0.668	1.550
	b. 200-575	1,462	1.141	1.668
	c. 100-200	613	0.657	0.403
	d. under 100 (S.E. Asia)	171	3.411	0.583
	e. under 100 (Africa, etc.)	149	0.534	0.080
	habitable areas	668	6.410	4.284
	difficult areas	620	0.010	0.006
	total world	667	6.420	4.290
2025	a. over 575$/cap.	3,204	0.910	2.916
	b. 200-575	2,174	1.631	3.546
	c. 100-200	1,283	1.140	1.463
	d. under 100 (S.E. Asia)	478	4.590	2.194
	e. under 100 (Africa, etc.)	361	0.938	0.339
	habitable areas	1,136	9.210	10.458
	difficult areas	1,164	0.240	0.279
	total world	1,136	9.450	10.737

(1960 U.S. $)

table 6.   global income projections — model S-20 /

2050	a. over 575$/cap.	4,267	1.345	5.739
	b. 200-575	3,002	2.188	6.568
	c. 100-200	1,898	1.924	3.652
	d. under 100 (S.E. Asia)	1,026	5.055	5.186
	e. under 100 (Africa, etc.)	906	1.630	1.476
	habitable areas	1,863	12.142	22.621
	difficult areas	2,135	0.588	1.255
	total world	1,876	12.730	23.876
2075	a. over 575$/cap.	5,678	1.674	9.505
	b. 200-575	4,045	2.657	10.748
	c. 100-200	3,175	2.560	8.128
	d. under 100 (S.E. Asia)	2,186	5.798	12.674
	e. under 100 (Africa, etc.)	1,390	2.194	3.050
	habitable areas	2,963	14.883	44.106
	difficult areas	3,173	0.817	2.592
	total world	2,974	15.700	46.698
2100	a. over 575$/cap.	7,557	1.975	14.925
	b. 200-575	5,519	3.101	17.114
	b. 100-200	4,384	2.885	12.648
	d. under 100 (S.E. Asia)	3,249	6.519	21.180
	e. under 100 (Africa, etc.)	2,132	2.465	5.255
	habitable areas	4,197	16.945	71.122
	difficult areas	4,718	0.955	4.506
	total world	4,225	17.900	75.628
2125	a. over 575$/cap.	10,600	2.076	22.006
	b. 200-575	7,860	3.272	25.718
	c. 100-200	5,686	3.157	17.951
	d. under 100 (S.E. Asia)	3,942	6.875	27.101
	e. under 100 (Africa, etc.)	3,650	2.709	9.888
	habitable areas	5,675	18.089	102.664
	difficult areas	7,257	1.011	7.337
	total world	5,759	19.100	110.001
2150	a. over 575$/cap.	13,104	2.186	28.645
	b. 200-575	9,772	3.435	33.567
	c. 100-200	7,112	3.310	23.541
	d. under 100 (S.E. Asia)	4,992	7.163	35.758
	e. Under 100 (Africa, etc.)	4,649	2.844	13.222
	habitable areas	7,114	18.938	134.733
	difficult areas	9,136	1.062	9.702
	total world	7,222	20.000	144.435

Date A.D.	groups of countries (arranged by income)	average income per capita	population (billions)	total income (billion $)
1960	a. over 575$/cap.	1,150	0.440	506
	b. 200 - 575	350	0.620	217
	c. 100 - 200	140	0.257	36
	d. under 100 (S.E. Asia)	80	1.444	116
	e. under 100 (Africa, etc.)	80	0.222	18
	habitable areas	300	2.982	893
1975	a. over 575$/cap.	2,415	0.506	1,222
	b. 200 - 575	816	0.796	650
	c. 100-200	201	0.370	74
	d. under 100 (S.E. Asia)	105	2.011	211
	e. under 100 (Africa, etc.)	98	0.316	31
	habitable areas	—	—	—
	difficult areas	—	—	—
	total world	547	4.000	2.188
2000	a. over 575$/cap.	6,820	0.667	4.549
	b. 200 - 575	2,855	1.139	3.252
	c. 100 - 200	664	0.656	0.436
	d. under 100 (S.E. Asia)	171	3.405	0.582
	e. under 100 (Africa, etc.)	149	0.533	0.079
	habitable areas	1,386	6.420	8.898
	difficult areas	1,293	0.010	0.013
	total world	1,386	6.430	8.911
2025	a. over 575$/cap.	17,330	0.917	15.892
	b. 200 - 575	7,798	1.644	12.820
	c. 100 - 200	2,358	1.164	2.745
	d. under 100 (S.E. Asia)	504	4.679	2.358
	e. under 100 (Africa, etc.)	370	0.945	0.350
	habitable areas	3,617	9.349	33.815
	difficult areas	3,771	0.251	0.946
	total world	3,621	9.600	34.761

(1960 U.S. $)

table 7.   global income projections – model income F-20 *m*

2050	a. over 575$/cap.	42.456	1.404	59.608
	b. 200 - 575	19,573	2.324	45.488
	c. 100 - 200	6,438	1.990	12.812
	d. under 100 (S.E. Asia)	1,811	5.538	10.029
	e. under 100 (Africa, etc.)	1,428	1.664	2.376
	habitable areas	10,086	12.920	130.313
	difficult areas	11,608	0.580	6.733
	total world	10,151	13.500	137.046
2075	a. over 575$/cap.	106,611	2.006	213.862
	b. 200 - 575	51,537	3.038	156.569
	c. 100 - 200	19,830	3.082	61.116
	d. under 100 (S.E. Asia)	5,954	5.996	35.700
	e. under 100 (Africa, etc.)	4,319	2.714	11.722
	habitable areas	28,449	16.836	478.969
	difficult areas	34,187	0.964	32.956
	total world	28,760	17.800	511.925
2100	a. over 575$/cap.	261,183	2.109	550.835
	b. 200 - 575	126,259	3.437	443.952
	c. 100 - 200	49,773	3.085	153.550
	d. under 100 (S.E. Asia)	16,263	7.743	125.924
	e. under 100 (Africa, etc.)	12,224	2.589	31.648
	habitable areas	68,866	18.963	1,305.909
	difficult areas	90,045	1.037	93.377
	total world	69,464	20.000	1,399.286
2125	a. over 575$/cap.	639,865	2.313	1,480.008
	b. 200 - 575	309,318	3.590	1,110.452
	c. 100 - 200	121,937	3.511	428.121
	d. under 100 (S.E. Asia)	40,820	7.753	316.477
	e. under 100 (Africa, etc.)	31,043	3.023	93.843
	habitable areas	169,832	20.190	3,428.901
	difficult areas	223,392	1.110	247.965
	total world	172,623	21.300	3,676.866
2150	a. over 575$/cap.	1,519,402	2.470	3,752.923
	b. 200 - 575	713,637	3.882	2,770.339
	c. 100 - 200	257,683	3.740	963.734
	d. under 100 (S.E. Asia)	85,475	8.094	691.835
	e. under 100 (Africa, etc.)	68,766	3.214	221.014
	habitable areas	392,516	21.400	8,399.845
	difficult areas	502,410	1.200	602.894
	total world	398,351	22.600	9,002.737

423

year	per capita income (in U.S. $ 1960 value)	projections of per capita energy consumption (in kg coal equivalent)
1960	300	1,404
1975	423	1,750
2010	667	2,200
2025	1,136	3,700
2050	1,876	5,000
2075	2,974	7,000
2100	4,225	9,000
2125	5,759	11,000
2150	7,222	13,400

table 8.   global energy consumption per capita
            model S-20 *l*

year	per capita income (in U.S. $, 1960 value)	projections of per capita energy consumption (in kg coal equivalent)
1960	300	1,404
1975	547	2,360
2010	1,386	4,167
2025	3,621	8,100
2050	10,151	17,300
2075	28,760	37,200
2100	69,464	72,500
2125	172,623	143,000
2150	398,349	300,000

table 9.   global energy consumption per capita
            model F-20 *m*

Appendix 3
A note on megalopolises

Introduction

Megalopolises started emerging in the 1940's as rudimentary, but real configurations showing the way towards the still larger types of settlements of the future (small eperopolis, eperopolis, Ecumenopolis), and have grown spectacularly both in size and in numbers ever since. Thus we now have over a generation of experience of their growth and development, and the corresponding knowledge, which although still quite imperfect, nevertheless does provide a first insight into the nature and structure of present megalopolises, and into the trends that point towards their future.

It is needless to stress the importance of this new concept in ekistics: it illustrates an altogether new and different type of settlement extending as a multiplicated, band-like formation over a vast region, one that already is predicted to acquire an extreme importance in the Near Future and to give us something of a hint, however imprecise, of the nature of Ecumenopolis. It also gives us a measure of both the unprecedented achievements (and advantages) of these new types of settlements, which justifies their unexpected attractiveness to large masses of people all over the globe, and of their extreme complexity, together with the novel and bewildering multiplicity of the large-scale problems they create. And we can say that we are privileged today in having for the first time in history a palpable reality for these new settlements which theorists, who might have tried to predict Ecumenopolis over a generation ago, entirely lacked.

This is why we thought it useful to try to assemble some basic facts on megalopolises in this Appendix, so that readers of this book may quickly locate some basic information about this type of settlement whenever they need it. More about megalopolises can be found in the bibliography.

The term "megalopolis" has been used in a variety of ways. It was the name of a (relatively) large city in ancient Arcadia that resulted from the consolidation of several smaller settlements into one unit. It was used by Jean Gottmann as a name for the specific, new, large-scale settlement that emerged recently along the Eastern seaboard of the U.S.A. Soon after the publication of J. Gottmann's book it became apparent that several other large-scale settlements around the earth resembled this one, and thus "megalopolis" began being used, although rather loosely, as a generic team defining this new type of large-scale, band-like, poly-nucleated settlement. The Athens Center of Ekistics has attempted to devise a set of definitions for this type of settlement[1] that bring together various previous attempts at such a definition. Throughout this book the word "megalopolis" has been used in two ways, first, to denote ekistic unit 12 of the ekistic scale, thus giving a simple size definition of megalopolis, and second, as a structural concept indicating various internal relations prevailing in this new type of settlement (e.g. connectivity, system of flows, axial development and polycentrality, regional development along specific lines, etc.).

We are still far from having fully understood the true nature and structure of megalopolises in detail, but at least a first approach to such an understanding is provided by the studies carried out so far. This is why a summary of the findings of such studies is presented here in an attempt to elucidate the structural defini-tions of megalopolises.

Definitions

Our current definitions of a true megalopolis must satisfy four criteria, which taken together constitute a necessary and sufficient set of conditions. First, there must be a substantial increase in size, scale, and complexity above that which is normal for the small megalopolis and the total population must be greater than 10 mil-lion. Second, there must be a number of distinct (but interconnected) major urban centers, generally at the metropolitan scale (population between one and 10 million). Third, these main centers must be in an essentially linear arrange-ment, distributed along a straight or slightly curving primary axis (fig. 39).

These three structural criteria, however, are by themselves still inadequate to distinguish a megalopolis from an unusually large and highly articulated small megalopolis. Since the particular characteristic of a megalopolis is the exceptional interaction which unifies each separate center with its immediate neighbors on the megalopolitan axis, there must be a certain minimum level of interaction or "connectivity" before the link between any pair of centers may be properly term-ed megalopolitan. This brings us to the fourth important criterion for the defini-tion of a megalopolis. It would be desirable to establish detailed criteria by measuring and quantifying the intensity of specific flows and types of interaction, but due to deficiencies in available data this remains beyond our capabilities. Within the limitations imposed by lack of data, an empirical comparison was made of center sizes, center separations, and other important features of the most fully-understood existing megalopolises, and it was found that the relationships between these phenomena could be adequately represented by a type of gravity model. Expressed in a simple formula, these relationships were tested for over 150 megalopolises — either in existence or predicted to emerge during the next generations — and the general formula was subsequently refined to its present level of sophistication[2].

As it now stands, the refined connectivity formula which expresses the interaction between any pair of adjacent major centers[3] in a megalopolitan chain may be stated as follows:

$$D = (100 \cdot \sqrt{P})\,(\sqrt{2})^{4-S} \cdot (\sqrt{2})^{N+T}, \text{ in which}$$

D is the distance[4] between two adjacent centers C_1 and C_2 expressed in kilometers;

P equals the square root of the product of the population of C_1 and C_2 ($\sqrt{P_1 P_2}$ with P_1 and P_2 expressed in millions of inhabitants);

N is a correction factor[5] based on the importance of smaller settlements located between C_1 and C_2;

T is a correction factor[6] reflecting the general quality of transportation links between C_1 and C_2, and

S is the desired index of interaction representing the connectivity conditions existing between C_1 and C_2.

Empirical research has determined that a value of S greater than or equal to 4 is a necessary and sufficient condition for the definition of a megalopolitan link, assuming that the three structural criteria stated before have been satisfied. As further data on megalopolises become available, it may be possible to bring the connectivity formula closer to a theoretical ideal (i.e. to define connectivity in terms of specific flows and levels of interaction between megalopolitan centers), but in the meantime this general approximation for connectivity seems to provide a reasonably reliable indicator of the appearance of megalopolitan formations and and an adequate index of the intensity of interaction between any pair of adjacent centers.

It is interesting to note that more detailed studies on megalopolises carried out recently by various groups in the U.S., Canada, Japan, Korea, W. Europe and elsewhere confirm with extremely close approximation the prediction based on the connectivity formula, proving this to be a good usable tool for investigating megalopolises in a first approach.

This formula has been used in the Athens Center of Ekistics in order to check whether present candidates to megalopolitan structure had actually acquired it and to make projections to the year 2000 (and slightly beyond it).

Results

The following tables give a summary of the results thus obtained. Table 1 gives our analysis of size definition for megalopolises and larger settlements; table 2 gives the number of megalopolises existing or projected to emerge by the year 2000 by types (sizes) of settlements, and by 5-year increments between 1960 and 2000; table 3 gives the names of the first megalopolises expected to emerge by 1975; and table 4 the names of the first "urbanized regions" (ekistic unit 13, "small eperopolis") expected to emerge by 2000. Fig. 153 gives a visual impression of the contents of table 2.

One sees how under present trends and high-level estimates the importance of megalopolises is anticipated to have grown by the year 2000 or after. The total population on this planet living in megalopolises (or still larger settlements) by that time is expected to reach, according to the various population projection models, between 40% and 50% of the total population of the earth, thus justifying the expression "the era of the megalopolis" for the period just after the year 2000.

Typology of megalopolises

In 1970, there were nineteen megalopolises (table 2) exhibiting an average annual growth rate for total population of about 3%. The growth rate of the populations of their metropolitan centers was generally higher — about 4% — but that of the smaller settlements which they included and of the areas surrounding their metropolitan centers was generally less than 3%. There is evidence that emerging megalopolises exhibit the highest rates of growth in population, while more mature specimens experience a progressive reduction in growth rates. There are, of course, vast differences in type and structure between the megalopolises which we can currently study. Density, for instance, varies from a low of 2-2.5 inh. per ha in the North American megalopolises to densities nearing or even exceeding 10 inh. per ha in those of Europe and Japan. In 1960, the maximum observed overall density of 12.8 inh. per ha (found in the Ruhr-Berlin Megalopolis) was almost equal to the theoretical future average. Megalopolitan areas range from a minimum of about 10,000 square kilometers (6,200 sq. mi.) in central Europe, Africa, and Southeast Asia, to a maximum of about 160,000 square kilometers (99,500 sq. mi.) in the Eastern Megalopolis of the U.S.A. — nearly twice the predicted future average for megalopolitan areas. Populations range from the lower theoretical limit of 10 million to the present maximum of about 70 million in the Japanese Megalopolis.

Despite the limited number of megalopolises available for study, a tentative typology may be attempted based primarily on geographic features, culture, and level of economic development:

Type I — North American (fig. 122)
— Large areas
— Lowest overall densities
— Highest per capita incomes
— Advanced urbanization
— Presence of many special functions and amenities
— Centers usually consisting of single or twin metropolises

Type II — West European (fig. 121)
— Much higher densities
— Higher order clustering of centers (multiple metropolises, or small megalopolises consisting of several centers intimately interconnected)
— Slightly lower per capita incomes
— More strongly influenced by historical structure and values
— More evidence of conservation activities in non built-up areas
— Increased importance of secondary centers.

Type III — Asian
— Low per capita income
— Low degree of urbanization
— Extensive slum areas and pronounced internal disparities
— Great shortage of Networks and utilities
— Existence of large numbers of villages adjacent to urban centers
— High densities, extending for large areas, combined with a lack of clear major centers.

The Japanese Megalopolis deserves mention as a special case, as its high densities, high incomes and highest degree of urbanization place it closer to the West European type than to the Asian, while still preserving its own rather unique features.

A fourth type just starting to emerge in Latin America[7] is not yet sufficiently advanced as a megalopolitan formation to permit a general description of its features, but it will probably represent an intermediate form midway between the Asian and the North American types.

stages of development		megalopolises		small eperopolises		eperopolises		Ecumenopolis	
		range	central value	range	central value	range	central value	range	central value
true	large	>250m	600m	>1,500m	3,500m	>6b	10b	≥25b	25b
	normal	35-250m	100m	250-1,500m	600m	1.5-6b	3.5b	10-25b	20b
	small	10-35m	18m	80-250m	150m	0.5-1.5b	0.85b	3-10b	6b
pre-		3-10m	6m	25-80m	45m	0.15-0.5b	0.3b	1-3b	2b

Note: "Normal" megalopolises are those corresponding to ekistic unit 12 of the ekistic scale. But in the previous, *formative stages,* megalopolises, before reaching their "normal" size, appear as smaller units (here classified as pre-megalopolises), with 3-10 million inh., or *small* true megalopolises, with 10-35 million inh. that exhibit some of the basic *structural features* of megalopolises (connectivity, regional development, relation of axes and centers, etc.), without having reached full size (and generally full development) yet. Similar comments are valid for the larger settlement units (small eperopolis, eperopolis, Ecumenopolis).

m = million
b = billion

table 1.   size definition for megalopolises and larger settlements

type of settlement and population range	1960	1965	1970	1975	1980	1985	1990	1995	2000
A. megalopolises*									
True: > 10m	11	14	19	30	43	55	68	81	95
of which: large > 250 m	—	—	—	—	—	—	—	—	—
normal 35-250m	2	4	6	10	15	20	25	30	35
small 10-35m	9	10	13	20	28	35	43	51	60
pre-megalopolises 3-10m	6	8	10	15	23	33	45	58	68
total (true + pre-megalopolises)	17	22	29	45	66	88	113	139	163
B. small eperopolises									
true 80m	—	1	2	3	4	6	8	10	12
of which: large 1500m	—	—	—	—	—	—	—	—	—
normal 250-1500m	—	—	—	—	—	—	—	—	1
small 80-250m	—	1	2	3	4	6	8	10	11
pre-small eperopolises 25-80m	1	2	2	3	4	5	6	8	10
total (true + pre-small eperopolises)	1	3	4	6	8	11	14	18	22

m = million

* All megalopolises are included here, whether isolated or forming part of small eperopolises.

table 2. emergence of the megalopolis, 1960-2000 number of megalopolises and small eperopolises

| | megalopolises added to those of the previous date | | |
1960	1965	1970	1975
N Japanese N Eastern (U.S.) S English S Great Lakes Megalopolis S Paris - Randstadt S Randstadt - Stuttgart S Ruhr - Hamburg S Ruhr - Berlin S Shanghai - Nanking S Peking - Tientsin S Shenyang - Dairen	S Berlin - Leipzig S Los Angeles - San Diego S Cairo - Alexandria	S Warsaw - Lodz S Yahata - Kumamoto S Rio - São Paulo S Hong Kong - Canton S Djakarta - Bandung	S Nurnberg - Munich S Stuttgart - Munich S Lodz - Katowice - Krakow S Rome - Naples S Detroit - Toronto S Chicago - St. Louis S Buenos Aires - Montevideo S Shenyang - Changchun S Changchun - Harbin S Witwatersrand - Pretoria S Milan - Turin
	"promoted" to "normal" N English N Randstadt - Stuttgart	"promoted" to "normal" N Great Lakes Megalopolis N Ruhr - Berlin	"promoted" to "normal" N Shanghai - Nanking N Rio - Sao Paulo N Paris - Randstadt N Ruhr - Hamburg
totals: 2N + 9S = 11 true megalopolises	4N + 10S = 14 true megalopolises	6N + 13S = 19 true megalopolises	10N + 20S = 30 true megalopolises

S = small megalopolis (10-35 million)
N = normal megalopolis (35-250 million)

table 3.   the first megalopolises
list of emerging "true megalopolises" (both "normal" and "small") 1960-1975

A. true "small" small eperopolises (80 - 250 million)

Name	Date of emergence
1. Rhine System	1965
2. Japanese System	1970
3. Great Lakes Megalopolis System	1975
4. Yangtse System	1980

Another 8 systems are expected to be added by 2000 A.D.

B. true "normal" small eperopolises (250 - 1500 million)

The first one projected to appear will be the Rhine System in the year 2000, by which time it is projected to have a population of 280 million.

table 4.   the first small eperopolises

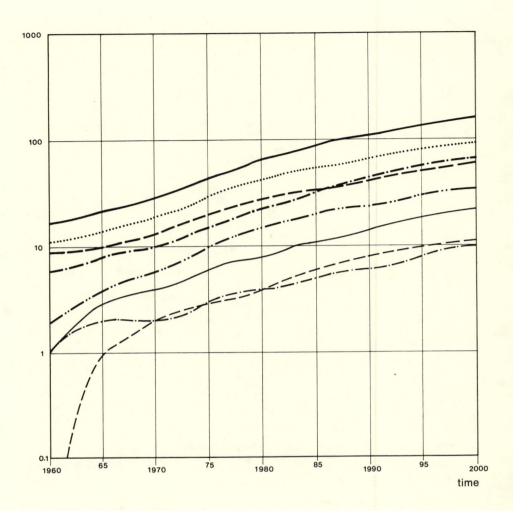

153. number of megalopolises and small eperopolises, 1960-
2000

Glossary

Anthroparea: Word coined by C.A. Doxiadis from the word *Anthropos* (human being) and *area*, meaning the built-up area in the broadest sense mostly used by Anthropos in his daily life.

Anthropocosmos: World of Anthropos as distinguished from the great world or cosmos beyond Anthropos' reach. Term coined by C.A. Doxiadis from the Greek words *anthropos* and *cosmos*, 'Man' and 'world'; first used in his lecture at the Swarthmore College Centennial Year Celebrations in 1964, entitled "The Human Crust of the Earth"

Anthropos: The Greek word for human being (Man), used in this book to indicate the individual with his own characteristics and problems as distinct from Society. (See also note 1, Part One).

Community class: Based on a systematic classification of human communities expressed in the Ekistic Logarithmic Scale (ELS), starting from class I, which corresponds to housegroup, and ending with class XII, corresponding to Ecumenopolis.

Deepways: The whole system of underground lines of transportation for private or mass-transportation vehicles, few or many, traveling at all speeds, which is indispensable for the solution of our urban problems. Term coined by C.A. Doxiadis, first used in his studies of 1965 and 1966 and in his book *Between Dystopia and Utopia*, 1966.

Dynapolis: Dynamic city or dynamic 'polis'. The ideal dynapolis is the city with a parabolic uni-directional growth which can expand in space and time. Term coined by C.A. Doxiadis and used since the early fifties in his teaching and writing. (C.A. Doxiadis, *Architecture in Transition,* Hutchinson, London, 1963, pp. 102-106).

Dystopia: From the Greek words *dys* and *topos*. *Dys* signifies difficulty or evil. It is the opposite of *eu* — good. In this combination and context, *dystopia* is another and much more precise word for what anti-utopia was supposed to mean. V.L. Parrington (1947) uses it instead of anti-utopia, and C.A. Doxiadis in his book *Between Dystopia and Utopia*, 1966.

Ecumenopolis: The coming city that will, together with the corresponding open land which is indispensable for Anthropos, cover the entire earth as a continuous system forming a universal settlement. It is derived from the Greek words *ecumene*, that is, the total inhabitable area of the world, and *polis*, or city, in the broadest sense of the word. Term coined by C.A. Doxiadis and first used in the October 1961 issue of EKISTICS. (See also note 1, Preface).

Ekistic elements: The five elements which compose human settlements: Anthropos, Nature, Society, Shells and Networks.

Ekistic Logarithmic Scale (ELS): A classification of settlements according to their size, presented on the basis of a logarithmic scale, running from Anthropos (unit 1), as the smallest unit of measurement, to the whole earth (unit 15). The ekistic logarithmic scale can be presented graphically, showing area or number of people corresponding to each unit, etc., so that it can be used as a basis for the measurement and classification of many dimensions in human settlements. (See also note 9, Part One).

Ekistics: The science of human settlements. It conceives the human settlement as a living organism having its own laws and, through the study of the evolution of human settlements from their most primitive phase to megalopolis and Ecumenopolis, develops the interdisciplinary approach necessary to its problems. Term coined by C.A. Doxiadis from the Greek words *oikos*, 'home', and *oikō*, 'settling down'; first used in his lectures of 1942 at the Athens Technical University.

Ekistic Unit: A classification of parts or whole human settlements, starting from unit 1, corresponding to Anthropos, and ending with unit 15, corresponding to Ecumenopolis. From unit 4, which corresponds to community class I, to unit 15, which corresponds to community class XII, the ekistic units coincide with the classification of human communities expressed in the ekistic logarithmic scale (ELS).

Entopia: Place that is practicable — that can exist. Term coined by C.A. Doxiadis from the Greek words *en* and *topos*, 'in' and 'place'. First used in the Trinity College Lectures, Hartford, Conn., 1966, and published in his book *Between Dystopia and Utopia*, 1966.

Eperopolis: Term coined by C.A. Doxiadis.
Corresponding to ekistic unit 14 and community class XI, with a population of

five thousand million, eperopolis replaces the old term "urbanized continent". It is derived from the Greek words *eperos* meaning "continent" and *polis* meaning "city".

ized continent". It is derived from the Greek words *eperos* meaning 'continent' and *polis* meaning 'city'.

Ergonomics: The physiological, anatomical and psychological aspects of Anthropos in his working environment. It is derived from two Greek words, *ergon* meaning 'work', and *nomoi* meaning 'laws' or 'habits' and 'customs'. The word was coined by O.G. Edholm and used, e.g., in his book *The Biology of Work*, World University Library, Weidenfeld & Nicolson, London, 1967.

Great Lakes Megalopolis (GLM): The megalopolitan formation which is emerging around the Great Lakes of North America involving parts of the States of Wisconsin, Illinois, Indiana, Michigan, Ohio, Pennsylvania and New York and a strip of the provinces of Ontario contiguous with the Great Lakes and the St. Lawrence Seaway. In 1960 this main part of GLM had a population of 22 million within an area of about 36 thousand square miles. It is encompassed by a secondary and outer zone, with about 36 million inhabitants within an area of 457.6 thousand square miles, extending into the states of Minnesota, Iowa, Missouri, Kentucky, West Virginia and Vermont, in addition to covering more area of the states and provinces mentioned above.

House, and housegroup: These terms replace "dwelling" and "dwelling group", corresponding to ekistic units 3 and 4, with a population of four and 40 people respectively. Housegroup corresponds to community class I.

Isolation of Dimensions and Elimination of Alternatives method (IDEA): The gradual isolation of dimensions and the selection, by elimination, of the alternatives, conceived along isolated dimensions, that satisfy certain ekistic criteria. It is an attempt to eliminate arbitrariness in the search of the many-dimensional parameter space of the urban system for the optimum alternative.

Method created by C.A. Doxiadis and published in Emergence and Growth of an Urban Region: the Developing Urban Detroit Area, Vol. 1, 1966, Vol. II, 1967, Vol. III, 1970, The Detroit Edison Company, Detroit, Michigan.

Kinetic field: The area Anthropos can move within a certain period by walking, by using animals or by using vehicles.

Megalopolis: A greater urbanized area resulting from the merging of metropolises and cities into one urban system. Its population is calculated in tens of millions. It is distinct from the metropolis, because its population exceeds ten million in which case it also covers a vast surface area, or because it has incorporated more than one metropolis. Term used since ancient Greek times when the small city of Megalopolis was created in Arcadia. Jean Gottman gave a special meaning to this ancient term in 1961 in his book *Megalopolis, the Urbanized Northeastern Seaboard of the United States*, a 20th Century Fund Study, the MIT Press, Massachusetts Institute of Technology, Cambridge, Mass., 1961. (See also Appendix 3).

Metropolis: A major, multi-center urban area with more than 50,000 people incorporating other small settlements, both urban and rural, growing dynamically to sizes as high as ten million people. A typical population of such settlements between 50,000 and ten million inhabitants is of the order of 2.0 million, while about one half of these settlements have a population varying between 50,000 and 100,000.

Nature: The natural environment of Anthropos as it exists before he starts re-modeling it by cultivation and construction. It provides the foundation upon which the settlement is created and the frame within which it can function.

Networks: Anthropos-made systems which facilitate the functioning of settlements, such as roads, water supply, electricity.

Shells: All types of structures within which Anthropos lives and carries out his various functions.

Society: Human society with all its characteristics, needs and problems, where every individual is examined only as one unit of it.

Standard Metropolitan Statistical Area (SMSA): In the U.S.A., human settlements containing at least one city with 50,000 inhabitans or more and having close economic and social relationships with contiguous settlements of metropolitan character. For a more detailed definition see the introduction to any of the *1960 Census of Population* reports, U.S. Bureau of the Census.

Utopia: An imaginary and indefinitely remote place, or state of ideal perfection, especially in laws, government, and social conditions. First used by Sir Thomas More for an imaginary and ideal country in his book *Utopia*, 1516; it is a Greek word, a combination of *ou*, 'not', and *topos*, 'place', meaning no-where or no-place.

Bibliography

Arendt, Hannah, *The Human Condition*, University of Chicago Press, Chicago, 1958.

Aristotle, *Politics*, trans. by H. Rackham, Loeb Classical Library, William Heinemann Publishers, London, 1944.

Arnfield, R.V. (ed.), *Technological Forecasting*, Edinburgh University Press, Edinburgh, 1969.

Baade, Fritz, *The Race to the Year 2000*, Cresset Press, London, 1963.

Bator, Francis M., *The Question of Government Spending*, Collier, New York, 1962.

Bell, Daniel, *The End of Ideology: on the Exhaustion of Political Ideas in the Fifties*, Free Press, Glencoe, Ill., 1960.

Berelson, Bernard (ed.), *Family Planning and Population Programs*, University of Chicago Press, Chicago, 1966.

Berneri, Marie-Louise, *Journey through Utopia*, Routledge & Kegan, London, 1950.

Borgstrom, George, *Too Many: the Biological Limitations of our Earth*, Macmillan, New York, 1969.

Bright, James R. (ed.), *Technological Forecasting of Industry and Government*, Prentice-Hall, Englewood Cliffs, N.J., 1968.

Brown, Harrison Scott, *The Challenge of Man's Future*, Viking, New York, 1954.

Brown, Harrison Scott, et al, *The Next Hundred Years*, Viking, New York, 1957.

Brown, Lester R., *In the Human Interest*, W.W. Norton, New York, 1974.

Calder, Nigel (ed.), *Unless Peace Comes*, Penguin, London, 1968.

Calder, Nigel (ed.), *The World in 1984*, 2 Vols., Penguin, London, 1965.

Carson, Rachel, *Silent Spring*, Hamish Hamilton, London, 1962.

Cetron, Marvin J., *Technological Forecasting: a Practical Approach*, Gordon & Breach Inc., New York, 1969.

Clark, Colin, *Starvation or Plenty?*, Secker & Warburg, London, 1970.

Clark, Grahame and Stuart Piggott, *Prehistoric Societies*, Hutchinson, London, 1965.

Clarke, Arthur C., *Profiles of the Future*, Harper & Row, New York, 1963.

Christaller, W., *Central Places in Southern Germany*, Prentice-Hall, Englewood Cliffs, N.J., 1966.

Coon, Carleton S., *The Hunting Peoples*, Jonathan Cape Ltd., London, 1972.

Coulborn, Rushton, *The Origin of Civilized Societies*, Princeton University Press, Princeton, N.J., 1959.

Doxiadis, C.A., *Anthropopolis: City for Human Development*, Athens Publishing Center, Athens, 1974.

Doxiadis, C.A., *Between Dystopia and Utopia*, Trinity College Press, Hartford, Conn., 1966; Faber & Faber, London, 1968; Athens Publishing Center, Athens, 1974.

Doxiadis, C.A., *Ecumenopolis: the Settlement of the Future*, Research Report No. 1, Athens Center of Ekistics, Athens Technological Organization, 1967.

Doxiadis, C.A., *Ekistics: an Introduction to the Science of Human Settlements*, Oxford University Press, New York, 1968.

Doxiadis, C.A., *Emergence and Growth of an Urban Region: the Developing Urban Detroit Area*, Vol. I, 1966, Vol. II, 1967, Vol. III, 1970, The Detroit Edison Company, Detroit, Michigan.

Doxiadis, C.A., *The Two-Headed Eagle: from the Past to the Future of Human Settlements*, Lycabettus Press, Athens, 1972.

Doxiadis, C.A., *Urban Renewal and the Future of the American City*, Public Administration Service, Chicago, Illinois, 1966.

Dubos, René, *The Dreams of Reason: Science and Utopias*, Columbia University Press, New York and London, 1961.

Dubos, René, *So Human an Animal*, Charles Scribner's Sons, New York, 1968.

Dumont, René and Bernard Rosier, *The Hungry Future*, Thomas Balogh, London, 1969.

Eckardt, Wolf von, *The Challenge of Megalopolis: a Graphic Presentation of the Urbanized Northeastern Seaboard of the U.S.*, Macmillan, New York, 1964.

Editors of FORTUNE,*The Mighty Force of Research*, McGraw-Hill, New York, 1956.

Eiseley, Loren, *The Immense Journey*, Vintage Books, New York, 1957.

Eiseley, Loren, *The Mind as Nature*, Harper & Row, New York, 1962.

Ellul, Jacques, *The Technological Society*, Knopf, New York, 1964.

Ecole Pratique des Hautes Etudes, *Villages Désertés et Histoire Economique XI - XVIII Siècle*, Série "Les Hommes et la Terre", tome XI, VIe Section, Centre de Recherches Historiques, S.E.V.P.E.N., Paris, 1965.

Etzioni, Amitai, *Modern Organizations*, Prentice-Hall, Englewood Cliffs, N.J., 1964.

Etzioni, Amitai, *Social Change: Sources, Patterns and Consequences*, Basic Books, New York, 1964.

Eurich, Nell, *Science in Utopia,* Harvard University Press, Cambridge, Mass., 1967.

Ewald, William R. Jr., *Environment and Policy: the Next Fifty Years,* Indiana University Press, Bloomington, 1968.

Gabor, Dennis, *Inventing the Future,* Secker & Warburg, London, 1963.

Gellner, Ernest, *Thought and Change,* Weidenfeld & Nicolson, London, 1964.

Glazer, Nathan, *Beyond the Melting Pot,* MIT Press, Cambridge, Mass., 1963.

Gordon, T.J. and Olaf Helmer, *A Report on a Long-Range Forecasting Study,* Rand Corporation, Santa Monica, Calif., 1964.

Gotschalk, D.W., *Human Aims in Modern Perspective,* Antioch Press, Yellow Springs, Ohio, 1966.

Gottmann, J., *Megalopolis: the Urbanized Northeastern Seaboard of the United States,* MIT Press, Cambridge, Mass., 1961.

Gottmann, J., *L'Urbanisation en Amérique du Nord et en Europe Occidentale: Notes Comparatives,* reprinted from *Social Science Information,* Social Science Information Council, UNESCO, Paris, Sept. 1963.

Gottmann, J., *Essais sur l'Aménagement de l'Espace Habité,* Mouton, Paris, 1966.

Gottmann, J., *Metropolis on the Move,* Wiley, London, 1967.

Goushev, Sergei and Mikhail Vassiliev, *Russian Science in the 21st Century,* McGraw-Hill, New York, 1960.

Greep, R.O. (ed.), *Human Fertility and Population Problems,* Schenkman, Cambridge, Mass., 1963.

Hall, E.T., *The Silent Language,* Doubleday, Garden City, New York, 1959.

Hall, E.T., *The Hidden Dimension,* Doubleday, Garden City, New York, 1966.

Hartung, Henri, *Unité de l'Homme,* Collection Sciences et Techniques Humaines, Fayard, Paris, 1963.

Hawkes, Jacquetta and Sir Leonard Woolley, *Prehistory and the Beginnings of Civilization, History of Mankind,* Vol. I, UNESCO, Allen & Unwin Ltd., London, 1963.

Heilbroner, R.L., *The Great Ascent: the Struggle for Economic Development in our Time,* Harper & Row, New York, 1962.

Heilbroner, R.L., *The Future as History,* Grove Press, New York, 1961.

Hoffer, Erik, *The Ordeal of Change,* Harper & Row, New York, 1963.

Hoffer, Erik, *The True Believer: Thoughts on the Nature of Mass Movements,* Harper & Row, New York, 1951.

Hoggart, Richard, *The Uses of Literacy,* Oxford University Press, New York, 1957.

Holler, Joanne, *Population Trends and Economic Development in the Far East,* George Washington University, Washington D.C., 1965.

Jantsch, E., *Technological Planning and Social Futures,* Cassell, London, 1972.

Jarvie, I.C., *The Revolution in Anthropology,* Routledge & Kegan, London, 1964.

Jouvenel, Bertrand de, *L'Art de la Conjecture,* Editions du Rocher, Monaco, 1964.

Jungk, Robert, *Tommorow is Already Here*, Simon & Schuster, New York, 1954.
Kahler, Erich, *Man the Measure: a New Approach to History*, Braziller, New York, 1956.
Kahler, Erich, *The Meaning of History*, Braziller, New York, 1964.
Kahler, Erich, *The Tower and the Abyss: an Inquiry into the Transformation of the Individual*, Braziller, New York, 1957.
Kahn, Herman and Anthony J. Wiener, *The Year 2000*, Macmillan, New York, 1968.
Kenyon, Kathleen, *Archaeology in the Holy Land*, Praeger, New York, 1970.
Levi, Lennart and Lars Andersson, *Population, Environment and Quality of Life*, Royal Ministry of Foreign Affairs, Sweden, 1974.
Lewinsohn, Richard, *Science, Prophecy and Prediction*, Fawcett, Greenwich, Conn., 1962.
Lozano, Eduardo E., *Thoughts on Urban Systems — (Megalopolis)*, Cambridge, Mass., 1965.
McClelland, David C., *The Achieving Society*, Van Nostrand, Princeton, 1961.
McHale, John, *The Future of the Future*, Braziller, New York, 1969.
Meadows, D., et al, *The Limits to Growth*, Potomac Associates, Earth Island Ltd., London, 1972.
Maheu, René, *La Civilisation de L'Universel*, Editions Gonthier, Paris, 1966.
Marcuse, Herbert, *One Dimensional Man*, Beacon, Boston, 1964.
Martin, Brian V., et al, *Principles and Techniques of Predicting Future Demand for Urban Area Transportation*, MIT Report No. 3. MIT Press, Cambridge, Mass., 1965.
Maslow, Abraham H. (ed.), *New Knowledge in Human Values*, Harper & Row, New York, 1959.
Mead, Margaret, *Culture and Commitment*, Natural History Press, Garden City, N.Y., 1970.
Medawar, P.B., *The Future of Man*, Basic Books, New York, 1960.
Meier, R.L., *Megalopolis Formation in the Midwest*, Dept of Conservation, University of Michigan, Ann Arbor, 1965.
Meier, R.L., *Communications Theory of Urban Growth*, MIT Press, Cambridge, Mass., 1962.
Meier, R.L., *Developmental Planning*, McGraw-Hill, New York, 1965.
Meier, R.L., *Science and Economic Development: New Patterns for Living*, (2nd ed.), MIT Press, Cambridge, Mass., 1966.
Mellaart, James, *Çatal Hüyük: a Neolithic Town in Anatolia*, Thames & Hudson, London, 1967.
Michael, Donald N., *The Next Generation*, Random House, New York, 1965.
Moller, Herbert (ed.), *Population Movements in Modern European History*, Macmillan, New York, 1964.
Morris, Desmond, *The Naked Ape*, McGraw-Hill, New York, 1967.

Mudd, S. (ed.), *The Population Crisis and the Use of World Resources*, Junk, The Hague, 1964.

Myrdal, Gunnar, *The Challenge of World Poverty*, Random House, New York, 1971.

Ozbekhan, H., *Technology and Man's Future*, Report SP. 2494, Systems Development Corp., Santa Monica, Calif., 1966.

Papaioannou, J.G., *Megalopolises: a First Definition*, Research Report No. 2, Athens Center of Ekistics, Athens Technological Organization, 1967.

Papaioannou, J.G., "Future Urbanization Patterns in Europe", *Mastery of Urban Growth*, Mens en Ruimte, Brussels, 1971.

Papaioannou, J.G. "Future Urbanization Patterns: a Long-Range, Worldwide View", *Challenges from the Future*, Vol. 2, Kodansha Ltd., Tokyo, 1970.

Papaioannou, J.G., "Some Highlights for A.D. 2000", *Mankind 2000*, ed. by R. Jungk and J. Galtung, Oslo, 1969.

Pell, Claiborne, *Megalopolis Unbound*, Praeger, New York, 1966.

Perloff, Harvey S. (ed.), *The Quality of the Urban Environment: Essays on "New Resources" in an Urban Age*, The Johns Hopkins Press, Baltimore, Md., 1969.

Philipson, Morris (ed.), *Automation*, Vintage Books, Random House, New York, 1962.

Pickard, J.P., "Population Land Area Projection in U.S. Megalopolis", URBAN LAND NEWS, February 1967.

Pickard, J.P., *Metropolitanization of the U.S.*, Urban Land Institute, Washington D.C., 1959.

Piggott, Stuart, *Ancient Europe*, Edinburgh University Press, Edinburgh, 1965.

Plato, *Theaetitus*, trans. Harold North Fowler, Loeb Classical Library, William Heinemann Publishers, London, 1961.

Polak, F., *Image of the Future*, 2 Vols., Oceana Press, New York, 1961.

Prehoda, R.W., *Designing the Future*, Chilton, London, 1967.

Price, Don K., *The Scientific Estate*, Harvard University Press, Cambridge, Mass., 1965.

Putnam, Palmer C., *Energy in the Future*, Van Nostrand, Princeton, N.J., 1956.

Rathjens, G.W., *The Future of the Strategic Arms Race*, Carnegie Endowment for International Peace, New York, 1969.

Runciman, S., *Fall of Constantinople*, Cambridge University Press, London, 1965.

Schurr, Sam H. and Bruce C. Netschert, *Energy in the American Economy, 1850-1975*, The Johns Hopkins Press, Baltimore, Md., 1960.

Shklovskii, I.S. and Carl Sagan, *Intelligent Life in the Universe*, Holden-Day Inc., New York, 1966.

Simon, Herbert, *The Shape of Automation for Man and Management*, Harper & Row, New York, 1965.

Srejović, Dragoslav, *Lepenski Vir,* Thames & Hudson, London, 1972.

Stanford Research Institute, *Basic Economic Projections: United States Population 1965-1980,* 1964.

Still, Henry, *Man: the Next 30 Years,* Hawthorn Books, New York, 1968.

Stover, Carl F., (ed.), *The Technological Order,* Wayne State University, Detroit, 1964.

Stravinsky, Igor, *Poetics of Music in the Form of Six Lessons,* Harvard University Press, Cambridge, Mass., 1970.

Taylor, Gordon Rattray, *The Biological Time-Bomb,* Thames & Hudson, London, 1968.

Teilhard de Chardin, Pierre, *L'Avenir de l'Homme,* Seuil, Paris, 1959.

Thomas, W.L., Jr. (ed.), *Man's Role in Changing the Face of the Earth,* University of Chicago Press, Chicago, 1956.

Thomson, Sir George, *The Foreseeable Future,* Cambridge University Press, Cambridge, 1965.

Time/Life Editors, *1973 Nature/Science Annual,* TIME-LIFE Books, New York, 1972.

Time/Life Editors, *The Plants,* LIFE Nature Library, TIME-LIFE Books, New York, 1965.

Time/Life Editors, *The Earth,* LIFE Nature Library, TIME-LIFE Books, New York, 1962.

Tiselius, Arne and Sam Nilsson (ed.), *The Place of Value in a World of Facts,* Wiley Interscience Division, John Wiley & Sons, London, 1970.

Toynbee, Arnold (ed.) *Cities of Destiny,* Thames & Hudson, London, 1967.

Toynbee, Arnold, *Some Problems of Greek History,* Oxford University Press, New York, 1969.

Toynbee, Arnold, *Cities on the Move,* Oxford University Press, London, 1970.

Toynbee, Arnold, et al, *On the Future of Art,* Viking Press, New York, 1970.

United Nations, *Proceedings of the International Conference on the Peaceful Uses of Atomic Energy,* 2 Vols., Geneva, 1955.

United Nations, *Review of Long-Term Economic Projections for Selected Countries in the ECAFE Region,* Development Programming Techniques Series No. 5, Bangkok, 1964.

U.S. Dept. of Housing and Urban Development, *Tomorrow's Transportation,* Washington, D.C., 1968.

Vassiliev, M. and S. Gouschev, *Life in the Twenty-first Century,* Penguin, London, 1961.

Vermot-Gauchy, Michel, *L'Education Nationale dans la France de Demain,* Editions du Rocher, Monaco, 1965.

Wagar, W., *The City of Man,* Houghton Mifflin, Boston, 1963.

Ward, Barbara and René Dubos, *Only One Earth: the Care and Maintenance of a Small Planet,* W.W. Norton, New York, 1972.

Wentworth Eldredge, H. (ed.), *Taming Megalopolis*, 2 Vols., Anchor Books, Doubleday, New York, 1967.

Whipple, Fred L., *Knowledge among Men*, Simon & Schuster, New York, 1966.

Wolstenholme, G. (ed.), *Man and his Future*, Ciba Foundation, Churchill, London, 1963.

Young, Michael (ed.), *Forecasting and the Social Sciences*, Social Science Research Council, London, 1968.

Notes and References

No. Page
Preface

1   XIII   We began with the term *settlement* in order to remain open-minded. Then we found that this settlement was to be an urban system, and in keeping with the ancient tradition which created the term *polis* and formed *metro-polis* and *megalo-polis*, we decided to use *polis* as the suffix of our new term since it would be universally understood. We examined several alternatives, such as *geo-polis* — which had to be excluded because the new city will cover the whole earth — or *cosmo-polis* — which had to be excluded because we do not at present foresee going into space beyond the moon, and if we do, then *cosmo-polis* will be needed for a much larger unit than this present one. We ended with the term Ecumenopolis, since it serves our realistic goals best. (See also Glossary).

2   XIII   C.A. Doxiadis, *Anthropopolis: City for Human Development*, Athens Publishing Center, Athens, 1974.

3   XIV   C.A. Doxiadis, *Ecumenopolis: the Settlement of the Future*, internal document published by Doxiadis Associates, R-ERES-18, June 23, 1961. C.A. Doxiadis, *Ecumenopolis: the Settlement of the Future*, Research Report No. 1, Athens Center of Ekistics, Athens Technological Organization, 1968.

4   XIV   Throughout this book we use the American billion, which is a thousand million (1,000,000,000), and not the British billion, which is a million million (1,000,000,000,000).

5   XIV   Lester R. Brown, *In the Human Interest*, W.W. Norton, New York, 1974.

Part one

1   2   For years I thought that "Anthropos" (the ancient Greek word for human) would be better than the English word "Man" to describe human beings or mankind, because the word "Man" is also confused with the masculine gender. Now the American Anthropological Association has passed a resolution (November 1973) and has taken the following decision: "In view of the fact that the founders of the discipline of anthropology were men socialized in a male-dominated society which systematically excluded women from the professions

No.	Page	

and thereby prevented their participation in the formation of our discipline, including its terminology; and being trained as anthropologists to understand that language reinforces and perpetuates the prevailing values and socio-economic patterns that contribute to the oppression of women; we move that the American Anthropological Association:

a. urge anthropologists to become aware in their writing and teaching that their wide use of the term "man" as genetic for the species is conceptually confusing (since "man" is also the term for the male) and that it be replaced by more comprehensive terms such as "people" and "human being" which include both sexes;

b. further urge that members of the Association select textbooks that have eliminated this form of sexism which has become increasingly offensive to more and more women both within and outside the disciplines.

I agree with this basic goal and throughout this book have used the word *Anthropos* (and where necessary the Greek plural *Anthropoi*) as meaning humans of both sexes. Unfortunately, however, because of the grammatical structure of the English language, in several instances it has been impossible to avoid the use of masculine pronouns when referring to *Anthropos*.

2 3 In autumn of 1971, under the sponsorship of two environmental organizations, "Operation Oxygen" and "Stamp out Smog", more than 100 companies in Los Angeles agreed to organize computerized car-sharing pools in an attempt to reduce the city's pollution from car exhaust fumes. Additionally, the city's bus company laid on special buses to take people to work and all vehicles cooperating in the experiment were asked to turn on their headlights to spread the cause. However, despite wide advance publicity in newspapers and on television and radio the result was zero — only five people turned up to ride in the buses and traffic monitors reported seeing one car with its headlights on.

3 6 S. Runciman, *Fall of Constantinople*, Cambridge University Press, London, 1965, p. 226.

4 6 C.A. Doxiadis, *Ecumenopolis: the Settlement of the Future*, internal document published by Doxiadis Associates, R-ERES-18, June 23, 1961. C.A. Doxiadis, *Ecumenopolis: Towards a Universal Settlement*, internal document published by Doxiadis Associates, R-GA 305, 1963.

5 7 The need for a science specifically devoted to the study of human settlements first because apparent to C.A. Doxiadis during the early days of World War II when he realized that existing practices in ar-

No.	Page	
		chitecture and community planning could not reclaim Greece from devastation, and he started teaching ekistics in the underground movement. After the war, as first Minister of Housing & Reconstruction, he was able to further develop his ideas through practical application and through many of his writings. Doxiadis Associates, which was formed in 1951, has continued to study and develop the science of ekistics through their innumerable building and study projects throughout the world. (See also Glossary).
6	8	Plato, *Theaetitus*, 152A, Loeb Classical Library, trans. Harold North Fowler, William Heinemann Publishers, London, 1961, p. 41.
7	8	Quoted in *The Mind as Nature* by Loren Eiseley, Harper & Row, New York, 1962, p. 36.
8	10	E.T. Hall, *The Silent Language*, Doubleday, Garden City, New York, 1959, Chapter 10. E.T. Hall, *The Hidden Dimension*, Doubleday, Garden City, New York, 1966.
9	11	Throughout this book we use this ekistic logarithmic scale which is the foundation for classification of all human settlements on the basis of their population. More information can be found in C.A. Doxiadis' book *Ekistics: an Introduction to the Science of Human Settlements*, Oxford University Press, New York, 1968, pp. 29, 31, fig. 22. During the many years this scale has been used, C.A. Doxiadis has been working on the nomenclature and finally concluded that the most proper names are those which we use in this series of four books. These are listed below together with the names used up until now in other ekistic studies:

1.   Anthropos — instead of Man (as explained in note 1, Part One)
2.   room
3.   house — instead of dwelling
4.   housegroup — instead of dwelling group
5.   small neighborhood
6.   neighborhood
7.   small polis — instead of small town
8.   polis — instead of town
9.   small metropolis — instead of large city
10. metropolis
11. small megalopolis — instead of conurbation
12. megalopolis
13. small eperopolis — instead of urbanized region
14. eperopolis — instead of urbanized continent
15. Ecumenopolis

No. Page

10   11   The "central place theory" was conceived by the Bavarian geographer Walter Christaller in the 1930's. In his own words it is a "general deductive theory" designed "to explain the size, number and distribution of towns" in the belief that "some ordering principles govern the distribution."

Christaller developed this theory in his book *Central Places in Southern Germany* (trans. by C.W. Baskin from the German original of 1933, *Die Zentralen Orte in Süddeutschland*), Prentice-Hall, Englewood-Cliffs, N.J., 1966.

11   17   C.A. Doxiadis, "The Future of Human Settlements", *The Place of Value in a World of Facts*, edited by Arne Tiselius and Sam Nilsson, Wiley Interscience Division, John Wiley & Sons, Inc., London, 1970, pp. 334-335.

12   19   Quoted in *The Mind as Nature* by Loren Eiseley, Harper & Row, New York, 1962 frontispiece, p. 13.

13   21   Barbara Ward and René Dubos, *Only One Earth: the Care and Maintenance of a Small Planet*, W.W. Norton & Co., Inc., New York, 1972.

14   23   Francis Bello, "The Young Scientists", FORTUNE, June 1960, pp. 152-159.

15   27   P.B. Medawar, *The Future of Man*, Basic Books, New York, 1960, p. 11.

16   27   *principles:* C.A. Doxiadis, "The Future of Human Settlements", *The Place of Value in a World of Facts*, edited by Arne Tiselius and Sam Nilsson, Wiley Interscience Division, John Wiley & Sons, Inc., New York, London, 1970, pp. 310-311.

laws: C.A. Doxiadis, *Ekistics: an Introduction to the Science of Human Settlements*, Oxford University Press, New York, 1968, pp. 287-316.

17   28   Quoted in *The Mind as Nature* by Loren Eiseley, Harper & Row, New York, 1962, p. 56.

18   29   Since 1959, Doxiadis Associates have been involved in the creation of Islamabad, the new capital of Pakistan. They advised on the location of the new capital, prepared the long-term and the first 5-year development programs, the plan of the metropolitan area including the city of Rawalpindi, the master plan of Islamabad, and detailed plans for a number of residential and commercial sectors of the city. Between 1966 and 1968, Doxiadis Associates prepared studies for types of houses and infrastructure works as well as of a number of road and traffic projects which were completed by 1969.

C.A. Doxiadis, "Islamabad: the Creation of a New Capital", THE TOWN PLANNING REVIEW, Vol. 36, No. 1, April 1965, pp. 1-17.

19   29   C.A. Doxiadis, *The Two-Headed Eagle: from the past to the future of human settlements*, Lycabettus Press, Athens, 1972.

No.	Page	
20	30	C.A. Doxiadis, *Ecumenopolis: the Settlement of the Future*, internal document published by Doxiadis Associates, R-ERES-18, June 23, 1961. C.A.Doxiadis, *Ecumenopolis: the Settlement of the Future*, Research Report No. 1, Athens Center of Ekistics, Athens Technological Organization, 1968.
21	33	In 1963 the first Delos Symposion organized by C.A. Doxiadis took place in Greece. It was attended by 34 experts of various disciplines from around the world who were bound together by their common concern for the future of cities. Since then, the Delos Symposia have taken place every year with the participation of an ever-widening circle of international experts. Additionally, from 1965-72, an International Seminar on Ekistics was organized annually by the Athens Center of Ekistics of the Athens Technological Organization, a sister institution of Doxiadis Associates.
22	33	Arnold Toynbee, *Cities of Destiny*, Thames & Hudson, London, 1967. Arnold Toynbee, *Cities on the Move*, Oxford University Press, London, 1970.
23	37	Arnold Toynbee, *Cities on the Move*, Oxford University Press, London, 1970, Chapter 10.

Part two

1	42	Dragoslav Srejović, *Lepenski Vir*, Thames & Hudson, London, 1972. James Mellaart, *Çatal Hüyük: a Neolithic Town in Anatolia*, Thames & Hudson, London, 1967.
2	43	C.A. Doxiadis, "The Formation of a Human Room", EKISTICS, March 1972, pp. 218-229. C.A. Doxiadis, "One Room for Every Human", paper presented at the Third International Symposium on Lower-Cost Housing Problems, May 27, 1974, Montreal, Canada.
3	44	The "Ancient Greek Settlements" project was begun by the Athens Center of Ekistics of the Athens Technological Organization in 1968 with the aim of creating a fully comprehensive archive of information on settlements in ancient Greece which would lead to a better understanding of the evolution of human settlements in general. The project, which is still continuing, has produced numerous reports.
4	45	ATLAS A LA DECOUVERTE DU MONDE, May 1971, p. 72.
5	45	Grahame Clark and Stuart Piggott, *Prehistoric Societies*, Hutchinson, London, 1965, p. 130.
6	45	Grahame Clark and Stuart Piggott, *Prehistoric Societies*, Hutchinson, London, 1965, p. 64.
7	45	Carleton S. Coon, *The Hunting Peoples*, Jonathan Cape Ltd., London, 1972, p. 191.

No.	Page	
8	45	Carleton S. Coon, *The Hunting Peoples*, Jonathan Cape Ltd., London, 1972, pp. 196-197.
9	46	Carleton S. Coon, *The Hunting Peoples*, Jonathan Cape Ltd., London, 1972, p. 25.
10	46	Grahame Clark and Stuart Piggott, *Prehistoric Societies*, Hutchinson, London, 1965, p. 45.
11	46	Grahame Clark and Stuart Piggott, *Prehistoric Societies*, Hutchinson, London, 1965, pp. 61-62.
12	48	Stuart Piggott, *Ancient Europe*, Edinburgh University Press, Edinburgh, 1965, p. 258.
13	48	Desmond Morris, *The Naked Ape*, McGraw-Hill, New York, 1967, pp. 196-197.
14	48	Grahame Clark and Stuart Piggott, *Prehistoric Societies*, Hutchinson, London, 1965, p. 166.
15	49	James Mellaart, *Çatal Hüyük: a Neolithic Town in Anatolia*, Thames & Hudson, London, 1967, pp. 15 and 30.
16	49	Rushton Coulborn, *The Origin of Civilized Societies*, Princeton University Press, Princeton, N.J., 1959, p. 10.
17	49	Grahame Clark and Stuart Piggott, *Prehistoric Societies*, Hutchinson, London, 1965, p. 245.
18	49	C.A. Doxiadis, "Ancient Greek Settlements", EKISTICS, January 1971, pp. 4-22. C.A. Doxiadis, "Ancient Greek Settlements: Second Annual Report", EKISTICS, February 1972, pp. 76-89.
19	49	W. Christaller, *Central Places in Southern Germany*, (trans. by C.W. Baskin from the German original of 1933, *Die Zentralen Orte in Süddeutschland*), Prentice-Hall, Englewood-Cliffs, N.J., 1966.
20	49	C.A. Doxiadis, "Ancient Greek Settlements: Third Report", EKISTICS, January 1973, pp. 7-16.
21	52	C.A. Doxiadis, *Ekistics: an Introduction to the Science of Human Settlements*, Oxford University Press, New York, 1968, pp. 138, 139, 224.
22	52	James Mellaart, *Çatal Hüyük: a Neolithic Town in Anatolia*, Thames & Hudson, London, 1967, p. 62, fig. 12.
23	53	Stuart Piggott, *Ancient Europe*, Edinburgh University Press, Edinburgh, 1965.
24	54	Victor Ehrenberg, "When did the polis rise?", JOURNAL OF HELLENIC STUDIES, 57, (1937), pp. 147-159.
25	55	C.A. Doxiadis, "Ancient Greek Settlements: Third Report", EKISTICS, January 1973, pp. 8-9.
26	55	Ibid.

No.	Page	
27	55	Kathleen Kenyon, *Archaeology in the Holy Land*, Praeger, New York, 1970, p. 261.
28	55	*Small Towns Study*, printed by Cambridgeshire and Ely County Council, Shire Hall, Cambridge, for the Economic Planning Council and the Consultative Committee, September 1972.
29	58	Grahame Clark and Stuart Piggott, *Prehistoric Societies*, Hutchinson, London, 1965, p. 106.
30	61	Pindar, *Pythia VII*, line 1, Pindari Carmina, Oxonii, 1935.
31	64	C.A. Doxiadis, *Ekistics: an Introduction to the Science of Human Settlements*, Oxford University Press, New York, 1968, p. 93.
32	64	*Proceedings of the First International Humanistic Symposium at Delphi*, 25 Sept.-4 Oct. 1969, First Volume, Athens, p. 169.
33	69	Grahame Clark and Stuart Piggott, *Prehistoric Societies*, Hutchinson, London, 1965, p. 112.
34	69	Walter P. Falcon, "Peasant Economics", (book review of *Subsistence Agriculture and Economic Development* by Clifton R. Wharton, Jr., Aldine, Chicago, 1969), SCIENCE, Vol. 170, November 6, 1970, pp. 616-617.
35.	76	Arnold Toynbee, *Cities on the Move*, Oxford University Press, New York, 1970, p. 186.
36	77	*1973 Nature/Science Annual*, TIME-LIFE Books, New York, 1972, p. 181.
37	77	C.A. Doxiadis, *Between Dystopia and Utopia*, Trinity College Press, Hartford, Conn., 1966; Faber & Faber, London, 1968; Athens Publishing Center, Athens, 1974, pp. 28-32.
38	77	Quoted in *Journey through Utopia* by Marie-Louise Berneri, Routledge & Kegan, London, 1950, p. 54.

Part three

1	85	C.A. Doxiadis, *Urban America and the Role of Industry*, report written for the National Association of Manufacturers, January 1971.
2	90	*Special Study on Social Conditions in Non-Self-Governing Territories*, United Nations, New York, 1953, pp. 75-76.
3	96	In Athens, Greece, this rate of increase was 5% between 1940 and 1973.
4	97	C.A. Doxiadis, *Urban America and the Role of Industry*, report written for the National Association of Manufacturers, January 1971.
5	97	The 1960 Census data recording movements of people in all major American cities was prepared by Brian J.L. Berry, University of Chicago, April 1967, for the Social Science Research Council Committee on Areas for Social and Economic Statistics, in cooperation with the Bureau of the Census, U.S. Department of Commerce. Project staff: L. Bourne, M. Earickson, P. Schwind. Cartographer: G. Pyle.

No. Page

6   ⁻97   G. Papageorgiou, "1940-1960 Growth of the Sample Metropolises", internal document RR-ACE 170, Athens Center of Ekistics, March 31, 1970.

7   97   C.A. Doxiadis, *Emergence and Growth of an Urban Region: the Developing Urban Detroit Area*, Vol. I, 1966, fig. 71, The Detroit Edison Company, Detroit, Michigan.
             Doxiadis Associates, Consultants on Development and Ekistics, *The Northern Ohio Urban System Research Project, Definition of the Study Area*, DOX-USA-A 78, October 1970, internal report.

8   101   Jean Gottmann, *Megalopolis: the Urbanized Northeastern Seaboard of the United States*, MIT Press, Cambridge, Mass., 1961.

9   112   *Villages Désertés et Histoire Economique XI-XVIII Siècle*, Série "Les Hommes et la Terre", tome XI, Ecole Pratique des Hautes Etudes, VIe Section, Centre de Recherches Historiques, S.E.V.P.E.N., Paris, 1965.

10   123   Rachel Carson, *Silent Spring*, Hamish Hamilton, London, 1962.

11   125   Brian J.L. Berry, *Megalopolitan Confluence Zones*, Athens Center of Ekistics Monograph Series, Research Report No. 10, 1971.

12   132   C.A. Doxiadis, *Anthropopolis: City for Human Development*, Athens Publishing Center, Athens, 1974, Chapter 5, fig. 73.

13   137   C.A. Doxiadis, *Urban Renewal and the Future of the American City*, Public Administration Service, Chicago, Illinois, 1966.

14   138   C.A. Doxiadis, *Between Dystopia and Utopia*, Trinity College Press, Hartford, Conn., 1966; Faber & Faber, London, 1968; Athens Publishing Center, Athens, 1974, pp. 31-34.

15   141   C.A. Doxiadis, *Ekistics: an Introduction to the Science of Human Settlements*, Oxford University Press, New York, 1968, fig. 432, p. 447.

16   150   Editors of FORTUNE, *The Mighty Force of Research*, McGraw-Hill, New York, 1956, p. 248.

17   151   Aristotle, *Politics, I.i*, 8-9, trans. by H. Rackham, Loeb Classical Library, William Heinemann Publishers, London, 1944, pp. 8-9.

18   154   D. Meadows, et al., *The Limits to Growth*, Potomac Associates, Earth Island Ltd., London, 1972.

19   154   University of Sussex, Science Policy Research Unit, *Thinking about the Future: a Critic of Limits to Growth*, Chatto & Windus, London, 1973.

Part four

1   159   C.A. Doxiadis, *Ekistics: an Introduction to the Science of Human Settlements*, Oxford University Press, New York, 1968, fig. 69.

2   160   Igor Stravinsky, *Poetics of Music in the Form of Six Lessons*, Harvard University Press, Cambridge, Mass., 1970, p. 89.

3   160   We call this the IDEA (Isolation of Dimensions and Elimination of

No. Page

        Alternatives) Method. It is presented in *Emergence and Growth of an Urban Region: the Developing Urban Detroit Area*, Vols. II, 1967, III, 1970, and its application is reviewed in EKISTICS, November 1966, p. 371 ff.

4   161   Herman Kahn and Anthony J. Wiener, *The Year 2000*, Macmillan, New York, 1968.

5   175   René Dubos, *So Human an Animal*, Charles Scribner's Sons, New York, 1968, p. 159.

6   177   Jacquetta Hawkes and Sir Leonard Woolley, *Prehistory and the Beginnings of Civilization*, *History of Mankind*, Volume I, UNESCO, Allen & Unwin Ltd., London, 1963, pp. 415-419.

7   177   Fred L. Whipple, *Knowledge among Men*, Simon & Schuster, New York, 1966, p. 179.

8   183   The reference to "snouts" comes from Loren Eiseley's image in his book *The Immense Journey*, Vintage Books, New York, 1957.

9   185   C.A. Doxiadis, "Water and Human Environment", *Water for Peace*, Vol. I, International Conference on Water for Peace, Washington D.C., May 23-31, 1967, U.S. Government Printing Office, Washington D.C., 20402, pp. 36-37, fig. 5.

10   186   Rachel Carson, *Silent Spring*, Hamish Hamilton, London, 1963, pp. 106-126.

11   187   The Editors of FORTUNE, *The Mighty Force of Research*, McGraw-Hill, New York, 1956, p. 175.

12   205   The Editors of FORTUNE, *The Mighty Force of Research*, McGraw-Hill, New York, 1956, p. 268.

13   209   The Editors of FORTUNE, *The Mighty Force of Research*, McGraw-Hill, New York, 1956, p. 195.

14   209   Ali Bulent Cambel, "Energy", SCIENCE JOURNAL, October 1967, Vol. 3, No. 10, pp. 57-62.

15   209   C.A. Doxiadis, "The Urban Systems of the Future", paper prepared for the Conference on "Technological Change and Human Environment", California Institute of Technology, Pasadena, California, October 20, 1970.

16   209   John McHale, *The Future of the Future*, Braziller, New York, 1969, p. 211.

17   209   Nigel Calder, ed., *The World in 1984*, Penguin, London, 1965, Vol. I, p. 73.

18   212   All these statements are taken from statistics given in Walker L. Cisler's "Energy, Production and Economic Growth" paper presented at the National Seminar on Total Energy and Energy Substitution, Vigyan Bhavan, New Delhi, India, March 26, 1973.

No. Page

19 212 The Editors of FORTUNE, *The Mighty Force of Research*, McGraw-Hill, New York, 1956, p. 178.

20 212 I.S. Shklovskii and Carl Sagan, *Intelligent Life in the Universe*, Holden-Day, Inc., New York, 1966, p. 394.

21 213 *1973 Nature/Science Annual*, TIME-LIFE Books, New York, 1972, p. 181.

22 214 John McHale, "World Energy Resources in the Future", FUTURES JOURNAL, 1968, p. 11.

23 214 L.K. Edwards, "High-Speed Tube Transportation", SCIENTIFIC AMERICAN, August 1965, pp. 30-40.

24 214 *1973 Nature/Science Annual*, TIME-LIFE Books, New York, 1972, pp. 112-123.

25 214 C.A. Doxiadis, *Emergence and Growth of an Urban Region: the Developing Urban Detroit Area*, Vols. II, 1967, III, 1970, The Detroit Edison Company, Detroit, Michigan.

26 222 Gunnar Myrdal, *The Challenge of World Poverty*, Random House, New York, 1971.

27 222 The Editors of FORTUNE, *The Mighty Force of Research*, McGraw-Hill, New York, 1956, p. 171.

28 223 Henry Still, *Man: the next 30 years*, Hawthorn Books, New York, 1968, p. 36.

29 224 "Wild Lands as a Scarce Resource", WORLD, January 2, 1973, p. 41.

30 225 LIFE Nature Library, *The Plants*, TIME-LIFE Books, New York, 1965, p. 166.

31 225 LIFE Nature Library, *The Earth*, TIME-LIFE Books, New York, 1962, p. 168.

32 225 Nigel Calder, ed., *The World in 1984*, Penguin, London, 1965, Vol. I, p. 133.

33 225 Yves La Prairie, "Exploiter L'Océan", REVUE 2000, No. 7, Mars 1968, p. 15.

34 226 René Dubos, "Humanizing the Earth", SCIENCE, Vol. 179, No. 4075, February 23, 1973, p. 771.

35 227 Senator Claiborne Pell, "The Oceans, Man's Last Great Resource", SATURDAY REVIEW, October 11, 1969.

36 228 W. Wagar, *The City of Man*, Houghton Mifflin, Boston, 1963, p. 22.

37 235 Arnold Toynbee, *Some Problems of Greek History*, Oxford University Press, New York, 1969, p. 486.

38 235 W. Wagar, *The City of Man*, Houghton Mifflin, Boston, 1963, p. 24.

39 238 This figure was derived from a Gallup Poll conducted in the U.S.A. in February 1971 using a sample of 1,571 adults interviewed in more than 300 scientifically selected localities.

No. Page

40 238 The nationwide referendum on a proposed constitutional amendment for the expulsion of 300,000 foreign workers from Switzerland was held on June 7, 1970, and was defeated by 54% to 46%. The Swiss government immediately imposed new restrictions whereby no more temporary seasonal workers were admitted into the country except in the hotel industry which had not yet filled its quota that summer and autumn.

41 238 Clara Pierre, "Refugees: the Modern Diaspora", WORLD, December 19, 1972, pp. 25-28.

42 243 Henry Still, *Man: the next 30 years*, Hawthorn Books, New York, 1968, pp. 9-10.

43 245 P.B. Medawar, *The Future of Man*, Basic Books, New York, 1960, p. 21.

44 246 H. von Foerster, P.M. Mora and Lawrence W. Amiot, "Doomsday: Friday, 13 November, A.D. 2026", SCIENCE, Vol. 132, No. 3436, November 4, 1960, pp. 1291-1295.

45 250 "The City of the Future", EKISTICS, Vol. 20, No. 116, July 1965.

46 251 Barbara Ward and René Dubos, *Only One Earth: the Care and Maintenance of a Small Planet*, W.W. Norton, New York, 1972, p. 213.

Part five

1 277 Werner Jager, *Paideia*, Oxford University Press, New York, 1st Vol. 1945 (reprint 1965), 2nd Vol. 1944 (reprint 1957), 3rd Vol. 1945 (reprint 1961).

2 283 C.A. Doxiadis, *Ekistics: an Introduction to the Science of Human Settlements*, Oxford University Press, New York, 1968, pp. 235-264.

3 283 Jean Gottmann, *Megalopolis: the Urbanized Northeastern Seaboard of the United States*, MIT Press, Cambridge, Mass., 1961.

4 285 C.A. Doxiadis, "Man's Movement and his City", SCIENCE, October 18, 1968, figs. 8, 9 and 4.

5 288 John G. Papaioannou, *Megalopolises: a First Definition*, Athens Center of Ekistics Monograph Series, Research Report No. 2, Athens, 1967.

6 290 These percentages are taken from BULLETIN STATISTIQUE published by the French Tourist Organization, Paris, 1960.

7 292 Richard K. Nelson, *Hunters of the Northern Ice*, University of Chicago Press, Chicago, 1965.

8 293 C.A. Doxiadis, *Emergence and Growth of an Urban Region: the Developing Urban Detroit Area*, Vol. I, 1966, Vol. II, 1967, Vol. III, 1970. A project of The Detroit Edison Company, Wayne State University and Doxiadis Associates, under the chairmanship of Walker

No. Page

L. Cisler, Chairman of the Board, the Detroit Edison Company, direct-
ed by C.A. Doxiadis, and published by the Detroit Edison Company.
Doxiadis Associates, Consultants on Development and Ekistics,
*The Northern Ohio Urban System Research Project, Definition
of the Study Area*, DOX-USA-A 78, October 1970, internal report.

9 293 *Etude Prospective de la Région Méditerranéenne*, internal documents
by EURDA, Société d'Etudes d'Urbanisme, de Développement et d'
Aménagement du Territoire, DOX-FRA-A 1, December 1967, DOX-
FRA-A 2, April 1969, DOX-FRA-A 4, October 1969, prepared for the
Délégation à l'Aménagement du Territoire et à l'Action Régionale et
le Ministère de l'Equipement et du Logement. Also document *La
Façade Méditerranéenne*, Schéma Général d'Aménagement de la
France, lère partie, réalisé par EURDA, Société d'Etudes d'Urbanisme,
de Développement et d'Aménagement du Territoire, "La Documentation Française", 29-31 quai Voltaire 75, Paris 7ème, November 1969.
Plan de Ordenación de la Provincia de Barcelona, internal report by
Doxiadis Iberica S.A., DOX-ESP-A 6 and DOX-ESP-A 7, November
1970, and *Plan de Ordenación de la Provincia de Gerona*, internal
report by Doxiadis Iberica S.A., DOX-ESP-A 9, February 1971, prepared
for the Diputación Provincial de Barcelona and the Diputación Provincial de Gerona respectively.

Internal research reports issued by the "Capital of Greece" research
project:
"Athens: a comparative study of a growing urban area; from recent
past to present: Man-Society", No. 135, August 8, 1968.
"Athens: a comparative study of a growing urban area; from present
to future: B. Nature;, No. 153, December 15, 1969.
"Athens: a comparative study of a growing urban area; from present
to future: A. An introduction to the last part of the study", No. 154,
December 23, 1969.
"Athens: a comparative study of a growing urban area; from present
to future: Man-Society, population and area in A.D. 2000", No. 165,
March 7, 1970.
"Athens: a comparative study of a growing urban area; from present
to future: Man-Society, economic data: a comparative picture around
2000", No. 167, March 13, 1970.
"1940-1960 growth of the sample metropolises", No. 170, March 31,
1970.
"1960-2000 Shells and Networks: size and cost", No. 172, May 8,
1970.
"Future Transportation", No. 173, May 8, 1970.

No.	Page	
		"A comparative analysis of growing urban areas: an account of conclusions", No. 176, October 13, 1970.
		"Final conclusion: a synthesis, three examples", No. 177, October 27, 1970.
10	302	K. Dahlström, "The Scandinavian Capital Triangle", S-ACE 101:281, July 30, 1972, internal report.
11	302	B.J. Rae, "Urban Development in New Zealand", S-ACE 101:271, February 11, 1972, internal report.
12	302	S.V. Singh, "Study of Urbanization along Amritsar-Calcutta Axis, India", S-ACE 101:287, September 12, 1972, internal report.
13	302	M.R. Perović, "Gulf Megalopolises: Investigation into highly urbanized clusters in the South of the United States of America", S-ACE 101:265, November 30, 1971, internal report.
14	308	Doxiadis Associates, Consultants on Development and Ekistics, *The Northern Ohio Urban System Research Project, Definition of the Study Area*, DOX-USA-A 78, October 1970, internal report.
15	308	The Great Lakes Megalopolis research project started in 1965, and was initiated within the framework of the Developing Urban Detroit Area research project when it was felt necessary to undertake a series of studies of the broader regions encompassing the Urban Detroit Area to place it in its proper setting and perspective. During the early stages of this work, a zone of more or less intense urban-type phenomena running from Illinois to Pennsylvania could be clearly distinguished from its surrounding area. It was then suggested that this Great Lakes zone might constitute an emerging megalopolis analogous to the Eastern Megalopolis, the urbanized northeastern corridor studied by Jean Gottmann. This view was soon confirmed by further findings and the study of this megalopolitan zone, due to its relevance to the Urban Detroit Area, became an important constituent element of the Urban Detroit Area research project.
16	314	The Editors of FORTUNE, *The Mighty Force of Research*, McGraw-Hill, New York, 1956, p. 182.
17	314	The extension to Cumbernauld, requested by Cumbernauld Development Corporation, was the subject of a public inquiry in September 1972 and was sanctioned by the Secretary of State for Scotland, Mr. Gordon Campbell, in April 1973. The target population was raised in 1960 from 50,000 to 70,000.
18	318	C.A. Doxiadis, "The Future of Human Settlements", *The Place of Value in a World of Facts*, edited by Arne Tiselius and Sam Nilsson, Wiley Interscience Division, John Wiley & Sons, Inc., New York, London, 1970, pp. 326-327.

No. Page

19 331 C.A. Doxiadis, *Emergence and Growth of an Urban Region: the Developing Urban Detroit Area*, Vol. II, 1967, The Detroit Edison Company, Detroit, Michigan, pp. 19-20.

20 332 C.A. Doxiadis, *Emergence and Growth of an Urban Region: the Developing Urban Detroit Area*, Vol. III, 1970, The Detroit Edison Company, Detroit, Michigan, figs. 373-376, 391-392.

21 333 R. Bugher, "Utilidor Project 68-2: Preliminary Findings and Observations", EKISTICS, October 1970, pp. 299-302.

22 333 C.A. Doxiadis, *Emergence and Growth of an Urban Region: the Developing Urban Detroit Area*, Vol. I, 1966, Vol. II, 1967, Vol. III, 1970, The Detroit Edison Company, Detroit, Michigan.
Doxiadis Associates, Consultants on Development and Ekistics, *The Northern Ohio Urban System Research Project, Definition of the Study Area*, DOX-USA-A 78, October 1970, internal report.

Part six

1 338 Aristotle, *Politics*, I.i, 8-9, trans. by H. Rackham, Loeb Classical Library, William Heinemann Publishers, London, 1944, pp. 8-9.

2 342 F. Zwicky, *Morphology of Propulsive Power*, Society for Morphological Research, Pasadena, California, 1962, Monograph No. 1, p. 369.

3 344 C.A. Doxiadis, "Global Action for Man's Water Resources", paper presented at the First World Congress on Water Resources, Chicago, Illinois, September 24-28, 1973, organized by the International Water Resources Association.

4 346 C.A. Doxiadis, *Ekistics: an Introduction to the Science of Human Settlements*, Oxford University Press, New York, 1968, pp. 287-316.

5 376 "The City of the Future", EKISTICS, Vol. 35, No. 207, February 1973.

6 392 Diogenes Laertius, *Diogenes*, Bk. VI, 63.

7 392 Quoted in *The City of Man* by W. Wagar, Houghton Mifflin, Boston, 1963, p. 80.

Appendix 2

1 414 John G. Papaioannou, *Population Projection for Ecumenopolis*, Athens Center of Ekistics Monograph Series, Research Report No. 9, Athens, 1970.

Appendix 3

1 426 John G. Papaioannou, *Megalopolises: a First Definition*, Athens Center of Ekistics Monograph Series, Research Report No. 2, Athens, 1967.

2 427 This refinement of the connectivity formula was based on the research of the Athens Center of Ekistics, which has produced detailed studies of the Great Lakes, Japanese, and future Greek Megalopolises, has examined in more summary form another dozen cases, and has

compiled a very generalized survey of some 160 specimens which practically exhausts the list of emergent megalopolises during the coming generations.

3 427 For the purposes of this discussion, the term "center" refers almost exclusively to large settlements with a population of over one million inhabitants (i.e., metropolises and small conurbations). Generally, settlements with less than this minimum population do not have the "critical mass" required for them to act as major megalopolitan centers.

4 427 The distance D is measured from the centroid of the core area of the central business district in the case of single metropolises for composite megalopolitan centers consisting of several settlements; the centroid of the total area (weighted by population distribution) is used as a base point for the measurement of D; and the total population of the several component settlements is taken as P for the composite center. To date, adjustments at the level of weighting have been executed intuitively rather than rigorously, with negligible loss of accuracy for the model.

5 427 The two centers C_1 and C_2, together with the portion of the megalopolitan axis which connects them, are said to form a "link", and an interconnected series of links made up a "chain", the linear nodal structure of the megalopolises (fig. 39). Only settlements with more than 100,000 inhabitants have been considered sufficiently important to warrant their inclusion in calculations of connectivity. For each settlement within the link under analysis which falls into the size category of 500,000-1,000,000 N is increased by 1.00, for each between 200,000 and 500,000 by 0.50, and for each between 100,000 and 200,000 by 0.25. (In the exceptional case that a settlement between 1,000,000 and 2,000,000 is not considered to act as an independent center but rather to fall within a link, N is augmented by 2.00). For example, a link containing two settlements of 600,000 and one settlement of 175,000 would be assigned a value of N = 1.00 + 1.00 + 0.25 = 2.25.

6 427 The transportation factor T for a link is assigned a value of 1.00 if good to excellent transportation connections exist and there are no major physical obstacles between the two major centers. Inferior transport facilities or the existence of serious obstacles such as mountain ranges between centers required that T be reduced to between 0.75 and 0.50, while the existence of severe obstacles such as major bodies of water separating centers implies still further reduction of the transportation factor to 0.25 or even 0.00. The determination of N and T is subject to a considerable latitude of personal judgement, but since their effect on the connectivity formula is only corrective and since the formula

Index

aborigines, 46
Accra, 106
administration of settlements, 130, 132
    problems of, 328-329
    see also, organization
Aegean Sea, 372, 373
Afghanistan, 48, 370
Africa, 133, 141, 224, 257, 373
    East, 45, 238, 305, 370
    East African Rift Valley, 370
    North, 370, 372
    Northwest, 372
    West, 305, 358
    West African Urban System, 302, 305
    West African Part of Ecumenopolis, 373, fig. 149, 376
agriculture, 48, 222
    land needed for, 222-223, fig. 94, 224, table 5
    subsistence, 69
    agricultural revolution, 68, 246
    agricultural technology, 205, 225-226
    see also, food
airplanes, 109, 215, 349
    see also, Supersonic Transportation
Alexander the Great, 235
Alexandria, 61
Alps, 2
Amazon basin, 223
    region, 140
    jungles, 9
America, 234, 293
    North, 257
    food production in North, 222
    North American part of Ecumenopolis, 373, fig. 148, 376
    South, 48, 257
    see also, U.S.A.
American Congress, 55
Amritsar-Calcutta axis (India), 302
"Ancient Greek Settlements" research project, 44
Angkor-Wat (Cambodia), 61, 66, 148
Ankara, 297
Antarctica, 297
Anthroparea, 52, 64
    see also, Glossary

Anthropocosmos, 176
    see also, Glossary
Anthropos (ekistic element), 9, 391
    predictions about, 27, 28
    experience of, 42
    problems of, 46, 122, 124, 324-326, 392
    opportunities and extension of, 130, fig. 54, 277
    physical condition of, 124, 277-278
    inequalities between, 234-235
    satisfaction of needs of, 320-321, fig. 132
    balance between the goals of, 384
        see also, balance
    Anthropos and his own evolution, 395-397
Apollo, 228
Aquinas, St. Thomas, 77
architecture, 213, 292, 389-390
Argentina, 305
Aristotle, 7-8, 151, 338, 394
Asia, 48, 55, 133, 293, 367, 370, 372
    Southeast, 222, 257, 263
    Southwest, 45
Asia Minor, 48, 370, 372, 373
Asian Highway, 370, 372, 373
Athens, 44, fig. 41, 111, 120, 151, fig. 63, 209, 293, 338, 373
    ancient, 265, 338, 383
    classical, 3, 61, 272, 277, 393
    "the megalopolis Athens", 61
    growth of production of energy and per capita incomes in,
        fig. 88
Athens Center of Ekistics, 4, 29, 88, 97, 101, 120, 141
Atlantic, 215
atmosphere, 175, 186-188
    pollution of, 186-187
    see also, biosphere
Atomic Energy Commission, 23
atomic explosions, 206
Australia, 46, 234, 257, 263, 305
automation, 205
automobiles, 109, 127, fig. 53, 133, 134, 150, 206, 214, 293,
    318, 320, 324, 331, 349
    antipollution standards of, 186
    car sharing pools, 3
Aztec Empire, 159

463

465